U.S. TAXATION
OF INTERNATIONAL OPERATIONS

KEY KNOWLEDGE

11292-356

Michael Tilton, CPA, JD

Notice to Readers

U.S. Taxation of International Operations: Key Knowledge does not represent an official position of the American Institute of Certified Public Accountants, and it is distributed with the understanding that the author and publisher are not rendering, legal, accounting, or other professional services in the publication. This work offers a detailed treatment of basic characteristics related to various statutes and regulations that address topics within the healthcare professional practices industry. This book is intended to be an overview of the topics discussed within, and the author has made every attempt to verify the completeness and accuracy of the information herein. However, neither the author nor publisher can guarantee the applicability of the information found herein. If legal advice or other expert assistance is required, the services of a competent professional should be sought.

Publisher: Amy M. Plent
Senior Managing Editor: Amy Krasnyanskaya
Acquisitions Editor: Amy Krasnyanskaya

Contents

Chapter 3: U.S. Foreign Tax Credit—Basic Concepts

Chapter 4: U.S. Foreign Tax Credit—Special Rules

Chapter 5: Initiation of Foreign Operations

Chapter 6: Foreign Branches and Affiliated Companies

Chapter 10: Foreign Business Provision of Services in the United States

Chapter 11: Exploitation of Business Assets Outside the United States

Chapter 12: Use of Foreign Tangible Property in the United States

Chapter 13: Use of Foreign Intangible Property in the United States

Chapter 1

Export Income

Taxation of Export Income

U.S. corporations, as well as citizens and permanent residents, are generally taxed on their export income in the same manner as on their income from the United States. This chapter focuses on the tax position of businesses that earn income outside the United States.

U.S. businesses report income and deductions from export activities on the same tax returns used to report income from domestic sales. However, there are two significant differences:

1. Income may be considered earned by a U.S. business for purposes of U.S. taxation even though exchange or capital controls imposed by foreign governments restrict the ability of the business to use the proceeds of the export sale, and

2. There are special forms and schedules to be completed that reflect specific issues that arise only in international transactions.

Recognition and Source of Income

Recognition of Income

In general, businesses are considered to recognize income and are required to report the income for tax purposes when the business receives the income, accrues the income under generally accepted accounting principles, or has the right to obtain the income.

Time of Payment

Generally, income is recognized when received or accrued. Recognition of income may take place earlier than actual receipt, however, when funds are deposited in a bank account in the name of the business or otherwise made freely available to the business. Similarly, recognition of income may take place later than actual receipt if the funds are subject to future contingencies.

A business may recognize income even though payment is made to another company. The determination of whether the recipient is acting solely for the business depends on whether the recipient is a real entity engaged in a real transaction.

U.S. businesses are on the cash method of accounting with respect to amounts owed to a related foreign person except where the related foreign person is a controlled foreign corporation, a passive foreign investment company or a foreign personal holding company, in which case the U.S. business can deduct accrued amounts as of the day on which a corresponding amount of income is recognized by the controlled foreign corporation, the passive foreign investment company or the foreign personal holding company.

Effective October 22, 2004, accrued but unpaid amounts due from a U.S. business to a related controlled foreign corporation or passive foreign investment company cannot be deducted by the U.S. business until a corresponding amount in included in the gross income of a U.S. person(s) who owns stock, directly or through a foreign entity, in the controlled foreign corporation or the passive foreign investment company.

Delivery of Goods

In some situations, a U.S. business will recognize income when goods are delivered to a foreign person. If the purchaser makes advance deposits with the seller or the purchaser pays with an irrevocable letter of credit, delivery of the goods may trigger recognition of income to the U.S. business. However if the U.S. business ships goods on consignment to a foreign dealer, the U.S. business will recognize income after the goods are sold by the dealer.

Receipts in Foreign Currency

U.S. tax liabilities are calculated and paid in U.S. dollars. When U.S. businesses transact in a foreign currency, foreign currency amounts must be translated into U.S. dollars. Also a U.S. business must account, for tax purposes, for gain or loss resulting from changes in relative values of the dollar and a foreign transactional currency while the U.S. business owns or has a position in a foreign transactional currency.

Generally transactions are reported for tax purposes in the business' functional currency. The functional currency of a U.S. citizen or resident or a domestic corporation is usually the U.S. dollar. A foreign currency is the functional currency if the economic environment of the business' "qualified business unit" (QBU) is in a foreign currency.

Qualified Business Unit

A QBU is a separate and clearly identified unit of a trade or business of a taxpayer that maintains separate books and records.

Every corporation, domestic or foreign, is a QBU. In addition, a particular activity of a corporation is a QBU if that activity is a trade or business and a separate set of books and records is maintained for it.

The currency of the economic environment of a QBU's activities is determined from facts and circumstances, the analysis of which is driven primarily by the currencies in which the QBU (1) accrues revenues and incurs expenses, (2) collects revenues and pays expenses, (3) borrows and lends, and (4) makes pricing and other financial decisions. The location of a QBU's principal place of business is also important, as are the duration of a QBU's activities and the volume of its independent activities, because use of a currency is premised upon a long-term commitment to a specific environment. Whether a foreign activity is of sufficient duration to be a QBU depends, in part, on whether the host country taxes those activities.

Example 1-1

The Sessions Group is a U.S. company and maintains headquarters in Delaware. Sessions opens a temporary office in London as part of an assessment of the European market. The London office is used by U.S. executives to support

---

marketing activities while the U.S. executives are in London for brief periods of time. No sales are transacted and Sessions closes the London office after nine months. Sessions deducts the London office start-up and closing expenses on its U.S. return. Sessions' London office is not a QBU.

Example 1-2

Assume, in Example 1-1, that several sales are closed in the United Kingdom and that the Sessions Group London office hires a permanent full-time employee to fulfill post-sale service requirements. Arguably, the presence of a full-time employee creates a taxable presence under United Kingdom tax law and, if so, the Sessions London office is a QBU.

The rate of inflation in a particular location is not considered. If a taxpayer has more than one trade or business, the economic environment analysis is applied to each trade or business.

Occasionally, more than one currency can comprise an economic environment because the QBU does significant business in more than one foreign currency. In this circumstance, a taxpayer may choose any one of the qualifying currencies as the functional currency.

A functional currency is a method of accounting, and adoption of or election of a new functional currency is a change of accounting method, normally accomplished only with consent of the Internal Revenue Service. Permission to change is usually given only if significant changes have occurred in the facts and circumstances of the QBU's economic environment.

A trade or business is a unified group of activities that constitutes an independent economic enterprise carried on for profit. A trade or business must ordinarily include every operation which forms a part of, or a step in, "a process by which an enterprise may earn income or profit...include[ing] the collection of income and payment of expenses." A vertical, functional or geographic division of the same trade or business is itself a trade or business if it is capable of producing income independently.

Example 1-3

Assume, in Example 1-2, that the Sessions Group manufactures goods in the United States and sells the goods to European customers through its London sales office. The London sales office may be a trade or business separate from the manufacturing operation because the sales office could be carried on as an independent economic enterprise.

Activities at a particular location may be a trade or business separate from identical activities at another location.

> **Example 1-4**
>
> Assume, in Example 1-3, that the Sessions Group also maintains sales offices in Paris and Frankfurt in addition to the London sales office. The London, Frankfurt, and Paris sales offices may be three separate trades or businesses.

Merely ancillary activities are not a trade or business.

> **Example 1-5**
>
> Assume, in Example 1-4, that the Sessions Group makes preliminary communications with potential Japanese customers from its headquarters in Delaware. Sessions needs to get documents to the potential Japanese customers to facilitate discussions. Sessions hires a contractor in Japan to deliver the documents. The contractor's activities in Japan are not a trade or business because the activities are ancillary to the communications originating in the United States.

> **Example 1-6**
>
> Assume, in Example 1-5, that Sessions creates a Japanese subsidiary to carry on the courier activities. The subsidiary is a QBU because a corporation, whether or not it has a trade or business, is a QBU.

An individual is not a QBU, but an individual may have a QBU consisting of a trade or business for which separate records are kept.

> **Example 1-7**
>
> U.S. citizen A distributes goods in Spain produced by various U.S. manufacturers. A's activities in Spain are a trade or business and therefore a QBU if separate records are kept for the activities.

However, an individual's activities as an employee are not a trade or business.

> **Example 1-8**
>
> Assume, in Example 1-7, that A hires B, also a U.S. citizen, to oversee A's distributorship in Spain. B's activities in Spain on behalf of A do not constitute a QBU.

A partner is deemed engaged in any business carried on by the partnership.

Foreign Currency Gain and Loss

Foreign currency gain or loss is usually accounted for transaction by transaction when a taxpayer or one of the taxpayer's QBUs engages in a transaction in a nonfunctional currency. A nonfunctional currency is a currency other than the functional currency of the taxpayer or QBU.

> **Example 1-9**
>
> Assume, in Example 1-4, that the Sessions Group, for which the overall functional currency is the dollar, has a QBU in Paris, for which the functional currency is the Euro.
>
> All currencies other than the Euro (including the U.S. dollar) are nonfunctional currencies for the Paris QBU. In contrast, for transactions not connected with any QBU of Sessions Group, all currencies other than the dollar (including the Euro) are nonfunctional currencies.

Treasury regulations provide that exchange gain or loss is calculated transaction by transaction and that gain or loss realized on separate transactions cannot be integrated regardless of whether the transactions are economically related. The transaction by transaction methodology to calculate exchange gain or loss is summarized below.

- A nonfunctional currency is generally treated as property other than money, and exchange gain or loss is recognized each time the currency is exchanged for a different currency or spent.

- A bank deposit in a nonfunctional currency is usually analyzed as currency.

- Interest income or expense on a debt instrument payable in a nonfunctional currency is translated at the exchange rate in effect when the debt is paid or accrued, and exchange gain or loss is recognized when principal or interest is paid or received.

- Revenues or costs other than interest are translated at the exchange rate on the date the revenue or expense is recognized under the taxpayer's method of accounting. If cash is not received or paid on the same date, exchange gain or loss is recognized when the income is received or the expense is paid.

- Income or loss under a forward, future, swap, or other hedging instrument in a nonfunctional currency is characterized as a gain or loss.

- If a currency contract or bank deposit in a nonfunctional currency hedges a taxpayer's obligation or entitlement under a contract to purchase or sell goods in the ordinary course of business, the hedge may be subsumed into the purchase contract.

- Individuals are usually exempted from recognizing exchange gain or loss with respect to nonfunctional currency used for personal (as distinguished from business and investment) transactions.

- Exchange gain or loss is usually income from sources within the taxpayer's country of residence, and a deduction for exchange loss is normally allocated to income from sources within that country.

Exchange gain or loss is usually ordinary income. Exchange gain or loss must be calculated using a fair market rate of exchange available to the public for currency under a spot contract in a free market and involving representative amounts. Exchange rates found in *International*

Financial Statistics (published by the International Monetary Fund) qualify as spot rates as do rates published in newspapers, financial journals and electronic financial news services.

A governmentally prescribed rate is used instead of a free market rate if the government rate more clearly reflects income in a particular transaction.

Effective for tax years beginning after December 31, 2004, taxpayers may elect to translate foreign income tax payments at the exchange rate in effect when the tax is paid instead of the average exchange rate in effect during the tax year in which the foreign taxes are accrued or paid.

This election applies to the tax year for which the election is made and to all subsequent years, unless revoked with the consent of the Treasury Secretary.

Example 1-10

Assume the government of country *X* establishes an exchange rate of 1u for $1, but the rate on a secondary market is 1u for 60 cents. U.S. corporation *D* purchases 100u for $60 on the secondary market and transfers 100u to its QBU in country *X*, which uses the country X currency as its functional currency and the QBU exchanges the 100u for $100 at the official rate.

The transfer of the 100u currency to *D* triggers recognition of gain or loss because the 100u are a nonfunctional currency to corporation *D*'s home office but the functional currency to the QBU. *D* has foreign currency gain on the transfer of $40 (dollar value of 100u at the official rate of 1u to $1 less $60 basis for the 100u). Corporation *D*'s income on the transfer to the QBU is most clearly reflected by the official rate because these transactions exploit the difference between the official and secondary market exchange rates.

Calculating Taxable Income for QBUs with Foreign Functional Currencies (Non-Hyperinflationary Currencies)

If a taxpayer has one or more QBUs with functional currencies that are different from the taxpayer's overall functional currency, taxable income or loss is calculated separately for each QBU. The calculation is completed in the QBU's functional currency, usually using a profit and loss method. A QBU is called a QBU branch if its functional currency differs from the taxpayer's overall functional currency and the QBU uses the profit and loss method. If a QBU's functional currency is hyperinflationary, a U.S. dollar approximate separate transaction method (DASTM) may be elected and is sometimes required.

Under the profit and loss method, taxable income or loss and earnings and profits are calculated in three steps, which are summarized below.

1.   A profit and loss statement is prepared from the branch's books and records in the branch's foreign functional currency.

2.   This statement is adjusted to conform to U.S. tax principles.

3.   The profit or loss shown on the adjusted statement is translated into dollars at the average exchange rate for the tax year, which is the simple average of daily exchange rates during the year exclusive of weekends and other nonbusiness days.

A loss calculated under the profit and loss method may be recognized even if the loss exceeds the taxpayer's investment in the branch.

Example 1-11

Assume a U.S. corporation organizes a branch in the foreign country X and funds the branch with $100, which is worth, at the time of funding, 100 units of the branch's functional currency (the country X u). The branch sustains a loss of $100u$ for the first year of operations, which is translated as $150 under the profit and loss method rules described above. The loss is fully recognized even though the dollar amount of the loss ($150) exceeds the dollar amount of the taxpayer's investment in the branch ($100).

However this excess loss is foreign currency gain that will subsequently be recognized as such through a recapture of the excess loss deduction when the branch makes a remittance to the taxpayer or terminates.

Calculating Taxable Income for QBUs with Hyperinflationary Foreign Functional Currencies

If the currency that would otherwise be a QBU's functional currency is hyperinflationary, the dollar must be used as the functional currency under a U.S. DASTM. Under DASTM, revenues and costs are translated into dollars as incurred and exchange gain and loss is recognized as it occurs.

In providing for this method, Congress recognized that for taxpayers operating in hyperinflationary currencies, local currency based accounting might not accurately reflect income or loss. More generally, tax calculations based on historical cost, including cost of goods sold, gain on sale of assets, interest income and expense, as well as depreciation, are distorted by inflation, and the distortion is most severe when inflation is high. DASTM largely insulates income calculations from the effects of inflation in hyperinflationary currency.

Example 1-12

Assume U.S. corporation D has a branch in country Z for which the functional currency is the country Z u. Country Z has experienced substantial inflation, and extraordinarily high interest rates reflect an expectation of continued inflation. D borrows 1000 u from a country Z lender at 45 percent interest. If corporation D is allowed to calculate branch taxable income under the profit and loss method, D would be allowed to deduct annual interest expense of $450u$ translated at the average exchange rate for the year. Most of the interest is effectively compensation to the country Z lender for erosion of the lender's principal through inflation. If cumulative inflation in the u is 40 percent during the year, the value of the principal falls by 40 percent during the year, and the interest cost in constant u's is only $50u$ ($450u$ nominal interest less $400u$ decrease in value of principal).

QBU's Required to Use DASTM

A QBU must adopt DASTM if its functional currency would otherwise be a hyperinflationary currency, that is, a currency in which cumulative inflation was at least 100 percent over the 36-month period immediately preceding the tax year. Cumulative inflation is determined with compounding. If inflation in a particular currency over the relevant 36-month period is 29 percent, 25 percent and 30 percent, the cumulative rate of inflation is 109.6 percent (129 percent of 125 percent of 130 percent, less 100 percent), not 84 percent (sum of 29, 25 and 30). The inflation rate is based on the consumer price index for the country issuing the currency, as given in *International Financial Statistics* (a publication of the International Monetary Fund).

A change to DASTM required by the regulations is deemed made with IRS consent. If a QBU is required to use DASTM for any year, DASTM becomes a method of accounting that can be changed only with IRS consent, except that the QBU must return to the profit and loss method, using the currency of its economic environment as functional currency, once that currency has not been hyperinflationary for three successive years.

General Application of DASTM

Under DASTM, annual income or loss, and earnings and profits or deficit, is calculated by following the steps listed below.

1. Prepare an income or loss statement from the QBU's books in the hyperinflationary currency.

2. Adjust the statement to conform to U.S. accounting principles.

3. Add or subtract DASTM gain or loss.

The translation into U.S. dollars is usually done by breaking each item on the income or loss statement into monthly amounts and translating the amount for each month at the exchange rate for the month. Taxpayers can adopt shorter translation periods but the periods must be equal in length, and, once elected, may be changed only with consent of the Internal Revenue Service.

DASTM Gain or Loss

Currency gain or loss (DASTM gain or loss) is ordinary income or loss and is the sum of the items listed below.

1. The QBU's net worth at the end of the year, plus

2. Any dividends or other remittances to the United States, credited income taxes or other adjustments that reduce net worth but do not affect income, less

3. Net worth at the end of the previous year, plus

4. The QBU's current year income, loss, earnings and profits or deficit, and

5. Net worth increases that do not affect income

Source of Income

U.S. businesses are generally taxed on worldwide income. To mitigate double taxation of foreign income, U.S. businesses may deduct foreign taxes, or, alternatively, elect to take a credit for taxes paid to foreign countries. Foreign taxes are creditable only against the U.S. income tax on foreign-source income. Therefore businesses exporting goods must determine whether profit earned from the sale of goods is foreign-source or U.S.-source income.

Purchase and Sale of Goods (Other Than Manufactured Inventory)

If export income is earned from the purchase and sale of inventory, other than manufactured inventory, then the location where right, title, and interest in the property are transferred to the purchaser will generally determine the source of income. For example, if a U.S. business purchases tiles in Mexico and sells the tiles in the United States, the income will be U.S.-source income. On the other hand, if the tiles are sold in France, the income will be foreign-source income.

If beneficial ownership and risk of loss are transferred to the buyer while the seller retains bare legal title, the sale will be deemed to have occurred at the time and place where beneficial ownership passed to the purchaser. For example, if the tiles are sold to a buyer in France and title to the tiles passes in France, the income will be foreign-source income. However, if the French buyer takes the risk of loss for the tiles at the moment the tiles are placed on a ship in New York and the French purchaser pays for tiles before the tiles arrive in France, the income should be U.S.-source income.

Factors to Be Examined

The principal factors to be examined in determining the source of income include the following:

- Does the purchaser or seller pay for insurance during shipping?

- Does the purchaser or seller pay for shipping?

- Does the seller retain a security interest in the goods pending payment?

- Does the seller have any additional obligations to perform in addition to transporting the goods?

In situations where the source of income is unclear, the point at which the buyer incurs an unconditional obligation to pay for the merchandise must be determined.

Sale of Manufactured Inventory

Income resulting from sales of inventory manufactured or produced by a U.S. business is divided between the locations of manufacture and sale. If inventory is manufactured or produced and sold in the United States, any income from sale of that inventory is sourced to the United States.

Gross income on a sale of inventory produced by a U.S. business outside of the United States, or a sale outside of the United States of inventory produced in the United States is sourced partly within and partly outside the United States.

The term "produced" includes manufactured, produced, created, fabricated, extracted, processed, cured or aged. Only production activities conducted directly by the taxpayer are considered for this purpose.

Relevant regulation describe two methods that may be used for allocating or apportioning income from these transactions (Section 863 sales)—a 50/50 method and an independent factory price (IFP) method. The 50/50 method applies to any Section 863 sale unless the taxpayer elects the IFP or books and records method for those sales. Whatever method a taxpayer utilizes for Section 863 sales must be applied separately to U.S. sales of goods produced outside of the United States and foreign sales of inventory produced in the United States.

50/50 METHOD

Under the 50/50 method, one half of the income from Section 863 sales is allocated to production activities and one half is allocated to the sales function.

Example 1-13

If Sessions Corporation produces inventory in the United States at a cost of $40 and sells that inventory in a foreign country for $100, the resulting income or $60 ($100 less $40) is allocated $30 to the United States as the place of production and $30 to the foreign country as the place of sale. The 50/50 method is the default method and is applicable unless the taxpayer elects the IFP method or the books and records method.

IFP METHOD

A taxpayer that fairly establishes an IFP may elect to apportion gross income from Section 863 sales by the IFP method, which operates as though the taxpayer's factory sold the inventory to its sales branch for the IFP. Gross receipts from the sale equal to the IFP are apportioned to production activities, and that amount, less the taxpayer's cost of goods sold (including only costs incurred at the place of production) is gross income from production activities and is sourced to the place of production. The remainder of the sales price, less any additional cost of goods sold incurred in sales activities is gross income sourced to the place of sale.

Example 1-14

Sessions Corporation is incorporated in the United States. Sessions Corporation produces inventory in the United States at a cost of $80. Sessions sales branch in London sells the inventory to retail stores in the U.K. for $110. Sessions sells identical inventory for $100 in transactions with unrelated buyers. These sales establish an IFP for $100. Under the IFP method, U.S. source income on Sessions sale to its retail store (income from production activities) is $20 ($100 sales revenue less $80 cost of goods sold), and foreign source income (income from sales activities) is $10.

An IFP is fairly established only if the taxpayer regularly sells a part of its manufactured inventory to independent distributors or other selling concerns in such a way as to reasonably establish the income earned from the production activity. Sales activities in connection with these sales may not be significant in relation to all of the activities undertaken with respect to the product. A particular IFP may only be used for sales that are reasonably contemporaneous with sales establishing the IFP and sales in geographic markets that are not substantially different from the markets in which the IFP sales are made.

The IFP method is elective. Once elected for any Section 863 sales, the IFP method must be used for all sales of inventory that are substantially similar in physical characteristics and function and sold at a similar level of distribution. All income from IFP sales is sourced where the inventory is produced. The IFP election is binding for all tax years subsequent to the year in which the IFP election is made. The taxpayer can abandon the IFP with IRS consent which will not be withheld unless the change would substantially distort the source of the taxpayer's income. Moreover the IFP method must be used for all sales of inventory for which IFPs are established during the election and any subsequent year.

Example 1-15

Assume Sessions Corporation manufactures three dissimilar products and establishes an IFP for one of the products. Sessions Corporation elects the IFP method for sales of that product and elects the 50/50 method for the other two products. Sessions Corporation must continue to use the IFP method for the first product as long as Sessions Corporation has an IFP for that product. If Sessions Corporation subsequently establishes an IFP for the second or third product, income on sales of that product must thereafter be apportioned by the IFP method.

BOOKS AND RECORDS METHOD

A taxpayer may apportion income from Section 863 sales by the method used to keep its books and records provided that the taxpayer has received advance permission from the Service. Once permission is granted, the books and records method must be used for all tax years unless the Service consents to a change. Permission to change will not be withheld unless the change would result in a substantial distortion of the source of the taxpayer's income. Permission to use the books and records method is granted only if the taxpayer demonstrates that the taxpayer will regularly employ in its books of account a detailed allocation of receipts and expenses that clearly reflects the amount of the taxpayer's income from production and sales activities.

SOURCES OF GROSS AND TAXABLE INCOME FROM PRODUCTION AND SALES ACTIVITIES

The 50/50, IFP, and books and records methods divide income between production and sales activities. The production share is sourced to the country or countries in which production activities occur and the sales share is sourced to the country or countries in which the sales occur.

The place of sale is presumed to be the United States if the inventory is wholly produced and sold for use, consumption or disposition in the United States. For this purpose, goods are considered produced wholly in the United States even if packaging, repackaging, labeling, or other minor assembly operations occur outside the United States. This presumption cannot be rebutted by transferring title to the buyer in a foreign country. It is not clear what evidence might rebut the presumption. The presumption was included in anticipation of possible abuses involving of inventory produced or sold in international waters or in space. However the express terms of the presumption are not so limited and appear to apply if, for example, inventory is produced in New York, exported to Canada, packaged and labeled and sold to the buyer in Michigan pursuant to a contract transferring title in Canada.

The production share is wholly from U.S. or foreign sources if the taxpayer's production assets are located only in the United States or only outside of the United States. Production assets include tangible and intangible assets owned directly by the taxpayer and used by the taxpayer to produce inventory sold in Section 863 sales. Production assets do not include accounts receivable, marketing intangibles and other intellectual property not related to the production of inventory, property used to transport inventory, warehouses, inventory itself, raw materials or work-in-process. Cash and other liquid assets, even if serving as working capital for production activity, are not production assets. Intangible production assts are deemed located where tangible assets are used in the same production activity.

If production assets are located both within and outside the United States, the production share is split between U.S. and foreign sources in proportion to the average adjusted basis of the production assets. If the assets are used to produce both inventory sold in Section 863 sales and other inventory (for example, inventory sold in the country in which the inventory is produced) only a portion of the adjusted basis of these assets is included, and this portion must be determined by some method that reasonably reflects the portion of the assets that produces inventory sold in Section 863 sales.

If a taxpayer enters into or structures a transaction with a principal purpose of reducing its U.S. tax liability by manipulating the basis formula, the Service may make appropriate adjustments so that the source of the taxpayer's income from production activity more clearly reflects the source of that income.

Example 1-16

Sessions Corporation owns production assets in the United States and the United Kingdom. Assets in both countries are used to manufacture inventory sold in Section 863 sales. In order to reduce the portion of production income apportioned to U.S. sources, Sessions Corporation sells its U.S. production assets. Immediately following the sale, Sessions Corporation leases the same production assets back from the purchaser.

Only production assets owned directly by the taxpayer are considered. No part of income allocated to production may be assigned to the place of manufacturing conducted by another person under contract to the taxpayer regardless of whether the contract manufacturer is related or unrelated to the taxpayer.

Manipulation of the Source of Income

The source of income may be particularly unclear where the taxpayer is in a position to control elements on both sides of a transaction or where one party makes adjustments to normal business practices solely to accommodate tax planning of the other party.

Where transactions are arranged in a particular manner primarily to avoid tax, the Internal Revenue Service will examine all factors of the transaction to determine where the substance of the sale occurred. In addition to the factors listed above, the IRS will look to the place where negotiations and execution of the agreement occurred, the location of the property that is the subject of the transaction, and the place of payment.

Example 1-17

The Sessions Group wishes to sell its aircraft parts to the Kingdom of Ukiah. Sessions is seriously concerned about the political stability of Ukiah and would ordinarily insist on receiving cash and completing the deal before the parts leave the Sessions plant in the United States. Sessions would also like to recognize foreign-source income on the transaction.

In order to try to accommodate both goals, the buyer and the seller agree to execute all documents of sale in Mexico. The planes remain in the United States in a public warehouse, but the seller will transfer the parts to the buyer by endorsing warehouse receipts to the buyer. Ukiah will make payment into a Mexican bank account in the name of Sessions.

Based on these facts, the IRS or a court could conclude that Sessions earned foreign-source income or that the arrangements in Mexico do not change the conclusion that beneficial ownership of the goods passed in the United States and that the seller recognized U.S.-source income.

Chapter 2

Allocation and Apportionment of Deductions

Allocation and Apportionment of Deductions

Until 1977, the requirement that expenses, losses and other deductions be apportioned or allocated among gross income from various sources was implemented through case law and vague regulations. In 1977 regulations were issued to ensure that foreign operations of U.S. businesses bear an appropriate share of the worldwide enterprise's deductions. But foreign corporations operating in the United States also use these rules to assign expenses to gross income effectively connected with a U.S. trade or business.

The regulations are based on the factual relationship of the expense, loss or other deduction to gross income. The analysis of this relationship is a two-step process.

1. Deductions are allocated to income from activities and investments in which the deductible costs are incurred. If the income class to which a deduction is allocated consists solely of income within or outside of the relevant taxable income category (for example, foreign-source taxable income) or statutory grouping, the allocation is complete.

2. A deduction allocated to a class of income including both income in the statutory grouping and other income (the residual grouping) is apportioned between the groupings on a basis that reflects the factual relationships between deductions and income.

Special allocation and apportionment rules apply to expenses incurred by shareholders, income taxes, losses on dispositions of personal property other than inventory, net operating loss (NOL) deductions unrelated to income-producing activities and investments, personal and dependency exemptions, interest and R&E expense.

Allocations to Gross Income Classes

A class of gross income may consist of one or more of the 15 items of gross income enumerated in Section 61 or other provisions of the Internal Revenue Code. The gross income items enumerated in Section 61 are listed below.

1. Compensation for provision of services.

2. Business income.

3. Gains from disposition of property.

4. Interest.

5.   Rents.

6.   Royalties.

7.   Dividends.

8.   Alimony.

9.   Annuities.

10.   Income from life insurance.

11.   Pensions.

12.   Income from discharge of indebtedness.

13.   Partnership income.

14.   Income in respect of decedent.

15.   Income from an interest in an estate or trust.

A deduction is definitely related to a class of gross income if it is incurred as a result of, or incident to, an activity or in connection with property from which such class of gross income is derived. A deduction may be definitely related to all of a business' gross income.

Example 2-1

Cage Consolidated Corp. is domiciled in Thetford, Vermont and maintains headquarters there. Cage Consolidated manufactures music synthesizers at its plant in the southern European country of Tarzana. The synthesizers are sold through sales branches in several European countries and in the United States.

Expenses of the U.S. sales branch are definitely related to gross income from sales by the U.S. sales branch because these expenses are incurred in an activity contributing to the production of this gross income. In contrast, expenses of sales achieved through Cage Consolidated European sales branches are definitely related to foreign-source gross income from those sales.

Cage Consolidated's general management expenses are definitely related to all of Cage Consolidated's gross income. Accordingly general management expenses are allocated to a class consisting of all gross income from business operations.

If an activity or item of property is expected to generate income of a particular class, expenses of the activity or property are allocated to that class regardless of whether the activity or property yields gross income for the tax year. If there is gross income, definitely related deductions are allocated regardless of whether the deductions are greater or less than the gross income.

Statutory and Residual Groupings

Gross income is also divided between statutory groupings and residual groupings. A statutory grouping consists of gross income of one or more of the 15 items of gross income enumerated in

Section 61 of the Internal Revenue Code or any other relevant Internal Revenue Code provision. The residual grouping is all gross income not in the statutory grouping.

If a deduction is definitely related to a class of gross income that is entirely within a statutory grouping, the deduction is allowed in full in calculating the relevant taxable amount. Conversely, none of the deduction is allowed if the gross income class is entirely within the residual grouping.

Example 2-2

Assume Cage Consolidated manufactures its music synthesizers in the United States and sells the music synthesizers through a sales branch in Tarzana. Cage Consolidated has an independent factory price (IFP) for the music synthesizers and elects to use the IFP method to divide gross income on sales between U.S. source manufacturing income and foreign-source sales income.

Expenses of the Tarzana branch are definitely related to foreign-source gross income and are therefore deducted in determining taxable income from foreign-sources. Expenses of manufacturing operations are definitely related to U.S. gross income from manufacturing, which is in the residual grouping and these expenses are therefore excluded in calculating foreign-source taxable income.

Apportionment

If a deduction is definitely related to a class of gross income that includes both gross income of a statutory grouping and the residual grouping, an apportionment is required.

Example 2-3

Assume, in Example 2-2, that Cage Consolidated incurs general management expenses in connection with the manufacture and sale of its music synthesizers, some of which are sold in the United States and some of which are sold through Cage Consolidated sales branches in Tarzana and other countries in southern Europe.

The U.S. sales create U.S. source income and the foreign sales create foreign-source income. If the general management expenses related to all Cage Consolidated sales, the general management expenses are definitely related to a class of gross income that includes both U.S. and foreign-source income and therefore must be apportioned.

The apportionment must be done in a way that reflects to a reasonably close extent the factual relationship between the deduction and the grouping of gross income. The regulations suggest, but do not require, that the factors listed below be considered in apportioning deductions between U.S. and foreign-source gross income.

1.   Number of units sold.

2.   Amount of gross sales.

3.   Cost of goods sold.

4. Relative share of profit contributed.

5. Expenses directly attributable to earning gross income.

6. Assets the use of which is directly attributable to earning gross income.

7. Administrative costs (including salaries, use of space, person hours spent) the use of which is directly attributable to earning gross income.

8. Gross income.

Example 2-4

Cage Consolidated Corp. manufactures music synthesizers at its plant in Thetford, Vermont (Cage-U.S.). In addition, Cage Consolidated Corp. manufactures and sells synthesizers through its Tarzana branch (Cage-Tarzana) and the Tarzana facility qualifies as a QBU. The synthesizers sold in the foreign market are more expensive than the synthesizers sold in the United States. For 2010, Cage-U.S. and Cage-Tarzana report the following the financial data shown below.

	Cage-U.S.	Cage-Tarzana
Units sold	247	645
Gross sales	$3,322,150	$7,256,250
Cost of goods sold	$1,068,275	$2,673,525
Gross income	$2,253,875	$4,582,725
Compensation paid	$115,000	$310,000
Shipping costs	$45,500	$22,500
Administrative costs	$29,500	$46,750
Total deductions	$190,000	$379,250
Net income	$2,063,875	$4,203,475

In order to apportion expenses based on the facts of this example, Cage Consolidated Corp. must place its gross income into appropriate gross income classes. Here both Cage-U.S. gross income and Cage-Tarzana gross income are in the business income class of gross income.

Next, Cage Consolidated Corp. must aggregate deductible expenses incurred in earning gross income. In this example, these expenses are $190,000 for Cage-U.S. and $379,250 for Cage-Tarzana or $569,250 in total.

Cage Consolidated Corp. can apportion these expenses under any of the apportionment methods shown below.

Apportionment Methods	Cage-Tarzana	Cage-U.S.
Units sold	411,621	157,629
Gross sales	$390,477	$178,773
Cost of goods sold	$406,730	$162,520
Compensation paid	$415,218	$154,032

The results among the four methods listed are not significantly different. In different situations the different apportionment method calculations could vary significantly. Before choosing an apportionment method, a judgment must be

---

made as to which apportionment method is most appropriate and defensible in the taxpayer's unique situation.

Variation

Assume the same facts, but Cage-Tarzana is operated as a separate, independent entity, the appropriate apportionment method to select would be the apportionment that most nearly reflects Cage-Tarzana's separate income statement. In the facts of Example 2-4, Cage-Tarzana's share of costs is approximately one third of total costs. Of the apportionment methods shown, gross sales, reflecting a ratio of 31:100, would most nearly approximate a separate income statement calculation and would therefore be the most appropriate and therefore defensible apportionment method.

Shareholder Expenses

Stewardship or shareholder expenses incurred in looking after an investment in stock are allocated to the class of gross income consisting of dividends received or to be received from the corporation. The same rule applies to expenses incurred by a corporation overseeing its investment in another corporation.

Activities undertaken for the corporation's own benefit in a related corporation are distinguished and handled differently from services performed by a shareholder corporation for a related corporation. If no charge is made, costs incurred in performing services for a related corporation are assigned as gross income to the entity performing the services under Code Sec. 482. Generally the distinction between oversight activities and services for a related corporation is that the former duplicate activities of the related corporation and the latter do not.

Example 2-5

Colgrass Corp. is a U.S. corporation that distributes wine in the United States. Colgrass has wholly owned subsidiaries in the Republics of Norco and Termo. Colgrass-Norco operated independently for 60 years before it was acquired by Colgrass in 2010. Colgrass made no significant changes to Colgrass-Norco personnel, management, or operations. Colgrass-Termo was formed in 2010 to acquire land and develop wine grapes. Colgrass-Termo is staffed with Termo and U.S. personnel and relies on Colgrass for many consulting services, for which Colgrass-Termo pays an arm's length fee. In 2010, Colgrass incurred $150,000 expenses to integrate the financial plan of Colgrass-Norco into the consolidated plan of the Colgrass Group. Colgrass incurred $200,000 expense preparing budgets and other financial material for Colgrass-Termo.

The $150,000 expense incurred to integrate the financial plan of Colgrass-Norco is allocable to dividends paid by Colgrass-Norco. The $200,000 expense incurred for Colgrass-Termo budgets and other financial materials are not allocable against Colgrass-Termo dividend income and can be deducted as stewardship on Colgrass Corp.'s U.S. income tax return.

Income Taxes

The general rule is to allocate the income tax deduction to gross income subject to the income tax. If a state taxes worldwide income, then a portion of the state income tax paid is allocated to foreign-source income. If a state taxes only U.S. source income, then that state's taxes are allocated only to U.S. source income.

Net Operating Losses

NOL deductions are allocated in the same manner as the deductions that created the NOL.

> **Example 2-6**
>
> Colgrass Corp. sustains a $10,000,000 net operating loss for 2010. The $10,000,000 NOL consists of $10,000,000 foreign-source taxable income and $20,000,000 U.S. Source loss. Colgrass Corp.'s deductions for the NOL in carryback and carryforward years are allocated entirely to U.S. source income because the NOL is entirely attributable to U.S. deductions.

Deductions Not Definitely Related to Any Gross Income

Deductions that are not related to business activities or investments are apportioned ratably among all gross income.

Personal and Dependency Exemptions

The deduction allocation and apportionment rules do not apply to personal and dependency exemptions. These exemptions are ignored in determining both foreign-source taxable and worldwide taxable income.

Interest

Generally interest expense is attributed to all of a business' activities and assets regardless of any specific reason for incurring a debt obligation. Interest expense is usually apportioned among all classes of gross income in proportion to the values of assets utilized in generating income.

Asset Method

Generally interest expense is apportioned according to the average of total assets producing income within the statutory and residual groupings.

> **Example 2-7**
>
> Colgrass Corp. has interest expense of $15,000,000 for 2010 and the average total value of Colgrass Corp.'s assets at the end of 2010 is $360,000,000, including $60,000,000 for assets used in activities producing gross income for foreign-sources. The interest expense allocated to foreign-source taxable income is calculated as $15,000,000 × $60,000,000 / $360,000,000 = $2,500,000. The remaining $12,500,000 interest expense ($15,000,000 − $2,500,000) is assigned to the residual grouping.

Assets are placed in a statutory grouping if the assets generate or have generated or are reasonably expected to generate income within that grouping and assets not matched with a statutory grouping are in the residual grouping. The physical location of the assets is not relevant. Generally, assets are divided into the three categories listed below.

1. Assets producing income exclusively within one statutory grouping or the residual grouping.

2. Assets producing income within two or more groupings.

3. Assets that produce no identifiable income yield or that contribute equally to all income of the taxpayer, such as assets used in general and administrative functions.

Assets in the second category are prorated according to gross income in the different groupings generated by the asset. If one-third of the income earned by the asset during the tax year is in a statutory grouping and two-thirds is in a residual grouping, the asset's value is split between the statutory and residual groupings in the same proportion. Assets in the third category, with no identifiable income, are disregarded.

The value used for assets to apportion interest under the asset method is either tax book value or fair market value. Once a business elects to use fair market value, the business and all related persons or entities must use fair market value until the IRS expressly authorizes a change. Tax book value is the asset's adjusted basis for tax (as opposed to financial) purposes.

For publicly-traded companies, fair market value is equal to the sum of the values of all outstanding stock plus the company's liabilities. Liabilities to related persons are excluded but the business' share of liabilities of related parties to third persons is included.

For companies that are not publicly traded, asset value is determined by capitalizing earnings. Tangible assets are valued by generally accepted valuation techniques. The value of intangible assets is calculated as the value of all assets less the value of tangible assets. Total intangible value is apportioned among intangible assets according to net income from operations before interest expense and income taxes.

If a business elects to use fair market value to apportion interest expense under the asset method but fails to establish fair market value of all assets, the IRS may determine asset value or require use of book value.

Generally the asset values selected, tax book or fair market value, are the arithmetic average of values as of the beginning and end of the tax year.

> **Example 2-8**
>
> Colgrass Corp.'s assets are valued at $200,000,000 at the end of 2009 and $200,200,000 at the end of 2010, of which $40,000,000 and $60,000,000 represent assets within a statutory grouping, respectively, at the end of 2009 and 2010. For 2009, the average asset value in the statutory group is $50,000,000, calculated as $40,000,000 value in 2009 plus $60,000,000 value in 2010 which equals $100,000,000. $100,000,000 divided by two equals $50,000,000 and the overall average is $200,100,000, calculated as $200,000,000 overall value in 2009

> plus $200,200,000 overall value in 2010, which equals $400,200,000. $400,200,000 divided by two equals $200,100,000.

If substantial distortion results from averaging beginning and end-of-year values, the averages must be calculated under a method that more clearly reflects the average value of assets weighted to reflect the time the assets are held.

Direct Allocations

In situations involving non-recourse debt, integrated financial transactions and loans to controlled foreign corporations, interest expense is allocated only to income from the asset financed with the non-recourse debt, integrated financial transactions or loans to a controlled foreign corporation. Similarly, bond premium amortization is allocated only to interest income generated by the bond.

Nonrecourse Debt

Interest is allocated exclusively to income generated by the asset secured by the debt if the requirements listed below are met.

1. The debt is incurred to purchase, construct or improve real or depreciable personal property (including amortizable intangibles) with a useful life in excess of one year.

2. The debt is so used.

3. The debt is entirely secured by the acquired, constructed, or improved property.

4. Expected cash income from the property can service the debt.

5. The loan agreement protects the lender's security interest and right to the cash income earned by the collateral.

If the secured assets do not generate income, interest expense is nevertheless allocated to the secured assets to the extent of income the assets could reasonably be expected to generate.

Integrated Financial Transaction

If a business borrows as part of an integrated financial transaction, interest on the borrowing is allocated entirely to income from the integrated financial transaction. An integrated financial transaction consists of an identified term investment and debt that finances the investment.

Example 2-9

Colgrass-Termo invests excess cash in a portfolio of stocks representing a stock index with a forward contract to sell a specified quantity of the stocks in the portfolio at a designated future date for a specified price. Colgrass-Termo might borrow money to finance its investment if the interest on the borrowing is lower than the implicit interest rate in the difference between the current and forward prices of the stock portfolio.

An integrated financial transaction must meet the requirements listed below.

1.   Debt must be incurred to finance an identified term investment.

2.   Simultaneous with the borrowing, the taxpayer must identify the debt as so incurred.

3.   The term investment must be acquired within 10 days of the borrowing.

4.   The projected return on the borrowing must be sufficient to service the debt.

5.   The income earned by the investment must be interest or interest equivalent.

6.   The maturities of the debt and the investment cannot differ by more than 10 days.

7.   The investment cannot be part of or related to normal, ongoing operations of the trade or business.

U.S. Shareholder Loans to CFCs

A U.S. shareholder lending money to a controlled foreign corporation may be required to allocate part of its interest expense to interest received from the CFC.

Bond Premium

Premium on the issuance of a debt instrument is amortized over the bond term and is recognized as gross income by the issuer and deducted by the bond holder. The issuer's deduction for interest is allocated to premium income, and the holder's deduction for the premium is allocated to interest on the bond.

Costs of Research and Experimentation

Costs incurred solely to meet legal requirements pertaining to improvement or marketing of products or processes are allocated solely to the jurisdiction imposing the requirement if the costs are not projected to generate more than a *de minimis* amount of gross income elsewhere. The remainder of a business' R&E expenses are allocated and apportioned, at the business' election, by sales or gross income.

Under the sales method, one-half of the R&E expenses is allocated to the country that is the situs of the activities in which the R&E expenses are incurred, and one-half of the R&E expenses is prorated according to sales. Under the sales apportionment, sales revenues and R&E expenses are grouped into broad product categories and expenses in each category are apportioned according to sales revenues in the category.

Under the gross income apportionment method, one-fourth of R&E expenses is allocated exclusively to the location in which the R&E activities take place and the remainder is apportioned according to gross income. However under the gross income apportionment method, the amounts assigned to statutory groupings and to residual gross income must be at least 50 percent of the amount assigned to this income under the sales apportionment method.

Local Legal Requirement

If research and development is undertaken solely to satisfy legal requirements imposed by a political entity with respect to improvement or marketing of special products or processes and the work is not reasonably expected to generate more than a *de minimis* amount of income outside the jurisdiction imposing the requirements, the R&E expenses are allocated only to income from sources in that country.

Example 2-10

Cortes Cybernetics, Inc. manufactures control devices for food preparation machines. During the past five years, Cortes has operated a branch that is a Qualified Business Unit (QBU) in the Kingdom of Hemet (Cortes-Hemet) and has drawn on an abundant pool of graduates of the Hemet Institute of Technology in order to build a research unit in the Kingdom of Hemet.

For 2010, the relevant financial data of Cortes Cybernetics are shown below.

	Cortes-U.S.	Cortes-Hemet	Total
Gross sales	$12,235,650	$15,360,000	$27,595,650
Cost of goods sold	$5,155,350	$4,545,500	$9,700,850
Gross income	$7,080,300	$10,814,500	$17,894,800
Research expenses	$2,745,000	$1,675,500	$4,420,500
Tentative net income	$4,335,300	$9,139,000	$13,474,300

Assuming that there is no obligation under Hemet law to incur R&E expense in Hemet, there is a 50 percent apportionment to Cortes-U.S. research and Cortes-Hemet, respectively. 50 percent of Cortes-U.S. research expense, $2,745,000 is $1,372,500. 50 percent of Cortes-Hemet research expenses is $1,675,500, is $837,750.

	Cortes-U.S.	Cortes-Hemet	Total
Gross sales	$12,235,650	$15,350,000	$27,585,650
Cost of goods sold	$5,155,350	$4,545,500	$9,700,850
Gross income	$7,080,300	$10,804,500	$17,884,800
Research expenses	$2,745,000	$1,675,500	$4,420,500
Tentative net income	$4,335,300	$9,129,000	$13,464,300
50 percent Situs allocation	$1,372,500		$1,372,500
50 percent Situs allocation		$837,750	$837,750

The remaining 50 percent of R&E expenses ($1,372,500 Cortes-U.S. and $837,750 Cortes-Hemet) can be apportioned on the basis of gross income or sales. A gross sales apportionment of the remaining R&E expense is shown below.

	Cortes-U.S.	Cortes-Hemet	Total
Gross sales	$12,235,650	$15,350,000	$27,585,650
Cost of goods sold	$5,155,350	$4,545,500	$9,700,850
Gross income	$7,080,300	$10,804,500	$17,884,800
Research expenses	$2,745,000	$1,675,500	$4,420,500
Tentative net income	$4,335,300	$9,129,000	$13,464,300
Hemet legal requirement			

---

50 percent Situs allocation	$1,372,500		$1,372,500
50 percent Situs allocation		$837,750	$837,750
Gross sales allocation	$980,359	$1,229,891	$2,210,250
Total allocation	$2,352,859	$2,067,641	$4,420,500

A gross income apportionment is shown below.

	Cortes-U.S.	Cortes-Hemet	Total
Gross sales	$12,235,650	$15,350,000	$27,585,650
Cost of goods sold	$5,155,350	$4,545,500	$9,700,850
Gross income	$7,080,300	$10,804,500	$17,884,800
Research expenses	$2,745,000	$1,675,500	$4,420,500
Tentative net income	$4,335,300	$9,129,000	$13,464,300
Hemet legal requirement			
50 percent Situs allocation	$1,372,500		$1,372,500
50 percent Situs allocation		$837,750	$837,750
Gross income allocation	$875,002	$1,335,248	$2,210,250
Total allocation	$2,247,502	$2,172,998	$4,420,500

Example 2-11

Assume, alternatively, the same facts as in Example 2-10 except that the Kingdom of Hemet law requires that R&E expense in the amount of 10 percent of current annual sales be incurred in Hemet. The apportionment process would now have three steps, beginning with the calculation of the Hemet legal requirement.

	Cortes-U.S.	Cortes-Hemet	Total
Gross sales	$12,235,650	$15,350,000	$27,585,650
Cost of goods sold	$5,155,350	$4,545,500	$9,700,850
Gross income	$7,080,300	$10,804,500	$17,884,800
Research expenses	$2,745,000	$1,675,500	$4,420,500
Tentative net income	$4,335,300	$9,129,000	$13,464,300
10 percent Hemet legal requirement		$1,535,000	$1,535,000

After substituting the amount allocated under the Hemet legal requirement, the remainder is subject to the situs rules. Again, there is a 50 percent apportionment to Cortes-U.S. research and Cortes-Hemet research, respectively. 50 percent of $2,745,000 is $1,372,500; 50 percent of $1,675,500 – $1,535,000 (amount allocated to Hemet pursuant to Hemet legal requirement) is $70,250.

	Cortes-U.S.	Cortes-Hemet	Total
Gross sales	$12,235,650	$15,350,000	$27,585,650
Cost of goods sold	$5,155,350	$4,545,500	$9,700,850
Gross income	$7,080,300	$10,804,500	$17,884,800
Research expenses	$2,745,000	$1,675,500	$4,420,500
Tentative net income	$4,335,300	$9,129,000	$13,464,300
10 percent Hemet legal requirement		$1,535,000	$1,535,000
50 percent Situs allocation	$1,372,500		$1,372,500

50 percent Situs allocation	$70,250	$70,250

Together the Hemet legal requirement and the situs allocations account for $2,977,750 of R&D expenses. The remaining expenses, $1,442,750 ($4,420,500 total R&E expenses less $2,977,750) are then apportioned on a gross income or a gross sales basis. A gross sales apportionment is shown below.

	Cortes-U.S.	Cortes-Hemet	Total
Gross sales	$12,235,650	$15,350,000	$27,585,650
Cost of goods sold	$5,155,350	$4,545,500	$9,700,850
Gross income	$7,080,300	$10,804,500	$17,884,800
Research expenses	$2,745,000	$1,675,500	$4,420,500
Tentative net income	$4,335,300	$9,129,000	$13,464,300
10 percent Hemet legal requirement		$1,535,000	$1,535,000
50 percent Situs allocation	$1,372,500		$1,372,500
50 percent Situs allocation		$70,250	$70,250
Gross sales allocation	$639,934	$802,816	$1,442,750
Total allocation	$2,012,434	$2,408,066	$4,420,500

A gross income apportionment is shown below.

	Cortes-U.S.	Cortes-Hemet	Total
Gross sales	$12,235,650	$15,350,000	$27,585,650
Cost of goods sold	$5,155,350	$4,545,500	$9,700,850
Gross income	$7,080,300	$10,804,500	$17,884,800
Research expenses	$2,745,000	$1,675,500	$4,420,500
Tentative net income	$4,335,300	$9,129,000	$13,464,300
10 percent Hemet legal requirement		$1,535,000	$1,535,000
50 percent Situs allocation	$1,372,500		$1,372,500
50 percent Situs allocation		$70,250	$70,250
Gross income allocation	$521,583	$921,167	$1,442,750
Total allocation	$1,894,083	$2,526,417	$4,420,500

Sales Method

Exclusive Allocation to Place of Research

Under the sales method, which applies unless the business elects to use the gross income method, one-half of a business' R&E expense not otherwise allocated is allocated to the country in which activities accounting for more than half of R&E expenses are located and one-half is apportioned ratably by sales.

If R&E activities are dispersed such that activities at no one geographic source account for more than 50 percent of the expenses, no exclusive apportionment is made and the entire amount is apportioned by sales.

Apportioned by Sales

R&E expenses not allocated exclusively to the place of research are apportioned by sales among product categories. The amount assigned to each category is split between statutory and residual groupings in proportion to sales of goods and services within the product category.

Product categories are taken from the Standard Industrial Classification (SIC) Manual, a publication of the Office of Management and Budget. Examples of product categories are engines and turbines, construction, mining and materials, handling machinery and equipment, electric lighting and wiring equipment, and drugs. A business carrying on R&E activities in more than one product category may combine categories but is not permitted to subdivide categories. Research and development not clearly identified with any product category is considered with any product category related to all of the business' product categories.

Under the sales apportionment, the deduction of R&E expenses, less amounts specifically allocated under rules described above, is apportioned to a statutory grouping in an amount equal to costs incurred multiplied by the ratio of sales revenues within the product category generating gross income in the statutory grouping overall sales revenues in the product category.

Example 2-12

Assume a U.S. corporation's deduction for R&E expenses is $100, $50 of which is allocated exclusively to U.S.-source income because the R&E activities are in the United States and within the product category in which the research is done. The corporation has sales revenues of $1,000, of which $600 is from U.S. sources and $400 is from foreign-sources. R&E expense apportioned to foreign-source taxable income is $20, calculated as $50 apportionable expense ($100 total R&E expense less $50 allocated exclusively to U.S.-source income) multiplied by $400 foreign-source sales revenues divided $1,000 total sales revenues.

The amount of R&E expense allocated to U.S.-source income is $80 ($50 under the exclusive allocation rule and $50 × $600 / $1,000 under the sales apportionment rule).

If R&E expense allocated to a particular product category exceeds the gross income of that category, the excess is allocated against other gross income in the statutory grouping.

Gross Income Method

R&E expenses not incurred to satisfy legal requirements are allocated in two steps as shown below.

1. If more than 50 percent of deductible R&E expenses are incurred in R&E activities located on one geographic location, 25 percent of the deduction is assigned to the location.

2. The remainder is apportioned ratably according to gross income in the statutory and residual groupings. The amount apportioned to the statutory grouping and the residual grouping must be at least 50 percent of what would go into this income under the sales method. If apportionment by gross income is not 50 percent of what would be apportioned to the statutory and residual grouping under the sales method, there is a forced allocation to the statutory or residual grouping, as necessary, of 50 percent of what would be allocated under the sales method and the remainder of the deduction goes to the other grouping. R&E expenses and gross income in all product categories are lumped together for this apportionment.

Election

A business must use the sales method unless the business elects the gross income method. The election must be made for the first tax year in which a business has R&E expenses. Once made, the election is binding for the election year and the following four years. The election is revocable only with IRS consent.

The gross income method must be elected for all R&E expenses or for none. Similarly, the sales method cannot be used for a portion of R&E expenses (for example, expenses relating to particular product categories) and the gross income method for the remainder.

Example 2-13

Cortes Cybernetics, Inc. is a U.S. corporation manufacturing and distributing control devices for food preparation machines. Cortes has R&E expenses of $60,000 in 2010, all of which are incurred in the United States and deducted under IRC §174. The expenses all fall within one product category, 333900, Other General Purpose Machinery Manufacturing, in the Machinery Manufacturing SIC Industry Group.

Cortes Cybernetics has a wholly owned foreign subsidiary, Cortes-Hemet, incorporated in the Republic of Hemet, that manufactures and sells food preparation machine control devices in other foreign countries using technology created by Cortes-U.S. and licensed to Cortes-Hemet. In 2010, Cortes-U.S. sales of food preparation machine control devices are $500,000, all of which are manufactured in the United States, and Cortes-Hemet sales, all transacted in foreign countries, are $300,000. Cortes-U.S. gross income for 2010 consists of $140,000 from U.S. food preparation machine control devices, $10,000 of royalties from Cortes-Hemet (foreign-sources), and $10,000 interest income from U.S. sources. Since Cortes Cybernetics allocated and apportioned deductions solely for purposes of the foreign tax credit limitation, the statutory grouping is gross income from foreign-sources and U.S.-income is residual gross income.

Under the sales method, one-half of the R&E expenses ($30,000) is allocated exclusively to the United States as the situs of R&D activities and the remainder is apportioned by sales as shown below.

$$\text{Statutory grouping:} \frac{\$30,000 \times \$300,000 \text{ (foreign sales)}}{\$800,000 \text{ total sales}} = \$11,250.$$

$$\text{Residual gross income: } \frac{\$30,000 \times \$500,000 \text{ (U.S. sales)}}{\$800,000 \text{ total sales}} = \$18,750.$$

Under the sales method, total R&E expense is apportioned $11,250 to the statutory grouping (foreign-source income) and $48,750 ($30,000 allocated to situs of R&E activities plus $18,750 calculated above) to U.S. income (residual gross income).

Under the gross income method, one-fourth of total R&E expense ($15,000) is allocated to the United States as the situs of R&E activities, and the remaining $45,000 is tentatively allocated by gross income from the product category ($140,000 U.S. source) and royalties ($10,000 foreign-source) as shown below.

Statutory Grouping

$45,000 (total R&E expense less $15,000 allocated and apportioned to U.S. R&E activity situs) × $10,000 foreign-source gross income / $150,000 total gross income ($140,000 U.S. source plus $10,000 foreign-source) = $3,000.

Residual Gross Income

$45,000 (calculated above) × $140,000 (U.S. source gross income) / $150,000 (calculated above) = $42,000.

However, the allocation to the statutory grouping is less than one-half of what it would be under the sales method ($11,250). Therefore, if Cortes Cybernetics elects the gross income method, the apportionment to the statutory grouping is $5,625, which is one-half of $11,250.

Form 1118, Schedule H

An illustration of what is reported on Form 1118, Schedule H can be constructed from the facts in the previous example.

Cortes Cybernetics reports the allocation and apportionment of its R&E expenses on Part I of Schedule H of Form 1118.

On Schedule H, Cortes Cybernetics reports apportionment of deductions alternatively under the sales and gross income methods. Under the sales method, Cortes Cybernetics must report the SIC code for the product line for which the R&E expenses are incurred, 333900, Other General Purpose Machinery Manufacturing.

Cortes Cybernetics reports $800,000 worldwide sales ($500,000 Cortes-U.S. sales plus $300,000 Cortes-Hemet sales) on line 1 of column (i). Since Cortes Cybernetics is allocating and apportioning R&E expenses solely for purposes of the foreign tax credit limitation, the statutory grouping is gross income from foreign-sources and U.S. income is residual income. Accordingly, Cortes Cybernetics enters $300,000 Cortes-Hemet foreign sales as the gross income from foreign-sources statutory grouping on line 3a, general limitation income, of column (i). Cortes Cybernetics completes column (i) of Part 1 of Schedule H of Form 1118 by totaling lines 3a through 3i of column (i), $300,000, on line 4 of column (i).

Cortes Cybernetics enters the total R&E expense incurred in 2010, $60,000, on line 1, column (ii) of Part 1 of Schedule H. Under the sales method, one-half of the R&E expense incurred in 2010, or $30,000, is allocated exclusively to the United States as the situs of R&E activities. The remainder, $60,000 total 2010 R&E expense less $30,000 allocated exclusively to the United States or $30,000, is the amount to be apportioned by sales and is entered on line 2 of column (ii).

R&E expenses allocated to the statutory grouping are calculated as $30,000 apportionable R&E expense × $300,000 foreign sales / $800,000 total sales or $11,250. $11,250 is entered on line 3a of column (ii) of Part 1 of Schedule H. Cortes Cybernetics completes column (ii) of Part 1 of Schedule H of Form 1118 by totaling lines 3a through 3i of column (ii), $11,250, on line 4 of column (ii).

Cortes Cybernetics totals R&E expenses allocated and apportioned under the sales methods in column (v) of Part 1 of Schedule H. Column (v) is completed by totaling columns (ii) and (iv). Cortes Cybernetics is allocating and apportioning R&E expenses attributable to one product line, Other General Purpose Machinery Manufacturing, only, and does not complete column (iv). Therefore, amounts in columns (ii) on lines 1, 2, 3, and 4 are carried to column (v), lines 1, 2, 3,

and 4. Upon completion of column (v), Cortes Cybernetics has reported that $11,250 of total 2010 R&E expense of $60,000 is apportioned to the foreign-source income statutory grouping under the sales method. The remaining 2010 R&E expenses, $48,750, consisting of $30,000 allocated to the United States as situs of 2010 R&E activities plus $18,750 ($30,000 apportionable expenses less $11,250 allocated to the foreign-source income statutory grouping) is allocated to U.S. or residual gross income.

Allocation and apportionment of expenses under the gross income method is reported in column (b) of Part 1 of Schedule H. Cortes Cybernetics checks Option 1 under column (b), under which the amount of R&E expense apportioned to the statutory and residual grouping under the gross income method must be at least 50 percent of the amount that would be apportioned under the sales method.

Cortes Cybernetics enters gross income from the product category, $150,000, ($140,000 Cortes-U.S. gross income from U.S. food preparation machine control devices plus $10,000 foreign-source royalty income from Cortes-Hemet) on line 1 of column (vi). Cortes-Cybernetics enters $60,000 of 2010 R&E expense incurred, in column (vii) line 1.

Under the gross income method, one-fourth of total R&E expense, $15,000, is allocated to the United States as the situs of R&E activities. The remaining $45,000 ($60,000 total R&E expense incurred in 2009 less $15,000 allocated to the United States) is entered in column (vii) line 2. Cortes Cybernetics enters the $10,000 foreign-source royalty from Cortes-Hemet on line 3a of column (vi). Similar to the sales method, foreign-source general limitation income is also the statutory grouping under the gross income method. Cortes Cybernetics totals lines 3a through 3i of column (vi), or $10,000, on line 4, column (vi).

Cortes Cybernetics calculates 2010 R&E expense apportioned to the foreign-source income statutory grouping as $45,000 ($60,000 total R&E expense less $15,000 allocated and apportioned to U.S. R&E activity situs) × $10,000 foreign-source income / $150,000 total gross income ($140,000 U.S.-source plus $10,000 foreign-source) = $3,000. However under option 1 of the gross income method the allocation of apportionable R&E expense must be at least half of what the allocation would be under the sales method ($11,250) or $5,625. Therefore, Cortes-Cybernetics enters $5,625 on line 3a of column (vii) as the amount of R&E expense apportioned to the statutory grouping. Cortes Cybernetics enters the total of lines 3a through 3i of column (vii), $5,625, on line 4. The remainder of apportionable R&E expense under the gross income method ($45,000 less $5,625 R&E expenses apportioned to the statutory grouping or $39,375) is apportioned to residual gross income.

Losses on Personal Property Other Than Inventory

Loss recognized with respect to personal property other than inventory is allocated to the class of gross income that would have included the gain from the transaction if gain had been realized. Loss includes a bad debt write-off or loss on property that is marked to market. Generally gain realized on a sale or exchange of such property is from sources in the business' country of residence. Accordingly, losses are typically deducted from gross income from resident country sources. For example, loss incurred on a U.S. resident's sale of a bond is usually deducted from U.S.-source income. Similarly, a resident's loss on a sale of corporate stock is usually allocated against U.S.-source income, even if gain on a sale of stock may have been characterized as a foreign-source dividend under IRC §1248.

Loss on sale of depreciable property is matched against hypothetical depreciation recapture that would have been recognized if gain had been realized.

Example 2-14

Assume that Cortes Cybernetics Corporation realizes a loss upon sale of food preparation machine control device manufacturing equipment used in the Republic of Hemet to manufacture food preparation machine control devices sold throughout the world, including the United States. Depreciation recapture is U.S.- or foreign-source income in the same proportion as depreciation deductions claimed against U.S.- and foreign-source income, except that all depreciation for any year in which the property was used predominantly outside the United States is deemed to have been deducted from foreign-source income.

Since Cortes Cybernetics used this equipment outside the United States exclusively, loss on the sale is allocated against foreign-source income, even if some of the depreciation was deducted against U.S.-source income.

Loss recognized by a U.S. citizen or resident alien is allocated to foreign-source income if the citizen's or resident alien's tax home is in a foreign country and the foreign country would tax gain on the sale or exchange at a marginal rate of at least 10 percent. A U.S. citizen or resident alien whose tax home is in a foreign country is not a U.S. resident and gain on a sale or exchange of personal property is foreign-sourced if taxed by a foreign country at a rate of at least 10 percent.

Anti-Abuse Rules

Transfer to Change Loss Allocation

If personal property (including stock) is transferred to another person or to a qualified business unit, office or other fixed place of business and if a principal purpose of the transfer is to change the allocation of a loss built into the property at the time of transfer, the transferee must allocated the built-in loss as if the loss had been recognized by the transferor immediately prior to the transfer.

Conversion into Other Property

If property is converted into other property with a principal purpose to change the allocation of loss built into the converted property, loss with respect to the converted property is allocated as if recognized on a sale of the property immediately prior to conversion.

A conversion could be effected, for example, by a like kind exchange qualifying for nonrecognition under IRC §1031.

Change of Residence

If a business changes country of residence with a principal purpose to change allocation of a loss, the loss is allocated as though the business' residence had not been changed.

Sample Form 2-1

Form **1118**
(Rev. December 2009)
Department of the Treasury
Internal Revenue Service

Foreign Tax Credit—Corporations

▶ See separate instructions.
▶ Attach to the corporation's tax return.

OMB No. 1545-0122

Name of corporation

Cortes Cybernetics, Inc.

Employer identification number

XX-XXXXXXX

For calendar year 20 **09**, or other tax year beginning _____ , 20 ____ , and ending _____ , 20 ____

Use a **separate** Form 1118 for each applicable category of income listed below. See **Categories of Income** in the instructions. Also, see **Specific Instructions.**
Check only one box on each form.

☐ Passive Category Income
☑ General Category Income
☐ Section 901(j) Income: Name of Sanctioned Country ▶ _____
☐ Income Re-sourced by Treaty: Name of Country ▶ _____

Schedule A Income or (Loss) Before Adjustments *(Report all amounts in U.S. dollars. See Specific Instructions.)*

Gross Income or (Loss) From Sources Outside the United States *(INCLUDE Foreign Branch Gross Income here and on Schedule F)*

1. Foreign Country or U.S. Possession (Enter two-letter code; see instructions. Use a separate line for each.)*	2. Deemed Dividends (see instructions)		3. Other Dividends		4. Interest	5. Gross Rents, Royalties, and License Fees	6. Gross Income From Performance of Services	7. Other (attach schedule)	8. Total (add columns 2(a) through 7)
	(a) Exclude gross-up	(b) Gross-up (sec. 78)	(a) Exclude gross-up	(b) Gross-up (sec. 78)					
A									
B									
C									
D									
E									
F									
Totals (add lines A through F)									

* For section 863(b) income, NOLs, income from RICs, and high-taxed income, use a single line (see instructions).

Deductions *(INCLUDE Foreign Branch Deductions here and on Schedule F)*

	9. Definitely Allocable Deductions					10. Apportioned Share of Deductions Not Definitely Allocable (enter amount from applicable line of Schedule H, Part II, column (d))	11. Net Operating Loss Deduction	12. Total Deductions (add columns 9(e) through 11)	13. Total Income or (Loss) Before Adjustments (subtract column 12 from column 8)
	Rental, Royalty, and Licensing Expenses		(c) Expenses Related to Gross Income From Performance of Services	(d) Other Definitely Allocable Deductions	(e) Total Definitely Allocable Deductions (add columns 9(a) through 9(d))				
	(a) Depreciation, Depletion, and Amortization	(b) Other Expenses							
A									
B									
C									
D									
E									
F									
Totals									

For Paperwork Reduction Act Notice, see separate instructions.

Cat. No. 10900F

Form **1118** (Rev. 12-2009)

Form 1118 (Rev. 12-2009)

Page **2**

Schedule B Foreign Tax Credit (Report all foreign tax amounts in U.S. dollars.)

Part I—Foreign Taxes Paid, Accrued, and Deemed Paid (see instructions)

1. Credit is Claimed for Taxes:		2. Foreign Taxes Paid or Accrued (attach schedule showing amounts in foreign currency and conversion rate(s) used)							3. Tax Deemed Paid (from Schedule C—Part I, column 10, Part II, column 8(b), and Part III, column 8)
☐ Paid ☐ Accrued		Tax Withheld at Source on:		Other Foreign Taxes Paid or Accrued on:				(h) Total Foreign Taxes Paid or Accrued (add columns 2(a) through 2(g))	
Date Paid	Date Accrued	(a) Dividends	(b) Interest	(c) Rents, Royalties, and License Fees	(d) Section 863(b) Income	(e) Foreign Branch Income	(f) Services Income	(g) Other	
A									
B									
C									
D									
E									
F									
Totals (add lines A through F)									

Part II—Separate Foreign Tax Credit (Complete a separate Part II for each applicable category of income.)

1	Total foreign taxes paid or accrued (total from Part I, column 2(h))	
2	Total taxes deemed paid (total from Part I, column 3)	
3	Reductions of taxes paid, accrued, or deemed paid (enter total from Schedule G)	( )
4	Taxes reclassified under high-tax kickout	
5	Enter the sum of any carryover of foreign taxes (from Schedule K, line 3, column (xiv)) plus any carrybacks to the current tax year	
6	Total foreign taxes (combine lines 1 through 5)	
7	Enter the amount from the applicable column of Schedule J, Part I, line 11 (see instructions). If Schedule J is **not** required to be completed, enter the result from the "Totals" line of column 13 of the applicable Schedule A	
8a	Total taxable income from all sources (enter taxable income from the corporation's tax return)	
b	Adjustments to line 8a (see instructions)	
c	Subtract line 8b from line 8a	
9	Divide line 7 by line 8c. Enter the resulting fraction as a decimal (see instructions). If line 7 is greater than line 8c, enter 1	
10	Total U.S. income tax against which credit is allowed (regular tax liability (see section 26(b)) minus American Samoa economic development credit)	
11	Credit limitation (multiply line 9 by line 10) (see instructions)	
12	**Separate foreign tax credit** (enter the smaller of line 6 or line 11 here and on the appropriate line of Part III)	

Part III—Summary of Separate Credits (Enter amounts from Part II, line 12 for **each** applicable category of income. **Do not** include taxes paid to sanctioned countries.)

1	Credit for taxes on passive category income	
2	Credit for taxes on general category income	
3	Credit for taxes on income re-sourced by treaty (combine all such credits on this line)	
4	Total (add lines 1 through 3)	
5	Reduction in credit for international boycott operations (see instructions)	
6	**Total foreign tax credit** (subtract line 5 from line 4). Enter here and on the appropriate line of the corporation's tax return	

Form **1118** (Rev. 12-2009)

Form 1118 (Rev. 12-2009)

Page **3**

Schedule C | **Tax Deemed Paid by Domestic Corporation Filing Return**

Use this schedule to figure the tax deemed paid by the corporation with respect to dividends from a first-tier foreign corporation under section 902(a), and deemed inclusions of earnings from a first- or lower-tier foreign corporation under section 960(a). **Report all amounts in U.S. dollars unless otherwise specified.**

Part I—Dividends and Deemed Inclusions From Post-1986 Undistributed Earnings

1. Name of Foreign Corporation (identify DISCs and former DISCs)	2. Tax Year End (Yr-Mo) (see instructions)	3. Country of Incorporation (enter country code from instructions)	4. Post-1986 Undistributed Earnings (in functional currency—attach schedule)	5. Opening Balance in Post-1986 Foreign Income Taxes	6. Foreign Taxes Paid and Deemed Paid for Tax Year Indicated		7. Post-1986 Foreign Income Taxes (add columns 5, 6(a), and 6(b))	8. Dividends and Deemed Inclusions		9. Divide Column 8(a) by Column 4	10. Tax Deemed Paid (multiply column 7 by column 9)
					(a) Taxes Paid	(b) Taxes Deemed Paid (from Schedule D, Part I—see instructions)		(a) Functional Currency	(b) U.S. Dollars		

Total (Add amounts in column 10. Enter the result here and include on "Totals" line of Schedule B, Part I, column 3.) . . . . ▲

Part II—Dividends Paid Out of Pre-1987 Accumulated Profits

1. Name of Foreign Corporation (identify DISCs and former DISCs)	2. Tax Year End (Yr-Mo) (see instructions)	3. Country of Incorporation (enter country code from instructions)	4. Accumulated Profits for Tax Year Indicated (in functional currency computed under section 902) (attach schedule)	5. Foreign Taxes Paid and Deemed Paid on Earnings and Profits (E&P) for Tax Year Indicated (in functional currency) (see instructions)	6. Dividends Paid		7. Divide Column 6(a) by Column 4	8. Tax Deemed Paid (see instructions)
					(a) Functional Currency	(b) U.S. Dollars		

Total (Add amounts in column 8b. Enter the result here and include on "Totals" line of Schedule B, Part I, column 3.) . . . . ▲

Part III—Deemed Inclusions From Pre-1987 Earnings and Profits

1. Name of Foreign Corporation (identify DISCs and former DISCs)	2. Tax Year End (Yr-Mo) (see instructions)	3. Country of Incorporation (enter country code from instructions)	4. E&P for Tax Year Indicated (in functional currency translated from U.S. dollars, computed under section 964) (attach schedule)	5. Foreign Taxes Paid and Deemed Paid for Tax Year Indicated (see instructions)	6. Deemed Inclusions		7. Divide Column 6(a) by Column 4	8. Tax Deemed Paid (multiply column 5 by column 7)
					(a) Functional Currency	(b) U.S. Dollars		

Total (Add amounts in column 8. Enter the result here and include on "Totals" line of Schedule B, Part I, column 3.) . . . . ▲

Form **1118** (Rev. 12-2009)

Form 1118 (Rev. 12-2009)

Page **4**

Schedule D Tax Deemed Paid by First- and Second-Tier Foreign Corporations under Section 902(b)

Use Part I to compute the tax deemed paid by a first-tier foreign corporation. Use Part II to compute the tax deemed paid by a second-tier foreign corporation with respect to dividends from a third-tier foreign corporation. **Report all amounts in U.S. dollars unless otherwise specified.**

Part I—Tax Deemed Paid by First-Tier Foreign Corporations

Section A—Dividends Paid Out of Post-1986 Undistributed Earnings (Include the column 10 results in Schedule C, Part I, column 6(b).)

1. Name of Second-Tier Foreign Corporation and Its Related First-Tier Foreign Corporation	2. Tax Year End (Yr-Mo) (see instructions)	3. Country of Incorporation (enter country code from instructions)	4. Post-1986 Undistributed Earnings (in functional currency—attach schedule)	5. Opening Balance in Post-1986 Foreign Income Taxes	6. Foreign Taxes Paid and Deemed Paid for Tax Year Indicated		7. Post-1986 Foreign Income Taxes (add columns 5, 6(a), and 6(b))	8. Dividends Paid (in functional currency)		9. Divide Column 8(a) by Column 4	10. Tax Deemed Paid (multiply column 7 by column 9)
					(a) Taxes Paid	(b) Taxes Deemed Paid (see instructions)		(a) of Second-tier Corporation	(b) of First-tier Corporation		

Section B—Dividends Paid Out of Pre-1987 Accumulated Profits (Include the column 8(b) results in Schedule C, Part I, column 6(b).)

1. Name of Second-Tier Foreign Corporation and Its Related First-Tier Foreign Corporation	2. Tax Year End (Yr-Mo) (see instructions)	3. Country of Incorporation (enter country code from instructions)	4. Accumulated Profits for Tax Year Indicated (in functional currency—attach schedule)	5. Foreign Taxes Paid and Deemed Paid for Tax Year Indicated (in functional currency—see instructions)	6. Dividends Paid (in functional currency)		7. Divide Column 6(a) by Column 4	8. Tax Deemed Paid (see instructions)	
					(a) of Second-tier Corporation	(b) of First-tier Corporation		(a) Functional Currency of Second-tier Corporation	(b) U.S. Dollars

Part II—Tax Deemed Paid by Second-Tier Foreign Corporations

Section A—Dividends Paid Out of Post-1986 Undistributed Earnings (Include the column 10 results in Section A, column 6(b), of Part I above.)

1. Name of Third-Tier Foreign Corporation and Its Related Second-Tier Foreign Corporation	2. Tax Year End (Yr-Mo) (see instructions)	3. Country of Incorporation (enter country code from instructions)	4. Post-1986 Undistributed Earnings (in functional currency—attach schedule)	5. Opening Balance in Post-1986 Foreign Income Taxes	6. Foreign Taxes Paid and Deemed Paid for Tax Year Indicated		7. Post-1986 Foreign Income Taxes (add columns 5, 6(a), and 6(b))	8. Dividends Paid (in functional currency)		9. Divide Column 8(a) by Column 4	10. Tax Deemed Paid (multiply column 7 by column 9)
					(a) Taxes Paid	(b) Taxes Deemed Paid (from Schedule E, Part I, column 10)		(a) of Third-tier Corporation	(b) of Second-tier Corporation		

Section B—Dividends Paid Out of Pre-1987 Accumulated Profits (Include the column 8(b) results in Section A, column 6(b), of Part I above.)

1. Name of Third-Tier Foreign Corporation and Its Related Second-Tier Foreign Corporation	2. Tax Year End (Yr-Mo) (see instructions)	3. Country of Incorporation (enter country code from instructions)	4. Accumulated Profits for Tax Year Indicated (in functional currency—attach schedule)	5. Foreign Taxes Paid and Deemed Paid for Tax Year Indicated (in functional currency—see instructions)	6. Dividends Paid (in functional currency)		7. Divide Column 6(a) by Column 4	8. Tax Deemed Paid (see instructions)	
					(a) of Third-tier Corporation	(b) of Second-tier Corporation		(a) In Functional Currency of Third-tier Corporation	(b) U.S. Dollars

Form **1118** (Rev. 12-2009)

Form 1118 (Rev. 12-2009)

Page **5**

Schedule E — Tax Deemed Paid by Certain Third-, Fourth-, and Fifth-Tier Foreign Corporations Under Section 902(b)

Use this schedule to report taxes deemed paid with respect to dividends paid from eligible post-1986 undistributed earnings of fourth-, fifth- and sixth-tier controlled foreign corporations. **Report all amounts in U.S. dollars unless otherwise specified.**

Part I—Tax Deemed Paid by Third-Tier Foreign Corporations (Include the column 10 results in Schedule D, Part II, Section A, column 6(b).)

1. Name of Fourth-Tier Foreign Corporation and Its Related Third-Tier Foreign Corporation	2. Tax Year End (Yr-Mo) (see instructions)	3. Country of Incorporation (enter country code from instructions)	4. Post-1986 Undistributed Earnings (in functional currency—attach schedule)	5. Opening Balance in Post-1986 Foreign Income Taxes	6. Foreign Taxes Paid and Deemed Paid for Tax Year Indicated		7. Post-1986 Foreign Income Taxes (add columns 5, 6(a), and 6(b))	8. Dividends Paid (in functional currency)		9. Divide Column 8(a) by Column 4	10. Tax Deemed Paid (multiply column 7 by column 9)
					(a) Taxes Paid	(b) Taxes Deemed Paid (from Part II, column 10)		(a) Of Fourth-tier CFC	(b) Of Third-tier CFC		

Part II—Tax Deemed Paid by Fourth-Tier Foreign Corporations (Include the column 10 results in column 6(b) of Part I above.)

1. Name of Fifth-Tier Foreign Corporation and Its Related Fourth-Tier Foreign Corporation	2. Tax Year End (Yr-Mo) (see instructions)	3. Country of Incorporation (enter country code from instructions)	4. Post-1986 Undistributed Earnings (in functional currency—attach schedule)	5. Opening Balance in Post-1986 Foreign Income Taxes	6. Foreign Taxes Paid and Deemed Paid for Tax Year Indicated		7. Post-1986 Foreign Income Taxes (add columns 5, 6(a), and 6(b))	8. Dividends Paid (in functional currency)		9. Divide Column 8(a) by Column 4	10. Tax Deemed Paid (multiply column 7 by column 9)
					(a) Taxes Paid	(b) Taxes Deemed Paid (from Part III, column 10)		(a) Of Fifth-tier CFC	(b) Of Fourth-tier CFC		

Part III—Tax Deemed Paid by Fifth-Tier Foreign Corporations (Include the column 10 results in column 6(b) of Part II above.)

1. Name of Sixth-Tier Foreign Corporation and Its Related Fifth-Tier Foreign Corporation	2. Tax Year End (Yr-Mo) (see instructions)	3. Country of Incorporation (enter country code from instructions)	4. Post-1986 Undistributed Earnings (in functional currency—attach schedule)	5. Opening Balance in Post-1986 Foreign Income Taxes	6. Foreign Taxes Paid For Tax Year Indicated	7. Post-1986 Foreign Income Taxes (add columns 5 and 6)	8. Dividends Paid (in functional currency)		9. Divide Column 8(a) by Column 4	10. Tax Deemed Paid (multiply column 7 by column 9)
							(a) Of Sixth-tier CFC	(b) Of Fifth-tier CFC		

Form **1118** (Rev. 12-2009)

Form 1118 (Rev. 12-2009)

Page **6**

Schedule F — Gross Income and Definitely Allocable Deductions for Foreign Branches

	1. Foreign Country or U.S. Possession (Enter two-letter code from Schedule A, column 1. Use a separate line for each).	2. Gross Income	3. Definitely Allocable Deductions
A			
B			
C			
D			
E			
F			

Totals (add lines A through F)* ▶

* **Note:** The Schedule F totals are not carried over to any other Form 1118 Schedule. (These totals were already included in Schedule A.) However, the IRS requires the corporation to complete Schedule F under the authority of section 905(b).

Schedule G — Reductions of Taxes Paid, Accrued, or Deemed Paid

A	Reduction of Taxes Under Section 901(e)—Attach separate schedule
B	Reduction of Foreign Oil and Gas Taxes—Enter amount from Schedule I, Part II, line 6
C	Reduction of Taxes Due to International Boycott Provisions— Enter appropriate portion of Schedule C (Form 5713), line 2b. **Important:** Enter only "specifically attributable taxes" here.
D	Reduction of Taxes for Section 6038(c) Penalty— Attach separate schedule
E	Other Reductions of Taxes—Attach schedule(s)

Total (add lines A through E). Enter here and on Schedule B, Part II, line 3 . . . . ▲

Form **1118** (Rev. 12-2009)

Form 1118 (Rev. 12-2009)

Schedule H Apportionment of Deductions Not Definitely Allocable *(complete only once)*

Part I—Research and Development Deductions

	(a) Sales Method					(b) Gross Income Method—Check method used: ☐ Option 1 ☐ Option 2 (See instructions)		(c) Total R&D Deductions Not Definitely Allocable (enter all amounts from column (a)(v) or all amounts from column (b)(vii))
	Product line #1 (SIC Code:)*		Product line #2 (SIC Code:)*		(v) Total R&D Deductions Under Sales Method (add columns (ii) and (iv))	(vi) Gross Income	(vii) Total R&D Deductions Under Gross Income Method	
	(i) Gross Sales	(ii) R&D Deductions	(iii) Gross Sales	(iv) R&D Deductions				
1 Totals (see instructions)	$800,000	$60,000			$60,000	$150,000	$60,000	
2 Total to be apportioned		$30,000			$30,000		$45,000	
3 Apportionment among statutory groupings:								
a General category income	$300,000	$11,250			$11,250	$10,000	$5,625	
b Passive category income								
c Section 901(j) income*								
d Income re-sourced by treaty*								
4 Total foreign (add lines 3a through 3d)	$300,000	$11,250			$11,250	$10,000	$5,625	

*Important: See *Computer-Generated Schedule H* in instructions.

* See instructions.

Form **1118** (Rev. 12-2009)

Form 1118 (Rev. 12-2009)

Schedule H — Apportionment of Deductions Not Definitely Allocable (continued)

Part II—Interest Deductions, All Other Deductions, and Total Deductions

	(a) Average Value of Assets—Check method used: ☐ Fair market value ☐ Tax book value ☐ Alternative tax book value		(b) Interest Deductions			(c) All Other Deductions Not Definitely Allocable	(d) Totals (add the corresponding amounts from column (c), Part I; columns (b)(iii) and (b)(iv), Part I; and column (c), Part II). Enter each amount from lines 3a through 3d below in column 10 of the corresponding Schedule A.
	(i) Nonfinancial Corporations	(ii) Financial Corporations	(iii) Nonfinancial Corporations	(iv) Financial Corporations			
1a Totals (see instructions)							
b Amounts specifically allocable under Temp. Regs. 1.861-10T(e)							
c Other specific allocations under Temp. Regs. 1.861-10T							
d Assets excluded from apportionment formula							
2 Total to be apportioned (subtract the sum of lines 1b, 1c, and 1d from line 1a)							
3 Apportionment among statutory groupings:							
a General category income							
b Passive category income							
c Section 901(j) income*							
d Income re-sourced by treaty*							
4 Total foreign (add lines 3a through 3d)							

* **Important:** See *Computer-Generated Schedule H* in instructions.

Form **1118** (Rev. 12-2009)

Chapter 3

U.S. Foreign Tax Credit—Basic Concepts

Choosing a Deduction or a Credit

A U.S. business that pays foreign taxes may be able to claim a deduction for those taxes against U.S. taxable income or, alternatively, directly credit foreign taxes paid against its U.S. tax liability. In most cases, it will be to a business' advantage to claim a direct credit.

Example 3-1

If C, a U.S. corporation, has taxable income of $100 in Country A calculated according to U.S. tax principles and no other income from any other source and pays $30 in income taxes to Country A, the following results occur if C takes a foreign tax credit or a deduction for the foreign income taxes paid, respectively:

Foreign Tax Credit

Taxable income	$100	
Country A tax	30	
U.S. tax	35	(35 percent of taxable income)
Credit for foreign taxes paid	30	
U.S. taxes paid	5	
Total taxes paid ($30 + $5)	35	
Net after tax income ($100 – $35)	65	

Deduction Taken for Foreign Taxes Paid

Taxable income	$100	
Deduction for Country A tax	30	
Net Taxable income	70	
U.S. tax paid	24.5	(35 percent of taxable income)
Total taxes paid ($24.50 + $30)	54.5	
Net after tax income ($100 – $54.50)	45.5	

Although a credit is often more valuable than a deduction, in some cases a business may elect to take the deduction. A credit may be claimed only against foreign taxes levied on net income, but a deduction may be taken against foreign real estate and other types of taxes. The credit is subject to a complex system of limitations designed, among other things, to prevent taxpayers from using foreign tax credits to reduce tax on U.S.-source income. The credit is also subject to a number of additional, policy-based limitations affecting businesses, and in particular, industries.

A business' election to claim a credit is made annually by completing Form 1120, Schedule J, Line 4a and Form 1118. This election is considered to be made for all foreign taxes for the year. A business may not pick some taxes to deduct and others to credit. Since the filing of the corporate tax return serves as the medium to elect between a credit and a deduction of foreign taxes, a business may elect a credit or a deduction for any year as long as it is entitled to file an amended tax return.

The Ten-Year Rule

The Internal Revenue Code provides a special statute of limitations of ten years to amend and correct foreign tax credit claims. This allows for the sometimes considerable time necessary to determine the actual amounts of foreign taxes paid.

Example 3-2

Foster Sales Corp. sells watches to customers in the Principality of Pacoima under circumstances where it is subject to tax by Pacoima on part of its income. In 2001, Foster was assessed and paid taxes of $55,000. In 2002, Pacoima fiscal authorities propose an additional assessment of $22,000. Foster contests the matter, and the case is settled in 2010 at $9,000.

Foster claimed a foreign tax credit on its Form 1120 for 2010. The limitations period for amending Foster's 2002 tax return has expired. Under the ten-year rule, Foster may amend its 2002 return by filing Form 1120X together with an amended Form 1118.

If, instead of an assessment, Pacoima were to issue Foster a refund of $13,000 in respect of 2002, Foster would be required to notify the Internal Revenue Service, by amended return, of the change in foreign taxes and foreign tax credit. For any change resulting from such a refund, there is no statute of limitations.

Scope of the Ten-Year Rule

Based on the facts in Example 3-2, a problem may exist where the business may not have been in a position to make an informed election in the original year. For example, suppose that in 2001 Foster was not assessed any income tax by Pacoima but did claim a deduction for property tax levied by Pacoima. In 2002, Foster has to pay $55,000 in respect of 2001 income and would like to claim a credit.

The IRS believes that the ten-year rule provides an extended limitations period for amended returns only to those businesses that have already elected to claim a credit during the regular three-year period. The IRS believes that the ten-year rule is not available for making an initial claim for a foreign tax credit.

In 1967 and 1968, the Court of Claims and the District Court for the Northern District of California held that the taxpayer had the full ten years to go back and file for a credit. In 1978, the Court of Claims held in *Hart v. United States* that the legislative history of the ten-year limit applies to initial filing for a credit on two bases: (1) the plain language of the statute and (2) the fact that a contrary holding would lead to an "absurd" result.

> **Note:** Although the issue remains unresolved, businesses should be aware that the IRS may challenge the filing of an initial claim for a foreign tax credit after three years but before ten years and that a court may agree with that challenge. Businesses should also be aware that the rule in *Hart* is supported by the language of the statute and that, on balance, it represents a reasonable filing position for businesses.

Creditable Foreign Taxes

The purpose of the credit is to avoid double taxation on the same income but not to reduce the net U.S. tax on the income below zero. In general, U.S. businesses may claim a credit against U.S. tax for the amount of foreign tax paid, directly or indirectly, on the same income.

Tax Imposed on Foreign-Source Income

The first requirement for creditability is that the foreign tax be imposed on foreign-source (as to the U.S.) income.

A payment is not a tax unless it is compulsory, and it is not deemed compulsory to the extent that the payment exceeds the amount of liability under foreign law for tax. The foreign tax credit regulations require that a business must take all reasonable steps to reduce, over time, the (business) reasonably expected foreign tax liability.

Example 3-3

Assume T's foreign income tax liabilities are less than the credit limitation. Country X undertakes an audit of T's return. In the absence of the compulsory payment rule, T would likely pay any additional tax assessed in the audit without protest. If T's country tax is increased, the credit against U.S. tax would increase in like amount, and T's worldwide tax liability and after-tax profits would remain unchanged. Expenses incurred in the country X examination are deductible but not creditable, and, therefore, reduce after-tax profits. T is therefore encouraged to incur no expense to protest the country X tax assessment and to simply pay any amount the country X authorities demand.

The regulations require that a business "exhaust…all effective and practical remedies" to minimize its foreign income taxes, including any available foreign audit adjustment and competent authority procedures available under applicable tax treaties. If a U.S. business qualifies for a treaty reduction of a foreign withholding tax, but foreign country law provides that the benefit of the reduction may be obtained only by a claim for refund of the excess of the statutory withholding rate over the reduced treaty rate, the U.S. foreign tax credit will be denied unless the business files a refund claim with the foreign country.

A remedy is considered effective and practical if the cost of the remedy is reasonable in light of the amount at issue and the likelihood of success. The risk that offsetting or additional tax might be assessed against a business is a cost that may be considered in deciding whether or not to pursue a remedy. If the statute of limitations has run on a business' right to a refund under foreign and treaty law when a U.S. IRS assessment occurs, the business need not press any claim because there is no effective remedy.

A business is not required to pursue all tax minimization opportunities. The foreign tax credit is not denied because a business does not defer foreign taxes as long as legally permitted. If foreign tax law allows capital equipment costs to be expensed immediately or be depreciated over two, four, six, or ten years, a business can elect a ten-year recovery period without jeopardizing the credit, even if, in later years, taxable income is insufficient to offset the depreciation deductions.

Similarly, a business is not required to alter its form of doing business or the form of any business transaction to reduce tax liability under foreign law.

Allocation and Apportionment of Expenses

A business is permitted to claim a credit only against its foreign-source taxable income. The business is required to allocate or apportion all deductible expenses to foreign-source gross income.

Types of Credits

There are two general types of credits that may be claimed by U.S. businesses: credit for taxes paid by a business (the Internal Revenue Code Section 901 credit) and credit for taxes paid by a foreign affiliate on income out of which a dividend is paid to a U.S. business (the Internal Revenue Code Section 902 credit). For some purposes, the computation of these two credits is made separately; for other purposes, the credits are lumped together.

Taxes on "Income"

The Internal Revenue Code allows a credit only for foreign *income* taxes. "Income tax" means a tax on net income, "the predominant character of which is that of an income tax in the U.S. sense." The regulations separate the definition of "tax" from the definition of "income tax." The regulations define "tax" as a subset of "levy" and state that "income tax" includes total payments to foreign governments, whether or not these payments are mandatory. Levies that are not taxes include fines, interest, penalties, and customs duties.

In addition to taxes, a company may make mandatory payments to a foreign government that derive from its business operations, and a company may pay royalties for use of a process or a percentage of gross or net income as part of a joint venture. This type of payment is described as coming from a *dual-capacity* business, one that is both a taxpayer in a foreign jurisdiction and in business with the foreign government.

Example 3-4

Marsalis Motors Corp. manufactures recreational vehicles (RVs) for worldwide consumption. In 2010, Marsalis contracted with the Republic of Snelling to build and to equip a factory in that country in order to build RVs for domestic sales and exports. Marsalis contributed its know-how and some secondhand machinery to the project; Snelling contributed the factory and the cash. The agreement called for Snelling to receive 40 percent of the net income from the venture, leaving the remainder to Marsalis. From its 60 percent share of net income, Marsalis must pay a 12 percent tax on any amounts remitted outside Snelling.

Marsalis may not claim the 40 percent payment as a foreign tax credit, but it may claim the 12 percent remittance levy as a credit.

Taxes on "Net Income"

A foreign tax does not have to be precisely a tax on "net income" as that term is understood for U.S. tax purposes. It is enough if the effect of the tax is similar to that of an income tax. A good rule of thumb is to ask if it is possible for a business to incur a loss after paying the tax. If so, the tax is probably not an income tax. There are numerous IRS rulings on the creditability of specific foreign taxes.

Computation of Foreign Pretax Income

Calculating foreign pretax income is critical for at least two purposes:

- Determining whether the foreign tax in question constitutes a creditable income tax, and

- Computing the effective foreign tax rate.

Historically, "accumulated profits" was the term of art in the foreign tax credit context. Regulations under Internal Revenue Code Section 902 still use the term "accumulated profits" and define it as the sum of a foreign corporation's earnings and profits and any foreign income tax thereon. The concept becomes a little fuzzy, however, when the regulations speak of distributing dividends out of accumulated profits rather than out of earnings and profits or out of accumulated profits net of foreign taxes.

Notwithstanding the terminology, the point is that while a foreign corporation must calculate its net income and foreign tax liability according to foreign tax principles, a U.S. corporation seeking to credit that same tax must calculate the same items according to U.S. tax accounting principles. This means that the true foreign tax rate cannot be known until net income is recomputed according to U.S. rules.

To state this another way, assume that a foreign subsidiary of a U.S. corporation earns $100, pays $27 in foreign tax, and distributes the remainder ($73) to its parent company. All other things being equal, the parent company would expect to pay, in U.S. tax, the difference between the company's U.S. tax ($34) and $27, or $7. However, this takes no account of the requirement that net income and foreign tax liability must be computed according to U.S. rules. These facts do not indicate whether earnings are $100 or a number that is greater or less than $100. If earnings are greater, then the amount of foreign tax paid must be spread ratably over that greater amount, and the foreign taxes allocable to the distribution will be reduced. The effect of this rule is illustrated by the following example.

Example 3-5

Moevs Machinery Corp., a U.S. parent corporation, has a wholly owned manufacturing subsidiary in the Principality of Proberta. In January, 2010, Moevs contributed $1.5 million in new machinery to Moevs-Proberta. As a result, Moevs-Proberta qualified for a special capital cost allowance (in addition to normal depreciation) of one-third of the cost each year for three years. For purposes of computing the net income of Moevs-Proberta according to U.S. standards, the capital cost allowance is not deducted from gross income. In December 2010, Moevs-Proberta made a profit, according to Proberta accounting standards, and declared a dividend of $50,000 to Moevs. The difference between Proberta's accounting principles and those of the United States in arriving at the amount of creditable tax is illustrated in the following table.

	Proberta	United States
Gross receipts	$1,050,000	$1,050,000
Cost of goods sold	$350,000	$350,000
Gross income	$700,000	$700,000
Shipping	$49,500	$49,500
Commissions	$5,500	$5,500
Capital Cost	$500,000	
Salaries	$45,000	$45,000
Net income (accumulated profits)	$100,000	$600,000
Proberta tax	$26,000	$26,000
Earnings and profits	$74,000	$574,000
Dividend to Moevs	$50,000	$50,000
Ratio of dividends to accumulated profits	1:2	1:12
Ratio times corporate tax	$13,000	$2,167

The first column of figures represents the computation of tax according to Proberta rules. The deduction for the capital cost allowance reduces Moevs-Proberta's taxable net income to $100,000, resulting in a tax of $26,000. For Proberta tax purposes, the corporation has earnings and profits of $74,000. Since the $500,000 deduction is a noncash item, however, Moevs-Proberta may have cash significantly in excess of $74,000. Using the Proberta tax accounting rules, the $50,000 dividend is divided by the $100,000 of pretax net income, which is 50 percent. This percentage is then applied to the amount of the Proberta tax actually paid ($26,000), resulting in $13,000 in theoretically creditable tax for U.S. income tax purposes.

The second column of figures represents the computation of tax according to U.S. accounting principles. Because the $500,000 is not a deductible expense, the taxable income becomes $600,000. The ratio between the dividend and taxable income now becomes 1:12, resulting in a creditable tax of $2,167.

Notional Computations of Income

A foreign country's tax rules and accounting standards for determining the net income of foreign business operations of U.S. corporations can have a significant effect on calculating the amount of creditable tax for U.S. income tax purposes. Even if a foreign country employs an unusual method of calculating the tax liability of a foreign branch operation, the entire amount of the foreign tax paid may be creditable as long as the tax itself is considered an income tax.

Example 3-6

Oliveros Organization, Inc., a U.S. parent corporation that produces and markets video games, maintains a number of foreign subsidiaries engaged in manufacturing or sales. Sales in Eastern Europe are high enough for Oliveros to have formed marketing corporations in five different countries. Because of the continued uncertainty of the economic climate in the five countries, Oliveros has formed a sixth company in the Republic of Pulga, located on an island in the Baltic Sea. Pulga is also a former Eastern bloc country, but its historical and commercial ties with other nations of northern Europe make it a much more secure business environment.

Where possible, funds are sent directly from wholesale customers in the five countries to Oliveros-Pulga. Funds received by any of the five subsidiaries are remitted to Oliveros-Pulga as quickly as possible. Oliveros-Pulga does not have title to the funds but merely serves as a holding vehicle, performing a service for a small fee. The fees received by Oliveros-Pulga are almost completely offset by its costs. The usual corporate tax rate in Pulga is 36 percent of net income. However, in cases where a business is considered to be "headquarters" or an "administrative" company, income is deemed to be the greater of 5 percent of the funds managed or 250 percent of the administrative expenses incurred in Pulga.

The following table describes the financial information for Oliveros-Pulga and the effect of the regular Pulga tax and each of the notional methods for determining the taxable income of Oliveros-Pulga for 2010.

Percent owned	100%
Receipts managed for others	$22,300,000
Fees received	$1,125,000
Office rent	$225,000
Telephone and fax	$375,000
Travel	$195,000
Salaries	$135,000
Net income	$195,000
Tax at 36 percent	$70,200
Notional net income (5 percent rule)	$1,115,000
Tax at 5 percent	$401,400
Notional net income (administration rule)	$2,325,000
Tax at 250 percent	$837,000

Based on the facts, for U.S. foreign tax credit purposes the net income of Oliveros-Pulga is still $195,000, and the amount of foreign tax paid is $837,000. If Oliveros-Pulga distributes a dividend of $100,000 at the end of 2010, the amount of creditable tax will be limited to the lesser of (1) the Pulga tax deemed paid on Pulga earnings or (2) the U.S. tax that would be paid on the same amount of earnings.

The Pulga tax is $837,000, but the Pulga earnings (for U.S. purposes) are only $195,000. The U.S. tax on $195,000 (at 35 percent) would be $68,250, which is the limit of the Pulga tax that is currently creditable. The remainder of the Pulga tax, $770,000, might, depending on the circumstances, be available for credit against other foreign income in the current year or against foreign income in other years.

Substitution Taxes

Taxes Imposed in Lieu of an Income Tax

Conceptually, the notional computation of taxable income is related to the so-called tax in lieu of an income tax (also known as a replacement tax). In general, a replacement tax is one that is imposed on a business instead of a foreign country's income tax. In order to be creditable as an in lieu of tax, the foreign levy must be a tax and it must meet the substitution requirements:

- The tax must be a tax in lieu of, and not in addition to, an income tax generally imposed by the foreign country.

- The base of this levy need not bear any relation to realized net income. The base for the levy may be gross income, gross receipts or sales, or the number of units produced or exported.

A foreign levy either is or is not a tax in lieu of an income tax in its entirety for all persons subject to the levy. A foreign levy satisfies the substitution requirement if the tax in fact operates as a tax imposed in substitution for, and not in addition to, an income tax or a series of income taxes otherwise generally imposed. Not all income derived by persons subject to the foreign tax need be exempt from the income tax.

Example 3-7

Owen Oscilloscope Corp. (Owen), a U.S. parent corporation, installs and services electronic equipment for hospitals and has customers in the nations of Central America. In 2010, Owen forms a corporation in the Republic of Pogo (Owen-Pogo). Owen-Pogo performs the service jobs formerly carried out directly by Owen, employing a combination of personnel who are sent periodically on a short-term basis to Pogo and Pogo residents.

Owen charges Owen-Pogo a management fee, in part for know-how and in part for the short-term lending of personnel. Pogo has a regular income tax that is roughly similar in its operation to the U.S. corporate income tax and is measured as 45 percent on net income. However, with respect to services income of foreign or foreign-controlled companies, Pogo imposes a tax of 22 percent on Pogo-source gross income.

The following table outlines Owen-Pogo's financial information for 2010, the effect of Pogo's regular 45 percent tax on net income, and the 22 percent tax computations on Owen-Pogo's gross income.

Percent owned	100%
Gross income	$2,500,000
Management fee to Owen	$460,000
Five salaries (Pogo)	$160,000
Net income	$1,880,000
Pogo regular tax (45 percent)	$846,000
Pogo special tax	$550,000
Effective Pogo tax rate	74%

Based on the facts, if Pogo were to impose the 22 percent tax on Owen-Pogo's gross income instead of its regular 45 percent tax on Owen-Pogo's net income, for U.S. income tax purposes, it would be regarded as having been clearly imposed as a "substitute" for the regular income tax. Therefore, it would be creditable under the foreign tax credit rules. The replacement tax rule would benefit Owen even if Owen-Pogo earned other income in Pogo that was taxed at the regular 45 percent rate.

Example 3-8

Assume the same facts as in Example 3-7, except that in 2010, Owen-Pogo not only performed service work but also sold video monitors and that Pogo taxed the services income and the sales income separately as follows:

Percent owned	100%
Gross income (services)	$2,500,000
Management fee to Owen	$460,000
Five salaries (Pogo)	$160,000
Net income (services)	$1,880,000
Receipts (TV monitors)	$600,000
Cost of goods sold	$375,000
Shipping	$27,500
Allocable salaries	$48,000
Net income (sales)	$149,500
Pogo regular tax (45 percent)	$423,000
Pogo special tax (22 percent)	$550,000
Tax on sales (regular tax)	$67,275
Tax on services (special tax)	$550,000
Total Pogo tax	$617,275
Net income for U.S. tax purposes	$2,029,500
Effective Pogo tax rate	30.4%

The key factor to be examined when testing a foreign tax for qualification under the replacement tax rule is whether the foreign country imposes an income tax and whether the tax being tested is imposed in place of that income tax (the "substitution" test).

Thus, based on the facts in this example, if Pogo did not impose its regular 45 percent tax on Owen-Pogo's net income (or a similar tax), then the 22 percent tax on Owen-Pogo's gross income would not qualify as a replacement tax for U.S. income tax purposes and, therefore, would not be creditable.

If Pogo had imposed an excise tax on the net worth of Owen-Pogo's local assets and had no generally imposed income tax, the excise tax would not qualify as a replacement tax for U.S. income tax purposes and, therefore, would not be creditable.

> On the other hand, if Pogo had both types of taxes and used the excise tax as a clear substitute for the income tax (on insurance companies, for example), the excise tax might qualify as a replacement tax for U.S. income tax purposes. If a company were subject to both types of tax, however, the excise tax would not qualify as a replacement tax for U.S. income tax purposes and, therefore, would not be creditable.

Example 3-9

The Kingdom of Poway imposes a tax of 25 percent on net income of all corporations but imposes an additional 5 percent excise tax on assets of foreigners engaged in the mining of uranium.

The 5 percent excise tax would not qualify as a replacement tax for U.S. income tax purposes and, therefore, would not be creditable. If, however, the 5 percent excise tax were imposed on gross income rather than on assets, it is possible that the excise tax might qualify for U.S. income tax purposes as an income tax, and, therefore, it might be creditable under the regular foreign tax credit rules.

Recognition Issue

Transactions That Are Not Realization Events

A foreign tax may be imposed on events that are not recognition events for purposes of U.S. federal income taxation. This presents at least two important considerations. First, the foreign levy must satisfy the realization test. This means that the event that triggers imposition of the tax must be a realization event under the Internal Revenue Code or an event that meets the test of the regulations.

Second, there is a practical problem of matching the foreign levy with the income to which it relates for purposes of the foreign tax credit limitation. Otherwise, the foreign tax credit limitation rules can leave the taxpayer with a foreign tax, which is paid or accrued in one tax period, but no income (or a reduced amount of income) for the same period for purposes of applying the foreign tax credit limitation.

Example 3-10

Rorem Rectifiers Corp. (Rorem), a U.S. parent corporation, manufactures and markets electronic devices in many countries. Its corporate structure includes a 50 percent-owned subsidiary in the Dominion of Dinuba (Rorem-Dinuba), a 50 percent interest in a partnership in the Federation of Fdant (Rorem-Fdant), and a foreign branch in the Commonwealth of Compton (Rorem-Compton).

In 2010, Rorem-Dinuba announces a one-for-one stock dividend. Since Rorem owns 500 of the 2,000 issued and outstanding shares of Rorem-Dinuba's stock, it receives another 500 shares. After the distribution, Rorem owns 1,000 of the 2,000 issued and outstanding shares. Dinuba treats the distribution as a taxable event and levies a dividend withholding tax of 10 percent on the value of the

---

distributed shares of stock. For U.S. income tax purposes, the distribution does not result in income.

In the same year, Rorem-Fdant makes a *pro rata* distribution of partnership property to all partners, including Rorem. Fdant revenue authorities treat the distribution as a taxable capital gain and levy a tax at 22 percent. For U.S. income tax purposes, the distribution is not income. In the same year, Rorem-Compton is assessed $500,000 in tax on the appreciation of its business assets. For U.S. income tax purposes, the appreciation is not a taxable event.

The problem for a U.S. business is that if there is no income for U.S. income tax purposes for the entire year, then a U.S. business loses its ability to claim that year's tax as a credit. Based on the facts in this example, therefore, the amount of creditable foreign tax equals the quotient of the dividend paid divided by accumulated profits, multiplied by the foreign tax. If the denominator of the fraction is zero, there can be no creditable tax.

Deemed Dividends

Conversely, a U.S. business may engage in a transaction that is treated for U.S. tax purposes as a dividend but for foreign tax purposes is treated as another type of transaction or as no transaction at all. A business reporting a deemed distribution of dividends under one of the tax rules governing foreign holding companies may claim a credit for foreign taxes deemed paid by the holding company in basically the same manner as if a real dividend were paid. Similarly, a transaction may be denominated a sale under foreign law and a dividend under U.S. law; this deemed dividend also carries with it a credit for foreign taxes deemed paid.

Taxpayers Qualifying for Credit

A U.S. business is allowed credit only for foreign income taxes paid or accrued during the tax year. Whether a particular foreign income tax is paid or accrued by a U.S. business, or is instead a tax liability of another company, can be difficult to determine. For U.S. income tax purposes, the effect of the rights and obligations of a business to pay tax on income is determined under U.S. income tax rules. The creation of those rights and obligations for a business to pay tax on income may be the product of either foreign income tax rules or U.S. income tax rules or both. The distinction becomes important when analyzing which entity in a transaction is considered the taxpayer.

Under the current regulations, a tax is considered paid or accrued only by the business on which foreign law imposes legal liability for tax, even if another company (for example, a withholding agent) remits the tax or if the tax liability is assumed by another company to the transaction by which the US business earns or receives the income subject to tax.

> **Example 3-11**
>
> Assume D, a US business, loans $1,000 to F, a resident of country X, under an agreement requiring F to pay interest at 6 percent, net of any withholding tax that may be imposed by country X. If country X imposes a 10 percent withholding tax on interest paid by country X residents to nonresidents and treats that tax as part

> of the interest income, the withholding tax on each $60 annual payment of net interest is $6.7 (10 percent of sum of $60 and $6.7), and for U.S. tax purposes, D has gross income of $66.7 and is treated as paying a foreign income tax of $6.7.

If a tax imposed on the combined income of two or more businesses that are jointly and severally liable for the tax, each of these businesses is considered the taxpayer with respect to the tax. If a U.S. business' subsidiaries in country X file a consolidated country X tax return, and the members of the country X group are jointly and severally liable for the tax on the group's income, each subsidiary is the taxpayer with respect to the country X tax on its portion of the consolidated income. However, if the country X parent is exclusively liable for the country X tax on all income of the country X group, the parent is deemed to have paid all of the group's country X tax.

In *Guardian Industries*, the Federal Claims court held that, under Luxembourg law, the parent of a Luxembourg group was exclusively liable for the group's Luxembourg income tax and was therefore considered to have paid all Luxembourg tax on the incomes of all members of the group. This result creates the possibility that a U.S. parent may claim credit for a Luxembourg group's Luxembourg tax, even though most of the group's income is not currently subject to U.S. tax.

Example 3-12

Assume USCo is the owner of a Luxembourg holding company, the assets of which are stock of an operating company, and the Luxembourg group elects to file a consolidated return in Luxembourg. For U.S. purposes, the Luxembourg parent holding company is disregarded as to USCo, but the Luxembourg operating company elects to be treated as a regarded controlled foreign corporation.

Under *Guardian Industries*, the Luxembourg holding company is exclusively liable for Luxembourg tax on the group's income. The Luxembourg holding company is disregarded as to USCo, therefore USCo is deemed to have paid the Luxembourg tax. However, because the Luxembourg operating company is treated as a controlled foreign corporation, the Luxembourg operating company's income is included in USCo's U.S. taxable income only to the extent that this income is distributed, actually or constructively, as a dividend. If no dividends are distributed, USCo is allowed a credit against U.S. tax for the Luxembourg tax on the Luxembourg operating subsidiary's income, subject to the credit limitation even though the income on which this tax is imposed is not currently subject to U.S. tax.

Proposed Regulations

Under the proposed regulations, an income tax is considered paid for U.S. income tax purposes by the business on which foreign law imposes legal liability for the tax. However, under the proposed regulations, foreign law is considered to impose legal liability for tax on income of the business that is required to account for the income under the foreign income tax law, even if another business is required to remit the tax or another company (for example, a withholding agent) actually remits the tax or foreign law permits the foreign taxing authority to proceed against another business to collect the tax, if not paid.

If U.S. and foreign tax laws conflict as to income ownership, foreign law characterization controls.

Example 3-13

Assume A, a U.S. business that owns a bond issued by a resident of country X, purports to sell the bond to B, also a U.S. business, under an agreement obligating A to repurchase the bond from B, and B to sell to A six years later for the same price. The agreement also requires B to make payments to A equal to the interest B receives on the bond. Legal title to the bond passes to B, which has the effect of transferring ownership of the bond to B for country X tax purposes, but A remains owner for U.S. income tax purposes. Country X imposes a 10 percent withholding tax on interest on the bond. Since B is owner of the income for country X tax purposes, B is considered legally liable for the tax, even though A, not B, recognizes the interest as gross income for U.S. tax purposes.

Affiliate as Agent

Generally, taxes paid by a U.S. parent corporation's foreign affiliated company to its host government are for the affiliated company's own account. In some circumstances, however, it is possible that a foreign government will treat the payments as being made on behalf of a U.S. parent corporation.

Example 3-14

Piston Products, Inc. (Piston), a U.S. parent corporation, manufactures trash compactors and markets them in a number of foreign countries. Piston forms a wholly owned sales subsidiary in one of its largest overseas markets, the Republic of Rovana.

Piston-Rovana maintains an inventory of compactors from which it makes bulk sales to distributors. In addition, Piston-Rovana takes orders that are filled by having Piston ship compactors directly from the United States. This after type of sale is indistinguishable from other sales on Piston-Rovana's books. Both Piston, and Piston Rovana, as well as the customer, consider the sales to have been made by Piston-Rovana.

Rovana law provides that the sale of goods by a foreign company is not taxable unless that company is engaged in business in Rovana. Rovana law also requires that the ownership of shares of a Rovana corporation does not constitute an act of engaging in business. Finally, Rovana law mandates that the transfer price for goods sold between related entities may be restated for Rovana tax purposes.

For the tax year 2010, Rovana revenue authorities seek not only to allocate more profit to Piston-Rovana for the compactors that were taken into its inventory and then resold but also to charge Piston with tax on compactors that were delivered directly by Piston to third-party customers.

With respect to the latter charge, Rovana claims unsuccessfully that the delivery mechanism is merely a cost-saving device and that Piston-Rovana serves as a purchaser and reseller of the compactors in all its sales.

> Assume that under U.S. income tax rules the income, and, therefore, the liability to tax belongs to Piston-Rovana. However, the Rovana revenue authorities claim that in respect of the direct shipments, Piston-Rovana acts as the agent of Piston, and, therefore, charge Piston $100,000 in tax. For 2010, Piston-Rovana makes no net profit (as computed by U.S. standards) and makes no distribution to Piston. For the same year, Piston earns foreign income from a number of different sources. Piston claims the $100,000 as a foreign tax credit.
>
> Based on these facts, the issue is whether Rovana law or U.S. law should be used to determine which company is the obligor for the Rovana tax. The general answer to this issue is that U.S. principles are used to identify the taxpayer. Therefore, the issues raised by this example should be whether Rovana revenue authorities consider Piston to be engaged in business in Rovana, whether Piston is legally liable for the tax under Rovana law and whether Rovana revenue authorities do not try to collect the same tax from Piston-Rovana (except as a surety). If the answer to these questions is yes, then the tax has been levied on Piston and it may claim a credit under the foreign tax credit rules. The *Guardian Industries* proposed regulations reverse this result.

Withholding

A similar problem exists when a U.S. company receives income from a foreign country that is subject to tax at the time of payment. This is called a withholding tax. A withholding tax is a convenient device that is used for a number of purposes, such as

- Imposing and collecting tax from a nonresident taxpayer deriving local-source income;

- Imposing and collecting tax on a local entity that is liable to tax on certain types of distributions; and

- Imposing and collecting taxes at different rates on different categories of income.

> **Example 3-15**
>
> In 2010, Farmers and Charmers Federal lent $10 million to a consortium of businessmen in the Republic of Termo. The loan was for fifteen years and called for annual payments of interest only at 12 percent net. The parties intended that "net" meant that any taxes levied by Termo were to be paid by the borrowers. Termo law provided for a 17 percent tax on interest paid to foreigners, which tax was required to be withheld and to be paid over by any resident payor of interest. Legally, however, the tax was imposed on the earner of the income. Consequently, the cost to the borrowers was greater than the product of the interest payment and the tax rate, as illustrated in the following tables.
>
> Tax Liability of Farmers and Charmers Federal
>
> | | |
> |---|---:|
> | Loan principal | $10,000,000 |
> | Annual interest payments | 1,200,000 |
> | Gross income to lender | 1,200,000 |
> | Tax imposed on lender at 17 percent | 204,000 |

Cost of tax	204,000

Tax Liability of the Borrowers

Loan principal	$10,000,000
Annual interest payment (gross interest divided by (1.00 – 0.17))	1,445,783
Cost of tax	245,783

Based on these facts, the borrowers' cost of the tax is about 20.5 percent of the net annual interest payment. The borrower's cost of funds is 14.46 percent. This arrangement also does not take into account the effect of the foreign tax credit. If the tax liability is considered to be Farmers and Charmers, it must report the full $1,445,783 and may claim a foreign tax credit or a deduction for the full $245,783 (17 percent of $1,445,783) considered to have been paid on its behalf (subject to all the usual restrictions and limitations of the credit).

Example 3-16

Assuming the same facts as in Example 3-15, if, in 2010, Farmers and Charmers Federal deducts foreign taxes paid, it will be economically in the position intended by the loan agreement. If Farmers and Charmers Federal claims a credit for the Termo taxes, the position may be quite different, as illustrated in the following table, which assumes that Farmers and Charmers Federal's cost of funds is 9 percent.

	Deduction of Tax	Credit of Tax
Cash income	$1,200,000	$1,200,000
Gross income	1,445,783	1,445,783
Interest expense	900,000	900,000
Net income	545,783	545,783
Tax paid on bank's behalf	245,783	245,783
Deduction of tax	245,783	
Net income after foreign tax	300,000	
Tentative U.S. tax	185,566	
Foreign tax to be credited		245,783
Net U.S. tax	105,000	

Based on these facts, not only does Farmers and Charmers Federal receive its interest-free of reductions for Termo tax, but it can make use of a foreign tax credit for taxes considered to have been paid on its behalf, thus effectively eliminating any U.S. income tax liability on the income.

Chapter 4

U.S. Foreign Tax Credit—Special Rules

Foreign Tax Credit as a Financing Device

Using the foreign tax credit to lower the cost of loans to borrowers or increase profits to lenders is occasionally possible. It depends on the ability of a U.S. lender to make use of any foreign tax credits generated by the loan transaction, which is frequently difficult.

Example 4-1

Assuming the same facts as in Example 3-16, suppose that 75 percent of any tax paid by the borrowers can be taken as a credit against other tax liability to Termo. Thus, the borrowers can pay the tax of $245,783 in respect of the interest deemed received by Farmers and Charmers Federal, but then the borrowers get a 76 percent credit against their overall tax bill to Termo. Thus, as illustrated in the table below, which still assumes that Farmers and Charmers Federal's cost of funds is 9 percent, the loan to the borrowers from Farmers and Charmers Federal becomes much cheaper, benefiting both the borrowers and Farmers and Charmers Federal.

	U.S. Credit of Tax	**With Special Termo Credit**
Cash income	$1,200,000	$1,200,000
Gross income	1,445,783	1,445,783
Interest expense	900,000	900,000
Net income	545,783	545,783
Tax paid on bank's behalf	245,783	245,783
Tentative U.S. tax	185,566	185,566
Foreign tax to be credited	245,783	245,783
Net U.S. tax	0	0
Tax benefit to borrower		184,337
Total tax cost	245,783	61,446

Based on these facts, the problem now is that the transaction generates only $61,446 in net foreign tax but, at least nominally, creates $245,783 in credits for Farmers and Charmers Federal. To the extent that a foreign tax is refunded or otherwise applied to reduce a withholding obligation, the foreign tax will not be considered a tax for purposes of any foreign tax credit claimed by a lender.

Thus, of the total foreign tax withheld and paid over (at least initially), only 25 percent, or $61,446, is creditable by Farmers and Charmers Federal under the foreign tax credit rules.

Tax Sparing

The payback arrangement in Example 4-1 illustrates an interesting characteristic of the U.S. foreign tax credit. The foreign tax credit is not designed to maximize U.S. income taxes. Leaving aside the issue of qualifying under the foreign tax credit rules, generally the higher the tax charged by a foreign government on a U.S. corporation's income the higher the credit granted against the corporation's U.S. tax liability will be.

However, this can work the other way as well. For example, the lower the tax charged by a foreign government on a U.S. corporation's income, the lower the credit granted against a corporation's U.S. tax liability will be. Even where a U.S. company is able to negotiate with a foreign country a lower tax rate on its income, that company may not derive any benefit from the reduced tax liability under the foreign tax credit rules.

Example 4-2

The newly created Republic of Corlera, which was formerly part of Eastern Siberia, wishes to attract foreign investment in order to give its oil fields the benefit of modern technology. Del Tredici Drilling Corp. promises to provide certain types of secondary extraction technology to a Corlera joint venture. In return, Corlera grants the corporation a ten-year tax holiday from its usual corporate tax rate of 31 percent on income. This will likely increase the noncreditable income taxes paid to Corlera and, therefore, the U.S. tax on income derived from the joint venture.

By contrast, some developed countries would allow a domestic company like Del Tredici a full foreign tax credit of 31 percent, even though that tax is not paid to Corlera. In this manner, Corlera would be in a position to create a meaningful tax incentive for foreign investments by companies in developed countries. The developed country's treasury is subsidizing the investment in Corlera to an extent, but it also gives its own companies an advantage in establishing commercial relations in Corlera. This granting of a foreign tax credit for foreign taxes not paid is usually called tax sparing. The United States has always refused to enact statutes or to enter into treaties creating such tax-sparing arrangements.

Example 4-3

Assuming the same facts as in Example 4-2, suppose that Corlera in fact charges the full corporate tax rate of 31 percent on Del Tredici's income that is derived from the joint venture. Del Tredici claims a foreign tax credit for the taxes paid to Corlera. In another tax year and in another form, Corlera confers benefits on Del Tredici equal in value to the amount of tax paid.

Based on these facts, the position of the IRS would be that there was no tax, creditable or otherwise, to the extent that the tax payment was offset by another financial benefit.

Integrated Income Tax System

Many of the most troublesome issues surrounding the foreign tax credit derive from dealing with income tax systems that are different from the U.S. income tax system. The foreign tax credit mechanism depends on the fundamental principle that U.S. businesses will encounter foreign income tax systems that are similar to the U.S. income tax system. Even when the foreign income tax system approximates the U.S. income tax system, however, there are serious issues.

Example 4-4

The Kingdom of Glendale has an income tax system that is designed to unify the taxation of corporations and shareholders. Both the corporate and the individual tax rates are 31 percent. When a corporation declares a dividend of after-tax earnings, the amount of the dividend is grossed up by the amount of corporate tax paid on those earnings and carries with it a credit against income tax on other Glendale income of the shareholder.

Arbuckle Artists, Inc., owns 5 percent of the equity of Lecuona, Ltd., a Glendale corporation that is engaged in film distribution. For 2009, Lecuona's earnings and distributions are as follows:

Gross income	$1,000,000
Expenses	375,000
Net income	625,000
Glendale tax (31 percent)	193,750
After-tax profits	431,250
Dividend declared	100,000
Arbuckle's cash dividend	5,000
"Attributable" Glendale tax	2,246

If the $2,246 in Glendale tax is considered to be levied on the shareholder, then Arbuckle can claim a foreign tax credit. Subject to the usual restrictions and limitations, Arbuckle reports $7,246 in income and may claim $2,246 as a credit. If, on the other hand, the tax is considered to be a charge on Lecuona, then there is no credit to Arbuckle.

The kind of problem described in Example 4-4 existed for many years with distributions from corporations in the United Kingdom and other countries using a U.K.-type of system. The foreign tax credit mechanism was inadequate to resolve this dilemma. The problem was finally dealt with, in the case of income from the United Kingdom, by a tax treaty provision giving the credit to a U.S. taxpayer notwithstanding the existing foreign tax credit rules.

Partnerships

For U.S. income tax purposes, a partnership is a reporting entity, but only partners, whether they are limited or general, are considered taxpayers. The partnership itself is considered to be the agent of the partners for purposes of tax liability and tax attributes. If a U.S. business is a partner in a foreign partnership (or similar entity), any foreign tax levied on the partnership itself is considered to be levied on the partners for U.S. income tax purposes.

The partners of a partnership may claim a foreign tax credit, and a distribution of profits is not a precondition to being able to claim the credit. From time to time, however, a foreign country will define "U.S. taxpayer" differently than the United States.

Example 4-5

Partch Products is an association of duck farm proprietorships formed in order to market the products of its four individual members, whose names are Lance, Vance, Chance and Bruce. Partch is considered to be an association taxable as a corporation by the Internal Revenue Service and reports its taxable income accordingly.

Partch maintains at least one employee in a number of Asian countries. One of these countries, the Dominion of Dulzura, considers Partch to be a partnership. Dulzura computes the taxable income of Partch from its Dulzura operations and bills Partch for tax payments on behalf of its "partners."

In 2010, Partch sells smoked duck breasts and frozen dressed ducks to unrelated customers in Dulzura. For 2010, Partch's financial information for sales in Dulzura is as follows:

Gross receipts	$225,000
Cost of goods sold	87,500
Gross income	137,500
Sales expenses	15,500
Shipping costs	23,500
Net income	98,500
Dulzura tax (26 percent)	25,610
After-tax income	72,890
Cash distributions	0

Based on these facts, if Partch is treated as a corporation for purposes of the foreign tax credit, then it may, subject to the usual restrictions and limitations, claim a credit for the Dulzura tax of $25,610. If Partch is treated as a partnership for purposes of the foreign tax credit, then only the partners may claim such a credit. The IRS has ruled that in this type of circumstance, the U.S. characterization of the entity will govern for purposes of the foreign tax credit. Thus, each partner must claim the foreign tax credit separately on Form 1116.

When Tax Is Considered Paid

There are a number of important timing issues involved in the foreign tax credit, stemming from the principle that a foreign tax cannot generally be claimed as a credit until that tax has been paid or accrued. A taxpayer cannot pay or accrue the tax until it figures out how much is owed. There is frequently an issue of which transfers are for payment of tax and which payments are mere deposits. Moreover, the term "accrued" has a different meaning in this context from normal accounting provisions.

FTC MINIMUM HOLDING PERIOD

Effective for amounts paid or accrued more than 30 days after October 22, 2004, the American Jobs Creation Act of 2004 requires that taxpayers hold property earning foreign tax credits through income or gain from property for more than 15 days (within a 31-day testing period), exclusive of periods during which the taxpayer is under an obligation to make related payments with respect to positions in substantially similar property. This minimum holding period applies to debt instruments as well as equity investments.

PAID OR ACCRUED

Originally, the foreign tax credit statute allowed a credit to a cash-basis taxpayer only for foreign taxes actually paid. That was impractical, however, and contrary to the purpose of the law, since it was not uncommon for U.S. taxpayers to fulfill their tax obligations in the following year. The rule was finally changed in 1924 to permit a cash-basis taxpayer to claim a credit for foreign taxes accrued on its books during the tax year.

The current statute makes the "accrual" rule clear for purposes of the direct credit. For purposes of the credit for deemed-paid taxes of foreign affiliates, however, the rule exists only in the regulations. The key for showing an accrual is to show that the all-events test has been met.

Example 4-6

The Codgliano Corp., a U.S. parent corporation, operates foreign branches in Chemeteka and Chilcoot. Chemeteka imposes a 27 percent income tax on branch profits. The tax is assessed annually but is payable as a withholding item from remittances abroad. Chilcoot imposes a 25 percent tax on branch profits that are remitted abroad.

In the case of Chemeteka, therefore, liability for tax occurs when the income is earned. In the case of Chilcoot, liability occurs when the income is remitted. In 2009, each branch earns $1 million. In 2010, each branch sends $500,000 to the head office in the United States.

Based on these facts, and under current case law, the Chemeteka tax liability may be credited in 2009, but the Chilcoot tax liability may be credited only in 2010.

Example 4-6 refers to the time when the liability to foreign tax accrues, but it may be difficult to ascertain when this liability occurs. There are still examples of situations where liability for tax is triggered only upon the distribution of earnings. Moreover, payments of estimated tax liability may not in and of themselves constitute "payment." On the other hand, if a taxpayer is permitted under local law to defer the payment of tax for one year, the liability for which has already become fixed in the current year, a foreign tax credit may be claimed in the current tax year.

CONTESTED FOREIGN TAXES

Theoretically, as long as the amount of tax is the subject of a legitimate dispute, there is no liability to pay and the foreign tax may not be accrued for purposes of the foreign tax credit. An accrual-basis taxpayer that pays a contested amount of taxes may claim a credit for those payments. If a taxpayer is successful in its claim against a foreign country's tax authorities, then its foreign income and corrected credits will be adjusted at that time.

Foreign Tax Credit Limitation

LIMITATION CATEGORIES

The principal purpose of the foreign tax credit limitation is to permit U.S. businesses to credit foreign taxes paid on income from foreign sources against U.S. taxes on the same income, limited to the amount of U.S. tax. A payment of foreign tax on income that exceeds the U.S. tax on the same income may be credited against U.S. taxes on other foreign income or in another taxable year. There are special rules for overall foreign losses.

The amount of foreign tax credited against U.S. tax is determined by multiplying U.S. tax on worldwide taxable income by a fraction. The numerator of the fraction is the business' taxable income from foreign sources, and the denominator is the business' worldwide taxable income. For this purpose, the business' foreign source taxable income cannot exceed the business' worldwide taxable income. In other words, the fraction cannot exceed one. The foreign tax credit limit applies to all foreign and possession taxes directly paid, withheld from payments received by the business or deemed paid by foreign corporations in which the business has an interest.

A three-step analysis is required to determine a business' foreign source taxable income. First, the business must identify each item of foreign source gross income. Second, the business must apportion and allocate deductions to that gross income to determine the net amount of taxable income from foreign sources. Finally, if the business has an overall foreign source loss (or domestic source loss incurred in tax years beginning after 2006), the business should determine whether any of the rules that change source of income apply.

If a business has no taxable income from foreign sources, no foreign tax credit may be claimed for that taxable year. The unused taxes may be carried back and then carried forward for possible use in another year. The business will not be able to use excess credits, however, in any other year in which the business has no foreign source taxable income.

Foreign source income that is excluded from gross income does not enter the numerator or the denominator of the limitation fraction. A foreign country may tax income that is exempt from U.S. tax, and the foreign tax paid may be credited against U.S. tax. However, the exempt income may not be used to determine the foreign tax credit limit. U.S. law defines the numerator of the foreign tax credit limitation fraction, even if amounts in the numerator are exempt under foreign law.

There are ten limitation categories (commonly called "baskets"). A business must compute a separate limit for each basket. The baskets are:

1. Passive income;

2. Interest subject to "high" withholding tax;

3. Income from provision of financial services, including any income earned by a company in the active conduct of a banking or insurance business, except for

a.　　High withholding tax interest,

b.　　Dividends from foreign corporations that are not controlled foreign corporations to a U.S. corporation entitled to claim an indirect foreign tax credit, and

c.　　Export financing interest that is not subject to high withholding tax;

4.　　Income from shipping operations;

5.　　Dividends from a noncontrolled foreign corporation to a U.S. shareholder eligible to claim an indirect foreign tax credit for taxes deemed paid;

6.　　Dividends from a domestic international sales corporation (DISC) or former DISC that are treated as foreign source income;

7.　　Taxable income "attributable" to foreign trading gross receipts of an FSC;

8.　　Distributions from an FSC (or former FSC) out of earnings and profits;

9.　　Foreign oil and gas income; and

10.　　All other income.

The purpose of the baskets is to prevent "averaging" or "cross-crediting" of high foreign taxes on one stream of income against U.S. taxes on another stream of income that has borne little or no foreign taxes.

Effective for tax years beginning after 2006, nine separate foreign tax credit limitation categories other than passive income are reduced to one, general limitation.

The most important of the baskets is the passive basket. By operation of the so-called high-tax kick-out rule, the taxable income in that basket has always been subject to foreign tax at an effective rate below the U.S. statutory rate. The United States collects tax with respect to the taxable income in the passive basket equal to the amount of that income multiplied by the difference between the U.S. tax rate and the average foreign effective tax rate on income in that basket. For example, if P, a U.S. corporation, has $400 of taxable income in its passive basket and that income was taxed by foreign countries at an average effective tax rate of 25 percent, then the United States would collect tax of $40 ($400 × (.35 − .25)) from P.

A similar result is obtained whenever the taxable income in a separate basket has been taxed by foreign jurisdictions at an average effective rate below the U.S. rate. In such circumstances, the separate basket limitation itself has no operative effect because the limitation is always greater than the amount of foreign taxes paid. The important effect of these low-tax separate baskets is that they allow the United States to collect its residual tax on taxable income in those baskets by preventing the cross-crediting of high foreign taxes attributable to other baskets.

Some separate baskets typically contain taxable income that has been subject to a high foreign tax rate. An example is the basket for foreign oil and gas extraction income. Another example is the high withholding tax interest basket. Other baskets, such as the financial services basket, may operate as a low-tax basket for some businesses and as a high-tax basket for other businesses. In the case of a high-tax basket, the separate basket limitation does have an operative effect in that it prevents the business from claiming a credit in excess of the tentative U.S. tax applicable to the income in that basket.

Separate baskets, other than the passive basket, may include some items of income that were subject to high foreign taxes and other items of income that were subject to low foreign taxes. In such circumstances, the business may offset the tentative U.S. tax on the lightly taxed income with the excess credits attributed to the highly taxed income.

To maintain the integrity of the special limitation rules, the Internal Revenue Code provides that certain income that would have been included in a particular separate limitation basket if it had been earned directly by a U.S. person will constitute separate basket limitation income even if it is channeled through one or more foreign affiliates. This result is achieved by the adoption of certain look-through rules that preserve the original character of income in certain cases. For example, income that is classified as royalty income when earned by a foreign affiliate would still be characterized as royalty income when it is received as a dividend by the U.S. parent corporation.

The operation of the separate basket limitation formula is illustrated by the following example.

Example 4-7

P, a U.S. parent corporation, has passive taxable income (one of the categories of separate basket taxable income) of $100, on which it paid a foreign income tax of $5. It has foreign-source taxable income of $300 from business operations, with respect to which it has paid a foreign income tax of $150. This income is included in the general (or residual) basket.

P has U.S.-source taxable income of $400. Under these conditions, P would lose $30 of credit because of the separate basket limitation rules. The amount of credit allowable under a separate basket limitation is calculated as follows:

- Worldwide taxable income = $800 (passive basket taxable income ($100) + general basket foreign-source taxable income ($300) + U.S.-source taxable income ($400))

- Tentative U.S. tax = $280 (35% × $800)

- Total foreign income taxes paid = $155 (foreign income taxes paid with respect to passive basket taxable income ($5) + other foreign income taxes paid with respect to general basket income ($150))

Tax Due without Special Basket Limitation (Overall Limitation)

- Total foreign-source taxable income = $400 (passive basket taxable income ($100) + general basket foreign-source taxable income ($300))

- Overall limitation = $140 (tentative U.S. tax ($280) × total foreign-source taxable income ($400) / worldwide taxable income ($800))

- Amount allowed as credit = $140 (lesser of total foreign income taxes paid ($155) or overall limitation ($140))

- Tax due = $140 (tentative U.S. tax ($280) less amount allowed as credit ($140))

- Excess credit = $15 (total foreign income taxes paid ($155) less overall limitation ($140))

Tax Due under Separate Basket Limitation

- Passive basket limitation = $35 (tentative U.S. tax ($280) × passive basket taxable income ($100) / worldwide taxable income ($800))

- Credit allowable with respect to passive basket taxable income = $5 (lesser of foreign income taxes paid with respect to passive basket taxable income ($5) or passive basket limitation ($35))

- General basket limitation = $105 (tentative U.S. tax ($280) × general basket foreign-source taxable income ($300) / worldwide taxable income ($800))

- Credit allowable with respect to general basket foreign-source taxable income = $105 (lesser of other foreign taxes paid with respect to general basket income ($150) or general basket limitation ($105))

- Total amount allowed as credit = $110 (credit allowable with respect to passive basket taxable income ($5) + credit allowable with respect to general basket foreign-source taxable income ($105))

- Tax due = $170 (tentative U.S. tax ($280) less total amount allowed as credit ($110))

- Excess credit = $45 (total foreign income taxes paid ($155) less total amount allowed as credit ($110))

In Example 4-7, the passive basket taxable income was taxable at an effective foreign tax rate below the U.S. effective tax rate, and the residual foreign-source taxable income subject to the general basket limitation was taxable at an effective foreign tax rate above the U.S. effective tax rate. In these circumstances, the passive basket limitation prevented the U.S. business from cross-crediting the excess foreign taxes imposed on the general basket limitation income against the tentative U.S. tax imposed on the passive basket taxable income. In this example, the important consequence of the passive basket limitation rule was its impact on the numerator of the general basket limitation fraction. The passive basket limitation itself had no operative effect in that the foreign taxes paid on the passive income were less than the limitation amount.

PASSIVE INCOME

The term "passive income" generally includes dividends, interest, rents, royalties, annuities, certain capital gains treated as foreign personal holding company income, any amount taxable to shareholders of a foreign personal holding company and certain amounts earned by qualified electing funds.

However, rents and royalties that are generated in a business' active conduct of business are excepted from passive income treatment. Dividends, interest, rents, and royalties from related entities incorporated in the same country as the payee are also excepted from passive income treatment.

HIGH WITHHOLDING TAX INTEREST

High withholding tax interest includes any type of passive income that is taxed at a high rate by a foreign government. "High" means at least 5 percent on gross interest income but does not include any export-financing interest.

FINANCIAL SERVICES INCOME

Financial services income includes any income earned by a company in the active conduct of a banking or insurance business, except for,

- High withholding tax interest;

- Dividends from foreign corporations that are not controlled foreign corporations to a U.S. corporation entitled to claim a credit for deemed-paid taxes under Internal Revenue Code Section 902; and

- Export-financing interest that is not subject to high withholding tax.

SHIPPING INCOME

Income from shipping operations includes income of all kinds from the use, exploitation, or disposition of any ship or aircraft in foreign commerce. Special *exclusions* cover (1) dividends paid by foreign corporations that are not controlled foreign corporations to a U.S. corporation entitled to claim a credit for deemed-paid taxes under Internal Revenue Code Section 902 and (2) financial services income.

DIVIDENDS FROM A "NONCONTROLLED SECTION 902 CORPORATION"

"Noncontrolled Section 902 corporation" means a foreign corporation (1) of which a U.S. business owns, directly or indirectly, enough equity to qualify to claim a credit for deemed-paid foreign taxes under Section 902 and (2) of which a U.S. business, together with other U.S. persons, does not own, directly or indirectly, enough equity to be considered a controlled foreign corporation.

INCOME FROM DOMESTIC INTERNATIONAL SALES CORPORATIONS AND FOREIGN SALES CORPORATIONS (FSC)

Taxable income that benefits from the special taxing rules for FSCs is placed in its own category. The same treatment is given collectively to

- Distributions of an FSC out of earnings and profits attributable to foreign trade income;

- Interest from a transaction resulting in foreign trade income; and

- Carrying charges from a transaction resulting in foreign trade income.

- Finally, distributions from a DISC or former DISC that are treated as foreign-source income are placed in a separate category.

CONSOLIDATION OF FOREIGN TAX CREDIT BASKETS

Effective for tax years beginning after December 31, 2006, 10 separate foreign tax credit limitation categories under current law are reduced to two—passive category and general limitation category income.

Other income is included in one of the two categories as appropriate. For example, shipping income generally falls into the general limitation category, whereas high withholding tax interest generally could fall into the passive income or the general limitation category, depending on the circumstances. Dividends from a domestic international sales corporation or former domestic international sales corporation, income attributable to certain foreign trade income and certain distributions from a foreign sales corporation or former foreign sales corporation all are assigned to the passive income limitation category.

In the case of a member of a financial services group or any other person predominantly engaged in the active conduct of a banking, insurance, financing or similar business, financial services income is considered to be general limitation category income.

Base Differences

Effective for tax years beginning after 2006, creditable foreign taxes imposed on amounts that do not constitute income under U.S. tax principles and which arose in tax years beginning after December 31, 2004 can be treated, at the taxpayer's election, as imposed on either general limitation category or passive category income. Once made, this election applies to all such taxes for these tax years and is revocable only with the consent of the Treasury Secretary.

CARRYOVERS OF UNUSED CREDITS

If a U.S. business is unable in the current year to claim a credit for all foreign taxes paid, it may be able to shift that unused amount to another tax year. Such unused taxes are first carried back two years and then forward five years.

The provision dealing with statutory categories makes it clear that any computation of carryovers is to be made *separately* for each category of income. This is reflected on Form 1118, Schedule B, Part II, Line 4. Thus, a single business earning income in all nine statutory categories should maintain nine different carryover accounts.

Effective for excess foreign taxes arising in tax years beginning October 22, 2004, and for excess foreign taxes that could be carried over prior to October 22, 2004, to any tax year ending after October 22, 2004, the carryover period is extended from five years to ten and the carryback period is reduced from two years to one.

FOREIGN OIL AND GAS INCOME

Foreign income from oil and gas operations is treated as a separate category. In fact, there are two subcategories that make up foreign oil and gas income.

The first subcategory is income from foreign oil and gas extraction income (FOGEI). FOGEI includes income from the lifting of such minerals and the sale or exchange of assets used to lift such minerals. For corporations, foreign taxes paid on this income may be credited only up to the amount of such income multiplied by the highest marginal U.S. tax rate on such income. For noncorporate businesses, the multiplier is the effective overall U.S. tax rate.

The second subcategory is foreign oil-related income (FORI). FORI includes refining, transportation, processing, performance of services, and distribution and sale of oil and gas and their products. The FORI limitation is aimed at circumstances where a foreign government chooses to tax oil and gas businesses in a manner that results in such businesses paying a higher effective tax rate than other businesses. The statute and regulations treat such extra amounts as deductible business expenses but not as creditable taxes.

COORDINATION WITH TREATIES

Where income earned by a U.S.-owned foreign corporation is resourced as U.S.-source income, and a U.S. tax treaty requires that the same income be treated as foreign-source income, a business may elect to treat the income as foreign-source income and calculate the direct or indirect foreign tax credit limitation separately with respect to the income.

Completion of Form 1118 for General Limitation Income

When there is only one statutory category of foreign income to be reported, only one Form 1118 is completed. However, if a U.S. business earns two or more types of foreign income, then the business must file a complete Form 1118 for each statutory category of foreign income. For example, if a business claims credit for taxes paid on income for all nine statutory categories of foreign income, then nine complete sets of Form 1118 must be prepared.

Example 4-8

Cramden Corporation, Inc., and its consolidated subsidiaries, a U.S.-based multi-national (Cramden) generated foreign-source income of varying types from numerous countries in 2010. Cramden's Southern Antilles-based financing subsidiaries, Global Funding, Inc. (Global) and Antilles Funding, Inc., were deemed to have remitted dividend payments to Cramden of $970,386 and $728,748, respectively. In addition, Global remitted actual dividends of $505,937 to which an indirect foreign tax credit of $227,375 attached (requiring a gross-up computation). Antilles Funding remitted $273,006 interest payments to its U.S. parent.

Cramden received trade income of $3,912,000 and interest income of $1,396,289 from the country of Carmel, and incurred $2,258,000 in expenses directly attributable to the trade income. A branch of Cramden generated $706,097 in the country of Cordura, and incurred $22,697 of expenses directly attributable to this income. Cramden received a dividend distribution of $16 million from a subsidiary operating in Cordura, to which an indirect foreign tax credit of $11,018,556 attached, while a second subsidiary of Cramden in the country of Cordura, Island Services, Inc., generated $4,480,572 of income and incurred directly attributable expenses of $530,016.

> Cramden Purchasing Corporation, in the land of Gardenia, generated $17,837,247, and incurred directly attributable expenses of $6,774,358. Cramden Export Corporation, also in Gardenia, generated $581,451, and incurred expenses of $430,699. Cramden Purchasing Corporation and Cramden Export Corporation remitted interest payments of $320,872 and $46,250, respectively, to the U.S. parent.
>
> A subsidiary of Cramden, Seascape, Inc. (Seascape), generated $173,527 in the island of Nauticus and $13,608 in the country of Bayland. A subsidiary in Bayland, Cramden Bayland, remitted dividend payments of $61,071 to which an indirect foreign tax credit of $10,777 attached, requiring a gross-up calculation. Cramden Bayland also remitted $277,469 interest to the U.S. parent.
>
> Finally, Cramden's catalog operation generated $854,000 abroad with directly related expenses of $67,000 while Cramden's portfolio investment activity outside the United States generated $2,575,283 of foreign-source investment income. Cramden Financing remitted $916,858 interest payments to the U.S. parent.

General Information Worksheet and Supporting Worksheets

In order to complete Form 1118, Cramden will need multiple copies of Form 1118. A separate Form 1118 will be required for each type of income generated.

Based on the facts in this example, Cramden will need to complete only one summary Schedule J, but it will need a separate Form 1118 for its passive income, general limitation income and financial services income.

SAMPLE FORMS

The following discussion is based on the facts provided in Example 4-8.

Prior to completing Form 1118, it is crucial to categorize income and expenses (both those directly attributable to a single class of income and those allocable to multiple classes of income) on a general information worksheet. The general information worksheet (see Sample Form 4-1—all sample forms are included in the Appendix to this chapter) categorizes the items of income in Example 4-8 as well as certain additional deductions not directly attributable to a single class of income.

The first step in completing Form 1118 should be to prepare supporting worksheets for the schedules that are to be completed. On the supporting worksheets for Cramden (see Sample Forms 4-2 through 4-4), the original information reflected on the general information worksheet has been segregated into separate work sheets, labeled Schedules A and B, for each of the three kinds of income that Cramden must report (1) passive income; (2) general limitation income and (3) financial services income. The accurate creation of these worksheets from source data is a critical step in completing Form 1118.

FORM 1118 FOR PASSIVE INCOME SCHEDULE A

Completion of page 1 of Form 1118 for the passive income follows closely the worksheet for passive income, in which the interest income from Cramden Corporation Investments abroad and from Cramden Financing Corporation are listed in Schedule A, line 4, and in the total column, line 8. Similarly, line 10 reflects the apportioned share of deductions not definitely allocable to other categories of income in the passive category. A final adjustment in the work sheet is the recharacterization of a prior loss.

FORM 1118 FOR PASSIVE INCOME SCHEDULE B

Schedule B of Form 1118 for passive income, on page 2, follows the worksheet and reflects no current foreign taxes paid or deemed paid. Part II of page 2, however, reflects a carryover of $1,649,986 of previously remitted foreign taxes. Part II of page 2 is where the limitation applies to the use of these foreign taxes paid (current and previously paid) against the U.S. tax liability. Line 6 represents total foreign taxes on passive income. Line 7 is the assumed total taxable income of Cramden from all sources for the taxable year. Line 8 is the fraction created when line 6 (total foreign taxes) is divided by line 7 (total taxable income from the year). Line 9 is Cramden's total U.S. income tax for the year and the fraction is multiplied by this amount to determine the amount of foreign tax from passive income creditable against U.S. tax in the current year. In Example 4-8, of the total foreign taxes previously paid of $1,649,986, $604,434 may be utilized the current year.

Finally, only one Part III of the three Forms 1118 is required to be completed. Assuming the Part III of the passive Form 1118 is to represent the summary schedule, the $604,434 amount derived in Part II, line 11, will be displayed on line 1 of Part III in the calculation of the total foreign tax credit eligible for use in the current year. The remainder of Part III will be completed following the completion of Part II on each of the other two Forms 1118 for the other types of income.

FORM 1118 FOR PASSIVE INCOME SCHEDULE H

Schedule H, page 6, of Form 1118 for passive income reflects assumed average values of assets at tax book value in Part II, section (a). Section (b) illustrates how total interest expense deductions of $4,569,016 are to be allocated to the three types of income for which Forms 1118 are to be completed. The total interest expense is allocated among the three categories of nonfinancial corporation income based on the nonfinancial corporation assets in each category (passive, general limitation and financial services) divided by the total assets in each category. Once the allocation is complete, all other deductions not definitely allocable in column (c) (separate work sheets are provided illustrating these expenses) are added to each category of income, and the result in column (d) of Part II of Schedule H provides the amounts to be included in line 10 of page 1 of each Form 1118. For a completed Form 1118 for Cramden's passive income, see Sample Form 4-5.

FORM 1118 FOR GENERAL LIMITATION INCOME SCHEDULES A AND B

The supporting worksheet for general limitation income will expedite completion of page 1 of Form 1118. Current year foreign taxes are reflected in Schedule B on page 2 of Form 1118. The limitation computation in Part II is calculated the same way as that for passive income, except that all current year foreign taxes are allowed in computing the total foreign tax credit. No carryover is created by the limitation, as was the case in the passive income Form 1118. The result in line 11 of Part II is carried to the summary schedule on the passive income Form 1118 Part III line 9.

FORM 1118 FOR GENERAL LIMITATION INCOME SCHEDULE C

The general limitation income Form 1118 illustrates a few additional concepts. Schedule C, page 3, reflects the source of the dividends received and reflected in the general limitation income basket. In this case, the dividends were declared from post-1986 earnings and profits. Notice line 5 of Part 1. The amount listed there is from page 4 of Form 1118, Schedule D, Part 1. The amount is described as foreign taxes deemed paid. The foreign taxes paid were actually remitted by a first-tier subsidiary of the entity listed on Schedule C (that is, the tax-paying entity is a second-tier foreign subsidiary of Cramden). Taxes paid by the second-tier subsidiary are deemed paid by the first-tier subsidiary and are utilized in the Schedule C (and ultimately Schedule B) amount of foreign taxes paid for use in determining the foreign tax credit limitation.

FORM 1118 FOR GENERAL LIMITATION INCOME SCHEDULE F

Finally, page 5 of Form 1118 for general limitation income reflects the foreign branch income received by Cramden and reflected on page 1 of the Form 1118. For a completed Form 1118 for Cramden's general limitation income, see Sample Form 4-6.

FORM 1118 FOR FINANCIAL SERVICES INCOME SCHEDULES A AND B

Note that Schedule A, page 1, and Schedule B, page 2, are completed in a similar manner as for the two preceding types of income. The result of line 11, Part II, is carried to the Part III summary of Form 1118 for passive income, page 2. For a completed Form 1118 for Cramden's financial services income, see Sample Form 4-7.

FORM 1118—TOTAL SEPARATE NET LIMITATION INCOME

A single Schedule J is completed displaying the total net separate limitation income amounts (the numerators of the foreign tax credit limitation fraction). These amounts correspond to the amounts listed on Line 6, Part II, of Form 1118, Schedule B, for each type of Cramden income. For a completed Schedule J, including instructions, see Sample Form 4-8.

After completing Schedule J, Cramden places the amount of the allowable foreign tax credit calculated in Schedule B, part II, Line 11, for each type of income on the appropriate line of the Form 1118 Master Schedule. Then, Cramden adds up the credits and transfers the sum to Form 1120. The resulting total credit amount for Cramden for 2010 is $4,561,278, as shown in Schedule B, Part III, Line 13, of Form 1118 for passive income. The Form 1118 Master Schedule summarizes the allowable foreign tax credits for the respective types of foreign-source income calculated on Schedule B, Part III, Line 13 of Form 1118. For a completed Form 1118 Master Schedule, see Sample Form 4-9.

FOREIGN OIL AND GAS EXTRACTION INCOME AND FOREIGN OIL-RELATED INCOME

As noted previously, FOGEI is treated as a separate limitation category of income for purposes of completing Form 1118. Specifically, FOGEI requires a separate limitation calculation for purposes of the foreign tax credit. FORI, on the other hand, involves a definition of what will constitute a foreign creditable tax. Except for the definitional issue, FORI is reported in the same manner as other types of income and tax.

Example 4-9

Engle Extractions operates oil fields in the Dominion of Bodfish. In 2010, Engle earns gross income of $4,250,000, pays tax to Bodfish in the amount of $2 million, and has direct expenses of $875,000. Engle's highest U.S. marginal tax rate is 35 percent.

Based on the facts of this example, Engle must complete Form 1118, Schedules I, G, and B.

SAMPLE FORMS

The following discussion is based on the facts provided in Example 4-9.

FORM 1118 SCHEDULE I

Engle begins completing Schedule I, Part 1, by entering its gross income, $4,250,000, in columns 2 and 7. Next Engle enters its deductions ($875,000) in columns 8 and 10. Engle subtracts column 10 from column 7 ($4,250,000 – $875,000 = $3,375,000) and enters the result in column 11. This amount represents Engle's taxable income. Engle now enters the Bodfish tax Engle paid ($2,000,000) in columns 12 and 14. On Part II, Engle enters its taxable income amount ($3,375,000) on Line 1. This amount is then multiplied by the highest marginal tax rate ($3,375,000 × 35% = $1,181,250) and enters the result on Line 2. Engle's tax payment to Bodfish ($2,000,000) is entered on Lines 3 and 5. Engle now subtracts Line 2 from Line 5 ($2,000,000 – $1,181,250 = $818,750) and enters the result on Line 6. This figure represents Engle's foreign tax credit reduction and is carried over to Schedule G, Part II, Line C. Once all the adjustments are added together in Part II, the total is entered on Schedule B, Part II, Line 3. For completed Form 1118 Schedule I illustrating Engle's income, see Sample Form 4-10.

Instructions for Form 1118
(Rev. December 2010)

Department of the Treasury
Internal Revenue Service

(Use with the December 2009 revision of Form 1118.)
Foreign Tax Credit—Corporations

Section references are to the Internal Revenue Code unless otherwise noted.

What's New for 2010

● Section 212 of P.L. 111-226 added new section 901(m), which provides for the denial of a foreign tax credit with respect to foreign income not subject to U.S. taxation by reason of covered asset acquisitions (as defined in new section 901(m)(2)). See *No Credit or Deduction* on page 3 for additional information.

● Section 213 of P.L. 111-226 added new section 904(d)(6), which provides for the separate application of the foreign tax credit rules with respect to certain items resourced under treaties. See *Income Re-sourced by Treaty* on page 2 for additional information.

● Section 214 of P.L. 111-226 added new section 960(c), which provides for a limitation with respect to section 956 inclusions. See the instructions for Schedule G, Line E on page 9 for additional information.

General Instructions

Purpose of Form

Use Form 1118 to compute a corporation's foreign tax credit for certain taxes paid or accrued to foreign countries or U.S. possessions. See *Taxes Eligible for a Credit* on page 3.

Who Must File

Any corporation that elects the benefits of the foreign tax credit under section 901 must complete and attach Form 1118 to its income tax return.

When to Make the Election

The election to claim the foreign tax credit (or a deduction in lieu of a credit) for any tax year may be made or changed at any time before the end of a special 10-year period described in section 6511(d)(3) (or section 6511(c) if the period is extended by agreement).

Computer-Generated Form 1118

The corporation may submit a computer-generated Form 1118 and schedules if they conform to the IRS version. However, if a software program

is used, it must be approved by the IRS for use in filing substitute forms. This ensures the proper placement of each item appearing on the IRS version. For more information, see Pub. 1167, General Rules and Specifications for Substitute Forms and Schedules.

How To Complete Form 1118

Important. Complete a separate Schedule A; Schedule B, Parts I & II; Schedules C through G; Schedule I; and Schedule K for each applicable separate category of income. See *Categories of Income* below. Complete Schedule B, Part III; Schedule H; and Schedule J only once.

● Use **Schedule A** to compute the corporation's income or loss before adjustments for each applicable category of income.

● Use **Schedule B** to determine the total foreign tax credit after certain limitations.

● Use **Schedule C** to compute taxes deemed paid by the domestic corporation filing the return.

● Use **Schedules D** and **E** to compute taxes deemed paid by lower-tier foreign corporations.

● Use **Schedule F** to report gross income and definitely allocable deductions from foreign branches.

● Use **Schedule G** to report required reductions of tax paid, accrued, or deemed paid.

● Use **Schedule H** to apportion deductions that cannot be definitely allocated to some item or class of income.

● Use **Schedule I** (a separate schedule) to compute reductions of taxes paid, accrued, or deemed paid on foreign oil and gas extraction income.

● Use **Schedule J** (a separate schedule) to compute adjustments to separate limitation income or losses in determining the numerators of limitation fractions, year-end recharacterization balances, and overall foreign and domestic loss account balances.

● Use **Schedule K** (a separate schedule) to reconcile the corporation's prior year foreign tax carryover with its current year foreign tax carryover.

Categories of Income

Compute a separate foreign tax credit for each applicable separate category described below.

Passive Category Income

Passive category income includes passive income and specified passive category income.

Passive income. Generally, passive income is:

● Any income received or accrued that would be foreign personal holding company income (defined in section 954(c)) if the corporation were a controlled foreign corporation (CFC) (defined in section 957). This includes any gain on the sale or exchange of stock that is more than the amount treated as a dividend under section 1248. However, in determining if any income would be foreign personal holding company income, the rules of section 864(d)(6) will apply only for income of a CFC.

● Any amount includible in gross income under section 1293 (which relates to certain passive foreign investment companies).

Passive income does **not** include:

● Any financial services income that is general category income (see *General Category Income* on page 2),

● Any export financing interest unless it is also related person factoring income (see section 904(d)(2)(G) and Temporary Regulations section 1.904-4T(h)(3)),

● Any high-taxed income (see *General Category Income* on page 2 and the instructions for Schedule A on page 5), or

● Any active rents or royalties. See Temporary Regulations section 1.904-4T(b)(2)(iii) for definitions and exceptions.

Note. Certain income received from a CFC and certain dividends from a 10/50 corporation that would otherwise be passive income may be assigned to another separate category under the look-through rules. See *Look-Through Rules* on page 2.

Specified passive category income. This term includes:

● Dividends from a DISC or former DISC (as defined in section 992(a)) to the extent such dividends are treated as foreign source income, and

● Distributions from a former FSC out of earnings and profits attributable to foreign trade income or interest or carrying charges (as defined in section 927(d)(1), before its repeal) derived from a transaction which results in foreign trade income (as defined in section 932(b), before its repeal).

Cat. No. 10905I

Section 901(j) Income

No credit is allowed for foreign taxes imposed by and paid or accrued to certain sanctioned countries. However, income derived from **each** such country is subject to a separate foreign tax credit limitation. Therefore, the corporation must use a separate Form 1118 for income derived from each such country. On each Form 1118, check the box for section 901(j) income at the top of page 1 and identify the applicable country in the space provided.

Sanctioned countries are those designated by the Secretary of State as countries that repeatedly provide support for acts of international terrorism, countries with which the United States does not have diplomatic relations, or countries whose governments are not recognized by the United States. As of the date these instructions were revised, section 901(j) applied to income derived from Cuba, Iran, North Korea, Sudan, and Syria. For more information, see section 901(j).

Note. The President of the United States has the authority to waive the application of section 901(j) with respect to a foreign country if it is (a) in the national interest of the United States and will expand trade and investment opportunities for U.S. companies in such foreign country and (b) the President reports to the Congress, not less than 30 days before the waiver is granted, the intention to grant such a waiver and the reason for such waiver.

Note. Effective December 10, 2004, the President waived the application of section 901(j) with respect to Libya.

If the corporation paid taxes to a country that ceased to be a sanctioned country during the tax year, see Rev. Rul. 92-62, 1992-2 C.B. 193, for details on how to figure the foreign tax credit for the period that begins after the end of the sanctioned period.

Income Re-sourced by Treaty

If a sourcing rule in an applicable income tax treaty treats any of the income described below as foreign source, and the corporation elects to apply the treaty, the income will be treated as foreign source.
• Dividends eligible for the dividends received deduction (section 245(a)(10)).
• Certain gains (section 865(h)).
• Certain income from a U.S.-owned foreign corporation (section 904(h)(10)). See Regulations section 1.904-5(m)(7) for an example.
• For tax years beginning after August 10, 2010, any item of income described in section 904(d)(6).

Important. The corporation must compute a separate foreign tax credit limitation for any such income for which it claims benefits under a treaty, using a separate Form 1118 for each amount of re-sourced income from a treaty country. On each Form 1118, check the box for income re-sourced by treaty at the top of

page 1 and identify the applicable country in the space provided.

General Category Income

This category includes all income not described above. This includes high-taxed income that would otherwise be passive category income. Usually, income is high-taxed if the total foreign income taxes paid, accrued, or deemed paid by the corporation for that income exceed the highest rate of tax specified in section 11 (and with reference to section 15, if applicable), multiplied by the amount of such income (including the amount treated as a dividend under section 78). For more information, see Regulations section 1.904-4(c). Also see the instructions for Schedule A on page 5 for additional reporting requirements.

This category also includes financial services income (defined below) if the corporation is a member of a financial services group (as defined in section 904(d)(2)(C)(ii)) or is predominantly engaged in the active conduct of a banking, insurance, financing, or similar business.

Financial services income. Financial services income is income received or accrued by a member of a financial services group or any corporation predominantly engaged in the active conduct of a banking, insurance, financing, or similar business, if the income is:
• Described in section 904(d)(2)(D)(ii),
• Passive income (determined without regard to section 904(d)(2)(B)(iii)(II)), or
• Incidental income described in Regulations section 1.904-4(e)(4).

Special Rules

Source Rules for Income

Determine income or (loss) for each separate category on Schedule A using the general source rules of sections 861 through 865 and related regulations; the special source rules of section 904(h) described below; and any applicable source rules contained in any applicable tax treaties.

Special source rules of section 904(h). Usually, the following income from a U.S.-owned foreign corporation, otherwise treated as foreign source income, must be treated as U.S. source income under section 904(h):
• Any subpart F income, foreign personal holding company income, or income from a qualified electing fund that a U.S. shareholder is required to include in its gross income, if such amount is attributable to the U.S.-owned foreign corporation's U.S. source income;
• Interest that is properly allocable to the U.S.-owned foreign corporation's U.S. source income; and
• Dividends equal to the U.S. source ratio (defined in section 904(h)(4)(B)).

The rules regarding interest and dividends described above do not apply

to a U.S.-owned foreign corporation if less than 10% of its E&P for the tax year is from U.S. sources.

Amounts That Do Not Constitute Income Under U.S. Tax Principles

For tax years beginning after December 31, 2006, creditable foreign taxes that are imposed on amounts that do not constitute income under U.S. tax principles are treated as imposed on general category income. See section 904(d)(2)(H).

Look-Through Rules

CFCs. Generally, dividends, interest, rents, and royalties received or accrued by the taxpayer are passive category income. However, if these items are received or accrued by a 10% U.S. shareholder from a CFC, they may be assigned to other separate categories under the look-through rules of section 904(d)(3). This includes:
• Interest, rents, and royalties based on the amount allocable to E&P of the CFC in a separate category and
• Dividends paid out of the E&P of a CFC in proportion to the ratio of the CFC's E&P in a separate category to its total E&P. Dividends include any amount included in gross income under section 951(a)(1)(B).

Look-through rules also apply to subpart F inclusions under section 951(a)(1)(A) to the extent attributable to E&P of the CFC in a separate category.

For more information and examples, see section 904(d)(3) and Regulations section 1.904-5.

10/50 corporations. Generally, dividends received or accrued by the taxpayer are passive category income. However, dividends received or accrued from a 10/50 corporation may be assigned to other separate categories under the look-through rules of section 904(d)(4). A 10/50 corporation is any foreign corporation in which the taxpayer (domestic corporation) meets the stock ownership requirements of section 902. See Regulations section 1.904-5(c)(4)(iii).

Certain amounts paid by a U.S. corporation to a related corporation. Look-through rules also apply to foreign source interest, rents, and royalties paid by a U.S. corporation to a related corporation. See Regulations section 1.904-5(g).

Other Rules

Certain transfers of intangible property. See section 367(d)(2)(C) for a rule that clarifies the treatment of certain transfers of intangible property.

Reporting Foreign Tax Information From Partnerships

If you received a Schedule K-1 from a partnership that includes foreign tax information, use the rules below to report that information on Form 1118.

Gross income sourced at partner level. This includes income from the sale of most personal property other than inventory, depreciable property, and certain intangible property sourced under section 865. This gross income will generally be U.S.-source and therefore will not be reported on Form 1118.

The remaining lines of the foreign tax section of the Schedule K-1 are reported on Form 1118 as follows:

Foreign gross income sourced at partnership level. Report on Schedule A.

Deductions allocated and apportioned at partner level and partnership level. Report on Schedule A or Schedule H.

Total foreign taxes paid or accrued. Report on Schedule B.

Reduction in taxes available for credit. Report on Schedule G.

Capital Gains

Foreign source taxable income or (loss) before adjustments in all separate categories in the aggregate should include gain from the sale or exchange of capital assets only up to the amount of foreign source capital gain net income (which is the smaller of capital gain net income from sources outside the United States or capital gain net income). Therefore, if the corporation has capital gain net income from sources outside the United States in excess of the capital gain net income reported on its tax return, enter a pro rata portion of the net U.S. source capital loss as a negative number on Schedule A, column 9(d) for each separate category with capital gain net income from sources outside the United States. To figure the pro rata portion of the net U.S. source capital loss attributable to a separate category, multiply the net U.S. source capital loss by the amount of capital gain net income from sources outside the United States in the separate category divided by the aggregate amount of capital gain net income from sources outside the United States in all separate categories with capital gain net income from sources outside the United States.

See section 904(b)(2)(B) for special rules regarding adjustments to account for capital gain rate differentials (as defined in section 904(b)(3)(D)) for any tax year. At the time these instructions went to print, there was no capital gain rate differential for corporations.

Credit Limitations

Taxes Eligible for a Credit

Domestic corporations. Generally, a domestic corporation may claim a foreign tax credit (subject to the limitation of section 904) for the following taxes:
• Income, war profits, and excess profits taxes (defined in Regulations section 1.901-2(a)) paid or accrued during the tax year to any foreign country or U.S. possession;

• Taxes deemed paid under sections 902 and 960; and
• Taxes paid in lieu of income taxes as described in section 903 and Regulations section 1.903-1.

Some foreign taxes that are otherwise eligible for the foreign tax credit must be reduced. These reductions are reported on Schedule G.

Note. A corporation may not claim a foreign tax credit for foreign taxes paid to a foreign country that the corporation does not legally owe, including amounts eligible for refund by the foreign country. If the corporation does not exercise its available remedies to reduce the amount of foreign tax to what it legally owes, a credit is not allowed for the excess amount.

Foreign corporations. Foreign corporations are allowed (under section 906) a foreign tax credit for income, war profits, and excess profits taxes paid or accrued (or deemed paid under section 902) to any foreign country or U.S. possession for income effectively connected with the conduct of a trade or business within the United States. The credit is not applicable, however, if a foreign country or U.S. possession imposes the tax on income from U.S. sources solely because the foreign corporation was created or organized under the law of the foreign country or U.S. possession or is domiciled there for tax purposes.

The credit may not be taken against any tax imposed on income not effectively connected with a U.S. business.

In computing the foreign tax credit limitation, the foreign corporation's taxable income includes only the taxable income that is effectively connected with the conduct of a trade or business within the United States.

A foreign corporation claiming a foreign tax credit will be treated as a domestic corporation in computing tax deemed paid (section 902(a)) and dividend gross-up (section 78).

Definition of foreign corporation for purposes of the deemed paid credit. In computing the deemed paid credit on Schedules C, D, and E, the term "foreign corporation" includes:
• A DISC or former DISC, but only for dividends from the DISC or former DISC that are treated as income from sources outside the United States and
• A contiguous country life insurance branch that has made an election to be treated as a foreign corporation under section 814(g).

Credit or Deduction

A corporation may choose to take either a credit or a deduction for eligible foreign taxes paid or accrued. The choice is made annually. Generally, if a corporation elects the benefits of the foreign tax credit for any tax year, no portion of the foreign taxes will be allowed as a deduction in that year or any subsequent tax year.

Exceptions. However, a corporation that elects the credit for eligible foreign taxes may be allowed a deduction for certain taxes for which a credit was not allowed. These include:
• Taxes for which the credit was denied because of the boycott provisions of section 908.
• Certain taxes on the purchase or sale of oil or gas (section 901(f)).
• Certain taxes used to provide subsidies (section 901(i)).
• Taxes paid to certain foreign countries for which a credit was denied under section 901(j).
• Certain taxes paid on dividends if the minimum holding period is not met with respect to the underlying stock, or if the corporation is obligated to make related payments with respect to positions in similar or related property (section 901(k)).
• Certain taxes paid on gain and income other than dividends if the minimum holding period is not met with respect to the underlying property, or if the corporation is obligated to make related payments with respect to positions in similar or related property (see section 901(l)).

No Credit or Deduction

No foreign tax credit (or deduction) is allowed for certain taxes including:
• Taxes on mineral income that were reduced under section 901(e).
• Certain taxes paid on distributions from possessions corporations (section 901(g)).
• Taxes on combined foreign oil and gas income that were reduced under section 907(a).
• Taxes attributable to income excluded under section 814(a) (relating to contiguous country branches of domestic life insurance companies).
• Taxes paid or accrued to a foreign country or U.S. possession with respect to income excluded from gross income on Form 8873, Extraterritorial Income Exclusion. However, see section 943(d) for an exception for certain withholding taxes.
• In the case of a covered asset acquisition (as defined in section 901(m)(2)), the disqualified portion of any tax determined with respect to the income or gain attributable to the relevant foreign assets (section 901(m)). **Note.** This rule generally applies to covered asset acquisitions after December 31, 2010.

Carryback and Carryforward of Excess Foreign Taxes

If the allowable foreign taxes paid, accrued, or deemed paid in a tax year in a separate category exceed the foreign tax credit limitation for the tax year for that separate category, the excess may be:
• Carried back 1 year to offset taxes imposed in the same category.
• Carried forward 10 years to offset taxes imposed in the same category (5 years for excess foreign taxes which may be

carried only to tax years ending before October 23, 2004).

The excess is applied first to the earliest of the years to which it may be carried, then to the next earliest year, etc. The corporation may not carry a credit to a tax year for which it claimed a deduction, rather than a credit, for foreign taxes paid or accrued. Furthermore, the corporation must reduce the amount of any carryback or carryforward by the amount it would have used if it had chosen to claim a credit rather than a deduction in that tax year. See section 904(c) and Regulations section 1.904-2 for more details.

How to claim the excess credit. If the corporation is carrying back the excess credit to an earlier year, file an amended tax return with a revised Form 1118 and schedules (including a revised Schedule K (Form 1118)).

Special rules apply to:
• The carryback and carryover of foreign taxes paid or accrued on combined foreign oil and gas income or related taxes (see section 907(f)) and
• An excess foreign tax credit for which an excess limitation account was established under section 960(b)(2).

Special rules for carryforwards of pre-2007 unused foreign taxes. The foreign taxes carried forward generally are allocated to the post-2006 separate categories to which those taxes would have been allocated if the taxes were paid or accrued in a tax year beginning after 2006. Alternatively, the corporation can allocate unused foreign taxes in its pre-2007 passive income category to the post-2006 separate category for passive category income, and can allocate all other unused foreign taxes in pre-2007 separate categories that were eliminated in 2007 to the post-2006 separate category for general category income.

Treaty-Based Return Positions

Corporations that adopt a return position that any U.S. treaty overrides or modifies any provision of the Internal Revenue Code, and causes (or potentially causes) a reduction of any tax incurred at any time, generally must disclose this position. Complete Form 8833, Treaty-Based Return Position Disclosure Under Section 6114 or Section 7701(b), and attach it to Form 1118. See section 6114 and Regulations section 301.6114-1 for details.

Failure to make such a report may result in a $10,000 penalty.

Proof of Credits

Form 1118 must be carefully filled in with all the information called for and with the calculations of credits indicated.

Important. Documentation (that is, receipts of payments or a foreign tax return for accrued taxes) is not required to be attached to Form 1118. However,

proof **must** be presented upon request by the IRS to substantiate the credit. See Regulations section 1.905-2.

If the corporation claims a foreign tax credit for tax accrued but not paid, the IRS may require a bond to be furnished on Form 1117, Income Tax Surety Bond, before the credit is allowed. See Regulations section 1.905-2(c).

Foreign Tax Credit Redeterminations

The corporation's foreign tax credit and U.S. tax liability generally must be redetermined if:
• Accrued foreign taxes when paid differ from the amounts claimed as credits;
• Accrued foreign taxes are not paid within 2 years after the close of the tax year to which they relate; or
• Any foreign tax paid is fully or partially refunded.

Except as provided in Temporary Regulations section 1.905-3T(d)(3), a redetermination of U.S. tax liability is not required to account for the effect of a redetermination of foreign tax paid or accrued by a foreign corporation on the amount of foreign taxes deemed paid under section 902 or 960. Instead, the foreign corporation's pools of E&P and foreign taxes are adjusted in the year of the foreign tax redetermination.

Reporting Requirements

If the corporation must redetermine its U.S. tax liability, the corporation must:
• File an amended return and Form 1118 with the Service Center where it filed the tax return on which it claimed the affected foreign tax credit and
• Provide identifying information such as the corporation's name, address, employer identification number (EIN), and the tax year or years that are affected by the redetermination.

Additional information required. If the redetermination was because of one of the following, the corporation must provide the additional information as indicated.
• **Refund of foreign taxes paid—**
1. The date or dates on which the foreign taxes were accrued, paid, and refunded;
2. The amount of foreign taxes accrued, paid, and refunded on each date (in foreign currency); and
3. The exchange rates used to translate such amounts.
• **Foreign taxes that when paid differ from the accrued amounts claimed as credits for a year beginning before 1998—**
1. The date on which the foreign taxes were accrued;
2. The dates on which the foreign taxes were paid;
3. The exchange rate for each date the foreign taxes were accrued and paid; and

4. The amount of foreign taxes accrued or paid on each such date (in foreign currency).
• **Foreign taxes that when paid differ from accrued amounts claimed as credits for a tax year beginning after 1997 because the corporation paid more or less foreign tax than was originally accrued or failed to pay accrued taxes within 2 years—**
1. The date on which the foreign taxes were accrued;
2. The dates on which the foreign taxes were paid;
3. The average exchange rate for the year for which the foreign taxes were accrued;
4. For taxes paid more than 2 years after the year to which they relate, the exchange rate at the time of payment; and
5. The amount of tax accrued or paid for each such date, and the amount of accrued tax that was not paid within 2 years (in foreign currency).
• **Foreign taxes deemed paid under section 902 or 960—**If the corporation is required to make a redetermination under Temporary Regulations section 1.905-3T(d)(3), include the following basic information as an attachment to the tax return for the year for which the redetermination applies:
1. The dates and amounts of any dividend distributions or other inclusions from E&P for the affected year or years;
2. The amount of E&P from which such dividends were paid for the affected year or years;
3. The current balances of the pools of E&P and foreign taxes before and after the foreign tax adjustment; and
4. The information described above for foreign taxes paid or accrued, as applicable.

If foreign taxes deemed paid under sections 902 or 960 are adjusted and the corporation is not required to redetermine its U.S. tax liability, adjust the appropriate pools of foreign taxes and E&P using the rules outlined in Temporary Regulations sections 1.905-3T(d)(2)(ii) and 1.905-4T(b)(2).

Amended returns for all years affected by foreign tax redeterminations that result in U.S. tax deficiencies and that occurred in the three tax years immediately preceding the corporation's first tax year beginning on or after November 7, 2007 (and tax years of foreign subsidiaries ending with or within such tax years of their domestic corporate shareholders), are due no later than the due date (with extensions) of the corporation's return for its second tax year beginning on or after November 7, 2007. Amended returns for all years affected by foreign tax redeterminations that result in U.S. tax deficiencies and that occur in tax years beginning after November 7, 2007 (and tax years of foreign subsidiaries ending with or within such tax years of their domestic corporate shareholders), are due no later than the due date (with extensions) of the corporation's return for its tax year in which the foreign tax redetermination occurs. For special rules relating to corporations under the jurisdiction of the Large Business & International Division, see Temporary Regulations sections 1.905-4T(b)(3) and 1.905-4T(f)(2)(iii).

Interest and Penalties

In most cases, interest is computed on the deficiency or overpayment that resulted from the foreign tax adjustment (sections 6601 and 6611 and the related regulations). See Temporary Regulations section 1.905-4T(e) for additional information.

If the corporation does not comply with the requirements discussed above within the time for filing specified, the penalty provisions of section 6689 (and the related regulations) will apply.

Specific Instructions

Report all amounts in U.S. dollars unless otherwise specified. If it is necessary to convert from a foreign currency, attach a statement explaining how the conversion rate was determined.

Separate Category of Income Boxes.

The corporation must complete a separate Form 1118 for each applicable category of income. See *Categories of Income* beginning on page 1.

Schedule A

Report gross income or (loss) from sources outside the United States for the applicable separate category in columns 2 through 7. Gross income equals gross receipts reduced by cost of goods sold. Report the applicable deductions to this gross income in columns 9 and 10. Report any net operating loss carryover in column 11. Be sure to include in all columns the gross income and deductions that pertain to foreign branches.

Section 863(b) gross income and deductions.

Aggregate **all** section 863(b) gross income and deductions and report the totals on a single line. It may be necessary to enter amounts in multiple columns on that single line, depending upon the nature of the section 863(b) gross income and deductions. For example, enter "863(b)" in column 1 and enter (as a positive number) all section 863(b) gross income (in columns 2 through 8) and all section 863(b) deductions (in columns 9a through 12). Also enter the net amount in column 13. Note that the totals are being reported on a single line because it is not necessary to report section 863(b) gross income and deductions on a per-country basis.

RIC pass-through amounts.

Aggregate **all** income passed through from regulated investment companies (RICs) and report the total on a single line. Enter "RIC" in column 1 and report the total in column 13. Note that the totals are being reported on a single line because it is not necessary to report the RIC pass-through amounts on a per-country basis.

Net operating losses.

Report any net operating loss carryover on a single line. Enter "NOL" in column 1 and report the total in column 11. Note that the totals are being reported on a single line because it is not necessary to report the NOL on a per-country basis.

Reclassifications of high-taxed income.

Aggregate all reclassifications of high-taxed income and report the total on a single line. With respect to passive category income, for items of income that have been included on Schedule A and that must be reclassified under the rules of Regulations section 1.904-4(c), enter "HTKO" in column 1 and enter (as a negative number) in column 13 the net amount of income that is being reclassified from passive category income. With respect to general category income, enter "HTKO" in column 1 and enter (as a positive number) in column 13 the net amount of income that is being reclassified to general category income. Note that the reclassifications are being reported on a single line because it is not necessary to report them on a per-country basis. Also note that tax reclassifications are needed on Schedule B. See those instructions for more information. Also see *General Category Income* on page 2 for general additional information about high-taxed income.

Column 1. Enter the two-letter codes (from the list at *www.IRS.gov/countrycodes* of all foreign countries and U.S. possessions within which income is sourced and/or to which taxes were paid, accrued, or deemed paid.

For section 863(b) income, enter "863(b)" instead of a two-letter code.

For income passed through from a RIC, enter "RIC" instead of a two-letter code.

For a net operating loss, enter "NOL" instead of a two-letter code.

For income adjustments for high-taxed income, enter "HTKO" instead of a two-letter code.

⚠️ *When you enter a country code in Schedule A, column 1, the information entered on the corresponding line of Schedule B, Part I, must pertain to that country code.*

Column 2(a). If the corporation is a U.S. shareholder in a CFC, report all income deemed received under section 951(a)(1)(A) (before gross-up). See section 904(d)(3) and *Look-Through Rules* on page 2 for more information. If the corporation is a U.S. shareholder in a passive foreign investment company (PFIC) and receives distributions from

stock in that PFIC, report all income deemed received (before gross-up) under section 1291.

Column 3(a). Report all other dividends (before gross-up) not included in column 2(a) from sources outside the United States for the applicable separate category. Other dividends include amounts included in gross income under section 951(a)(1)(B).

Note. All dividends from a domestic corporation are of U.S. source, including dividends from a domestic corporation which has 80% or more of its gross income from sources outside the United States.

Columns 2(b) and 3(b). Include taxes deemed paid by a domestic corporation under section 902 or section 960 on distributions by a foreign corporation in income as dividend gross-up. See Regulations section 1.960-3(b) for exceptions.

Column 4. Enter all interest received from foreign sources. See section 861(c) for the treatment of interest from a domestic corporation that meets the foreign business requirement.

Column 6. Include gross income, including compensation, commissions, fees, etc., for technical, managerial, engineering, construction, scientific, or similar services outside the United States. Be sure to include gross income from services performed through a foreign branch.

Column 7. Include all other gross income from sources outside the United States for the applicable separate category, including all other gross income of foreign branches and pass-through entities and any exchange gain or loss recognized under sections 986(c) or 987(3) on a distribution or remittance of previously taxed amounts. Attach a schedule identifying the gross income by type and by the foreign country or U.S. possession from which it was sourced.

Column 9(d). Include all other deductions definitely allocable to income from sources outside the United States (dividends, interest, etc.) for the applicable separate category. Include deductions allocable to income of foreign branches.

Include any reduction of foreign source capital gain net income. If foreign source capital gain net income from all separate categories is more than the capital gain net income reported on the corporation's tax return, enter a pro rata portion of the excess as a negative number in each separate category. See *Capital Gains* on page 3.

Column 10. Enter only the apportioned share from Schedule H, Part II, column (d) that relates to gross income reported in columns 2 through 7.

Note. If the corporation qualified as a financial services entity because it treated certain amounts as active financing income that are not listed in Regulations sections 1.904-4(e)(2)(i)(A) through (X), but that are described as similar items in Regulations section 1.904-4(e)(2)(i)(Y), attach a statement to Form 1118 showing the types and amounts of the similar items.

Column 11. Enter the corporation's net operating loss as defined in section 172 that is attributable to foreign source income in the separate limitation category. If the net operating loss is part of an overall foreign loss, see Temporary Regulations section 1.904(g)-3T for allocation rules that apply in determining the amount to enter in column 11.

It is not necessary to report the NOL adjustment on a per-country basis. See *Net Operating Losses* on page 5.

Schedule B

Part I—Foreign Taxes Paid, Accrued, and Deemed Paid

Report only foreign taxes paid, accrued, or deemed paid for the separate category for which this Form 1118 is being completed. Report all amounts in U.S. dollars. If the corporation must convert from foreign currency, attach a schedule showing the amounts in foreign currency and the exchange rate used.

For corporations claiming the credit on the accrual basis, the exchange rate for translating foreign taxes into U.S. dollars will generally be an average exchange rate for the tax year to which the taxes relate. However, the exchange rate on the date of payment must be used if the foreign taxes (a) are paid more than 2 years after the close of the tax year to which they relate or (b) are paid in a tax year prior to which they relate. In addition, for tax years beginning after December 31, 2004, taxpayers may elect to use the exchange rate on the date of payment. Taxpayers may elect to use the payment date exchange rates for all creditable foreign income taxes or only those taxes that are attributable to qualified business units with U.S. dollar functional currencies. The election is made by attaching a statement to a timely-filed (including extensions) Form 1118 that indicates the corporation is making the election under section 986(a)(1)(D). Once made, the election applies for all subsequent tax years and is revocable only with the consent of the IRS. See section 986(a).

 The information entered on each line of Schedule B, Part I must pertain to the country code specified on the corresponding line of Schedule A, column 1.

Column 1. Claim the foreign tax credit for the tax year in which the taxes were paid or accrued, depending on the method of accounting used. If a credit for taxes accrued is claimed, show both the date accrued and the date paid (if paid).

If the cash method of accounting is used, an election under section 905(a) may be made to claim the credit based on accrued taxes. If this election is made, figure the foreign tax credit for all subsequent tax years on the same basis. Also, the credits are subject to the redetermination provisions of section 905(c). See page 4 for details.

Column 2(d). Include foreign taxes paid or accrued on foreign branch taxable income to which the rules of section 863(b) apply.

Note. Do not include these overlapping amounts in column 2(e).

Part II—Separate Foreign Tax Credit

Line 4. If the corporation is reclassifying high-taxed income from passive category income to general category income, enter the related tax adjustment on line 4. Indicate whether adjustment is positive or (negative). See *General Category Income* on page 2 for additional information.

Line 5. Enter the total amount of foreign taxes carried forward or back to the current year. The amount of foreign taxes carried forward to the current tax year is the amount from Schedule K (Form 1118), line 3, column (xiv). Attach Schedule K (Form 1118) to Form 1118.

Line 7. If the corporation has a current year overall domestic loss or recapture of an overall domestic loss account, or, in any of its separate categories, a current year separate limitation loss, an overall foreign loss, recapture of an overall foreign loss, or current year separate limitation income in a category in which it has a beginning balance of income that must be recharacterized, adjustments must be made. See the separate instructions for Schedule J to determine if that schedule must be filed.

Line 8b. Enter taxable income that should not be taken into account in computing the foreign tax credit limitation.

Line 9. Divide line 7 by line 8c to determine the limitation fraction. Enter the fraction on line 9 as a decimal with the same number of places as the number of digits to the left of the decimal in adjusted taxable income on line 8c. For example, if adjusted taxable income on line 8c is $100,000, compute the limitation fraction to 6 decimal places.

Line 11. The limitation may be increased under section 960(b) for any tax year that the corporation receives a distribution of previously taxed E&P. See section 960(b).

Part III—Summary of Separate Credits

Complete Part III only once. Enter on lines 1 through 3 the separate foreign tax credits from Part II, line 12, for each applicable separate category.

Note. Complete Part III only on the Form 1118 with the largest amount entered on Part II, line 12.

Line 5. If the corporation participates in or cooperates with an international boycott, the foreign tax credit may be reduced. Complete Form 5713,

International Boycott Report. If the corporation chooses to apply the international boycott factor to calculate the reduction in the credit, enter the amount from line 2a(3) of Schedule C (Form 5713) on line 5.

Schedules C, D, and E

If the corporation is a partner in a partnership, for taxes of foreign corporations for tax years beginning after October 22, 2004, stock owned directly or indirectly, by or for a partnership shall be considered as being owned proportionately by its partners. See section 902(c)(7).

Schedule C

Part I—Dividends and Deemed Inclusions From Post-1986 Undistributed Earnings

Column 1. Enter the name of the foreign corporation (or DISC or former DISC) whose earnings were distributed to, or included in income by, the domestic corporation filing the return.

Column 2. Enter the year and month in which the foreign corporation's U.S. tax year ended.

Example. When figuring foreign taxes deemed paid in 2009 by a calendar year domestic corporation with respect to dividends and inclusions out of post-1986 undistributed earnings for the foreign corporation's tax year that ended June 30, 2009, enter "0906."

Column 3. Enter the applicable two-letter codes from the list at *www.IRS. gov/countrycodes*.

Column 4. Enter the distributing corporation's post-1986 undistributed earnings pool for the separate category for which the schedule is being completed. Generally, this amount is the corporation's E&P (computed in the corporation's functional currency according to sections 964(a) and 986) accumulated in tax years beginning after 1986, determined as of the close of the corporation's tax year without reduction for any earnings distributed or otherwise included in income (that is, under section 304, 367(b), 951(a), 1248, or 1293) during the current tax year.

Post-1986 undistributed earnings are reduced to account for distributions or deemed distributions that reduced E&P and inclusions that resulted in previously taxed amounts described in section 959(c)(1) and (2) or section 1293(c) in prior tax years beginning after 1986. See Regulations section 1.902-1(a)(9). Also, see section 902(c)(3) and Regulations section 1.902-1(a)(13) for special rules treating earnings accumulated in post-1986 years as pre-1987 accumulated profits when no U.S. shareholder was eligible to claim a section 902 credit with respect to taxes paid by the foreign corporation.

Column 5. Enter the opening balance in the distributing corporation's post-1986 foreign income taxes pool for the tax year indicated. This amount is the foreign income taxes paid, accrued, or deemed paid (in U.S. dollars) by the foreign corporation for prior tax years beginning after 1986, reduced by foreign taxes attributable to distributions or deemed inclusions of earnings in prior tax years. See Regulations section 1.902-1(a)(8)(i).

Column 6(a). Enter the foreign income taxes paid or accrued by the foreign corporation for the tax year indicated, translated into U.S. dollars using the exchange rate specified in section 986(a).

Column 6(b). Enter the foreign income taxes deemed paid (under section 902(b)) by the corporation for the tax year indicated (from Schedule D, Part I, Section A, column 10, and Section B, column 8(b)).

Column 8(a). Report the sum (in the foreign corporation's functional currency) of all dividends paid and deemed inclusions out of post-1986 undistributed earnings for the tax year indicated.

Column 8(b). Report the column 8(a) amounts, translated into U.S. dollars at the appropriate exchange rates (as defined in section 989(b)). If the foreign corporation's functional currency is the U.S. dollar, **do not** complete column 8(b).

Part II—Dividends Paid Out of Pre-1987 Accumulated Profits

Use a separate line for each dividend paid. If a dividend is paid out of the accumulated profits of more than one pre-1987 tax year, figure and show the tax deemed paid on a separate line for each tax year. In applying section 902, the IRS may determine from which tax year's accumulated profits the dividends were paid. See Regulations section 1.902-3(g)(4).

Important. The formula for calculating foreign taxes deemed paid under section 902 with respect to dividends paid in a post-1987 year out of pre-1987 accumulated profits requires that all components (dividends, accumulated profits, and taxes) be maintained in the foreign corporation's functional currency and translated into U.S. dollars at the exchange rate in effect on the date of the dividend distribution. See Regulations section 1.902-1(a)(10)(ii) and (iii).

Column 1. Enter the name of the first-tier foreign corporation (or DISC or former DISC) that paid a dividend out of pre-1987 profits to the domestic corporation filing the return.

Column 2. Enter the year and month in which the foreign corporation's pre-1987 tax year ended.

Column 3. Enter the applicable two-letter codes from the list at *www.IRS. gov/countrycodes*.

Column 4. For each line, enter the pre-1987 accumulated profits for the tax year indicated in column 2, computed in functional currency under section 902.

See Regulations section 1.902-1(a)(10)(i) and (ii).

Column 5. Enter the foreign taxes paid and deemed paid (in functional currency) with respect to the pre-1987 accumulated profits entered in column 4 for the tax year indicated in column 2. See the instructions for Schedule G on page 8 for information on reduction of foreign taxes for failure to furnish information required under section 6038.

Column 6(a). Enter the amount of each dividend paid by the first-tier foreign corporation (or DISC or former DISC) to the domestic corporation (in functional currency) out of the accumulated profits of the pre-1987 tax year indicated in column 2.

Column 6(b). Enter the amount from column 6(a) translated into U.S. dollars using the spot exchange rate in effect on the date of distribution. See Regulations sections 1.902-1(a)(10)(ii) and 1.902-3(g)(1).

Column 8(a). Multiply column 5 by column 7. Enter this amount in column 8(a) in functional currency.

Column 8(b). Enter the amount from column 8(a) translated into U.S. dollars at the spot exchange rate in effect on the date of distribution. See Regulations section 1.902-1(a)(10)(iii).

Part III—Deemed Inclusions From Pre-1987 Earnings and Profits

Important. The formula for calculating foreign taxes deemed paid under section 960 with respect to deemed inclusions (that is, under section 956 or 1248) in a post-1986 year out of pre-1987 E&P requires that earnings and profits and foreign taxes be calculated in U.S. dollars under the rules of Regulations section 1.964-1(a) through (e), and then translated into the foreign corporation's functional currency at the exchange rate in effect on the first day of the foreign corporation's first post-1986 tax year. See Notice 88-70, 1988-2 C.B. 369. The deemed inclusion is then translated into U.S. dollars at the appropriate exchange rate specified in section 989(b). Foreign income taxes paid in pre-1987 tax years are translated into U.S. dollars for purposes of section 960 at the exchange rate in effect when the foreign taxes were paid. See Regulations section 1.964-1(d) and Temporary Regulations section 1.905-5T(b)(1).

Column 1. Enter the name of the first- or lower-tier foreign corporation whose earnings were deemed included in the income of the domestic corporation filing the return.

Column 2. Enter the year and month in which the corporation's pre-1987 tax year ended. If the deemed inclusion is from accumulated E&P of more than one tax year, figure and show the tax deemed paid on a separate line for each year.

Column 3. Enter the applicable two-letter codes from the list at *www.IRS. gov/countrycodes*.

Column 4. For each line, enter the E&P calculated in U.S. dollars under Regulations sections 1.964-1(a) through (e), translated into functional currency under Notice 88-70 for the tax year indicated in column 2.

Column 5. Enter foreign taxes paid and deemed paid (in U.S. dollars) with respect to the E&P entered in column 4. See the instructions for Schedule G on page 8 for information on reduction of foreign taxes for failure to furnish information required under section 6038.

Column 6(b). Enter the amount from column 6(a) translated into U.S. dollars at the appropriate exchange rate specified in section 989(b).

Schedule D

Part I—Tax Deemed Paid by First-Tier Foreign Corporations

Section A—Dividends Paid Out of Post-1986 Undistributed Earnings

Column 1. Enter the name of the second-tier foreign corporation and the name of the first-tier foreign corporation to which it paid a dividend out of post-1986 undistributed earnings.

Example. The U.S. corporation filing the return owns all of the stock of CFC1 and CFC2. CFC1 and CFC2 each own 50% of the stock of CFC3. In 2010, CFC3 pays a dividend to CFC1 and CFC2. Use one line to report dividends from CFC3 to CFC1 and another line to report dividends from CFC3 to CFC2.

Column 2. Enter the year and month in which the distributing second-tier foreign corporation's tax year ended.

Example. If a first-tier foreign corporation that uses the calendar year 2010 as its tax year receives dividends out of post-1986 undistributed earnings of a second-tier foreign corporation for a tax year that ended June 30, 2010, enter "1006."

Column 3. Enter the applicable two-letter codes from the list at *www.IRS. gov/countrycodes*.

Column 4. Enter the second-tier foreign corporation's post-1986 undistributed earnings pool (in functional currency) for the separate category for which the schedule is being completed. See the instructions for Schedule C, Part I, column 4.

Column 5. Enter the opening balance in the second-tier foreign corporation's post-1986 foreign income taxes pool for the tax year indicated. See the instructions for Schedule C, Part I, column 5.

Column 6(a). Enter the foreign income taxes paid or accrued by the second-tier foreign corporation for the tax year indicated, translated from foreign currency into U.S. dollars using the exchange rate specified in section 986(a).

Column 6(b). Enter the foreign income taxes deemed paid (under section 902(b)) by the second-tier foreign corporation for the tax year indicated (from Schedule D, Part II, Section A, column 10, and Part II, Section B, column 8(b)).

Column 8(a). Report the sum (in the second-tier foreign corporation's functional currency) of all dividends paid out of its post-1986 undistributed earnings for the tax year indicated.

Column 8(b). Report the sum of the column 8(a) amounts translated into the functional currency of the first-tier foreign corporation at the spot rate in effect on the date of each distribution.

Section B—Dividends Paid Out of Pre-1987 Accumulated Profits

Use a separate line for each dividend paid. If a dividend is paid out of the accumulated profits of more than one pre-1987 tax year, figure and show the tax deemed paid on a separate line for each tax year. In applying section 902, the IRS may determine from which tax year's accumulated profits the dividends were paid. See Regulations section 1.902-3(g)(4).

Important. The formula for calculating foreign taxes deemed paid by a first-tier foreign corporation under section 902(b) with respect to dividends paid by a second-tier foreign corporation in a post-1986 year out of pre-1987 accumulated profits requires that all components (dividends, accumulated profits, and taxes) be maintained in the second-tier foreign corporation's functional currency. Dividends are translated into the first-tier foreign corporation's functional currency and added to its post-1986 undistributed earnings at the exchange rate in effect on the date of the dividend distribution. See Regulations section 1.902-1(a)(9)(ii). Foreign taxes are translated into U.S. dollars, and added to the first-tier foreign corporation's post-1986 foreign income taxes, at the exchange rate in effect on the date of the dividend distribution. See Regulations section 1.902-1(a)(8)(ii).

Column 1. Enter the name of the second-tier foreign corporation and the name of the first-tier foreign corporation to which it paid a dividend out of pre-1987 accumulated profits.

Column 2. For each pre-1987 tax year, enter the year and month in which the second-tier foreign corporation's tax year ended.

Column 3. Enter the applicable two-letter codes from the list at *www.IRS. gov/countrycodes*.

Column 4. For each line, enter the pre-1987 accumulated profits for the tax year indicated in column 2, computed in the second-tier corporation's functional currency under section 902. See Regulations sections 1.902-1(a)(10)(i) and (ii).

Column 5. Enter the foreign taxes paid and deemed paid under section 902(b) (in functional currency) with respect to the accumulated profits entered in column 4 for the pre-1987 tax year indicated in column 2. See the instructions for Schedule G below for information on reduction of foreign taxes for failure to furnish information required under section 6038.

Column 6(a). Enter each dividend paid by the second-tier foreign corporation (in functional currency) to the first-tier foreign corporation out of the accumulated profits of the pre-1987 tax year indicated in column 2.

Column 6(b). Enter the amount from column 6(a), translated into the first-tier foreign corporation's functional currency using the spot exchange rate in effect on the date of distribution. See Regulations sections 1.902-1(a)(10)(ii) and 1.902-3(g)(1).

Column 8(a). Multiply column 5 by column 7. Enter the result in column 8(a).

Column 8(b). Enter the amount from column 8(a), translated in U.S. dollars at the spot exchange rate in effect on the date of distribution. See Regulations section 1.902-1(a)(10)(iii).

Part II—Tax Deemed Paid by Second-Tier Foreign Corporations

Follow the instructions for the corresponding columns of Schedule D, Part I, substituting "second-tier foreign corporation" for references to the "first-tier foreign corporation" and "third-tier foreign corporation" for references to the "second-tier foreign corporation."

Note. In completing Section A, column 5, note that section 902(b) as in effect prior to the Taxpayer Relief Act of 1997 did not treat any foreign taxes as deemed paid by a third- or lower-tier foreign corporation with respect to dividends received from lower-tier foreign corporations.

Schedule E

Use Schedule E to report foreign taxes deemed paid with respect to dividends from certain fourth-, fifth-, and sixth-tier controlled foreign corporations out of earnings accumulated in tax years beginning after August 5, 1997. Follow the instructions for the corresponding columns of Schedule D, Part I, Section A, substituting references to the next lower-tier foreign corporation as appropriate.

The post-1986 undistributed earnings and taxes pools for the eligible CFCs begin on the first day of the CFC's first tax year beginning after August 5, 1997. Earnings accumulated in tax years beginning before August 6, 1997, will be treated as pre-1987 accumulated profits for section 902 purposes. See section 902(c)(6) and Regulations section 1.902-1(a)(10)(i). Foreign income taxes attributable to these pre-pooling profits

must be reduced when the associated earnings are distributed. However, such taxes are generally not eligible for the deemed paid credit. See Regulations sections 1.902-1(a)(10)(iii) and 1.902-1(c)(8).

Note. In completing Part III, column 5, note that, under section 902(b) as amended by the Taxpayer Relief Act of 1997, no taxes are deemed paid by a sixth- or lower-tier foreign corporation with respect to dividends received from lower-tier foreign corporations.

Schedule F

Enter the gross income and definitely allocable deductions for each foreign branch (including a disregarded entity) as indicated. For each such foreign branch for which Form 8858, Information Return of U.S. Persons With Respect To Foreign Disregarded Entities, is not filed, attach an income statement, balance sheet, and schedule of remittances.

Schedule G

Line A. If the corporation claims a deduction for percentage depletion under section 613 with respect to any part of its foreign mineral income (as defined in section 901(e)(2)) for the tax year, any foreign taxes on that income must be reduced by the smaller of:

1. The foreign taxes minus the tax on that income or
2. The tax on that income determined without regard to the deduction for percentage depletion minus the tax on that income.

The reduction must be made on a country-by-country basis (Regulations section 1.901-3(a)(1)). Attach a separate schedule showing the reduction.

Line C. If the corporation chooses to calculate the reduction in the foreign tax by identifying taxes specifically attributable to participation in or cooperation with an international boycott, enter the amount from Form 5713, Schedule C, line 2b. See Form 5713 and its separate Schedule C and instructions.

Line D. If the corporation controls a foreign corporation or partnership and fails to furnish any return or any information in any return required under section 6038(a) by the due date, reduce the foreign taxes available for credit under sections 901, 902, and 960 by 10%. If the failure continues for 90 days or more after the date of written notice by the IRS, reduce the tax by an additional 5% for each 3-month period or fraction thereof during which the failure continues after the 90-day period has expired. See section 6038(c) for limitations and special rules.

In addition, a $10,000 penalty is imposed under section 6038(b) for failure to supply the information required under section 6038(a) for each entity within the time prescribed. If the required information is not submitted within 90 days after the IRS has mailed notice to the U.S. person, additional penalties may apply.

Note. The reduction in foreign taxes available for credit is reduced by any dollar penalty imposed under section 6038(b).

Line E. Include the reduction described under section 960(c), as applicable.

Schedule H

Computer-Generated Schedule H

A computer-generated Schedule H may be filed if it conforms to the IRS version. In some cases, Schedule H can be expanded to properly apportioned deductions. This applies in cases such as when the corporation:
- Has more than two product lines (under the sales method of apportioning R&D deductions),
- Has section 901(j) income from more than one sanctioned country, or
- Has income re-sourced by treaty for more than one country.

Part I—Research and Development Deductions

Use Part I to apportion the research and development (R&D) deductions that cannot be definitely allocated to some item or class of gross income. Use **either** the sales method **or** one of the gross income methods described in Regulations section 1.861-17.

Note. The line 4 totals will generally be less than the totals on lines 1 and 2 because the line 4 totals do not include the gross income and deductions that are implicitly apportioned to the residual grouping.

Column (a) Sales Method

Complete these columns only if the corporation elects the sales method of apportioning R&D deductions described in Regulations section 1.861-17(c). Enter in the spaces provided the SIC Code numbers (based upon the Standard Industrial Classification System) of the product lines to which the R&D deductions relate. See Regulations section 1.861-17(a)(2)(ii) and (iii) for details on choosing SIC codes and changing a product category.

Note. If the corporation has more than two product lines, see *Computer-Generated Schedule H* above.

Columns (a)(i) and (a)(iii)

Line 1. Enter the worldwide gross sales for the product lines.

Lines 3a through 3d. Enter the gross sales that resulted in gross income for each statutory grouping.

Columns (a)(ii) and (a)(iv)

Line 1. Enter the total R&D deductions connected with the product lines.

Line 2. Reduce the line 1 totals by legally mandated R&D (Regulations section 1.861-17(a)(4)), and a 50% exclusive apportionment amount (Regulations section 1.861-17(b)(1)(i)) if applicable.

The legally mandated R&D rules apply to R&D undertaken solely to meet legal requirements imposed by a particular political entity for improvement or marketing of specific products or processes **if** the corporation does not reasonably expect the results of that research to generate gross income (beyond de minimis amounts) outside a single geographic source.

Under the exclusive apportionment rules, 50% of the R&D deductions are apportioned exclusively to the statutory grouping of gross income, or the residual grouping of gross income, as the case may be, from the geographic source where the R&D activities which account for more than 50% of the amount of such deduction were performed. If the 50% test is **not** met, then no part of the deduction is apportioned under these rules.

Lines 3a through 3d. To figure the amount of R&D deductions to apportion to each statutory grouping, divide the gross sales apportioned to the statutory grouping by the worldwide gross sales for the product line. Multiply the result by the R&D deductions to be apportioned.

Note. If the corporation had section 901(j) income from more than one sanctioned country or had income re-sourced by treaty for more than one country, see *Computer-Generated Schedule H above.*

Example 1. To determine the amount to enter on line 3a, column (a)(ii):

1. Divide the amount on line 3a, column (a)(i) by the amount on line 1, column (a)(i).
2. Multiply the result by the amount on line 2, column (a)(ii).

Example 2. To determine the amount to enter on line 3b, column (a)(iv):

1. Divide the amount on line 3b, column (a)(iii) by the amount on line 1, column (a)(iii).
2. Multiply the result by the amount on line 2, column (a)(iv).

Column (b) Gross Income Methods

Complete these columns only if the corporation elects one of the gross income methods of apportioning R&D deductions described in Regulations section 1.861-17(d)(2) and (3). Check the box for the option used. Use Option 1 only if certain conditions are met. See Regulations section 1.861-17(d)(2).

Note. If the corporation has more than one product line, separately determine for each product line the apportionment of R&D deductions relating to such product

line and enter the total amounts apportioned to each statutory grouping in the appropriate line of column (b)(vii).

Column (b)(vi)

Line 1. Enter the total gross income (excluding exempt income according to Temporary Regulations section 1.861-8T(d)(2)).

Lines 3a through 3d. Enter the gross income within each statutory grouping.

Column (b)(vii)

Line 1. Enter the total R&D deductions.

Line 2. Reduce the line 1 totals by legally mandated R&D (Regulations section 1.861-17(a)(4)), and a 25% exclusive apportionment amount (Regulations section 1.861-17(b)(1)(ii)).

Lines 3a through 3d. If Option 1 is checked, divide the gross income apportioned to the statutory grouping by the total gross income and multiply the result by the R&D deductions to be apportioned. If Option 2 is checked, enter the appropriate amount as described in Regulations section 1.861-17(d)(3).

Part II—Interest Deductions, All Other Deductions, and Total Deductions

Note. The line 4 totals will generally be less than the totals on lines 1 and 2 because the line 4 totals do not include the gross income and deductions that are implicitly apportioned to the residual grouping.

Columns (a)(i) through (b)(iv)

Use these columns to apportion interest deductions. See Temporary Regulations sections 1.861-8T through 1.861-13T for rules on the apportionment of interest deductions based on the fair market value, tax book value, or adjusted tax book value of assets.

If the corporation elected to use the fair market value method to apportion interest expense, see Temporary Regulations section 1.861-9T(h). Also see Rev. Proc. 2003-37, 2003-1 C.B. 950, for procedures for supplying certain documentation and information.

For tax years beginning on or after March 26, 2004, a corporation may elect to use the alternative tax book value method. See Regulations section 1.861-9(i).

Columns (a) and (b) are subdivided into "Nonfinancial Corporations" and "Financial Corporations." In allocating interest deductions, members of an affiliated group that are financial corporations must be treated as a separate affiliated group. Complete columns (a)(ii) and (b)(iv) for members of the corporation's affiliated group that are financial corporations and columns (a)(i) and (b)(iii) for members that are nonfinancial corporations.

See Regulations section 1.861-11 for the definition of an affiliated group.

Columns (a)(i) and (a)(ii)

Line 1a. Enter the average of the total assets of the affiliated group. See Temporary Regulations section 1.861-9T(g)(2) for the definition of average for these purposes.

Line 1b. Enter the assets included on line 1a that are characterized as excess related party indebtedness. See Temporary Regulations section 1.861-10T(e) for an exception to the general rule of fungibility for excess related party indebtedness.

Line 1c. Enter all other assets that attract specifically allocable interest deductions. See Temporary Regulations section 1.861-10T for other exceptions to the general rule of fungibility (such as qualified nonrecourse indebtedness and integrated financial transactions).

Line 1d. Enter the total of the exempt assets and assets without directly identifiable yield that are to be excluded from the interest apportionment formula (Temporary Regulations sections 1.861-8T(d)(2) and 1.861-9T(g)(3)).

Lines 3a through 3d. The assets on line 2 are characterized as assets in one of the statutory groupings or as belonging to the residual grouping. Enter the value of the assets in each of the statutory groupings on line 3a through 3d. See Temporary Regulations sections 1.861-9T(g)(3), 1.861-12T(g)(2), and 1.861-12T(h)(2) for the rules for characterizing the assets.

Columns (b)(iii) and (b)(iv)

Line 1a. Enter the total interest deductions for the members of the corporation's affiliated group. These include any expense that is currently deductible under section 163 (including original issue discount), and interest equivalents. See Temporary Regulations section 1.861-9T for the definition of interest equivalents and a list of the sections that disallow or suspend interest deductions or require the capitalization of interest deductions.

Line 1b. Enter the interest deductions associated with the assets on line 1b of columns (a)(i) and (a)(ii), respectively, that attract specifically allocable interest deductions under Temporary Regulations section 1.861-10T(e).

Note. These interest deductions will be divided among the statutory groupings and will appear as a definitely allocable deduction in Schedule A, column 9(d).

Line 1c. Enter the interest deductions associated with the assets on line 1c of columns (a)(i) and (a)(ii), respectively, that attract specifically allocable interest deductions.

Lines 3a through 3d. To figure the amount of interest deductions to apportion to each statutory grouping, divide the assets apportioned to the grouping by the total assets apportioned and multiply the result by the interest deductions to be apportioned.

Example 1. To figure the amount to enter on line 3a, column (b)(iii): (a) divide the amount entered on line 3a, column (a)(i), by the amount on line 2, column (a)(i); and (b) multiply the result by the amount on line 2, column (b)(iii).

Example 2. To figure the amount to enter on line 3b, column (b)(iv): (a) divide the amount on line 3b, column (a)(ii) by the amount on line 2, column (a)(ii); and (b) multiply the result by the amount on line 2, column (b)(iv).

Column (c)

Complete this column to apportion all other deductions not definitely allocable (other than interest deductions and R&D deductions). See Regulations sections 1.861-8 and 1.861-14 and Temporary Regulations sections 1.861-8T and 1.861-14T.

Line 1a. Enter the total other deductions. Examples include: stewardship expenses; legal and accounting expenses; and other expenses related to certain supportive functions such as overhead, general and administrative, advertising, and marketing. Deductions for charitable contributions made on or after July 28, 2004, generally are definitely related and allocable to all gross income and apportioned solely to domestic source income.

Lines 3a through 3d. Enter the amounts apportioned to each statutory grouping.

Schedules I, J, and K

See the separate instructions for Schedule I, Schedule J, and Schedule K to see if the corporation must file these schedules.

Paperwork Reduction Act Notice. We ask for the information on this form to carry out the Internal Revenue laws of the United States. You are required to give us the information. We need it to ensure that you are complying with these laws and to allow us to figure and collect the right amount of tax.

You are not required to provide the information requested on a form that is subject to the Paperwork Reduction Act unless the form displays a valid OMB control number. Books or records relating to a form or its instructions must be retained as long as their contents may become material in the administration of any Internal Revenue law. Generally, tax returns and return information are confidential, as required by section 6103.

The time needed to complete and file this form and related schedules will vary depending on individual circumstances. The estimated average times are:

Form	Recordkeeping	Learning about the law or the form	Preparing and sending the form to the IRS
1118	71 hr., 16 min.	17 hr., 44 min.	20 hr., 53 min.
Sch. I (Form 1118)	9 hr., 19 min.	1 hr.	1 hr., 11 min.
Sch. J (Form 1118)	22 hr., 43 min.	1 hr., 23 min.	1 hr., 49 min.

If you have comments concerning the accuracy of these time estimates or suggestions for making this form and related schedules simpler, we would be happy to hear from you. See the instructions for the tax return with which this form is filed.

4-26

SAMPLE FORM 4-1, Page 1
Cramden Corporation, Inc. & Consolidated Subsidiaries
Computation of Foreign Tax Credit
Foreign Source Income
Calendar Year

GENERAL INFORMATION WORKSHEET FOR FORM 1118

SUBSIDIARY BY FOREIGN COUNTRY	TYPE OF INCOME					CLASSIFICATION				Expenses Directly Allocable to a Single Class of Income	Total Income Before Treas. Reg. Sec. 1.861 Allocations
	Other Income	Dividends	IRC Sec. 78 Gross-Up	Interest	Rents and Royalties	Passive Income	General Limitation Income	Financial Services Income	High Tax Income		
Southern Antilles											
Cramden Corporation, Inc.											
Global Funding, Inc.							733,312				733,312
Antilles Funding, Inc.		505,937	227,375	273,006				273,006			273,006
Carmel											
Cramden Corporation, Inc.	3,912,000			1,396,289			3,912,000	1,396,289		2,258,000	3,050,289
Bayland											
Cramden Corporation, Inc.											
Cramden Bayland		61,071	10,777	277,469			71,848	277,469			349,317
Seascape, Inc.	13,608						13,608				13,608
Cordura											
Cramden Corporation, Inc.	706,097						706,097			22,697	683,400
Cramden Cordura, Inc.	4,480,572	16,000,000	11,018,556				27,018,556				27,018,556
Island Services, Inc.							4,480,572			530,016	3,950,556
Gardenia											
Cramden Purchasing Corporation	17,837,247			320,872			17,837,247	320,872		6,774,358	11,383,761
Cramden Export Corporation	581,451			46,250			581,451	46,250		430,699	197,002
Nauticus											
Seascape, Inc.	173,527						173,527				173,527
Other											
Cramden Corporation-investments				2,575,283		2,575,283					2,575,283
Cramden Corporation, Inc. -- Catalog	854,000						854,000			67,000	787,000
Cramden Financing				916,858		916,858					916,858
Total	28,558,502	16,567,008	11,256,708	5,806,027	None	3,492,141	56,382,218	2,313,886	None	10,082,770	52,105,475

SAMPLE FORM 4-1, Page 2
Cramden Corporation, Inc. & Consolidated Subsidiaries
Computation of Foreign Tax Credit
Foreign Source Income
Calendar Year

GENERAL INFORMATION WORKSHEET FOR FORM 1118

	Directly Allocable to Multiple Classes of Income	Allocated Deductions	Subtotal Expenses	Dividends	Interest	Rents and Royalties	Branch	Services	Foreign Source Income
Southern Antilles									
Cramden Corporation, Inc.	16	29,500	29,516						970,386
Global Funding, Inc.									728,748
Antilles Funding, Inc.		198,438	198,438						
Carmel									
Cramden Corporation, Inc.		966,480	966,480						
Bayland									
Cramden Corporation, Inc.		207,180	207,180						
Cramden Bayland	6,541	1,610	8,151						
Seascape, Inc.									
Cordura									
Cramden Corporation, Inc.	17,924	20,933	38,857				1,810,809		11,018,556
Cramden Cordura, Inc.	35,332	1,056,191	1,091,523						
Island Services, Inc.	5,958	140,147	146,105						
Gardenia									
Cramden Purchasing Corporation	1,186,101	425,009	1,611,110						
Cramden Export Corporation	10,184	32,013	42,197						
Nauticus									
Seascape, Inc.						17,353			
Other									
Cramden Corporation-Investments		282,837	282,837						
Cramden Corporation, Inc. -- Catalog									
Cramden Financing		1,217,677	1,217,677						
Total	1,262,056	4,578,015	5,840,071			17,353	1,810,809		12,717,690

Net Income   46,265,404

Total Taxes 14,545,852

SAMPLE FORM 4-1, Page 3
Cramden Corporation, Inc. & Consolidated Subsidiaries
Computation of Foreign Tax Credit
Foreign Source Income
Calendar Year

GENERAL INFORMATION WORKSHEET FOR FORM 1118

Description	International Development	Foreign Travel	Duplicated Expenses	Financing Expense	Accounting/ Legal	General Limitation Total
Compensation of Officers	326,235	371,394	(273,794)			423,835
Repairs	4,636					4,636
Taxes	20,927					20,927
Interest				1,449,679		1,449,679
Employee Benefits	17,112					17,112
Other Deductions	640,290	(83,756)				556,534
Total Deductions	1,009,200	287,638	(273,794)	1,449,679		2,472,723

CLASSIFICATION

	Passive	General Limitation	Financial Services
		423,835	
		4,636	
		20,927	
	1,502,125	1,449,679	1,617,212
		17,112	
		556,534	
Total Foreign	1,502,125	2,472,723	1,617,212

5,832,973

Sample Form 4-2, Page 1
EIN: XX-XXXXXXX
Cramden Corporation, Inc. and Consolidated Subsidiaries
Supporting Worksheet for Form 1118 -- Passive Income
Calendar Year

Schedule A	Separate Limitation Income or (Loss) Before Adjustments							
	Deemed Dividends	Other Dividends				Gross Rents Royalties & License Fees Col. 5	Services Income Col. 6	Other Income Col. 7	Total Col. 8
Foreign Country or US Possession	Exclude Gross Up Col 2 (a)	Include Gross Up Col 2(b)	Gross Up Col 3(a)	Include Gross Up Col 3(b)	Interest Col. 4				
Carmel Cramden Corporation									
Bayland Cramden-Bayland									
Southern Antilles Antilles Funding Global Funding									
Other Cramden Corporation-Investments Cramden Financing					2,575,283 916,858				2,575,283 916,858
					3,492,141				3,492,141

Sample Form 4-2, Page 2
Cramden Corporation, Inc. and Consolidated Subsidiaries
Supporting Worksheet for Form 1118 -- Passive Income
Calendar Year

Schedule B — Foreign Tax Credit

Part 1 - Foreign Taxes Paid, Accrued and Deemed Paid

Foreign Country	Credit Is Claimed For Taxes — Date Paid Date Accrued Col. 1	Foreign Tax Paid or Accrued						Taxes Deemed To Have Been Paid Col. 3
		TAX WITHHELD AT SOURCE			OTHER TAXES PAID OR ACCRUED		Total Foreign Taxes Col. 2h	
		Dividends Col. 2a	Interest Col. 2b	Rents/Royalties Col. 2c	Branch Income Col. 2d	Service Income Col. 2e	Other Income Col. 2g	
Carmel								
Cramden Corporation								
Bayland								
Cramden-Bayland								
Southern Antilles								
Antilles Funding								
Global Funding								
Other								
Cramden Corporation -- Investments								
Cramden Financing								
Total		-0-	-0-	-0-	-0-	-0-	-0-	-0-

Sample Form 4-3
Cramden Corporation, Inc. and Consolidated Subsidiaries
EIN XX-XXXXXXX
Form 1118 Supporting Worksheet (General Limitation Income)
Calendar Year
Schedule A

Foreign Country or US Possession	Separate Limitation Income or (Loss) B/F Adj.				Interest Col. 4	Gross Rents Royalties & License Fees Col. 5	Income From Performance of Services Col. 6	Other Income Col. 7	Total Col. 8
	Deemed Dividends		Other Dividends						
	Exclude Gross-Up Col. 2(a)	Include Gross-Up Col. 2(b)	Exclude Gross-Up Col. 3(a)	Include Gross-Up Col. 3(b)					
Gardenia									
Cramden Purchasing Corporation							17,837,247		17,837,247
Cramden Export Corporation							581,451		581,451
Carmel									
Cramden Corporation									
Cordura									
Cramden Corporation			16,000,000					706,097	706,097
Cramden Cordura, Inc. Island Services, Inc.				11,018,556				4,480,572	4,480,572
Bayland									
Seascape, Inc.									
Cramden SA de C.V.	505,937	227,375				13,608			13,608
Southern Antilles									
Antilles Funding									
Global Funding									733,312
Nauticus									
Seascape, Inc.						173,527			173,527
Other									
Cramden Corporation-Investments								854,000	854,000
Cramden Financing									
Total	505,937	227,375	16,000,000	11,018,556	-0-	187,135	18,418,698	9,952,669	56,310,370

Sample Form 4-4, Page 1
Cramden Corporation, Inc. and Consolidated Subsidiaries
EIN: XX-XXXXXXX
Form 1118 Supporting Workpaper (Financial Services Income)
Calendar Year

Schedule A

Foreign Country or US Possession	Separate Limitation or (Loss) Before Adjustments									
	Deemed Dividends	Other Dividends				Gross Rents Royalties & License Fees Col. 5	Income From Performance of Service Col. 6	Other Income Col. 7	Total Col. 8
	Exclude Gross-Up Col. 2(a)	Include Gross-Up Col. 2(b)	Exclude Gross-Up Col. 3(a)	Include Gross-Up Col. 3(b)	Interest Col. 4				
Gardenia									
Cramden Purchasing Corporation					320,872				320,872
Cramden Export Corporation					46,250				46,250
Carmel									
Cramden Corporation									
Cordura									
Cramden Corporation					1,396,289				1,396,289
Cramden Cordura, Inc.									
Island Services, Inc.									
Bayland									
Cramden-Bayland	61,071	10,777			227,469				299,317
Cramden SA de C.V.									
Southern Antilles									
Antilles Funding		8,400			265,286				273,686
Global Funding									
Nauticus									
Seascape, Inc.									
Other									
Cramden Corporation--Investments									
Cramden Financing									
Total	61,071	19,177	-0-	-0-	2,256,166	-0-	-0-	-0-	2,336,414

Sample Form 4-4, Page 2
Cramden Corporation, Inc. and Consolidated Subsidiaries
Form 1118 Supporting Worksheet (Financial Services Income)
Calendar Year

Schedule B	Foreign Tax Credit					Reliable Part of Deductions Not Def. Allocable Col. 10	Total Deductions Col. 11	Total Separate Limitation Income of (Loss) Before Adj. Col.12
Foreign Country	Definitely Allocable Deductions							
	Depreciation and Amortization Col. 9(a)	Other Expenses Col. 9(b)	Expenses Related to Gross Income From Performance of Services Col. 9 c	Other Def. Allocable Deductions Col. 9(d)	Total Def. Allocable Deductions Col. 9(e)			
Gardenia								
Cramden Purchasing Corporation						222,100	222,100	98,772
Cramden Export Corporation						32,013	32,013	14,237
Carmel								
Cramden Corporation						966,480	966,480	429,809
Cramden Cordura, Inc.								
Island Services, Inc.								
Bayland								
Cramden-Bayland	207,180					207,180	207,180	92,137
Cramden SA de C.V.								
Southern Antilles								
Antilles Funding						189,439	189,439	84,247
Global Funding								
Nauticus								
Seascape, Inc.								
Other								
Cramden Corporation -- Investments								
Cramden Financing								
Total	207,180	-0-	-0-	-0-	-0-	1,617,212	1,617,212	719,202

256520

975722

Recharacterization of prior-year loss pursuant to IRC § 904 f (5) c

Sample From 4-4, Page 3
Cramden Corporation, Inc. and Consolidated Subsidiaries
EIN: XX-XXXXXXX
Form 1118 Supporting Worksheet (Financial Services Income)

Schedule B — Foreign Tax Credit
Part 1 -- Foreign Taxes Paid, Accrued and Deemed Paid

Foreign Country	Credit Is Claimed For Taxes Date Paid Col. 1	Date Accrued Col. 1	Foreign Tax Paid or Accrued TAX WITHHELD AT SOURCE Dividends Col. 2(a)	Interest Col. 2(b)	Rents & Royalties Col. 2c	OTHER TAXES PAID OR ACCRUED ON: Branch Income Col. 2(d)	Service Income Col. 2(e)	Other Income Col. 2(g)	Total Foreign Taxes Col. 2(h)	Taxes Deemed To Have Been Paid Col. 3
Gardenia										
Cramden Purchasing Corporation										
Cramden Export Corporation		1,992		80,218					80,218	
Carmel										
Cramden Corporation				59,773					59,773	
Cordura										
Cramden Corporation										
Cramden Cordura, Inc.										
Island Services, Inc.										
Bayland										
Cramden-Bayland										
Cramden SA de C.V.			10,777	34,120					44,897	
Southern Antilles										
Antilles Funding										
Global Fuunding										
Nauticus										
Seacape, Inc.										
Other										
Cramden Corporation -- Investments										
Cramden Financing										
Total		1,992	10,777	174,111	-0-	-0-	-0-	-0-	184,888	-0-

Sample Form 4-5

Form 1118
(Rev. December 2009)
Department of the Treasury
Internal Revenue Service

Foreign Tax Credit—Corporations

▶ See separate instructions.
▶ Attach to the corporation's tax return.

OMB No. 1545-0122

Name of corporation

Cramden Corporation

Employer identification number

For calendar year 20 **10** , or other tax year beginning ____ , 20 ____ , and ending ____ , 20 ____

Use a **separate** Form 1118 for each applicable category of income listed below. See **Categories of Income** in the instructions. Also, see **Specific Instructions**.
Check only one box on each form.

☑ Passive Category Income
☐ General Category Income
☐ Section 901(j) Income: Name of Sanctioned Country ▶ ____
☐ Income Re-sourced by Treaty: Name of Country ▶ ____

Schedule A   Income or (Loss) Before Adjustments *(Report all amounts in U.S. dollars. See Specific Instructions.)*

Gross Income or (Loss) From Sources Outside the United States (*INCLUDE* Foreign Branch Gross Income here *and* on Schedule F)

1. Foreign Country or U.S. Possession (Enter two-letter code; see instructions. Use a separate line for each.) *	2. Deemed Dividends (see instructions)		3. Other Dividends		4. Interest	5. Gross Rents, Royalties, and License Fees	6. Gross Income From Performance of Services	7. Other (attach schedule)	8. Total (add columns 2(a) through 7)
	(a) Exclude gross-up	(b) Gross-up (sec. 78)	(a) Exclude gross-up	(b) Gross-up (sec. 78)					
A									
B									
C See									
D Attached									
E Schedules									
F									
Totals (add lines A through F)	-0-	-0-	-0-	-0-	-0-	1,508,665	-0-	-0-	3,492,141

* For section 863(b) income, NOLs, income from RICs, and high-taxed income, use a single line (see instructions).

Deductions (*INCLUDE* Foreign Branch Deductions here *and* on Schedule F)

	9. Definitely Allocable Deductions					10. Apportioned Share of Deductions Not Definitely Allocable (enter amount from applicable line of Schedule H, Part II, column (d))	11. Net Operating Loss Deduction	12. Total Deductions (add columns 9(e) through 11)	13. Total Income or (Loss) Before Adjustments (subtract column 12 from column 8)
Rental, Royalty, and Licensing Expenses		(b) Other Expenses	(c) Expenses Related to Gross Income From Performance of Services	(d) Other Definitely Allocable Deductions	(e) Total Definitely Allocable Deductions (add columns 9(a) through 9(d))				
(a) Depreciation, Depletion, and Amortization									
A									
B									
C	See								
D	Attached								
E	Schedules								
F									
Totals	-0-		-0-	-0-	-0-	-0-	-0-	1,508,665	1,983,476

For Paperwork Reduction Act Notice, see separate instructions.

Cat. No. 10900F

Form **1118** (Rev. 12-2009)

Form 1118 (Rev. 12-2009)　　　　　　　　　　　　　　　　　　　　　　　　　　Page **2**

Schedule B　Foreign Tax Credit (Report all foreign tax amounts in U.S. dollars.)

Part I—Foreign Taxes Paid, Accrued, and Deemed Paid (see instructions)

1. Credit is Claimed for Taxes:		2. Foreign Taxes Paid or Accrued (attach schedule showing amounts in foreign currency and conversion rate(s) used)							3. Tax Deemed Paid (from Schedule C—Part I, column 10, Part II, column 8(b), and Part III, column 8)
☐ Paid ☐ Accrued		Tax Withheld at Source on:		Other Foreign Taxes Paid or Accrued on:				(h) Total Foreign Taxes Paid or Accrued (add columns 2(a) through 2(g))	
Date Paid	Date Accrued	(a) Dividends	(b) Interest	(c) Rents, Royalties, and License Fees	(d) Section 863(b) Income	(e) Foreign Branch Income	(f) Services Income	(g) Other	
A									
B									
C		See							
D		Attached							
E		Schedules							
F									
Totals (add lines A through F)		-0-	-0-	-0-	-0-	-0-	-0-	-0-	-0-

Part II—Separate Foreign Tax Credit (Complete a *separate* Part II for *each* applicable category of income.)

1	Total foreign taxes paid or accrued (total from Part I, column 2(h))	
2	Total taxes deemed paid (total from Part I, column 3)	
3	Reductions of taxes paid, accrued, or deemed paid (enter total from Schedule G)	( )
4	Taxes reclassified under high-tax kickout	
5	Enter the sum of any carryover of foreign taxes (from Schedule K, line 3, column (xiv)) plus any carrybacks to the current tax year	1,649,986
6	Total foreign taxes (combine lines 1 through 5)	1,649,986
7	Enter the amount from the applicable column of Schedule J, Part I, line 11 (see instructions). If Schedule J is **not** required to be completed, enter the result from the "Totals" line of column 13 of the applicable Schedule A	1,983,476
8a	Total taxable income from all sources (enter taxable income from the corporation's tax return)	78,045,642
b	Adjustments to line 8a (see instructions)	
c	Subtract line 8b from line 8a	78,045,642
9	Divide line 7 by line 8c. Enter the resulting fraction as a decimal (see instructions). If line 7 is greater than line 8c, enter 1	.025414
10	Total U.S. income tax against which credit is allowed (regular tax liability (see section 26(b)) minus American Samoa economic development credit)	27,315,974
11	Credit limitation (multiply line 9 by line 10) (see instructions)	694,208
12	**Separate foreign tax credit** (enter the smaller of line 6 or line 11 here and on the appropriate line of Part III)	694,208

Part III—Summary of Separate Credits (Enter amounts from Part II, line 12 for **each** applicable category of income. **Do not** include taxes paid to sanctioned countries.)

1	Credit for taxes on passive category income	694,208
2	Credit for taxes on general category income	3,956,844
3	Credit for taxes on income re-sourced by treaty (combine all such credits on this line)	
4	Total (add lines 1 through 3)	4,651,052
5	Reduction in credit for international boycott operations (see instructions)	
6	**Total foreign tax credit** (subtract line 5 from line 4). Enter here and on the appropriate line of the corporation's tax return	4,651,052

Form **1118** (Rev. 12-2009)

Form 1118 (Rev. 12-2009)

Page **3**

Schedule C — Tax Deemed Paid by Domestic Corporation Filing Return

Use this schedule to figure the tax deemed paid by the corporation with respect to dividends from a first-tier foreign corporation under section 902(a), and deemed inclusions of earnings from a first- or lower-tier foreign corporation under section 960(a). **Report all amounts in U.S. dollars unless otherwise specified.**

Part I—Dividends and Deemed Inclusions From Post-1986 Undistributed Earnings

1. Name of Foreign Corporation (identify DISCs and former DISCs)	2. Tax Year End (Yr-Mo) (see instructions)	3. Country of Incorporation (enter country code from instructions)	4. Post-1986 Undistributed Earnings (in functional currency—attach schedule)	5. Opening Balance in Post-1986 Foreign Income Taxes	6. Foreign Taxes Paid and Deemed Paid for Tax Year Indicated		7. Post-1986 Foreign Income Taxes (add columns 5, 6(a), and 6(b))	8. Dividends and Deemed Inclusions		9. Divide Column 8(a) by Column 4	10. Tax Deemed Paid (multiply column 7 by column 9)
					(a) Taxes Paid	**(b)** Taxes Deemed Paid (from Schedule D, Part I—see instructions)		**(a)** Functional Currency	**(b)** U.S. Dollars		

Total (Add amounts in column 10. Enter the result here and include on "Totals" line of Schedule B, Part I, column 3.) . . . . ▲

Part II—Dividends Paid Out of Pre-1987 Accumulated Profits

1. Name of Foreign Corporation (identify DISCs and former DISCs)	2. Tax Year End (Yr-Mo) (see instructions)	3. Country of Incorporation (enter country code from instructions)	4. Accumulated Profits for Tax Year Indicated (in functional currency computed under section 902) (attach schedule)	5. Foreign Taxes Paid and Deemed Paid on Earnings and Profits (E&P) for Tax Year Indicated (in functional currency) (see instructions)	6. Dividends Paid		7. Divide Column 6(a) by Column 4	8. Tax Deemed Paid (see instructions)
					(a) Functional Currency	**(b)** U.S. Dollars		

Total (Add amounts in column 8b. Enter the result here and include on "Totals" line of Schedule B, Part I, column 3.) . . . . ▲

Part III—Deemed Inclusions From Pre-1987 Earnings and Profits

1. Name of Foreign Corporation (identify DISCs and former DISCs)	2. Tax Year End (Yr-Mo) (see instructions)	3. Country of Incorporation (enter country code from instructions)	4. E&P for Tax Year Indicated (in functional currency translated from U.S. dollars, computed under section 964) (attach schedule)	5. Foreign Taxes Paid and Deemed Paid for Tax Year Indicated (see instructions)	6. Deemed Inclusions		7. Divide Column 6(a) by Column 4	8. Tax Deemed Paid (multiply column 5 by column 7)
					(a) Functional Currency	**(b)** U.S. Dollars		

Total (Add amounts in column 8. Enter the result here and include on "Totals" line of Schedule B, Part I, column 3.) . . . . ▲

Form **1118** (Rev. 12-2009)

Schedule D Tax Deemed Paid by First- and Second-Tier Foreign Corporations under Section 902(b)

Use Part I to compute the tax deemed paid by a first-tier foreign corporation with respect to dividends from a second-tier foreign corporation. Use Part II to compute the tax deemed paid by a second-tier foreign corporation with respect to dividends from a third-tier foreign corporation. **Report all amounts in U.S. dollars unless otherwise specified.**

Part I—Tax Deemed Paid by First-Tier Foreign Corporations

Section A—Dividends Paid Out of Post-1986 Undistributed Earnings (Include the column 10 results in Schedule C, Part I, column 6(b).)

1. Name of Second-Tier Foreign Corporation and Its Related First-Tier Foreign Corporation	2. Tax Year End (Yr-Mo) (see instructions)	3. Country of Incorporation (enter country code from instructions)	4. Post-1986 Undistributed Earnings (in functional currency—attach schedule)	5. Opening Balance in Post-1986 Foreign Income Taxes	6. Foreign Taxes Paid and Deemed Paid for Tax Year Indicated		7. Post-1986 Foreign Income Taxes (add columns 5, 6(a), and 6(b))	8. Dividends Paid (in functional currency)		9. Divide Column 8(a) by Column 4	10. Tax Deemed Paid (multiply column 7 by column 9)
					(a) Taxes Paid	(b) Taxes Deemed Paid (see instructions)		(a) of Second-tier Corporation	(b) of First-tier Corporation		

Section B—Dividends Paid Out of Pre-1987 Accumulated Profits (Include the column 8(b) results in Schedule C, Part I, column 6(b).)

1. Name of Second-Tier Foreign Corporation and Its Related First-Tier Foreign Corporation	2. Tax Year End (Yr-Mo) (see instructions)	3. Country of Incorporation (enter country code from instructions)	4. Accumulated Profits for Tax Year Indicated (in functional currency—attach schedule)	5. Foreign Taxes Paid and Deemed Paid for Tax Year Indicated (in functional currency—see instructions)	6. Dividends Paid (in functional currency)		7. Divide Column 6(a) by Column 4	8. Tax Deemed Paid (see instructions)	
					(a) of Second-tier Corporation	(b) of First-tier Corporation		(a) Functional Currency of Second-tier Corporation	(b) U.S. Dollars

Part II—Tax Deemed Paid by Second-Tier Foreign Corporations

Section A—Dividends Paid Out of Post-1986 Undistributed Earnings (Include the column 10 results in Section A, column 6(b), of Part I above.)

1. Name of Third-Tier Foreign Corporation and Its Related Second-Tier Foreign Corporation	2. Tax Year End (Yr-Mo) (see instructions)	3. Country of Incorporation (enter country code from instructions)	4. Post-1986 Undistributed Earnings (in functional currency—attach schedule)	5. Opening Balance in Post-1986 Foreign Income Taxes	6. Foreign Taxes Paid and Deemed Paid for Tax Year Indicated		7. Post-1986 Foreign Income Taxes (add columns 5, 6(a), and 6(b))	8. Dividends Paid (in functional currency)		9. Divide Column 8(a) by Column 4	10. Tax Deemed Paid (multiply column 7 by column 9)
					(a) Taxes Paid	(b) Taxes Deemed Paid (from Schedule E, Part I, column 10)		(a) of Third-tier Corporation	(b) of Second-tier Corporation		

Section B—Dividends Paid Out of Pre-1987 Accumulated Profits (Include the column 8(b) results in Section A, column 6(b), of Part I above.)

1. Name of Third-Tier Foreign Corporation and Its Related Second-Tier Foreign Corporation	2. Tax Year End (Yr-Mo) (see instructions)	3. Country of Incorporation (enter country code from instructions)	4. Accumulated Profits for Tax Year Indicated (in functional currency—attach schedule)	5. Foreign Taxes Paid and Deemed Paid for Tax Year Indicated (in functional currency—see instructions)	6. Dividends Paid (in functional currency)		7. Divide Column 6(a) by Column 4	8. Tax Deemed Paid (see instructions)	
					(a) of Third-tier Corporation	(b) of Second-tier Corporation		(a) In Functional Currency of Third-tier Corporation	(b) U.S. Dollars

Form **1118** (Rev. 12-2009)

Form 1118 (Rev. 12-2009)

Schedule E — Tax Deemed Paid by Certain Third-, Fourth-, and Fifth-Tier Foreign Corporations Under Section 902(b)

Use this schedule to report taxes deemed paid with respect to dividends paid from eligible post-1986 undistributed earnings of fourth-, fifth- and sixth-tier controlled foreign corporations. **Report all amounts in U.S. dollars unless otherwise specified.**

Part I—Tax Deemed Paid by Third-Tier Foreign Corporations (Include the column 10 results in Schedule D, Part II, Section A, column 6(b).)

1. Name of Fourth-Tier Foreign Corporation and Its Related Third-Tier Foreign Corporation	2. Tax Year End (Yr-Mo) (see instructions)	3. Country of Incorporation (enter country code from instructions)	4. Post-1986 Undistributed Earnings (in functional currency—attach schedule)	5. Opening Balance in Post-1986 Foreign Income Taxes	6. Foreign Taxes Paid and Deemed Paid for Tax Year Indicated		7. Post-1986 Foreign Income Taxes (add columns 5, 6(a), and 6(b))	8. Dividends Paid (in functional currency)		9. Divide Column 8(a) by Column 4	10. Tax Deemed Paid (multiply column 7 by column 9)
					(a) Taxes Paid	(b) Taxes Deemed Paid (from Part II, column 10)		(a) Of Fourth-tier CFC	(b) Of Third-tier CFC		

Part II—Tax Deemed Paid by Fourth-Tier Foreign Corporations (Include the column 10 results in column 6(b) of Part I above.)

1. Name of Fifth-Tier Foreign Corporation and Its Related Fourth-Tier Foreign Corporation	2. Tax Year End (Yr-Mo) (see instructions)	3. Country of Incorporation (enter country code from instructions)	4. Post-1986 Undistributed Earnings (in functional currency—attach schedule)	5. Opening Balance in Post-1986 Foreign Income Taxes	6. Foreign Taxes Paid and Deemed Paid for Tax Year Indicated		7. Post-1986 Foreign Income Taxes (add columns 5, 6(a), and 6(b))	8. Dividends Paid (in functional currency)		9. Divide Column 8(a) by Column 4	10. Tax Deemed Paid (multiply column 7 by column 9)
					(a) Taxes Paid	(b) Taxes Deemed Paid (from Part III, column 10)		(a) Of Fifth-tier CFC	(b) Of Fourth-tier CFC		

Part III—Tax Deemed Paid by Fifth-Tier Foreign Corporations (Include the column 10 results in column 6(b) of Part II above.)

1. Name of Sixth-Tier Foreign Corporation and Its Related Fifth-Tier Foreign Corporation	2. Tax Year End (Yr-Mo) (see instructions)	3. Country of Incorporation (enter country code from instructions)	4. Post-1986 Undistributed Earnings (in functional currency—attach schedule)	5. Opening Balance in Post-1986 Foreign Income Taxes	6. Foreign Taxes Paid For Tax Year Indicated	7. Post-1986 Foreign Income Taxes (add columns 5 and 6)	8. Dividends Paid (in functional currency)		9. Divide Column 8(a) by Column 4	10. Tax Deemed Paid (multiply column 7 by column 9)
							(a) Of Sixth-tier CFC	(b) Of Fifth-tier CFC		

Form **1118** (Rev. 12-2009)

Form 1118 (Rev. 12-2009)

Page **6**

Schedule F — Gross Income and Definitely Allocable Deductions for Foreign Branches

1. Foreign Country or U.S. Possession (Enter two-letter code from Schedule A, column 1. Use a separate line for each.)	2. Gross Income	3. Definitely Allocable Deductions
A		
B		
C		
D		
E		
F		
Totals (add lines A through F)* ▲		

* Note: The Schedule F totals are not carried over to any other Form 1118 Schedule. (These totals were already included in Schedule A.) However, the IRS requires the corporation to complete Schedule F under the authority of section 905(b).

Schedule G — Reductions of Taxes Paid, Accrued, or Deemed Paid

A	Reduction of Taxes Under Section 901(e)—Attach separate schedule	
B	Reduction of Foreign Oil and Gas Taxes—Enter amount from Schedule I, Part II, line 6	
C	Reduction of Taxes Due to International Boycott Provisions—Enter appropriate portion of Schedule C (Form 5713), line 2b. **Important:** Enter only "specifically attributable taxes" here.	
D	Reduction of Taxes for Section 6038(c) Penalty—Attach separate schedule	
E	Other Reductions of Taxes—Attach schedule(s)	
	Total (add lines A through E). Enter here and on Schedule B, Part II, line 3 . . . . ▲	

Form **1118** (Rev. 12-2009)

| Schedule H | Apportionment of Deductions Not Definitely Allocable *(complete only once)* |

Part I—Research and Development Deductions

		(a) Sales Method				(b) Gross Income Method—Check method used: □ Option 1 □ Option 2 (See instructions.)		(c) Total R&D Deductions Not Definitely Allocable (enter all amounts from column (a)(v) or all amounts from column (b)(vii))
	Product line #1 (SIC Code:)*		Product line #2 (SIC Code:)*		(v) Total R&D Deductions Under Sales Method (add columns (ii) and (iv))	(vi) Gross Income	(vii) Total R&D Deductions Under Gross Income Method	
	(i) Gross Sales	(ii) R&D Deductions	(iii) Gross Sales	(iv) R&D Deductions				
1 Totals (see instructions)								
2 Total to be apportioned								
3 Apportionment among statutory groupings:								
a General category income								
b Passive category income								
c Section 901(j) income*								
d Income re-sourced by treaty*								
4 Total foreign (add lines 3a through 3d)								

* **Important:** See *Computer-Generated Schedule H* in *instructions.*

Form **1118** (Rev. 12-2009)

Schedule H   Apportionment of Deductions Not Definitely Allocable *(continued)*
Part II—Interest Deductions, All Other Deductions, and Total Deductions

| | (a) Average Value of Assets—Check method used: ☐ Fair market value ☑ Tax book value ☐ Alternative tax book value | | (b) Interest Deductions | | (c) All Other Deductions Not Definitely Allocable | (d) Totals (add the corresponding amounts from column (c), Part I; columns (b)(iii) and (b)(iv), Part II; and column (c), Part II). Enter each amount from lines 3a through 3d below in column 10 of the corresponding Schedule A. |
	(i) Nonfinancial Corporations	(ii) Financial Corporations	(iii) Nonfinancial Corporations	(iv) Financial Corporations		
1a Totals (see instructions)	22,879,832	3,506,341	13,085,978	533,611	1,263,957	
b Amounts specifically allocable under Temp. Regs. 1.861-10T(e)						
c Other specific allocations under Temp. Regs. 1.861-10T						
d Assets excluded from apportionment formula	3,117,240					
2 Total to be apportioned (subtract the sum of lines 1b, 1c, and 1d from line 1a)	19,762,592	3,506,341	13,095,078	533,611		
3 Apportionment among statutory groupings:						
a General category income	17,164,062		3,066,892		1,257,416	4,324,308
b Passive category income	8,406,735		1,502,892		6,541	1,508,665
c Section 901(j) income*						
d Income re-sourced by treaty*						
4 Total foreign (add lines 3a through 3d)	25,570,797	None	4,569,016	None	1,263,957	5,832,973

*Important: See *Computer-Generated Schedule H* in instructions.*

Form **1118** (Rev. 12-2009)

Sample Form 4-6

Form 1118
(Rev. December 2009)
Department of the Treasury
Internal Revenue Service

Foreign Tax Credit—Corporations

▶ See separate instructions.
▶ Attach to the corporation's tax return.

OMB No. 1545-0122

Name of corporation

Cramden Corporation and Consolidated Subsidiaries

Employer identification number

XX-XXXXXXX

For calendar year 20 __10__ , or other tax year beginning _____ , 20 ___ , and ending _____ , 20 ___

Use a **separate** Form 1118 for each applicable category of income listed below. See **Categories of Income** in the instructions. Also, see **Specific Instructions.**
Check only one box on each form.

☐ Passive Category Income
☑ General Category Income
☐ Section 901(j) Income: Name of Sanctioned Country ▶ _____
☐ Income Re-sourced by Treaty: Name of Country ▶ _____

Schedule A **Income or (Loss) Before Adjustments** *(Report all amounts in U.S. dollars. See Specific Instructions.)*

Gross Income or (Loss) From Sources Outside the United States (*INCLUDE* Foreign Branch Gross Income here *and* on Schedule F)

1. Foreign Country or U.S. Possession (Enter two-letter code; see instructions. Use a separate line for each.) *	2. Deemed Dividends (see instructions)		3. Other Dividends		4. Interest	5. Gross Rents, Royalties, and License Fees	6. Gross Income From Performance of Services	7. Other (attach schedule)	8. Total (add columns 2(a) through 7)
	(a) Exclude gross-up	(b) Gross-up (sec. 78)	(a) Exclude gross-up	(b) Gross-up (sec. 78)					
A									
B		See							
C		Attached							
D		Schedules							
E									
F									
Totals (add lines A through F)	505,937	227,375	16,000,000	11,018,556	-0-	187,135	18,418,698	9,592,669	56,310,370

* For section 863(b) income, NOLs, income from RICs, and high-taxed income, use a single line (see instructions).

Deductions (*INCLUDE* Foreign Branch Deductions here *and* on Schedule F)

9. Definitely Allocable Deductions					10. Apportioned Share of Deductions Not Definitely Allocable (enter amount from applicable line of Schedule H, Part II, column (d))	11. Net Operating Loss Deduction	12. Total Deductions (add columns 9(e) through 11)	13. Total Income or (Loss) Before Adjustments (subtract column 12 from column 8)
Rental, Royalty, and Licensing Expenses		(c) Expenses Related to Gross Income From Performance of Services	(d) Other Definitely Allocable Deductions	(e) Total Definitely Allocable Deductions (add columns 9(a) through 9(d))				
(a) Depreciation, Depletion, and Amortization	(b) Other Expenses							
A								
B		See						
C		Attached						
D		Schedules						
E								
F								
Totals	-0-	-0-	6,248,537	3,577,713	9,826,250	2,707,096		12,533,346	43,777,024

For Paperwork Reduction Act Notice, see separate instructions.

Cat. No. 10900F

Form **1118** (Rev. 12-2009)

Form 1118 (Rev. 12-2009)

Page **2**

Schedule B — Foreign Tax Credit (Report all foreign tax amounts in U.S. dollars.)

Part I—Foreign Taxes Paid, Accrued, and Deemed Paid (see instructions)

	1. Credit is Claimed for Taxes:		2. Foreign Taxes Paid or Accrued (attach schedule showing amounts in foreign currency and conversion rate(s) used)							
	Paid	Accrued	Tax Withheld at Source on:			Other Foreign Taxes Paid or Accrued on:			(h) Total Foreign Taxes Paid or Accrued (add columns 2(a) through 2(g))	3. Tax Deemed Paid (from Schedule C—Part I, column 10, Part II, column 8(b), and Part III, column 8)
	Date Paid	Date Accrued	(a) Dividends	(b) Interest	(c) Rents, Royalties, and License Fees	(d) Section 863(b) Income	(e) Foreign Branch Income	(f) Services Income	(g) Other		
A											
B											
C			See								
D			Attached								
E			Schedules								
F											
Totals (add lines A through F)			-0-	-0-	17,353	-0-				1,828,162	12,717,690

Part II—Separate Foreign Tax Credit (Complete a separate Part II for each applicable category of income.)

1	Total foreign taxes paid or accrued (total from Part I, column 2(h))	1,828,162
2	Total taxes deemed paid (total from Part I, column 3)	12,717,690
3	Reductions of taxes paid, accrued, or deemed paid (enter total from Schedule G)	( )
4	Taxes reclassified under high-tax kickout	
5	Enter the sum of any carryover of foreign taxes (from Schedule K, line 3, column (xiv)) plus any carrybacks to the current tax year	14,545,752
6	Total foreign taxes (combine lines 1 through 5)	43,777,024
7	Enter the amount from the applicable column of Schedule J, Part I, line 11 (see instructions). If Schedule J is **not** required to be completed, enter the result from the "Totals" line of column 13 of the applicable Schedule A	
8a	Total taxable income from all sources (enter taxable income from the corporation's tax return)	78,045,642
b	Adjustments to line 8a (see instructions)	
c	Subtract line 8b from line 8a	78,045,642
9	Divide line 7 by line 8c. Enter the resulting fraction as a decimal (see instructions). If line 7 is greater than line 8c, enter 1	.5609
10	Total U.S. income tax against which credit is allowed (regular tax liability (see section 26(b)) minus American Samoa economic development credit)	27,315,974
11	Credit limitation (multiply line 9 by line 10) (see instructions)	15,321,956
12	**Separate foreign tax credit** (enter the smaller of line 6 or line 11 here and on the appropriate line of Part III)	14,545,752

Part III—Summary of Separate Credits (Enter amounts from Part II, line 12 for **each** applicable category of income. **Do not** include taxes paid to sanctioned countries.)

1	Credit for taxes on passive category income	
2	Credit for taxes on general category income	
3	Credit for taxes on income re-sourced by treaty (combine all such credits on this line)	
4	Total (add lines 1 through 3)	
5	Reduction in credit for international boycott operations (see instructions)	
6	**Total foreign tax credit** (subtract line 5 from line 4). Enter here and on the appropriate line of the corporation's tax return	

Form **1118** (Rev. 12-2009)

Page **3**

Schedule C — Tax Deemed Paid by Domestic Corporation Filing Return

Use this schedule to figure the tax deemed paid by the corporation with respect to dividends from a first-tier foreign corporation under section 902(a), and deemed inclusions of earnings from a first- or lower-tier foreign corporation under section 960(a). **Report all amounts in U.S. dollars unless otherwise specified.**

Part I—Dividends and Deemed Inclusions From Post-1986 Undistributed Earnings

1. Name of Foreign Corporation (identify DISCs and former DISCs)	2. Tax Year End (Yr-Mo) (see instructions)	3. Country of Incorporation (enter country code from instructions)	4. Post-1986 Undistributed Earnings (in functional currency—attach schedule)	5. Opening Balance in Post-1986 Foreign Income Taxes	6. Foreign Taxes Paid and Deemed Paid for Tax Year Indicated		7. Post-1986 Foreign Income Taxes (add columns 5, 6(a), and 6(b))	8. Dividends and Deemed Inclusions		9. Divide Column 8(a) by Column 4	10. Tax Deemed Paid (multiply column 7 by column 9)
					(a) Taxes Paid	(b) Taxes Deemed Paid (from Schedule D, Part I—see instructions)		(a) Functional Currency	(b) U.S. Dollars		
Cramden-Cordura	0312	CD	16,452,692	11,273,311			11,273,311	16,000,000	16,000,000	.97837	11,018,556
Cramden-Antilles	0312	NA	2,541,573	748,748	950,386		1,699,134	2,541,573	2,541,573	1.00	1,699,134

Total (Add amounts in column 10. Enter the result here and include on "Totals" line of Schedule B, Part I, column 3.) . . . . ▲   12,717,690

Part II—Dividends Paid Out of Pre-1987 Accumulated Profits

1. Name of Foreign Corporation (identify DISCs and former DISCs)	2. Tax Year End (Yr-Mo) (see instructions)	3. Country of Incorporation (enter country code from instructions)	4. Accumulated Profits for Tax Year Indicated (in functional currency computed under section 902) (attach schedule)	5. Foreign Taxes Paid and Deemed Paid on Earnings and Profits (E&P) for Tax Year Indicated (in functional currency) (see instructions)	6. Dividends Paid		7. Divide Column 6(a) by Column 4	8. Tax Deemed Paid (see instructions)
					(a) Functional Currency	(b) U.S. Dollars		

Total (Add amounts in column 8b. Enter the result here and include on "Totals" line of Schedule B, Part I, column 3.) . . . . ▲

Part III—Deemed Inclusions From Pre-1987 Earnings and Profits

1. Name of Foreign Corporation (identify DISCs and former DISCs)	2. Tax Year End (Yr-Mo) (see instructions)	3. Country of Incorporation (enter country code from instructions)	4. E&P for Tax Year Indicated (in functional currency translated from U.S. dollars, computed under section 964) (attach schedule)	5. Foreign Taxes Paid and Deemed Paid for Tax Year Indicated (see instructions)	6. Deemed Inclusions		7. Divide Column 6(a) by Column 4	8. Tax Deemed Paid (multiply column 5 by column 7)
					(a) Functional Currency	(b) U.S. Dollars		

Total (Add amounts in column 8. Enter the result here and include on "Totals" line of Schedule B, Part I, column 3.) . . . . ▲

Form **1118** (Rev. 12-2009)

Form 1118 (Rev. 12-2009)

Schedule D Tax Deemed Paid by First- and Second-Tier Foreign Corporations under Section 902(b)

Use Part I to compute the tax deemed paid by a first-tier foreign corporation with respect to dividends from a second-tier foreign corporation. Use Part II to compute the tax deemed paid by a second-tier foreign corporation with respect to dividends from a third-tier foreign corporation. **Report all amounts in U.S. dollars unless otherwise specified.**

Part I—Tax Deemed Paid by First-Tier Foreign Corporations

Section A—Dividends Paid Out of Post-1986 Undistributed Earnings (Include the column 10 results in Schedule C, Part I, column 6(b).)

1. Name of Second-Tier Foreign Corporation and Its Related First-Tier Foreign Corporation	2. Tax Year End (Yr-Mo) (see instructions)	3. Country of Incorporation (enter country code from instructions)	4. Post-1986 Undistributed Earnings (in functional currency—attach schedule)	5. Opening Balance in Post-1986 Foreign Income Taxes	6. Foreign Taxes Paid and Deemed Paid for Tax Year Indicated		7. Post-1986 Foreign Income Taxes (add columns 5, 6(a), and 6(b))	8. Dividends Paid (in functional currency)		9. Divide Column 8(a) by Column 4	10. Tax Deemed Paid (multiply column 7 by column 9)
					(a) Taxes Paid	(b) Taxes Deemed Paid (see instructions)		(a) of Second-tier Corporation	(b) of First-tier Corporation		
Cramden-Global NV	0312	SA	3,250,000	950,386		-0-	950,386	3,250,000	3,250,000	1.00	950,386

Section B—Dividends Paid Out of Pre-1987 Accumulated Profits (Include the column 8(b) results in Schedule C, Part I, column 6(b).)

1. Name of Second-Tier Foreign Corporation and Its Related First-Tier Foreign Corporation	2. Tax Year End (Yr-Mo) (see instructions)	3. Country of Incorporation (enter country code from instructions)	4. Accumulated Profits for Tax Year Indicated (in functional currency—attach schedule)	5. Foreign Taxes Paid and Deemed Paid for Tax Year Indicated (in functional currency—see instructions)	6. Dividends Paid (in functional currency)		7. Divide Column 6(a) by Column 4	8. Tax Deemed Paid (see instructions)	
					(a) of Second-tier Corporation	(b) of First-tier Corporation		(a) Functional Currency of Second-tier Corporation	(b) U.S. Dollars

Part II—Tax Deemed Paid by Second-Tier Foreign Corporations

Section A—Dividends Paid Out of Post-1986 Undistributed Earnings (Include the column 10 results in Section A, column 6(b), of Part I above.)

1. Name of Third-Tier Foreign Corporation and Its Related Second-Tier Foreign Corporation	2. Tax Year End (Yr-Mo) (see instructions)	3. Country of Incorporation (enter country code from instructions)	4. Post-1986 Undistributed Earnings (in functional currency—attach schedule)	5. Opening Balance in Post-1986 Foreign Income Taxes	6. Foreign Taxes Paid and Deemed Paid for Tax Year Indicated		7. Post-1986 Foreign Income Taxes (add columns 5, 6(a), and 6(b))	8. Dividends Paid (in functional currency)		9. Divide Column 8(a) by Column 4	10. Tax Deemed Paid (multiply column 7 by column 9)
					(a) Taxes Paid	(b) Taxes Deemed Paid (from Schedule E, Part I, column 10)		(a) of Third-tier Corporation	(b) of Second-tier Corporation		

Section B—Dividends Paid Out of Pre-1987 Accumulated Profits (Include the column 8(b) results in Section A, column 6(b), of Part I above.)

1. Name of Third-Tier Foreign Corporation and Its Related Second-Tier Foreign Corporation	2. Tax Year End (Yr-Mo) (see instructions)	3. Country of Incorporation (enter country code from instructions)	4. Accumulated Profits for Tax Year Indicated (in functional currency—attach schedule)	5. Foreign Taxes Paid and Deemed Paid for Tax Year Indicated (in functional currency—see instructions)	6. Dividends Paid (in functional currency)		7. Divide Column 6(a) by Column 4	8. Tax Deemed Paid (see instructions)	
					(a) of Third-tier Corporation	(b) of Second-tier Corporation		(a) In Functional Currency of Third-tier Corporation	(b) U.S. Dollars

Form **1118** (Rev. 12-2009)

Form 1118 (Rev. 12-2009)

Schedule E — Tax Deemed Paid by Certain Third-, Fourth-, and Fifth-Tier Foreign Corporations Under Section 902(b)

Use this schedule to report taxes deemed paid with respect to dividends paid from eligible post-1986 undistributed earnings of fourth-, fifth- and sixth-tier controlled foreign corporations. **Report all amounts in U.S. dollars unless otherwise specified.**

Part I—Tax Deemed Paid by Third-Tier Foreign Corporations (Include the column 10 results in Schedule D, Part II, Section A, column 6(b).)

| 1. Name of Fourth-Tier Foreign Corporation and Its Related Third-Tier Foreign Corporation | 2. Tax Year End (Yr-Mo) (see instructions) | 3. Country of Incorporation (enter country code from instructions) | 4. Post-1986 Undistributed Earnings (in functional currency—attach schedule) | 5. Opening Balance in Post-1986 Foreign Income Taxes | 6. Foreign Taxes Paid and Deemed Paid for Tax Year Indicated | | 7. Post-1986 Foreign Income Taxes (add columns 5, 6(a), and 6(b)) | 8. Dividends Paid (in functional currency) | | 9. Divide Column 8(a) by Column 4 | 10. Tax Deemed Paid (multiply column 7 by column 9) |
| | | | | | (a) Taxes Paid | (b) Taxes Deemed Paid (from Part II, column 10) | | (a) Of Fourth-tier CFC | (b) Of Third-tier CFC | | |

Part II—Tax Deemed Paid by Fourth-Tier Foreign Corporations (Include the column 10 results in column 6(b) of Part I above.)

| 1. Name of Fifth-Tier Foreign Corporation and Its Related Fourth-Tier Foreign Corporation | 2. Tax Year End (Yr-Mo) (see instructions) | 3. Country of Incorporation (enter country code from instructions) | 4. Post-1986 Undistributed Earnings (in functional currency—attach schedule) | 5. Opening Balance in Post-1986 Foreign Income Taxes | 6. Foreign Taxes Paid and Deemed Paid for Tax Year Indicated | | 7. Post-1986 Foreign Income Taxes (add columns 5, 6(a), and 6(b)) | 8. Dividends Paid (in functional currency) | | 9. Divide Column 8(a) by Column 4 | 10. Tax Deemed Paid (multiply column 7 by column 9) |
| | | | | | (a) Taxes Paid | (b) Taxes Deemed Paid (from Part III, column 10) | | (a) Of Fifth-tier CFC | (b) Of Fourth-tier CFC | | |

Part III—Tax Deemed Paid by Fifth-Tier Foreign Corporations (Include the column 10 results in column 6(b) of Part II above.)

| 1. Name of Sixth-Tier Foreign Corporation and Its Related Fifth-Tier Foreign Corporation | 2. Tax Year End (Yr-Mo) (see instructions) | 3. Country of Incorporation (enter country code from instructions) | 4. Post-1986 Undistributed Earnings (in functional currency—attach schedule) | 5. Opening Balance in Post-1986 Foreign Income Taxes | 6. Foreign Taxes Paid For Tax Year Indicated | 7. Post-1986 Foreign Income Taxes (add columns 5 and 6) | 8. Dividends Paid (in functional currency) | | 9. Divide Column 8(a) by Column 4 | 10. Tax Deemed Paid (multiply column 7 by column 9) |
| | | | | | | | (a) Of Sixth-tier CFC | (b) Of Fifth-tier CFC | | |

Form **1118** (Rev. 12-2009)

Form 1118 (Rev. 12-2009)

Page **6**

Schedule F — Gross Income and Definitely Allocable Deductions for Foreign Branches

	1. Foreign Country or U.S. Possession (Enter two-letter code from Schedule A, column 1. Use a separate line for each.)	2. Gross Income	3. Definitely Allocable Deductions
A	Cramden-Cordura	706,097	22,957
B	Cramden-Island	4,480,572	530,016
C			
D			
E			
F			
Totals (add lines A through F)* ▲		5,186,669	552,983

Note: *The Schedule F totals are not carried over to any other Form 1118 Schedule. (These totals were already included in Schedule A.) However, the IRS requires the corporation to complete Schedule F under the authority of section 905(b).*

Schedule G — Reductions of Taxes Paid, Accrued, or Deemed Paid

A	Reduction of Taxes Under Section 901(e)—Attach separate schedule
B	Reduction of Foreign Oil and Gas Taxes—Enter amount from Schedule I, Part II, line 6
C	Reduction of Taxes Due to International Boycott Provisions— Enter appropriate portion of Schedule C (Form 5713), line 2b. **Important:** Enter only "specifically attributable taxes" here.
D	Reduction of Taxes for Section 6038(c) Penalty— Attach separate schedule
E	Other Reductions of Taxes—Attach schedule(s)
Total (add lines A through E). Enter here and on Schedule B, Part II, line 3 . . . . ▲	

Form **1118** (Rev. 12-2009)

Schedule H   Apportionment of Deductions Not Definitely Allocable *(complete only once)*

Part I—Research and Development Deductions

	(a) Sales Method					(b) Gross Income Method—Check method used: ☐ Option 1 ☐ Option 2 (See instructions.)		(c) Total R&D Deductions Not Definitely Allocable (enter all amounts from column (a)(v) or all amounts from column (b)(vii).)
	Product line #1 (SIC Code: _____) *		Product line #2 (SIC Code: _____) *		(v) Total R&D Deductions Under Sales Method (add columns (ii) and (iv))	(vi) Gross Income	(vii) Total R&D Deductions Under Gross Income Method	
	(i) Gross Sales	(ii) R&D Deductions	(iii) Gross Sales	(iv) R&D Deductions				
1 Totals (see instructions)	▓		▓			▓		▓
2 Total to be apportioned								
3 Apportionment among statutory groupings:								
a General category income								
b Passive category income								
c Section 901(j) income*								
d Income re-sourced by treaty*								
4 Total foreign (add lines 3a through 3d)								

* Important: See *Computer-Generated Schedule H in instructions.*

Form 1118 (Rev. 12-2009)

Schedule H Apportionment of Deductions Not Definitely Allocable *(continued)*
Part II—Interest Deductions, All Other Deductions, and Total Deductions

| | (a) Average Value of Assets—Check method used: ☐ Fair market value ☑ Tax book value ☐ Alternative tax book value | | (b) Interest Deductions | | (c) All Other Deductions Not Definitely Allocable | (d) Totals (add the corresponding amounts from column (c), Part I; columns (b)(ii) and (b)(iv), Part II; and column (c), Part II). Enter each amount from lines 3a through 3d below in column 10 of the corresponding Schedule A. |
	(i) Nonfinancial Corporations	(ii) Financial Corporations	(iii) Nonfinancial Corporations	(iv) Financial Corporations		
1a Totals (see instructions)	22,879,832	3,506,341	13,085,978	533,611	1,263,957	
b Amounts specifically allocable under Temp. Regs. 1.861-10T(e)						
c Other specific allocations under Temp. Regs. 1.861-10T						
d Assets excluded from apportionment formula	3,117,240					
2 Total to be apportioned (subtract the sum of lines 1b, 1c, and 1d from line 1a)	19,762,592		13,085,978	533,611		
3 Apportionment among statutory groupings:						
a General category income	17,164,062		3,066,892		1,257,416	4,324,308
b Passive category income	8,406,735		1,502,124		6,541	1,508,665
c Section 901(j) income*						
d Income re-sourced by treaty*						
4 Total foreign (add lines 3a through 3d)	25,570,797	None	4,569,016	None	1,263,957	5,832,973

* **Important:** See *Computer-Generated Schedule H in instructions.*

Form **1118** (Rev. 12-2009)

Page **8**

Sample Form 4-7

Form 1118
(Rev. December 2009)
Department of the Treasury
Internal Revenue Service

Foreign Tax Credit—Corporations

▶ See separate instructions.
▶ Attach to the corporation's tax return.

OMB No. 1545-0122

Name of corporation

Cramden Corporation and Consolidated Subsidiaries

For calendar year 20 **10**, or other tax year beginning _____ , 20 ___ , and ending _____ , 20 ___

Employer identification number

XX-XXXXXXX

Use a **separate** Form 1118 for each applicable category of income listed below. See **Categories of Income** in the instructions. Also, see **Specific Instructions.**
Check only one box on each form.

☐ Passive Category Income   ☐ Section 901(j) Income: Name of Sanctioned Country ▶ _____
☑ General Category Income   ☐ Income Re-sourced by Treaty: Name of Country ▶ _____

Schedule A   Income or (Loss) Before Adjustments *(Report all amounts in U.S. dollars. See Specific Instructions.)*

Gross Income or (Loss) From Sources Outside the United States *(INCLUDE Foreign Branch Gross Income here and on Schedule F)*

1. Foreign Country or U.S. Possession (Enter two-letter code; see instructions. Use a separate line for each.)*	2. Deemed Dividends (see instructions)		3. Other Dividends		4. Interest	5. Gross Rents, Royalties, and License Fees	6. Gross Income From Performance of Services	7. Other (attach schedule)	8. Total (add columns 2(a) through 7)
	(a) Exclude gross-up	(b) Gross-up (sec. 78)	(a) Exclude gross-up	(b) Gross-up (sec. 78)					
A					1,396,289				1,396,289
B BL			61,071	10,777	227,469				299,317
C GS					320,872				320,872
D GA					46,250				46,250
E SA			8,400		265,286				273,686
F									
Totals (add lines A through F)			69,471	10,777	2,256,166				2,336,414

* For section 863(b) income, NOLs, income from RICs, and high-taxed income, use a single line (see instructions).

Deductions *(INCLUDE Foreign Branch Deductions here and on Schedule F)*

	9. Definitely Allocable Deductions				10. Apportioned Share of Deductions Not Definitely Allocable (enter amount from applicable line of Schedule H, Part II, column (d))	11. Net Operating Loss Deduction	12. Total Deductions (add columns 9(e) through 11)	13. Total Income or (Loss) Before Adjustments (subtract column 12 from column 8)
	Rental, Royalty, and Licensing Expenses		(c) Expenses Related to Gross Income From Performance of Services	(d) Other Definitely Allocable Deductions	(e) Total Definitely Allocable Deductions (add columns 9(a) through 9(d))				
	(a) Depreciation, Depletion, and Amortization	(b) Other Expenses							
A								966,480	429,809
B								207,180	92,137
C								222,100	98,772
D								32,013	14,237
E								189,439	84,247
F									
Totals								1,617,212	719,202

For Paperwork Reduction Act Notice, see separate instructions.   Cat. No. 10900F   Form **1118** (Rev. 12-2009)

Form 1118 (Rev. 12-2009)

Schedule B — Foreign Tax Credit (Report all foreign tax amounts in U.S. dollars.)

Part I—Foreign Taxes Paid, Accrued, and Deemed Paid (see instructions)

1. Credit is Claimed for Taxes: ☑ Paid ☐ Accrued		2. Foreign Taxes Paid or Accrued (attach schedule showing amounts in foreign currency and conversion rate(s) used)								3. Tax Deemed Paid (from Schedule C— Part I, column 10, Part II, column 8(b), and Part III, column 8)
		Tax Withheld at Source on:		Other Foreign Taxes Paid or Accrued on:					(h) Total Foreign Taxes Paid or Accrued (add columns 2(a) through 2(g))	
Date Paid	Date Accrued	(a) Dividends	(b) Interest	(c) Rents, Royalties, and License Fees	(d) Section 863(b) Income	(e) Foreign Branch Income	(f) Services Income	(g) Other		
A 2010			59,773						59,773	
B 2010		10,777	34,120						44,897	
C			80,218						80,218	
D										
E										
F										
Totals (add lines A through F)		10,777	174,111						184,888	184,888

Part II—Separate Foreign Tax Credit (Complete a separate Part II for each applicable category of income.)

1	Total foreign taxes paid or accrued (total from Part I, column 2(h))	184,888
2	Total taxes deemed paid (total from Part I, column 3)	
3	Reductions of taxes paid, accrued, or deemed paid (enter total from Schedule G)	( )
4	Taxes reclassified under high-tax kickout	
5	Enter the sum of any carryover of foreign taxes (from Schedule K, line 3, column (xiv)) plus any carrybacks to the current tax year	
6	Total foreign taxes (combine lines 1 through 5)	184,888
7	Enter the amount from the applicable column of Schedule J, Part I, line 11 (see instructions). If Schedule J is **not** required to be completed, enter the result from the "Totals" line of column 13 of the applicable Schedule A	719,202
8a	Total taxable income from all sources (enter taxable income from the corporation's tax return)	78,045,642
b	Adjustments to line 8a (see instructions)	
c	Subtract line 8b from line 8a	78,045,642
9	Divide line 7 by line 8c. Enter the resulting fraction as a decimal (see instructions). If line 7 is greater than line 8c, enter 1	.009215
10	Total U.S. income tax against which credit is allowed (regular tax liability (see section 26(b)) minus American Samoa economic development credit)	27,315,974
11	Credit limitation (multiply line 9 by line 10) (see instructions)	251,719
12	**Separate foreign tax credit** (enter the smaller of line 6 or line 11 here and on the appropriate line of Part III)	184,888

Part III—Summary of Separate Credits (Enter amounts from Part II, line 12 for **each** applicable category of income. **Do not** include taxes paid to sanctioned countries.)

1	Credit for taxes on passive category income	
2	Credit for taxes on general category income	
3	Credit for taxes on income re-sourced by treaty (combine all such credits on this line)	
4	Total (add lines 1 through 3)	
5	Reduction in credit for international boycott operations (see instructions)	
6	**Total foreign tax credit** (subtract line 5 from line 4). Enter here and on the appropriate line of the corporation's tax return	

Form **1118** (Rev. 12-2009)

Form 1118 (Rev. 12-2009)

Schedule C — Tax Deemed Paid by Domestic Corporation Filing Return

Use this schedule to figure the tax deemed paid by the corporation with respect to dividends from a first-tier foreign corporation under section 902(a), and deemed inclusions of earnings from a first- or lower-tier foreign corporation under section 960(a). **Report all amounts in U.S. dollars unless otherwise specified.**

Part I—Dividends and Deemed Inclusions From Post-1986 Undistributed Earnings

1. Name of Foreign Corporation (identify DISCs and former DISCs)	2. Tax Year End (Yr-Mo) (see instructions)	3. Country of Incorporation (enter country code from instructions)	4. Post-1986 Undistributed Earnings (in functional currency—attach schedule)	5. Opening Balance in Post-1986 Foreign Income Taxes	6. Foreign Taxes Paid and Deemed Paid for Tax Year Indicated		7. Post-1986 Foreign Income Taxes (add columns 5, 6(a), and 6(b))	8. Dividends and Deemed Inclusions		9. Divide Column 8(a) by Column 4	10. Tax Deemed Paid (multiply column 7 by column 9)
					(a) Taxes Paid	(b) Taxes Deemed Paid (from Schedule D, Part I—see instructions)		(a) Functional Currency	(b) U.S. Dollars		
Cramden-Cordura	0312	CD	16,452,692	11,273,311			11,273,311	16,000,000	16,000,000	.97837	11,018,556
Cramden-Antilles	0312	NA	2,541,573	748,748		950,386	1,699,134	2,541,573	2,541,573	1.00	1,699,134

Total (Add amounts in column 10. Enter the result here and include on "Totals" line of Schedule B, Part I, column 3.) . . . . . . ▲ | 12,717,690

Part II—Dividends Paid Out of Pre-1987 Accumulated Profits

1. Name of Foreign Corporation (identify DISCs and former DISCs)	2. Tax Year End (Yr-Mo) (see instructions)	3. Country of Incorporation (enter country code from instructions)	4. Accumulated Profits for Tax Year Indicated (in functional currency computed under section 902) (attach schedule)	5. Foreign Taxes Paid and Deemed Paid on Earnings and Profits (E&P) for Tax Year Indicated (in functional currency) (see instructions)	6. Dividends Paid		7. Divide Column 6(a) by Column 4	8. Tax Deemed Paid (see instructions)	
					(a) Functional Currency	(b) U.S. Dollars		(a) Functional Currency	(b) U.S. Dollars

Total (Add amounts in column 8b. Enter the result here and include on "Totals" line of Schedule B, Part I, column 3.) . . . . . . ▲

Part III—Deemed Inclusions From Pre-1987 Earnings and Profits

1. Name of Foreign Corporation (identify DISCs and former DISCs)	2. Tax Year End (Yr-Mo) (see instructions)	3. Country of Incorporation (enter country code from instructions)	4. E&P for Tax Year Indicated (in functional currency translated from U.S. dollars, computed under section 964) (attach schedule)	5. Foreign Taxes Paid and Deemed Paid for Tax Year Indicated (in functional currency) (see instructions)	6. Deemed Inclusions		7. Divide Column 6(a) by Column 4	8. Tax Deemed Paid (multiply column 5 by column 7)
					(a) Functional Currency	(b) U.S. Dollars		

Total (Add amounts in column 8. Enter the result here and include on "Totals" line of Schedule B, Part I, column 3.) . . . . . . ▲

Form **1118** (Rev. 12-2009)

Form 1118 (Rev. 12-2009)

Page **4**

Schedule D   Tax Deemed Paid by First- and Second-Tier Foreign Corporations under Section 902(b)

*Use Part I to compute the tax deemed paid by a first-tier foreign corporation with respect to dividends from a second-tier foreign corporation. Use Part II to compute the tax deemed paid by a second-tier foreign corporation with respect to dividends from a third-tier foreign corporation. **Report all amounts in U.S. dollars unless otherwise specified.***

Part I—Tax Deemed Paid by First-Tier Foreign Corporations

Section A—Dividends Paid Out of Post-1986 Undistributed Earnings (Include the column 10 results in Schedule C, Part I, column 6(b).)

1. Name of Second-Tier Foreign Corporation and Its Related First-Tier Foreign Corporation	2. Tax Year End (Yr-Mo) (see instructions)	3. Country of Incorporation (enter country code from instructions)	4. Post-1986 Undistributed Earnings (in functional currency—attach schedule)	5. Opening Balance in Post-1986 Foreign Income Taxes	6. Foreign Taxes Paid and Deemed Paid for Tax Year Indicated		7. Post-1986 Foreign Income Taxes (add columns 5, 6(a), and 6(b))	8. Dividends Paid (in functional currency)		9. Divide Column 8(a) by Column 4	10. Tax Deemed Paid (multiply column 7 by column 9)
					(a) Taxes Paid	(b) Taxes Deemed Paid (see instructions)		(a) of Second-tier Corporation	(b) of First-tier Corporation		
Cramden-Global NV	0312	SA	3,250,000	950,386	-0-		950,386	3,250,000	3,250,000	1.00	950,386

Section B—Dividends Paid Out of Pre-1987 Accumulated Profits (Include the column 8(b) results in Schedule C, Part I, column 6(b).)

1. Name of Second-Tier Foreign Corporation and Its Related First-Tier Foreign Corporation	2. Tax Year End (Yr-Mo) (see instructions)	3. Country of Incorporation (enter country code from instructions)	4. Accumulated Profits for Tax Year Indicated (in functional currency—attach schedule)	5. Foreign Taxes Paid and Deemed Paid for Tax Year Indicated (in functional currency—see instructions)	6. Dividends Paid (in functional currency)		7. Divide Column 6(a) by Column 4	8. Tax Deemed Paid (see instructions)	
					(a) of Second-tier Corporation	(b) of First-tier Corporation		(a) Functional Currency of Second-tier Corporation	(b) U.S. Dollars

Part II—Tax Deemed Paid by Second-Tier Foreign Corporations

Section A—Dividends Paid Out of Post-1986 Undistributed Earnings (Include the column 10 results in Section A, column 6(b), of Part I above.)

1. Name of Third-Tier Foreign Corporation and Its Related Second-Tier Foreign Corporation	2. Tax Year End (Yr-Mo) (see instructions)	3. Country of Incorporation (enter country code from instructions)	4. Post-1986 Undistributed Earnings (in functional currency—attach schedule)	5. Opening Balance in Post-1986 Foreign Income Taxes	6. Foreign Taxes Paid and Deemed Paid for Tax Year Indicated		7. Post-1986 Foreign Income Taxes (add columns 5, 6(a), and 6(b))	8. Dividends Paid (in functional currency)		9. Divide Column 8(a) by Column 4	10. Tax Deemed Paid (multiply column 7 by column 9)
					(a) Taxes Paid	(b) Taxes Deemed Paid (from Schedule E, Part I, column 10)		(a) of Third-tier Corporation	(b) of Second-tier Corporation		

Section B—Dividends Paid Out of Pre-1987 Accumulated Profits (Include the column 8(b) results in Section A, column 6(b), of Part I above.)

1. Name of Third-Tier Foreign Corporation and Its Related Second-Tier Foreign Corporation	2. Tax Year End (Yr-Mo) (see instructions)	3. Country of Incorporation (enter country code from instructions)	4. Accumulated Profits for Tax Year Indicated (in functional currency—attach schedule)	5. Foreign Taxes Paid and Deemed Paid for Tax Year Indicated (in functional currency—see instructions)	6. Dividends Paid (in functional currency)		7. Divide Column 6(a) by Column 4	8. Tax Deemed Paid (see instructions)	
					(a) of Third-tier Corporation	(b) of Second-tier Corporation		(a) In Functional Currency of Third-tier Corporation	(b) U.S. Dollars

Form **1118** (Rev. 12-2009)

Schedule E — Tax Deemed Paid by Certain Third-, Fourth-, and Fifth-Tier Foreign Corporations Under Section 902(b)

Use this schedule to report taxes deemed paid with respect to dividends deemed paid from eligible post-1986 undistributed earnings of fourth-, fifth- and sixth-tier controlled foreign corporations. **Report all amounts in U.S. dollars unless otherwise specified.**

Part I—Tax Deemed Paid by Third-Tier Foreign Corporations (Include the column 10 results in Schedule D, Part II, Section A, column 6(b).)

1. Name of Fourth-Tier Foreign Corporation and Its Related Third-Tier Foreign Corporation	2. Tax Year End (Yr-Mo) (see Instructions)	3. Country of Incorporation (enter country code from instructions)	4. Post-1986 Undistributed Earnings (in functional currency—attach schedule)	5. Opening Balance in Post-1986 Foreign Income Taxes	6. Foreign Taxes Paid and Deemed Paid for Tax Year Indicated		7. Post-1986 Foreign Income Taxes (add columns 5, 6(a), and 6(b))	8. Dividends Paid (in functional currency)		9. Divide Column 8(a) by Column 4	10. Tax Deemed Paid (multiply column 7 by column 9)
					(a) Taxes Paid	(b) Taxes Deemed Paid (from Part II, column 10)		(a) Of Fourth-tier CFC	(b) Of Third-tier CFC		

Part II—Tax Deemed Paid by Fourth-Tier Foreign Corporations (Include the column 10 results in column 6(b) of Part I above.)

1. Name of Fifth-Tier Foreign Corporation and Its Related Fourth-Tier Foreign Corporation	2. Tax Year End (Yr-Mo) (see Instructions)	3. Country of Incorporation (enter country code from instructions)	4. Post-1986 Undistributed Earnings (in functional currency—attach schedule)	5. Opening Balance in Post-1986 Foreign Income Taxes	6. Foreign Taxes Paid and Deemed Paid for Tax Year Indicated		7. Post-1986 Foreign Income Taxes (add columns 5, 6(a), and 6(b))	8. Dividends Paid (in functional currency)		9. Divide Column 8(a) by Column 4	10. Tax Deemed Paid (multiply column 7 by column 9)
					(a) Taxes Paid	(b) Taxes Deemed Paid (from Part III, column 10)		(a) Of Fifth-tier CFC	(b) Of Fourth-tier CFC		

Part III—Tax Deemed Paid by Fifth-Tier Foreign Corporations (Include the column 10 results in column 6(b) of Part II above.)

1. Name of Sixth-Tier Foreign Corporation and Its Related Fifth-Tier Foreign Corporation	2. Tax Year End (Yr-Mo) (see Instructions)	3. Country of Incorporation (enter country code from instructions)	4. Post-1986 Undistributed Earnings (in functional currency—attach schedule)	5. Opening Balance in Post-1986 Foreign Income Taxes	6. Foreign Taxes Paid For Tax Year Indicated	7. Post-1986 Foreign Income Taxes (add columns 5 and 6)	8. Dividends Paid (in functional currency)		9. Divide Column 8(a) by Column 4	10. Tax Deemed Paid (multiply column 7 by column 9)
							(a) Of Sixth-tier CFC	(b) Of Fifth-tier CFC		

Form 1118 (Rev. 12-2009)

Page **6**

Schedule F — Gross Income and Definitely Allocable Deductions for Foreign Branches

1. Foreign Country or U.S. Possession (Enter two-letter code from Schedule A, column 1. Use a separate line for each.)	2. Gross Income	3. Definitely Allocable Deductions
A		
B		
C		
D		
E		
F		

Totals (add lines A through F)* ▶

*Note: The Schedule F totals are not carried over to any other Form 1118 Schedule. (These totals were already included in Schedule A.) However, the IRS requires the corporation to complete Schedule F under the authority of section 905(b).

Schedule G — Reductions of Taxes Paid, Accrued, or Deemed Paid

A	Reduction of Taxes Under Section 901(e)—Attach separate schedule
B	Reduction of Foreign Oil and Gas Taxes—Enter amount from Schedule I, Part II, line 6
C	Reduction of Taxes Due to International Boycott Provisions—Enter appropriate portion of Schedule C (Form 5713), line 2b. **Important:** Enter only "specifically attributable taxes" here.
D	Reduction of Taxes for Section 6038(c) Penalty—Attach separate schedule
E	Other Reductions of Taxes—Attach schedule(s)

Total (add lines A through E). Enter here and on Schedule B, Part II, line 3 . . . . ▶

Form **1118** (Rev. 12-2009)

Schedule H — Apportionment of Deductions Not Definitely Allocable (complete only once)

Part I—Research and Development Deductions

	(a) Sales Method					(b) Gross Income Method—Check method used: ☐ Option 1 ☐ Option 2 (See instructions.)		(c) Total R&D Deductions Not Definitely Allocable (enter all amounts from column (a)(v) or all amounts from column (b)(vii))
	Product line #1 (SIC Code: ___)*		Product line #2 (SIC Code: ___)*		(v) Total R&D Deductions Under Sales Method (add columns (ii) and (iv))	(vi) Gross Income	(vii) Total R&D Deductions Under Gross Income Method	
	(i) Gross Sales	(ii) R&D Deductions	(iii) Gross Sales	(iv) R&D Deductions				
1 Totals (see instructions)								
2 Total to be apportioned								
3 Apportionment among statutory groupings:								
a General category income								
b Passive category income								
c Section 901(j) income*								
d Income re-sourced by treaty*								
4 Total foreign (add lines 3a through 3d)								

* Important: See *Computer-Generated Schedule H in instructions.*

Form **1118** (Rev. 12-2009)

Schedule H   Apportionment of Deductions Not Definitely Allocable (continued)

Part II—Interest Deductions, All Other Deductions, and Total Deductions

(a) Average Value of Assets—Check method used:
- ☐ Fair market value
- ☑ Tax book value
- ☐ Alternative tax book value

	(a) Average Value of Assets		(b) Interest Deductions		(c) All Other Deductions Not Definitely Allocable	(d) Totals (add the corresponding amounts from column (c), Part I; columns (b)(iii) and (b)(iv), Part II; and column (c), Part II). Enter each amount from lines 3a through 3d below in column 10 of the corresponding Schedule A.
	(i) Nonfinancial Corporations	(ii) Financial Corporations	(iii) Nonfinancial Corporations	(iv) Financial Corporations		
1a Totals (see instructions)	22,879,832	3,506,341	13,085,978	533,611	1,263,957	
b Amounts specifically allocable under Temp. Regs. 1.861-10T(e)						
c Other specific allocations under Temp. Regs. 1.861-10T						
d Assets excluded from apportionment formula	3,117,240					
2 Total to be apportioned (subtract the sum of lines 1b, 1c, and 1d from line 1a)	19,762,592	3,506,341	13,085,978	533,611		
3 Apportionment among statutory groupings:						
a General category income	17,164,062		3,066,892		1,257,416	4,324,308
b Passive category income	8,406,735		1,502,124		6,541	1,508,665
c Section 901(j) income*						
d Income re-sourced by treaty*						
4 Total foreign (add lines 3a through 3d)	25,570,797	None	4,569,016	None	1,263,957	5,832,973

*Important: See **Computer-Generated Schedule H** in instructions.

Form **1118** (Rev. 12-2009)

Sample Form 4-8

Schedule J (Form 1118) (Rev. January 2009) Department of the Treasury Internal Revenue Service	Adjustments to Separate Limitation Income (Loss) Categories for Determining Numerators of Limitation Fractions, Year-End Recharacterization Balances, and Overall Foreign and Domestic Loss Account Balances For calendar year 20 __10__ , or other tax year beginning _____ , 20 _____ , and ending _____ , 20 _____ ▶ Attach to Form 1118. For Paperwork Reduction Act Notice, see the Instructions for Form 1118.	OMB No. 1545-0122

Name of corporation	Employer identification number
Cramden Corporation and Consolidated Subsidiaries	XX-XXXXX

Part I   Adjustments to Separate Limitation Income or (Losses) in Determining Numerators of Limitation Fractions (see instructions)

		(i) General category income	(ii) Passive category income	(iii) Other income*	(iv) U.S. income
1	Income or (loss) before adjustments	44,239,706	1,983,476		
2	Allocation of separate limitation losses:				
a	General category income		( )	( )	
b	Passive category income	( )		( )	
c	Other income*	( )	( )		
3	Subtotal— Combine lines 1 through 2c.				
4	Allocation of overall foreign losses				( )
5	Allocation of domestic losses	( )	( )	( )	
6	Subtotal— Combine lines 3 through 5.				
7	Recapture of overall foreign losses	( )	( )	( )	
8	Subtotal— Combine lines 6 and 7.				
9	Recharacterization of separate limitation income:				
a	General category income	( )			
b	Passive category income		( )		
c	Other income*			( )	
10	Recapture of overall domestic losses				( )
11	Numerator of Limitation Fraction— Combine lines 8 through 10. Enter each result here and on Schedule B, Part II, line 7, of corresponding Form 1118.				

Part II   Year-End Balances of Future Separate Limitation Income That Must Be Recharacterized (section 904(f)(5)(C))

a	General category income				
b	Passive category income				
c	Other income*				

Part III   Overall Foreign Loss Account Balances (section 904(f)(1))
Complete for each separate limitation income category.

1	Beginning balance				
2	Current year additions				
3	Current year reductions (other than recapture)	( )	( )	( )	
4	Current year recapture (from Part I, line 7)	( )	( )	( )	
5	Ending balance—Combine lines 1 through 4.				

Part IV   Overall Domestic Loss Account Balances (section 904(g)(1))

1	Beginning balance				
2	Current year additions				
3	Current year reductions (other than recapture)	( )	( )	( )	
4	Subtotal—Combine lines 1 through 3.				
5	Current year recapture (from Part I, line 10)				
6	Ending balance—Subtract line 5 from line 4.				

* Important: See Computer-Generated Schedule J in instructions.   Cat. No. 10309U   Schedule J (Form 1118) (Rev. 1-2009)

Sample Form 4-9

FORM 1118   **Master Schedule**
Foreign Tax Credit -- Corporations

This Schedule comprises the summary of all foreign tax credits and duplicates or replaces the information in Schedule B, Part III.

Name: Cramden Corp.	Employer I.D. Number: XX-XXXXXXX

1. Credit with respect to passive income.	604,434
2. Credit with respect to high withholding tax interest.	
3. Credit with respect to financial services income.	184,888
4. Credit with respect to shipping income.	
5. Credit with respect to dividends from each non-controlled corporation (Sec. 902).	
6. Credit with respect to dividends from a DISC or a former DISC.	
7. Credit with respect to taxable income attributable to foreign trade income.	
8. Credit with respect to certain distributions from a FSC or a former DISC.	
9. Credit withrespect to all other income from sources outside the United States.	3,771,956
10. Total of 1 through 9.	4,561,278
11. Reduction in credit for international boycott operations. (See specific instructions.)	
12. Total foreign tax credit (subtract line 11 from line 10). Enter here and on Form 1120, Schedule J, line 4a.	4,561,278

Sample Form 4-10

Reduction of Foreign Oil and Gas Taxes

SCHEDULE I (Form 1118)
(Rev. December 2010)
Department of the Treasury
Internal Revenue Service

OMB No. 1545-0122

▶ Attach to Form 1118.

For calendar year 20 10 , or other tax year beginning , 20 , and ending , 20

Name of corporation

Employer identification number
xx-XXXXXXXX

Engle Extractions

Use a separate Schedule I (Form 1118) for each applicable category of income listed below. Check only one box on each schedule.

☐ Passive Category Income   ☐ Section 901(j) Income: Name of Sanctioned Country ▶
☑ General Category Income   ☐ Income Re-sourced by Treaty: Name of Country ▶

Report all amounts in U.S. dollars.

Part I   **Combined Foreign Oil and Gas Income and Taxes**

Gross Foreign Oil and Gas Income From Sources Outside the United States and its Possessions (see instructions)

1. Name of foreign country (Use a separate line for each country.)	2. Gross foreign oil and gas extraction income	3. Gross foreign oil related income	4. Certain dividends from foreign corporations	5. Constructive distributions under section 951(a)	6. Other	7. Total (add columns 2 through 6)
A Bodfish	4,250,000					4,250,000
B						
C						
D						
E						
F						
Totals (add lines A through F)	4,250,000					4,250,000

Deductions

	8. Definitely allocable deductions	9. Ratable part of deductions not definitely allocable	10. Total (add columns 8 and 9)	11. Taxable income (column 7 minus column 10)
A	875,000		875,000	3,375,000
B				
C				
D				
E				
F				
Totals	875,000		875,000	3,375,000

Foreign Oil and Gas Taxes (attach schedule)

	12. Paid or accrued	13. Deemed paid	14. Total (add columns 12 and 13)
A	2,000,000		2,000,000
B			
C			
D			
E			
F			
Totals	2,000,000		2,000,000

For Paperwork Reduction Act Notice, see the Instructions for Form 1118.   Cat. No. 10237L   **Schedule I (Form 1118) (Rev. 12-2010)**

Part II	**Reduction Under Section 907(a)**	
1	Combined foreign oil and gas income. (See the instructions for line 1 below.)	3,375,000
2	Multiply line 1 by the highest rate of tax under section 11(b). (See the instructions for line 2 below.)	1,181,250
3	Total taxes (from Part I, column 14, "Totals" line)	2,000,000
4	Carryover or carryback of disallowed credits. (See section 907(f)—attach schedule.)	
5	Total taxes before reduction (add line 3 and line 4)	2,000,000
6	Reduction (subtract line 2 from line 5; if zero or less, enter -0-). Enter here and on Schedule G, line B of the corresponding Form 1118	818,750

General Instructions

Section references are to the Internal Revenue Code unless otherwise noted.

Who Must File

If the corporation claims a credit for any income taxes paid, accrued, or deemed paid during the tax year on combined foreign oil and gas income, the amount of such taxes eligible for credit may be reduced. See section 907(a) and Regulations section 1.907(a)-1 for details.

Method of Reporting

Report all amounts in U.S. dollars. If it is necessary to convert from foreign currency, attach a statement explaining how the rate was determined.

Specific Instructions

Part I

See section 907(c) and underlying regulations for rules on the income to include in Part I.

Note. Do not include any dividend or interest income that is passive income. See the Instructions for Form 1118 for the definition of passive income.

Column 2. Enter gross income from sources outside the United States and its possessions from the following:

• The extraction (by the corporation or any other person) of minerals from oil or gas wells located outside the United States and its possessions.

• The sale or exchange of assets used in the trade or business of extracting minerals from oil or gas wells located outside the United States and its possessions.

See section 907(c)(1).

Column 3. Enter gross income from sources outside the United States and its possessions from the following:

• The processing of minerals extracted (by the corporation or any other person) from oil or gas wells (located outside the United States and its possessions) into their primary products.

• The transportation of such minerals or primary products.

• The distribution or sale of such minerals or primary products.

• The disposition of assets used in the trade or business described in the three previous bulleted items.

• The performance of any other related service.

See section 907(c)(2).

Column 4. Enter dividends (including section 78 gross-up) from a foreign corporation on which taxes are deemed paid under section 902 only if the dividends are paid out of foreign oil and gas extraction income or foreign oil related income of the distributing corporation and are not passive income. Dividends from foreign corporations for which the corporation is not entitled to compute a deemed paid credit are passive income and are not included in Part I.

Column 5. Enter amounts taxable under section 951(a) (including section 78 gross-up) that are attributable to the controlled foreign corporation's combined foreign oil and gas income.

Column 6. Include the corporation's distributive share of partnership combined foreign oil and gas income. Also include in column 6 interest income paid by a foreign corporation on which taxes are deemed paid under section 902, to the extent it is paid out of foreign oil related income. However, do not include interest income paid by a foreign subsidiary out of foreign oil and gas extraction income of the payor, even if it is not passive income.

See section 907(c)(3).

Column 11. For each country, subtract column 10 from column 7 and enter the result in column 11. When totaling the column 11 amounts, note that a taxable loss from a foreign country offsets taxable income from other countries.

Columns 12 and 13. Attach a schedule to show how the foreign taxes paid, accrued, or deemed paid with respect to combined foreign oil and gas income were figured.

Part II

Line 1. Enter the total from Part I, column 11, minus any recapture described in section 907(c)(4).

Line 2. At the time this schedule went to print, the highest rate of tax specified under section 11(b) was 35%.

Chapter 5

Initiation of Foreign Operations

Blocked Income

In general, income that is not received or does not come within the control of a U.S. business is not taxed by the United States. Income is not taxable income unless and until the income is actually or constructively received.

Example 5-1

Babbitt Bros. sells goods to a buyer in the Republic of Milpitas in return for a 120-day note. If the note is not negotiable or cannot be sold or pledged (pursuant to its terms or prevailing market conditions) to a third-party, Babbitt Bros. will recognize income only when or if the note is actually paid. However, if Babbitt receives as payment a stack of freely exchangeable or otherwise negotiable Milpitas Bluebacks, Babbitt will realize income in the amount of the current fair market value of the Milpitas Bluebacks, even if Babbitt can neither convert the Bluebacks nor transfer the Bluebacks out of Milpitas.

Treatment of Blocked Income

All foreign income, blocked or otherwise, is presumed realized and recognized, unless considered "deferrable income." Deferrable income is income received by, credited to the account of or accrued to a business which, owing to monetary exchange or other restrictions imposed by a foreign country, is not readily convertible into United States dollars or into other money or property which is readily convertible into United States dollars.

Release of Funds

Income ceases to be deferrable (1) when the currency becomes readily convertible; (2) when the U.S. business, notwithstanding the foreign restrictions, manages to convert the funds; or (3) when the U.S. business uses the funds for nondeductible personal expenses or disposes of the funds by gift, dividend, or other type of distribution. When only part of the blocked funds is released, the U.S. business recognizes that amount as income.

Accounting for Expenses

Expenses allocable to blocked income are not deductible until the blocked income is recognized. These expenses may be incurred either abroad or in the United States. As blocked income is recognized, allocable expenses may be deducted.

Method of Reporting

Once deferral has been elected, a business may not report its blocked income without the consent of the IRS. This consent should be requested on Form 3115, Application to Change Accounting Method.

Taxation in Foreign Countries

General Rules

Under most circumstances, a U.S. business must pay U.S. tax on all income from export sales regardless of the source, timing, or nature of that income. In addition, a U.S. business may be liable for income tax in one or more foreign countries.

The Distributorship Risk

U.S. businesses may be subject to taxation in foreign countries solely from sales activities. This is known as the distributorship risk.

Example 5-2

The law in the Commonwealth of Covina provides that sales of goods are subject to Covina income tax if the seller engages in sales activities in Covina with regularity, continuity and frequency or if the seller maintains a place of business in Covina.

On January 10, Handy Industries, a U.S. business, begins shipping electronic keyboards to customers in Covina. The sale is arranged by fax communication; the buyer has no representative in the United States and Handy Industries has no representative or office in Covina. Under the terms of the sale contract, title to the keyboards passes on receipt. Buyers pay by bank transfer in U.S. dollars within fifteen days of receipt. On the basis of these facts, it is unlikely that Handy Industries will be liable for income tax in Covina.

On April 10, Handy Industries begins shipping its keyboards to three distributors in Covina, X, Y, and Z. Each distributor takes title to the keyboards and pays Handy Industries on 120-day terms. On the basis of these facts, it is still unlikely that Handy Industries will be liable for income tax in Covina.

On July 10, Handy Industries contracts with X to provide after-sale service for the keyboards. In order to fulfill its obligation, Handy sends U.S. technicians on three-month tours of duty to Covina. After one year, increased sales, combined with frequent breakdowns of the keyboards, result in the presence of three technicians in Covina at any given time.

On July 11, Y agrees to carry Handy Industries' keyboards exclusively. In return, Y is granted certain discounts and shipping and manufacturing priorities.

On July 12, Z and Handy Industries agree that Z will not pay Handy Industries for each keyboard shipped but that Handy will be compensated by receiving 50 percent of the gross profit on each sale by Z.

> Each of the arrangements in this example brings Handy Industries closer to the status of being taxed on its keyboard income. As to X, Covina might find, as a matter of fact, that the service activity is a major component of the sales effort and that the technicians are maintaining an office of Handy Industries on the premises of X.
>
> As to Y, Covina might find that Y has become a dependent agent of Handy Industries, so that all its activities are imputed to Handy Industries.
>
> As to Z, while the receipt of a profit share would not ordinarily make Handy Industries taxable, Covina might find that Handy Industries has agreed to share in the losses as well, thus creating a partnership arrangement between Handy Industries and Covina.

Protective Measures

Example 5-2 illustrates the difficulty of resolving these issues clearly. This is frequently the case where there are no specific rules on foreign country tax liability. U.S. businesses should consider implementing protective measures. As to the contract with X in Example 5-2, Handy Industries could set up a service corporation, either in the United States or in Covina, to hire the technicians (either as employees or as consultants). This corporation would provide the services on the keyboards in return for a fee from Handy Industries. In this way, only the service corporation, not Handy Industries, would be exposed to Covina tax.

As to Y, the contract should ensure that neither party has the power to affect business decisions of the other and that the mutual obligations are of reasonably equal value.

As to Z, the contract should ensure that (1) Handy Industries' only right is a percentage of profit, if any; (2) there is no common management of business activity; (3) Handy Industries has no interest in the assets of Z nor is there an intention by the parties to form a partnership or other joint venture; and (4) Handy Industries has no liability to share in the losses of Z.

Treaties and Export Income

Tax treaties, like other international agreements, create or amend laws of the United States and laws of a foreign jurisdiction. Presently, the United States is party to approximately fifty-four tax treaties. Of that number, those treaties in effect as of this writing include the countries listed below.

Australia	India	Poland
Austria	Indonesia	Portugal
Barbados	Ireland	Republic of Korea
Belgium	Israel	Romania
Canada	Italy	Russian Federation

China	Jamaica	Slovak Republic
Commonwealth of Independent States and Georgia (formerly Union of Soviet Socialist Republics)	Japan	Slovenia
Cyprus	Kazakhstan	South Africa
Czech Republic	Latvia	Spain
Denmark	Lithuania	Sweden
Egypt	Luxembourg	Switzerland
Estonia	Mexico	Thailand
Finland	Morocco	Trinidad and Tobago
France	Netherlands	Tunisia
Germany	New Zealand	Turkey
Greece	Norway	Ukraine
Hungary	Pakistan	United Kingdom
Iceland	Philippines	Venezuela

The principal purpose of tax treaties is to prevent transactions from being taxed by more than one jurisdiction. This purpose is accomplished through a number of methods, including the following:

- Forbearance from tax by one of the treaty parties.

- Allowance of a tax credit by one of the treaty parties.

- Reduction in rate of tax by a treaty party.

Because there are inconsistencies between countries in determining taxable income, tax treaties are often used to establish (1) consistent definitions of "permanent establishment;" (2) consistent treatment of personal service income; and (3) consistent rules on industrial and commercial profits. Tax treaties often deal with the issue of allocation and apportionment of expenses to the income of a permanent establishment. Also, under Competent Authority provisions, tax treaties provide a mechanism for treaty parties to resolve problems resulting from inconsistent tax treatment. Other purposes of tax treaties include providing procedures for reporting and withholding and permitting the exchange of information between treaty parties, which enables treaty parties to assist each other in enforcing their respective tax laws and provides taxpayers with a means of resolving conflicts resulting from inconsistent taxation of the same transaction.

Taxes Covered

U.S. tax treaties address the federal income tax. The foreign taxes covered in the treaties are income taxes, but some treaties with certain countries cover other taxes as well. Tax treaties can also cover taxes that are not yet in existence. An automatic extension clause is included in most of the newer treaties, providing that if the existing income tax in a country is replaced by a different statute that performs much the same function, it will automatically be covered by the existing treaty provisions.

In general, the beneficiaries of tax treaties are the individuals and businesses considered resident in one of the countries. In addition, the United States always reserves the right in treaties to tax its citizens and corporations on worldwide income, although it may also stipulate treating a certain foreign tax as a creditable tax. Definitions of what constitutes a "resident" for purposes of a tax treaty are provided in the treaty itself. More precise determinations of this issue must be made under the laws of the treaty parties.

Jurisdictions Covered

The territory covered by the treaty is specified first in the language of the treaty itself and then under the provisions of local law of each treaty party. In some cases, colonies of existing states have, when achieving independent status, agreed to continue the rights and obligations of certain existing treaties made by the former government. In some cases, these new nations conclude mini-treaties, called protocols, which often succeed in preserving some but not all of the provisions of a master treaty.

Treaties and the Internal Revenue Code

In general, treaties and federal statutes have equal status under law, with the later-in-time rule prevailing in cases of conflicts. The U.S. Supreme Court, however, has also held that the history of both the statute and the treaty should be considered to determine whether the drafters intended to override the existing law.

Claiming That a Treaty Provision Overrides the Code

If there is a conflict, a U.S. business may claim the benefit of the conflicting treaty on its tax return, subject to one requirement: the taxpayer must describe in detail the treaty rule and the U.S. law to be overridden on its return. A corporation making a claim for a treaty benefit that does not provide the required disclosure will be fined $10,000.

Treatment of Export Income

BUSINESS PROFITS

For a U.S. business engaged solely in direct exports, the key treaty provisions are those that relate to permanent establishment and business profits (also called industrial and commercial profits). According to the model treaties of both the United States and the Organization for Economic Cooperation and Development (OECD), a resident in one country will not be taxed on its business income in the other country unless it maintains a permanent establishment in the other state and the income is attributable to that permanent establishment.

PERMANENT ESTABLISHMENT

"Permanent establishment" is a venerable term and is described variously as a "factory, office or other fixed place of business" and "a fixed place of business in which the business of the enterprise is wholly or partially carried on."

The OECD model treaty specifically excludes the following from the definition of "permanent establishment:"

- The use of facilities solely for the purpose of storage, display, or delivery of goods or merchandise belonging to the enterprise.

- The maintenance of goods solely for display, storage, or delivery.

- The maintenance of a stock of goods solely for the purpose of processing by another enterprise.

- The maintenance of a fixed place of business solely to purchase goods or to collect information for the enterprise.

- The maintenance of a fixed place of business solely for advertising, supply of information, scientific research, or similar activities.

U.S. Competent Authority Aid

The tax treaty Competent Authority provision creates a mechanism for countries to resolve problems resulting from inconsistent tax treatment of income or expenses or both between the treaty signatories. Unless a tax treaty permits otherwise, only U.S. persons can request U.S. competent authority assistance. The request can be filed at any time following an action giving rise to a claim for competent authority. Taxpayers have discretion over the time for filing a request for competent authority assistance but delays may preclude effective relief (Rev. Proc. 2002-52).

If the situation involves a U.S.-initiated adjustment of tax or income resulting from a tax examination, the request can be submitted after the amount of the proposed adjustment is put in writing to the taxpayer. If the request is not put in writing, the U.S. competent authority will generally deny the request as premature. When a foreign examination is involved, the request may be submitted when the business believes the filing is needed based on actions of the country proposing the adjustment. When there is a reallocation of income or deductions between related entities, the request should be filed when the business can establish probability of double taxation. If the situation does not involve an examination, the request can be made when the business believes competent authority is warranted.

Payments to Foreign Officials

In order to export goods to certain countries, it is sometimes desirable, even necessary, to make payments to government officials that would be illegal if made in the United States. The general rule under Internal Revenue Code Section 162 is that illegal payments are not deductible as business expenses. However, in the case of payments to foreign officials, the rule in the Foreign

Corrupt Practices Act is substituted. This latter rule distinguishes outright bribes from two categories of payment that are deductible:

1. Payments made to foreign officials to encourage compliance or to expedite the processing of nondiscretionary "routine administrative actions." These are sometimes referred to as "grease."

2. Payments made to foreign officials for any purpose that is lawful in the foreign jurisdiction even though it might be illegal under U.S. law.

Example 5-3

Porter Manufacturing, Inc. sells paper for photocopy machines to three island countries that were formerly part of the Dutch East Indies: Jacumba, Ramona and Azusa. In Jacumba, Porter's agents regularly pay off customs agents to ensure that their paper will pass through customs within a reasonable period of time. In Ramona, Porter's agents make payments to government purchasing officials to guarantee that Ramona buys Porter paper instead of the paper made by Schubert A.G. In Azusa, Porter's agents pay a percentage commission to government officials to take care of all customs, transshipment, and regulatory responsibilities. These officials receive only a nominal salary in Azusa, and they are entitled and expected to earn their principal compensation in this manner.

Based on these facts, under Internal Revenue Code Section 162 and the Foreign Corrupt Practices Act, the payments to Azusa may be deductible, and the payments to Ramona and Jacumba would not be deductible.

Export Incentives

Since 1942, Congress has enacted various legislative regimes creating special companies to export goods and services from the United States. Different legislative regimes have been created and replaced in response to changes in U.S. policy on exports and foreign investment and, more recently, to comply with U.S. obligations under the General Agreement on Trades and Tariffs (GATT).

The most recent incentive, an exclusion for certain "extraterritorial income" realized in transactions after September 30, 2000, is considered to violate the GATT by a panel of the Dispute Resolution Body of the World Trade Organization (WTO). The United States has appealed the WTO decision and could resolve the issue in trade discussions with WTO member countries. Congress may rewrite the extraterritorial income exclusion legislation in a manner that satisfies the WTO and WTO member countries or the issue could go to arbitration if the U.S. appeal fails. Prior to the appeal, WTO member countries asserted that they would impose $4 billion of trade sanctions against U.S. products if the United States fails to revise the extraterritorial income exclusion to comply with the WTO decision.

To understand the extraterritorial exclusion, why the incentive is considered to violate the GATT and the likely resolution of this dispute, it is helpful to briefly review the history of U.S. export incentives.

Western Hemisphere Trade Corporations

Congress created the Western Hemisphere Trade Corporation (WHTC) in 1942 to spur direct U.S. investment throughout the Western Hemisphere. WHTCs were taxed at a marginal rate that was 14 percentage points less than the normal corporate tax rate but the incentive did not increase direct U.S. investment in the Western Hemisphere as most WHTCs were export arms of U.S. manufacturers. Congress ended the WHTC incentive in 1980.

Domestic International Sales Corporations

Congress enacted the domestic international sales corporation (DISC) provisions in 1971 to more directly stimulate export of goods manufactured in the United States and to encourage exporting through U.S. rather than foreign affiliates. The DISC was tax-exempt and, to maintain this status, usually had to limit its activities to exporting goods produced by U.S. manufacturers.

A portion of DISC income was taxed immediately to the DISC's shareholders, whether or not distributed. U.S. tax on the remainder was deferred until distribution as a dividend. The tax-deferred earnings could be loaned to the producer of the goods by the DISC (usually its parent corporation) or invested in other assets related to the producer's export activities indefinitely.

The DISC incentive caused complaints from other countries that the DISC subsidized U.S. exports, in violation of the GATT. A GATT panel of experts and a majority of the members of the GATT council argued that the DISC incentive was an export subsidy because the DISC incentive allowed an indefinite deferral of tax on income from activities located in the United States and no interest was charged on the deferred tax. The European community requested authority from the GATT council to take retaliatory action. Fearing a breakdown in the GATT dispute settlement process, the U.S. treasury proposed legislation to replace the DISC incentive with a new company, the Foreign Sales Corporation (FSC) in 1984.

Foreign Sales Corporation

A FSC is a foreign company, typically a subsidiary of a U.S. corporation, that elects to be taxed as a FSC. A portion of a FSC's income from exporting goods produced in the United States is exempt from U.S. taxation, even if effectively connected with a trade or business carried on by the FSC in the United States. A U.S. company owning stock of a FSC is allowed a 100 percent dividends-received deduction for dividends paid from the FSC's foreign trade income. Accordingly, neither the FSC nor its U.S parent pay U.S. tax on the exempt portion of foreign trade income and the non-exempt portion of this income is taxed only once.

Under the GATT rules, a country need not tax income from economic processes occurring outside its territory. Congress believed that income attributable to economic activities occurring outside the United States should be exempt from U.S. tax to afford U.S. exporters comparable taxation to their competitors, typically headquartered in countries with territorial tax systems. Congress intended that the activities and economic processes related to the exempt portion of foreign trade income would be undertaken by a FSC outside the U.S. customs territory.

In February 2000, the Appellate Body of the WTO found that the FSC incentive illegally subsidized U.S. exports in violation of GATT and ordered the United States to remove this subsidy no later than October 1, 2000. Congress repealed the FSC incentive and, as a substitute, enacted an incentive that excludes "extraterritorial income" from gross income to the extent these receipts are "qualifying foreign trade income."

The Senate Finance Committee report on the legislation enacting the extraterritorial income exclusion states that the objectives of the extraterritorial income exclusion incentive are to retain a competitive balance for U.S. businesses that compete in the world market and to comply with the decisions of the WTO.

The committee's report states that the extraterritorial income exclusion incentive fundamentally amends the definition of gross income by excluding income from certain activities performed outside the United States and applying this exclusion to all foreign trade income, whether or not the goods are manufactured in the United States.

However, the actual extraterritorial income exclusion legislation favors goods produced in, and exported from, the United States. Excludable extraterritorial income can usually arise from a sale or lease only if not more than 50 percent of the value of the goods sold or leased is attributable to articles produced outside the United States and the direct cost of labor performed outside the United States. Moreover, excludable income is calculated by percentages that need not reasonably reflect income derived from activities performed outside the United States. Although a company can benefit from the extraterritorial income exclusion without directly involving itself in exporting, the company can usually only benefit from the extraterritorial income exclusion if the company deals with goods that have been exported from the United States.

Foreign Trade Income

The extraterritorial income exclusion excludes "qualifying foreign trade income," which reduces taxable income by either

- 30 percent of "foreign sale and leasing income,"

- 1.2 percent of "foreign trading gross receipts," or

- 15 percent of "foreign trade income" from the transaction, but in no event more than 30 percent of foreign trade income.

Foreign trade income is taxable income attributable to "foreign trading gross receipts," and foreign trading gross receipts derive from transactions in "qualifying foreign trade property."

Qualifying Foreign Trade Property

Qualifying foreign trade property is property held primarily for sale, lease, or rental for use outside the United States if not more than 50 percent of the property's value is attributable to articles sourced outside the United States, direct costs for labor performed outside the United States and if the manufacturer or producer is a U.S. corporation, citizen or resident, a foreign corporation electing to be taxed as a U.S. corporation or a partnership or pass-through entity, whose owners are in one of these categories.

Puerto Rico is considered part of the United States for purposes of the extraterritorial income exclusion. Therefore articles sourced in Puerto Rico are considered to be from the United States.

Foreign Trading Gross Receipts

Foreign trading gross receipts are sales, leases, or rentals of qualifying foreign trade property, services that are related and subsidiary to sales, leases and rentals of qualifying foreign trade property, engineering and architectural services performed outside the United States and managerial services performed to further transactions yielding foreign trading gross receipts provided that the qualifying foreign trade property or services will not ultimately be used in the United States.

Foreign Economic Processes

As noted, foreign trading gross receipts do not exist unless economic processes with respect to a transaction occur outside the United States. Generally this means that (1) the taxpayer, the taxpayer's agent or a related party participate outside the United States in the solicitation (other than advertising), negotiation and making the contract for the transaction yielding the foreign trading gross receipts and (2) the taxpayer's foreign direct costs are at least 50 percent of total direct costs.

Example 5-4

If a manufacturer sells goods the manufacturer has produced to a related distributor, which resells the goods to unrelated persons in foreign countries, the manufacturer is considered to satisfy the foreign economic process test even if the manufacturer has no activities outside the United States.

Total direct costs are transaction costs attributable to

- Advertising and sales promotion.

- Order processing and delivery arrangements.

- Delivery transportation outside the United States.

- Invoicing and credit risk.

- Foreign direct costs that are costs attributable to the activities that take place outside the United States.

Alternatively, the foreign economic processes requirement is satisfied if the taxpayer's foreign direct costs are 85 percent or more of total direct costs in two or more categories of total direct costs.

Foreign Trade Income

One of the alternative calculations of the extraterritorial income exclusion is an exclusion reducing taxable income by 15 percent of foreign trade income. Also, in no event may any of the alternative exclusion calculations reduce taxable income by more than 30 percent of foreign trade income.

Foreign trade income is taxable income attributable to foreign trading gross receipts, calculated as foreign trading gross receipts, less

- Cost of goods sold in transactions generating foreign trading gross receipts.

- Direct expenses of the transactions.

- A portion of the taxpayer's overhead costs.

Overhead expenses must be apportioned between the taxpayer's foreign trading gross receipts and other revenues in a reasonable manner that does not materially distort income.

Example 5-5

Assume X Corp.'s foreign trading gross receipts are $1,000, X Corp.'s cost of goods sold in transactions yielding foreign trading gross receipts is $600, direct expenses of the foreign gross trading receipt transactions are $275 and apportioned overhead expenses are $25. X Corp.'s foreign trade income is $100 ($1,000 less the listed expenses).

Foreign Sale and Leasing Income

Another of the alternative calculations of the extraterritorial income exclusion is an exclusion reducing taxable income by 30 percent of foreign sale and leasing income. Foreign sale and leasing income is foreign trade income allocable to a foreign economic process undertaken by the taxpayer or his agent.

Foreign economic processes include advertising, sales promotion or soliciting, negotiating or making the transaction contract as well as order processing and delivery, transportation, invoicing, payment receipt and assumption of credit risk.

Foreign sale and leasing income is also foreign trade income from leasing or renting qualifying foreign trade property to a lessee using the property outside the United States as well as foreign trade income resulting from the sale of qualifying foreign trade income held for sale or lease.

Foreign sale and leasing income from the sale, rent or lease of qualifying foreign trade property produced, manufactured, grown or extracted by the taxpayer or a related party cannot exceed the amount that would have been so characterized if the taxpayer acquired the qualifying foreign trade property from a third party at market value.

If a manufacturer leases qualifying foreign trade property that the manufacturer produced or acquired from a related party, the foreign sale and leasing income derived from the lease cannot exceed the amount of foreign sale and leasing income that the manufacturer would have earned with respect to the lease if the manufacturer had purchased the property at market value the day the manufacturer entered the lease.

In calculating foreign sale and leasing income, only directly allocable expenses are included in the calculation of foreign trade income.

Example 5-6

If X Corp. has foreign trading gross receipts of $1,000 and costs allocable to these receipts consisting of $600 cost of goods sold, other direct expenses of $275 and apportioned overhead of $25, X Corp.'s foreign trade income is $100, or $1,000 less the listed costs. Foreign sale and leasing income is that portion of $100 foreign trade income that foreign economic processes bear to foreign trade income. If X Corp.'s foreign solicitation, negotiation, advertising, transportation and other foreign economic processes comprise 28 percent of foreign trade income, foreign sale and leasing income is $28 or 28 percent of $100.

Calculation of Exclusion

As noted the extraterritorial income exclusion reduces taxable income from a transaction by, alternatively, (1) 30 percent of foreign sale and leasing income; (2) 1.2 percent of foreign trading gross receipts or (3) 15 percent of foreign trade income, but in no event more than (4) 30 percent of foreign trade income. A taxpayer may choose the alternative that reduces taxable income by the greatest amount or a lesser measure. The excluded gross income is the sum of the chosen alternative plus a gross-up for related expenses that are not otherwise deductible. The extraterritorial income exclusion applies in the calculation of regular and alternative minimum tax.

Example 5-7

In 2010, X Corp. has $10,000 foreign trading gross receipts, cost of goods sold attributable to these receipts of $6,000, direct transaction expenses of $2,750, and apportioned indirect expenses of $250. X Corp.'s foreign trade income (FTI) for 2010 is $1,000 ($10,000 less the listed expenses). Alternative calculations of the extraterritorial income exclusion are shown below. Assume that foreign sales and lease income is $350.

	30% FS & LI	1.2% FTGR	15% FTI
Reduction of taxable income	$105	$120	$150
Gross-up for disallowed deductions:			
Disallowed Deductions	$2,750	$3,000	$3,000
Excluded Taxable Income	$105	$120	$150
Divided by FTI	$1,000	$1,000	$1,000
Equals Gross-Up Factor	.105	.120	.150
Times Disallowed Deductions	$289	$360	$450
Equals Qualifying FTI	$394	$480	$600

X Corp.'s qualifying foreign trade income is $600 unless X elects not to use the maximum calculated alternative.

Foreign taxes on the excluded income are not allowed as foreign tax credits.

Qualifying foreign trade income is determined transaction-by-transaction. Forthcoming treasury regulations may allow transaction grouping based on product lines or trade or industry convention. Taxpayer grouping of products that fall within more than one Standard Industrial Code will be accepted if reasonable.

Qualifying foreign trade income for any tax year is reduced by the sum of the following adjustments:

- The product of the qualifying foreign trade income multiplied by the international boycott factor, plus

- Any illegal bribe, kickback, or other payment made by or on behalf of the taxpayer directly or indirectly to an official, employee, or agent of a government.

PHASE-OUT OF EXTRATERRITORIAL INCOME EXCLUSION

The ETI rules are repealed for transactions entered after December 31, 2004, subject to a phase-out that allows 80 percent and 60 percent, respectively, benefits to be claimed in 2005 and 2006. ETI benefits are fully available for transactions undertaken pursuant to binding contracts in effect September 17, 2003.

DOMESTIC PRODUCTION DEDUCTION

Corporations, partnerships, other pass-through entities and individuals earning income from qualified domestic production activities (without regard to exporting) may deduct a percentage of income otherwise taxable in the United States. The deduction is a percentage of the lesser of qualified production activities income or taxable income as otherwise calculated for the year. The deduction is phased in beginning at 3 percent in 2005 and 2006, going to 6 percent in 2007-2009, and topping out at 9 percent thereafter. The deduction is also limited to 50 percent of W-2 wages attributable to domestic production paid by the business, which is defined as all members of an affiliated group determined with a 50 percent vote/value threshold rather an 80 percent vote/value threshold.

Qualified production activities income is domestic production gross receipts reduced by directly allocable expenses plus an appropriate share of other expenses that are not directly allocable.

Domestic production gross receipts are gross receipts resulting from sale, rental, or license of tangible personal property and any computer software or sound recording manufactured, produced, grown, or extracted in whole or in significant part in the United States, excluding any gross receipts derived from lease, sale, or rental to a related person. "Manufactured in significant part in the United States" requires that more than 50 of the aggregate development and production costs are incurred in the United States.

Domestic production gross receipts must be reduced by directly allocable costs of goods sold, other deductions, expenses and losses and a proportionate share of indirectly related deductions, losses, and expenses. Current law expense allocation and apportionment rules will apply.

Reporting Foreign Bank Accounts

U.S. businesses are subject to two general requirements. First, businesses must report each transfer, either into or from the United States, of more than $10,000 in currency to the U.S. Customs authorities. Second, all U.S. businesses, except for U.S. subsidiaries of foreign corporations, must report all foreign bank accounts with a value of more than $10,000 in which the business has a financial interest or management authority. The report on foreign bank accounts (Form TD F 90-22.1) is filed with the Treasury Department (not the IRS) by June 30 each year.

Completed forms should be sent to the following address:

U.S Department of the Treasury
P.O. Box 32621
Detroit, MI 48232-0621

You can, however, hand-deliver the form to any local IRS office, and they will forward it to the Department of Treasury for processing.

Foreign bank accounts with a value of more than $10,000 in which a business has a financial interest or management authority are disclosed on the business' annual income tax return.

> **Note:** The Treasury Department tracks interest earned in foreign accounts through Form TD F 90-22.1. It is unclear, however, whether businesses that report the existence of accounts on Schedule K of Form 1120 and the current balance on Form TD F 90-22.1 also report the interest on Line 18 of Form 1120.

Filing Requirements

Form TD F 90-22.1 is filed for any foreign account in which a U.S. person has a financial interest or signatory authority. Filing is required for an account in a foreign branch of a U.S. bank, but it is not necessary for an account with a U.S. branch of a foreign bank.

If the business is incorporated, the form should be filed for all foreign bank accounts (up to twenty-five foreign accounts can be reported on a single form). A form should be filed on behalf of the corporation as a whole by the person who usually signs the corporate tax return.

In addition, any person who has signatory authority over the foreign accounts should file the form. This latter filing need not be as detailed as the corporate filing as long as the filer has no financial interest in the account.

Example 5-8

The Sessions Group has a regular banking relationship with the Monetary and Momentary Trust Co. of Los Angeles. To effect a sale of aircraft parts in the Kingdom of Ukiah, Sessions opens an account in the bank's branch in Guadalajara, Mexico (Account A) and opens an account with the Los Angeles branch of Banco de Chavez, headquartered in Guadalajara, Mexico (Account B). Account A is used to receive the funds from the export transaction. Since all transfers are made by wire, no corporate office has individual signatory authority over Account A. Account B was opened to establish a relationship with the Mexican bank; two officers of Sessions have signatory authority.

Based on these facts, Sessions must file one Form TDF 90-22.1 for Account A, completing Items 1 through 4 and 9 through 12. No filing is required for Account B.

An individual who has signatory authority over a foreign account for which the owner already files a Form TD F 90-22.1 should file his or her own Form TD F 90-22.1, completing Items 1 through 5 and 10 through 12. An individual who has a financial interest in a foreign account for which a Form TD F 90-22.1 has already been filed should file his or her own Form TD F 90-22.1, completing Items 1 through 4, 6, and 10 through 12. This latter situation would exist in Example 5-8 if an individual had entered into a joint venture with Sessions to sell the aircraft parts.

Even if the June 30th deadline is missed, the form should be filed as soon as possible, as there are very significant penalties for willfully failing to file the form. The law provides for a penalty of up to $10,000 per violation for willfully failing to file the form.

Corporate Income Tax Return

All of a corporation's tax-related items, whether domestic or foreign, are reported on Form 1120. Foreign items are reported in much the same manner as domestic items, but there are a few differences. First, the foreign tax credit is computed on Form 1118 and entered on Form 1120, Schedule J, Line 4a. Second, deferrable income because of foreign blockage is reported on a phantom Form 1120. Third, deduction of foreign tax is entered on Form 1120, Line 17.

Filing Requirements

The filled-in Forms 1120 illustrate the reporting of blocked income and the placement of summary foreign tax credit information. (See Sample Forms 5-1 and 5-2. All sample forms are included in the Appendix to this chapter.)

Example 5-9

Assume the same facts as in Example 5-1, except that in 2010, Babbitt Bros. earns a total of $364,711,000 gross sales from the Republic of Milpitas. Of this amount, $37,846,000 is paid in Milpitas Bluebacks, one of the world's least attractive currencies. The Bluebacks are subject to Milpitas exchange controls and may not be converted into a major currency or transferred out of Milpitas. The entire amount of Babbitt's income in Milpitas is subject to Milpitas tax at 20 percent of net income. The following table illustrates Babbitt's unblocked and blocked income, deductions, and tax:

	A—Unblocked	B—Blocked	C—Total
Gross Receipts			
(Form 1120, Page 1, Line lc)	$327,225,000	$37,486,000	$364,711,000
Cost of Goods Sold			
(Form 1120, Page 1, Line 2)	156,573,000	18,564,000	175,137,000
Gross Profit			
(Form 1120, Page 1, Line 3)	170,652,000	18,922,000	189,574,000
Dividends			
(Form 1120, Page 1, Line 4)	3,038,000		3,038,000
Interest			
(Form 1120, Page 1, Line 5)	451,000	15,000	466,000
Net Gain (Loss)			
(Form 1120, Page1, Line 9)	(129,000)	358,000	229,000

Other Income			
(Form 1120, Page 1, Line 10)	310,000		310,000
Total Income			
(Form 1120, Page 1, Line 11)	174,322,000	19,295,000	193,617,000
Officers Compensation			
(Form 1120, Page 1, Line 12)	1,619,000	160,000	1,779,000
Salaries and Wages less employment credits			
(Form 1120, Page 1, Line 13a)	54,608,000	4,894,000	59,502,000
Repairs and Maintenance			
(Form 1120, Page 1, Line 14)	833,000	47,000	880,000
Bad Debts			
(Form 1120, Page 1, Line 15)	331,000	56,000	387,000
Rents			
(Form 1120, Page 1, Line 16)	34,406,000	3,976,000	38,382,000
Taxes			
(Form 1120, Page 1, Line 17)	8,165,000	312,000	8,477,000
Interest			
(Form 1120, Page 1, Line18)	7,898,000	29,000	7,927,000
Depreciation			
(Form 1120, Page 1, Line 20)	9,983,000	796,000	10,779,000
Less Other Depreciation			
(Form 1120, Page 1, Line 21a)	(984,000)		(984,000)
Advertising			
(Form 1120, Page 1, Line 23)	17,485,000	2,282,000	19,767,000
Employee Benefits			
(Form 1120, Page 1, Line 25)	2,642,000	207,000	2,849,000
Other Deductions			
(Form 1120, Page 1, Line 26)	12,815,000	4,635,000	17,450,000
Total Deductions			
(Form 1120, Page 1, Line 27)	149,801,000	17,394,000	167,195,000
Taxable Income			
(Form 1120, Page 1, Line 28)	24,521,000	1,901,000	26,422,000
Special Deductions			
(Form 1120, Page 1, Line 29b)	(2,120,000)		(2,120,000)
Net Taxable Income			
(Form 1120, Page 1, Line 30)	22,401,000	1,901,000	24,302,000
Income Tax			
(Form 1120, Page 3, Schedule J, Line 3)	7,840,000	665,000	8,505,000
Foreign Tax Credit			
(Form 1120, Page 3, Schedule J, Line 4a)	(4,479,000)	(380,000)	(4,859,000)
Net Tax			
(Form 1120, Page 3, Schedule J, Line 10)	3,361,000	285,000	3,646,000
Total Tax			
(Form 1120, Page 1, Line 31)	3,361,000	285,000	3,646,000

For 2010, Babbitt reports its unblocked income, deductions, and tax (the amounts in Column A) on Form 1120; then, it reports its blocked income, deductions, and tax (the amounts in Column B) on a separate Form 1120 that Babbitt marks as "Reporting of Blocked Income Under Revenue Ruling 74-351." For completed Forms 1120, see Sample Forms 5-1 and 5-2.

International Boycotts

Businesses that participate directly or indirectly in any international boycott by one foreign country as a condition to doing business in or with that foreign country must report the income from this participation on Form 5713.

Participation in a boycott is reported in one or more of three categories: (1) boycotts maintained against Israel by one of the countries on a list published by the Treasury Department; (2) boycotts maintained against Israel by countries not on that list; and (3) boycotts against countries other than Israel.

"Boycott" is defined generally as an agreement to refrain from

1. Doing business with or in a specific third country or countries.

2. Doing business with U.S. persons that do business with or in such third countries.

3. Doing business with companies whose management or ownership consists in part of members of any particular racial, ethnic, religious, or national groups.

4. Hiring members of any particular racial, ethnic, religious, or national groups.

5. Shipping goods on carriers owned or managed by persons not participating in such boycotts.

The statute provides exceptions for two situations: (1) where the United States sanctions participation with respect to a particular foreign country and (2) where the taxpayer exports goods to or imports goods from a country that is the victim of an international boycott. The sanction imposed is a reduction in certain benefits granted by Congress with respect to the taxation of foreign-source income.

In general, businesses calculate the ratio of their activity with the boycotting country to their total foreign activity (the "international boycott factor"). This factor is then applied to reduce the availability of certain benefits, such as the foreign tax credit.

Mechanically, the computation consists of the ratio of the total of (1) purchases made from boycotting countries; (2) sales made to boycotting countries; and (3) the cost of services performed in boycotting countries to the total of the three items for all foreign countries. The resulting factors, for each foreign boycotting country, are reported annually on Form 5713.

A business may request a determination from the Treasury Department as to whether any particular transactions constitute participation in an international boycott. Some information is given in Treasury guidelines.

Filing Requirements

Form 5713 is basically divided into four parts: the master form, Schedule A, Schedule B, and Schedule C. The master form is essentially a questionnaire on the taxpayer's foreign operations in countries that require businesses to participate in a commercial boycott of Israel or of any other country.

Schedule A is completed if a taxpayer elects to compute the amount of benefits to be foregone by an apportionment method.

Schedule B, on the other hand, is completed if the taxpayer elects to identify and to forego those tax benefits specifically attributable to activities in boycotting countries.

Schedule C is filed by shareholders of interest-charge domestic international sales corporations (IC-DISCs). It summarizes the information provided on Schedule A or Schedule B and provides, in Items 2, 3, and 4, the adjustments resulting from application of the boycott factor penalty to foreign tax credits, certain deferrals under Subpart F, and deferrals of certain IC-DISCS.

Form 5713 is filed with a taxpayer's annual income tax return and is mailed separately to the Service center in Philadelphia.

Example 5-10

Joplin Farm Machinery, Inc. exports tractors to three European Republics: Boron, Modoc, and Trona. In order to obtain its contract to sell tractors in Boron, Joplin Farm Machinery, Inc. agreed to participate in Boron's commercial boycott against Israel. Assume also that Boron is not on the Treasury Department's list as a boycotting country. Assume further that Joplin sells a total of $60 million worth of tractors to Boron, Modoc and Trona ($20 million to each country).

Based on these facts, Joplin fills out Form 5713 by entering the identification information requested at the top of the front page of the form (name, address, type of filer, and so on). Next, on Line 4a, Joplin enters the type of form filed (Form 1120) for the corporation. On Line 4c, Joplin enters its total assets, which is assumed to be $4 million. Joplin must answer questions 7a through 8. Joplin must answer Question 9 and report Boron's boycott of Israel on Line 9a, which is where nonlisted countries boycotting Israel, such as Boron, are listed. Then, Joplin answers Questions 10, 11, and 12, all of which are "Yes." In addition, Joplin must answer Questions 13a(1)(i) through 13a(1)(iv), and 13a(2) in Part II, all of which are "No."

Because the answers to Questions 11 and 12 are "Yes," Joplin must fill out Schedules A and C, which are reproduced. Joplin does not fill out Schedule B because it is not computing a loss of tax benefits using the specifically attributable taxes and income method.

Schedule A is dedicated to calculating the international boycott factor. The schedule is very straightforward. Basically, Joplin enters its name at the top and checks the appropriate box for the name of the country being boycotted (Israel). Next, Joplin enters the name of the boycotting country (Boron) in Column 1. In Column 3, Joplin lists the sales of tractors to Boron ($20,000,000), which is totaled at the base of that column and then entered on Line I below it. Now, Joplin enters the total sales to Boron, Modoc and Trona ($60,000,000) on Line 2b, which is totaled on Line 2d. On Line 3, Joplin computes the international boycott factor by dividing Line I by Line 2d ($20,000,000/$60,000,000 = .33). Thus, Joplin's foreign tax credit that is otherwise available will be reduced by one-third (which represents the ratio of the Boron-source income to all foreign-source income). The international boycott factor is also entered on Line 2a(2) of Schedule C.

Schedule C is completed to determine the tax effect of the international boycott on the foreign tax credit. Again, Joplin enters its name at the top and checks the box for 1a because it is using the international boycott factor from Schedule A as the method of computing its loss of tax benefits for doing business in Boron. The figure on Line 2a(1) is the assumed foreign tax credit before adjustment ($933,000). Since Joplin has already entered the international boycott factor on Line 2a(2), Joplin now multiplies 2a(1) by 2a(2) ($933,000 × .33 = $307,890), and the result, which represents the reduction of Joplin's foreign tax credit, is entered on Line 2a(3). Now, Line 2a(3) is subtracted from Line 2a(1) ($933,000 – $307,890 = $625,110), and the result, which represents Joplin's adjusted foreign tax credit, is entered on Line 2a(4). Joplin does not fill out the rest of Schedule C, basically because it answered "No" to Questions 7b, 7c and 7i on Form 5713. For a filled-in Form 5713, see Sample Form 5-3. For Schedules A through C, see Sample Forms 5-4, 5-5 and 5-6, respectively.

International Transportation of Currency

The vast majority of transfers of money and securities in and out of the United States occur through the U.S. banking system and are reported by financial institutions. In cases where cash or securities in bearer form are transferred, both the transferor and the transferee are required, if U.S. persons, to report the act of transfer (either in or out) on FinCen Form 105 to the U.S. Customs Service.

Filing Requirements

FinCen Form 105 must be filed for each transfer or for groups of transfers. It need not be filed for any transfer by wire, interbank deposit, or other transaction that does not involve the physical transfer of currency or bearer securities. Nor is a financial institution required to file the form.

In part, this filing requirement is aimed at people carrying sacks of currency in or out of the United States, but the rules are aimed at taxpayers engaged in legitimate business activities as well. For example, a U.S. business might make a direct transfer of bearer bonds to a European agent for sale abroad.

Example 5-11

Assume the same facts as in Example 5-8, except that the Sessions Group has taken part of its proceeds from the bank in Mexico in the form of bearer bonds and has sent them by bonded carrier to its office in the United States.

Based on these facts, the Sessions Group must fill out FinCen Form 105 because a monetary instrument is being transported internationally. In this example, the Sessions Group must fill out Part II, which requests some identification information. Then, Sessions fills out Part III, which requests information regarding the monetary instrument. For a completed FinCen Form 105, see Sample Form 5-7.

Sample Form 5-1

Form 1120

U.S. Corporation Income Tax Return

Department of the Treasury
Internal Revenue Service

For calendar year 2010 or tax year beginning _____ , 2010, ending _____ , 20 ____

▶ See separate instructions.

OMB No. 1545-0123

2010

A Check if:
1a Consolidated return (attach Form 851) ☐
b Life/nonlife consolidated return ☐
2 Personal holding co. (attach Sch. PH) ☐
3 Personal service corp. (see instructions) ☐
4 Schedule M-3 attached ☐

Print or type

Name: Babbitt Brothers, Inc.
Number, street, and room or suite no. If a P.O. box, see instructions.
280 North Residual Drive
City or town, state, and ZIP code
Slippery Hills, CA 90217

B Employer identification number XX-XXXXXXX
C Date incorporated 1/8/85
D Total assets (see instructions) $ 257,970,000

E Check if: (1) ☐ Initial return (2) ☐ Final return (3) ☐ Name change (4) ☐ Address change

Income

			Amount
1a	Gross receipts or sales	b Less returns and allowances	c Bal ▶ 1c	327,225,000
2	Cost of goods sold (Schedule A, line 8)		2	156,573,000
3	Gross profit. Subtract line 2 from line 1c		3	170,652,000
4	Dividends (Schedule C, line 19)		4	3,038,000
5	Interest		5	451,000
6	Gross rents		6	
7	Gross royalties		7	
8	Capital gain net income (attach Schedule D (Form 1120))		8	
9	Net gain or (loss) from Form 4797, Part II, line 17 (attach Form 4797)		9	(129,000)
10	Other income (see instructions—attach schedule)		10	310,000
11	**Total income.** Add lines 3 through 10	▶	11	174,322,000

Deductions (See instructions for limitations on deductions.)

12	Compensation of officers (Schedule E, line 4)	▶	12	1,619,000
13	Salaries and wages (less employment credits)		13	54,608,000
14	Repairs and maintenance		14	883,000
15	Bad debts		15	331,000
16	Rents		16	34,406,000
17	Taxes and licenses		17	8,165,000
18	Interest		18	7,898,000
19	Charitable contributions		19	
20	Depreciation from Form 4562 not claimed on Schedule A or elsewhere on return (attach Form 4562)		20	8,999,000
21	Depletion		21	
22	Advertising		22	
23	Pension, profit-sharing, etc., plans		23	17,485,000
24	Employee benefit programs		24	
25	Domestic production activities deduction (attach Form 8903)		25	2,642,000
26	Other deductions (attach schedule)		26	12,815,000
27	**Total deductions.** Add lines 12 through 26	▶	27	149,801,000
28	Taxable income before net operating loss deduction and special deductions. Subtract line 27 from line 11		28	24,521,000
29	**Less: a** Net operating loss deduction (see instructions)	29a		
	b Special deductions (Schedule C, line 20)	29b 2,119,000	29c	2,119,000

Tax, Refundable Credits, and Payments

			Amount
30	**Taxable income.** Subtract line 29c from line 28 (see instructions)		30	22,401,000
31	**Total tax** (Schedule J, line 10)		31	3,361,000
32a	2009 overpayment credited to 2010	32a 1,121,000		
b	2010 estimated tax payments	32b 2,956,000		
c	2010 refund applied for on Form 4466	32c ( ) d Bal ▶ 32d 4,077,000		
e	Tax deposited with Form 7004	32e		
f	Credits: (1) Form 2439	(2) Form 4136	32f	
g	Refundable credits from Form 3800, line 19c, and Form 8827, line 8c	32g	32h	4,077,000
33	Estimated tax penalty (see instructions). Check if Form 2220 is attached ▶ ☐		33	
34	**Amount owed.** If line 32h is smaller than the total of lines 31 and 33, enter amount owed		34	
35	**Overpayment.** If line 32h is larger than the total of lines 31 and 33, enter amount overpaid		35	715,510
36	Enter amount from line 35 you want: **Credited to 2011 estimated tax** ▶ Refunded ▶		36	

Sign Here

Under penalties of perjury, I declare that I have examined this return, including accompanying schedules and statements, and to the best of my knowledge and belief, it is true, correct, and complete. Declaration of preparer (other than taxpayer) is based on all information of which preparer has any knowledge.

Signature of officer ____ Date ____ ▶ Title ____

May the IRS discuss this return with the preparer shown below (see instructions)? ☐ Yes ☐ No

Paid Preparer Use Only

Print/Type preparer's name	Preparer's signature	Date	Check ☐ if self-employed	PTIN
Firm's name ▶			Firm's EIN ▶	
Firm's address ▶			Phone no.	

For Paperwork Reduction Act Notice, see separate instructions. Cat. No. 11450Q Form **1120** (2010)

Form 1120 (2010)   Page **2**

Schedule A	**Cost of Goods Sold** (see instructions)		
1	Inventory at beginning of year	1	75,719,000
2	Purchases	2	167,888,000
3	Cost of labor	3	
4	Additional section 263A costs (attach schedule)	4	16,491,000
5	Other costs (attach schedule)	5	
6	**Total.** Add lines 1 through 5	6	260,098,000
7	Inventory at end of year	7	103,525,000
8	**Cost of goods sold.** Subtract line 7 from line 6. Enter here and on page 1, line 2	8	156,573,000

9a Check all methods used for valuing closing inventory:

    (i) ☐ Cost

    (ii) ☐ Lower of cost or market

    (iii) ☐ Other (Specify method used and attach explanation.) ▶ _____

  b Check if there was a writedown of subnormal goods   ▶ ☐

  c Check if the LIFO inventory method was adopted this tax year for any goods (if checked, attach Form 970)   ▶ ☐

  d If the LIFO inventory method was used for this tax year, enter percentage (or amounts) of closing inventory computed under LIFO | 9d |

  e If property is produced or acquired for resale, do the rules of section 263A apply to the corporation?   ☐ Yes   ☐ No

  f Was there any change in determining quantities, cost, or valuations between opening and closing inventory? If "Yes," attach explanation   ☐ Yes   ☐ No

Schedule C	**Dividends and Special Deductions** (see instructions)	(a) Dividends received	(b) %	(c) Special deductions (a) × (b)
1	Dividends from less-than-20%-owned domestic corporations (other than debt-financed stock)	3,028,000	70	2,119,600
2	Dividends from 20%-or-more-owned domestic corporations (other than debt-financed stock)		80	
3	Dividends on debt-financed stock of domestic and foreign corporations		see instructions	
4	Dividends on certain preferred stock of less-than-20%-owned public utilities		42	
5	Dividends on certain preferred stock of 20%-or-more-owned public utilities		48	
6	Dividends from less-than-20%-owned foreign corporations and certain FSCs		70	
7	Dividends from 20%-or-more-owned foreign corporations and certain FSCs		80	
8	Dividends from wholly owned foreign subsidiaries		100	
9	**Total.** Add lines 1 through 8. See instructions for limitation			
10	Dividends from domestic corporations received by a small business investment company operating under the Small Business Investment Act of 1958		100	
11	Dividends from affiliated group members		100	
12	Dividends from certain FSCs		100	
13	Dividends from foreign corporations not included on lines 3, 6, 7, 8, 11, or 12			
14	Income from controlled foreign corporations under subpart F (attach Form(s) 5471)			
15	Foreign dividend gross-up			
16	IC-DISC and former DISC dividends not included on lines 1, 2, or 3			
17	Other dividends			
18	Deduction for dividends paid on certain preferred stock of public utilities			
19	**Total dividends.** Add lines 1 through 17. Enter here and on page 1, line 4 ▶	3,028,000		
20	**Total special deductions.** Add lines 9, 10, 11, 12, and 18. Enter here and on page 1, line 29b ▶			2,119,000

Schedule E	**Compensation of Officers** (see instructions for page 1, line 12)

Note: *Complete Schedule E only if total receipts (line 1a plus lines 4 through 10 on page 1) are $500,000 or more.*

(a) Name of officer	(b) Social security number	(c) Percent of time devoted to business	(d) Common	(e) Preferred	(f) Amount of compensation
1 See attached statements		%	%	%	1,619,000
		%	%	%	
		%	%	%	
		%	%	%	
		%	%	%	
2	Total compensation of officers				1,619,000
3	Compensation of officers claimed on Schedule A and elsewhere on return				
4	Subtract line 3 from line 2. Enter the result here and on page 1, line 12				1,619,000

Form **1120** (2010)

Form 1120 (2010)   Page **3**

Schedule J	**Tax Computation** (see instructions)				
1	Check if the corporation is a member of a controlled group (attach Schedule O (Form 1120)) . . . . ▶ ☐				
2	Income tax. Check if a qualified personal service corporation (see instructions) . . . . ▶ ☐		**2**	7,840,490	
3	Alternative minimum tax (attach Form 4626)		**3**		
4	Add lines 2 and 3		**4**	7,840,490	
5a	Foreign tax credit (attach Form 1118)	**5a**	4,479,000		
b	Credit from Form 8834, line 29	**5b**			
c	General business credit (attach Form 3800)	**5c**			
d	Credit for prior year minimum tax (attach Form 8827)	**5d**			
e	Bond credits from Form 8912	**5e**			
6	**Total credits.** Add lines 5a through 5e		**6**	4,479,000	
7	Subtract line 6 from line 4		**7**	3,361,490	
8	Personal holding company tax (attach Schedule PH (Form 1120))		**8**		
9	Other taxes. Check if from: ☐ Form 4255 ☐ Form 8611 ☐ Form 8697 ☐ Form 8866 ☐ Form 8902 ☐ Other (attach schedule) . . .		**9**		
10	**Total tax.** Add lines 7 through 9. Enter here and on page 1, line 31		**10**	3,361,490	

Schedule K	**Other Information** (see instructions)		**Yes**	**No**
1	Check accounting method: **a** ☐ Cash **b** ☐ Accrual **c** ☐ Other (specify) ▶ _____			
2	See the instructions and enter the:			
a	Business activity code no. ▶ _____			
b	Business activity ▶ Transportation			
c	Product or service ▶ Aircraft Parts			
3	Is the corporation a subsidiary in an affiliated group or a parent-subsidiary controlled group?			✓
	If "Yes," enter name and EIN of the parent corporation ▶ _____			
4	At the end of the tax year:			
a	Did any foreign or domestic corporation, partnership (including any entity treated as a partnership), trust, or tax-exempt organization own directly 20% or more, or own, directly or indirectly, 50% or more of the total voting power of all classes of the corporation's stock entitled to vote? If "Yes," complete Part I of Schedule G (Form 1120) (attach Schedule G)			✓
b	Did any individual or estate own directly 20% or more, or own, directly or indirectly, 50% or more of the total voting power of all classes of the corporation's stock entitled to vote? If "Yes," complete Part II of Schedule G (Form 1120) (attach Schedule G) .			✓
5	At the end of the tax year, did the corporation:			
a	Own directly 20% or more, or own, directly or indirectly, 50% or more of the total voting power of all classes of stock entitled to vote of any foreign or domestic corporation not included on **Form 851,** Affiliations Schedule? For rules of constructive ownership, see instructions If "Yes," complete (i) through (iv).			✓

(i) Name of Corporation	(ii) Employer Identification Number (if any)	(iii) Country of Incorporation	(iv) Percentage Owned in Voting Stock

Form **1120** (2010)

Form 1120 (2010)   Page **4**

Schedule K   *Continued*

		Yes	No
b	Own directly an interest of 20% or more, or own, directly or indirectly, an interest of 50% or more in any foreign or domestic partnership (including an entity treated as a partnership) or in the beneficial interest of a trust? For rules of constructive ownership, see instructions		✓

If "Yes," complete (i) through (iv).

(i) Name of Entity	(ii) Employer Identification Number (if any)	(iii) Country of Organization	(iv) Maximum Percentage Owned in Profit, Loss, or Capital

		Yes	No
6	During this tax year, did the corporation pay dividends (other than stock dividends and distributions in exchange for stock) in excess of the corporation's current and accumulated earnings and profits? (See sections 301 and 316.)		✓

If "Yes," file **Form 5452,** Corporate Report of Nondividend Distributions.

If this is a consolidated return, answer here for the parent corporation and on Form 851 for each subsidiary.

		Yes	No
7	At any time during the tax year, did one foreign person own, directly or indirectly, at least 25% of **(a)** the total voting power of all classes of the corporation's stock entitled to vote or **(b)** the total value of all classes of the corporation's stock?		✓

For rules of attribution, see section 318. If "Yes," enter:

(i) Percentage owned ▶ _____ and **(ii)** Owner's country ▶ _____

(c) The corporation may have to file **Form 5472,** Information Return of a 25% Foreign-Owned U.S. Corporation or a Foreign Corporation Engaged in a U.S. Trade or Business. Enter the number of Forms 5472 attached ▶ _____

8 Check this box if the corporation issued publicly offered debt instruments with original issue discount . . . . ▶ ☐

If checked, the corporation may have to file **Form 8281,** Information Return for Publicly Offered Original Issue Discount Instruments.

9 Enter the amount of tax-exempt interest received or accrued during the tax year ▶ $ _____

10 Enter the number of shareholders at the end of the tax year (if 100 or fewer) ▶ _____

11 If the corporation has an NOL for the tax year and is electing to forego the carryback period, check here . . . . . ▶ ☐

If the corporation is filing a consolidated return, the statement required by Regulations section 1.1502-21(b)(3) must be attached or the election will not be valid.

12 Enter the available NOL carryover from prior tax years (do not reduce it by any deduction on line 29a.) ▶ $ _____

		Yes	No
13	Are the corporation's total receipts (line 1a plus lines 4 through 10 on page 1) for the tax year **and** its total assets at the end of the tax year less than $250,000?		✓

If "Yes," the corporation is not required to complete Schedules L, M-1, and M-2 on page 5. Instead, enter the total amount of cash distributions and the book value of property distributions (other than cash) made during the tax year. ▶ $ _____

		Yes	No
14	Is the corporation required to file Schedule UTP (Form 1120), Uncertain Tax Position Statement (see instructions)?		✓

If "Yes," complete and attach Schedule UTP.

Form **1120** (2010)

U.S. Taxation of International Operations: Key Knowledge

Form 1120 (2010)

Page 5

Schedule L — Balance Sheets per Books

	Assets	(a) Beginning of tax year	(b)	(c) End of tax year	(d)
1	Cash		7,001,000		8,218,000
2a	Trade notes and accounts receivable	1,134,000		5,588,000	
b	Less allowance for bad debts	( )	1,134,000	( )	5,588,000
3	Inventories		75,719,000		103,525,000
4	U.S. government obligations		42,885,000		36,488,000
5	Tax-exempt securities (see instructions)				
6	Other current assets (attach schedule)				
7	Loans to shareholders				
8	Mortgage and real estate loans				
9	Other investments (attach schedule)		23,000		
10a	Buildings and other depreciable assets	50,447,000		90,023,000	
b	Less accumulated depreciation	(14,904,000)	35,543,000	(22,857,000)	67,166,000
11a	Depletable assets				
b	Less accumulated depletion	( )		( )	
12	Land (net of any amortization)		5,306,000		7,681,000
13a	Intangible assets (amortizable only)	234,000		1,158,000	
b	Less accumulated amortization	(117,000)	117,000	(579,000)	579,000
14	Other assets (attach schedule)		52,757,000		28,725,000
15	Total assets		220,485,000		257,970,000

	Liabilities and Shareholders' Equity	(a)	(b)	(c)	(d)
16	Accounts payable		9,591,000		15,448,000
17	Mortgages, notes, bonds payable in less than 1 year				27,812,000
18	Other current liabilities (attach schedule)		17,935,000		17,368,000
19	Loans from shareholders				
20	Mortgages, notes, bonds payable in 1 year or more		115,845,000		102,203,000
21	Other liabilities (attach schedule)				
22	Capital stock: a Preferred stock	957,999		1,499,000	
	b Common stock	18,926,000	19,883,000	30,399,000	31,898,000
23	Additional paid-in capital		47,257,000		43,336,000
24	Retained earnings—Appropriated (attach schedule)				
25	Retained earnings—Unappropriated		10,372,000		22,166,000
26	Adjustments to shareholders' equity (attach schedule)				
27	Less cost of treasury stock		(398,000)		(3,261,000)
28	Total liabilities and shareholders' equity		220,485,000		257,970,000

Schedule M-1 — Reconciliation of Income (Loss) per Books With Income per Return

Note: Schedule M-3 required instead of Schedule M-1 if total assets are $10 million or more—see instructions

1	Net income (loss) per books	16,073,000	7	Income recorded on books this year not included on this return (itemize):	
2	Federal income tax per books	7,161,000		Tax-exempt interest $ _____	
3	Excess of capital losses over capital gains	736,000			
4	Income subject to tax not recorded on books this year (itemize): _____ See Attached	3,307,000		See Attached	235,000
			8	Deductions on this return not charged against book income this year (itemize):	
5	Expenses recorded on books this year not deducted on this return (itemize):		a	Depreciation $ _____	
a	Depreciation $ _____		b	Charitable contributions $ _____	
b	Charitable contributions $ _____				
c	Travel and entertainment $ _____ See Attached	3,438,000		See Attached	5,959,000
			9	Add lines 7 and 8	6,194,000
6	Add lines 1 through 5	30,715,000	10	Income (page 1, line 28)—line 6 less line 9	24,521,000

Schedule M-2 — Analysis of Unappropriated Retained Earnings per Books (Line 25, Schedule L)

1	Balance at beginning of year	10,372,000	5	Distributions: a Cash	4,432,000
2	Net income (loss) per books	16,073,000		b Stock	
3	Other increases (itemize): _____ See Attached	153,000		c Property	
			6	Other decreases (itemize): _____	
			7	Add lines 5 and 6	4,432,000
4	Add lines 1, 2, and 3	26,598,000	8	Balance at end of year (line 4 less line 7)	22,166,000

Form **1120** (2010)

5-24

Sample Form 5-2

Form **1120**	**U.S. Corporation Income Tax Return**	OMB No. 1545-0123

Department of the Treasury
Internal Revenue Service

For calendar year 2010 or tax year beginning _____, 2010, ending _____, 20 ___

▶ See separate instructions.

2010

A Check if:
1a Consolidated return (attach Form 851) . ☐
b Life/nonlife consolidated return . . ☐
2 Personal holding co. (attach Sch. PH) . ☐
3 Personal service corp. (see instructions) . ☐
4 Schedule M-3 attached ☐

Print or type

Name: Babbitt Brothers, Inc.

Number, street, and room or suite no. If a P.O. box, see instructions.
280 North Residual Drive

City or town, state, and ZIP code
Slippery Hills, CA 90217

B Employer identification number
XX-XXXXXXX

C Date incorporated
1/5/85

D Total assets (see instructions)
$ 22,558,000

E Check if: (1) ☐ Initial return (2) ☐ Final return (3) ☐ Name change (4) ☐ Address change

Income

1a	Gross receipts or sales 37,486,000	b Less returns and allowances	c Bal ▶ 1c 37,486,000
2	Cost of goods sold (Schedule A, line 8)	2	18,564,000
3	Gross profit. Subtract line 2 from line 1c	3	18,922,000
4	Dividends (Schedule C, line 19)	4	
5	Interest	5	15,000
6	Gross rents	6	
7	Gross royalties	7	
8	Capital gain net income (attach Schedule D (Form 1120))	8	
9	Net gain or (loss) from Form 4797, Part II, line 17 (attach Form 4797)	9	358,000
10	Other income (see instructions—attach schedule)	10	None
11	**Total income.** Add lines 3 through 10 . . . . ▶	11	19,295,000

Deductions (See instructions for limitations on deductions.)

12	Compensation of officers (Schedule E, line 4) . . . . ▶	12	160,000
13	Salaries and wages (less employment credits)	13	4,894,000
14	Repairs and maintenance	14	47,000
15	Bad debts	15	56,000
16	Rents	16	3,976,000
17	Taxes and licenses	17	312,000
18	Interest	18	7,898,000
19	Charitable contributions	19	
20	Depreciation from Form 4562 not claimed on Schedule A or elsewhere on return (attach Form 4562)	20	796,000
21	Depletion	21	
22	Advertising	22	
23	Pension, profit-sharing, etc., plans	23	2,282,000
24	Employee benefit programs	24	
25	Domestic production activities deduction (attach Form 8903)	25	207,000
26	Other deductions (attach schedule)	26	4,635,000
27	**Total deductions.** Add lines 12 through 26 . . . . ▶	27	17,394,000
28	Taxable income before net operating loss deduction and special deductions. Subtract line 27 from line 11.	28	1,901,000
29	**Less: a** Net operating loss deduction (see instructions) 29a		
	b Special deductions (Schedule C, line 20) . . . 29b	29c	

Tax, Refundable Credits, and Payments

30	**Taxable income.** Subtract line 29c from line 28 (see instructions)	30	1,901,000
31	**Total tax** (Schedule J, line 10)	31	285,350
32a	2009 overpayment credited to 2010 . 32a		
b	2010 estimated tax payments . . . 32b 370,000		
c	2010 refund applied for on Form 4466 32c ( ) d Bal ▶ 32d 370,000		
e	Tax deposited with Form 7004 . . . . 32e		
f	Credits: (1) Form 2439 ____ (2) Form 4136 ____ 32f		
g	Refundable credits from Form 3800, line 19c, and Form 8827, line 8c . . . 32g	32h	
33	Estimated tax penalty (see instructions). Check if Form 2220 is attached . . . . . . ▶ ☐	33	
34	**Amount owed.** If line 32h is smaller than the total of lines 31 and 33, enter amount owed	34	None
35	**Overpayment.** If line 32h is larger than the total of lines 31 and 33, enter amount overpaid	35	84,650
36	Enter amount from line 35 you want: **Credited to 2011 estimated tax** ▶ ____ **Refunded** ▶	36	

Sign Here

Under penalties of perjury, I declare that I have examined this return, including accompanying schedules and statements, and to the best of my knowledge and belief, it is true, correct, and complete. Declaration of preparer (other than taxpayer) is based on all information of which preparer has any knowledge.

▶ _____ _____ ▶ _____
Signature of officer   Date   Title

May the IRS discuss this return with the preparer shown below (see instructions)? ☐ Yes ☐ No

Paid Preparer Use Only

Print/Type preparer's name	Preparer's signature	Date	Check ☐ if self-employed	PTIN

Firm's name ▶
Firm's address ▶

Firm's EIN ▶
Phone no.

For Paperwork Reduction Act Notice, see separate instructions.   Cat. No. 11450Q   Form **1120** (2010)

Form 1120 (2010)
Page **2**

Schedule A — Cost of Goods Sold (see instructions)

1	Inventory at beginning of year	1	8,426,000
2	Purchases	2	20,054,000
3	Cost of labor	3	
4	Additional section 263A costs (attach schedule)	4	1,198,000
5	Other costs (attach schedule)	5	
6	**Total.** Add lines 1 through 5	6	29,678,000
7	Inventory at end of year	7	11,114,000
8	**Cost of goods sold.** Subtract line 7 from line 6. Enter here and on page 1, line 2	8	18,564,000

9a Check all methods used for valuing closing inventory:

   (i) ☐ Cost

   (ii) ☐ Lower of cost or market

   (iii) ☐ Other (Specify method used and attach explanation.) ▶ _____

b Check if there was a writedown of subnormal goods . . . . ▶ ☐

c Check if the LIFO inventory method was adopted this tax year for any goods (if checked, attach Form 970) . . . . . . ▶ ☐

d If the LIFO inventory method was used for this tax year, enter percentage (or amounts) of closing inventory computed under LIFO . . . . 9d | |

e If property is produced or acquired for resale, do the rules of section 263A apply to the corporation? . . . . . ☐ Yes ☐ No

f Was there any change in determining quantities, cost, or valuations between opening and closing inventory? If "Yes," attach explanation . . . . ☐ Yes ☐ No

Schedule C — Dividends and Special Deductions (see instructions)

		(a) Dividends received	(b) %	(c) Special deductions (a) × (b)
1	Dividends from less-than-20%-owned domestic corporations (other than debt-financed stock)		70	
2	Dividends from 20%-or-more-owned domestic corporations (other than debt-financed stock)		80	
3	Dividends on debt-financed stock of domestic and foreign corporations		see instructions	
4	Dividends on certain preferred stock of less-than-20%-owned public utilities		42	
5	Dividends on certain preferred stock of 20%-or-more-owned public utilities		48	
6	Dividends from less-than-20%-owned foreign corporations and certain FSCs		70	
7	Dividends from 20%-or-more-owned foreign corporations and certain FSCs		80	
8	Dividends from wholly owned foreign subsidiaries		100	
9	**Total.** Add lines 1 through 8. See instructions for limitation			
10	Dividends from domestic corporations received by a small business investment company operating under the Small Business Investment Act of 1958		100	
11	Dividends from affiliated group members		100	
12	Dividends from certain FSCs		100	
13	Dividends from foreign corporations not included on lines 3, 6, 7, 8, 11, or 12			
14	Income from controlled foreign corporations under subpart F (attach Form(s) 5471)			
15	Foreign dividend gross-up			
16	IC-DISC and former DISC dividends not included on lines 1, 2, or 3			
17	Other dividends			
18	Deduction for dividends paid on certain preferred stock of public utilities			
19	**Total dividends.** Add lines 1 through 17. Enter here and on page 1, line 4 ▶			
20	**Total special deductions.** Add lines 9, 10, 11, 12, and 18. Enter here and on page 1, line 29b . . . . . . ▶			

Schedule E — Compensation of Officers (see instructions for page 1, line 12)

Note: *Complete Schedule E only if total receipts (line 1a plus lines 4 through 10 on page 1) are $500,000 or more.*

(a) Name of officer	(b) Social security number	(c) Percent of time devoted to business	Percent of corporation stock owned		(f) Amount of compensation
			(d) Common	(e) Preferred	
1 See attached statements		%	%	%	160,000
		%	%	%	
		%	%	%	
		%	%	%	
		%	%	%	

2	Total compensation of officers	160,000
3	Compensation of officers claimed on Schedule A and elsewhere on return	
4	Subtract line 3 from line 2. Enter the result here and on page 1, line 12	160,000

Form **1120** (2010)

Form 1120 (2010)   Page **3**

Schedule J	**Tax Computation** (see instructions)			

1	Check if the corporation is a member of a controlled group (attach Schedule O (Form 1120)) . . . . ▶ ☐		
2	Income tax. Check if a qualified personal service corporation (see instructions) . . . . ▶ ☐	**2**	665,350
3	Alternative minimum tax (attach Form 4626)	**3**	
4	Add lines 2 and 3	**4**	665,350

5a	Foreign tax credit (attach Form 1118)	**5a**	380,000	
b	Credit from Form 8834, line 29	**5b**		
c	General business credit (attach Form 3800)	**5c**		
d	Credit for prior year minimum tax (attach Form 8827)	**5d**		
e	Bond credits from Form 8912	**5e**		

6	**Total credits.** Add lines 5a through 5e	**6**	380,000
7	Subtract line 6 from line 4	**7**	285,350
8	Personal holding company tax (attach Schedule PH (Form 1120))	**8**	
9	Other taxes. Check if from: ☐ Form 4255 ☐ Form 8611 ☐ Form 8697		
	☐ Form 8866 ☐ Form 8902 ☐ Other (attach schedule)	**9**	
10	**Total tax.** Add lines 7 through 9. Enter here and on page 1, line 31	**10**	285,350

Schedule K	**Other Information** (see instructions)		

		Yes	No
1	Check accounting method: **a** ☐ Cash **b** ☐ Accrual **c** ☐ Other (specify) ▶ _____		
2	See the instructions and enter the:		
a	Business activity code no. ▶ _____		
b	Business activity ▶ Transportation		
c	Product or service ▶ Aircraft Parts		
3	Is the corporation a subsidiary in an affiliated group or a parent-subsidiary controlled group?		✓
	If "Yes," enter name and EIN of the parent corporation ▶ _____		
	_____		
4	At the end of the tax year:		
a	Did any foreign or domestic corporation, partnership (including any entity treated as a partnership), trust, or tax-exempt organization own directly 20% or more, or own, directly or indirectly, 50% or more of the total voting power of all classes of the corporation's stock entitled to vote? If "Yes," complete Part I of Schedule G (Form 1120) (attach Schedule G)		✓
b	Did any individual or estate own directly 20% or more, or own, directly or indirectly, 50% or more of the total voting power of all classes of the corporation's stock entitled to vote? If "Yes," complete Part II of Schedule G (Form 1120) (attach Schedule G) .		✓
5	At the end of the tax year, did the corporation:		
a	Own directly 20% or more, or own, directly or indirectly, 50% or more of the total voting power of all classes of stock entitled to vote of any foreign or domestic corporation not included on **Form 851,** Affiliations Schedule? For rules of constructive ownership, see instructions If "Yes," complete (i) through (iv).		✓

(i) Name of Corporation	(ii) Employer Identification Number (if any)	(iii) Country of Incorporation	(iv) Percentage Owned in Voting Stock

Form **1120** (2010)

Schedule K   *Continued*

				Yes	No
b	Own directly an interest of 20% or more, or own, directly or indirectly, an interest of 50% or more in any foreign or domestic partnership (including an entity treated as a partnership) or in the beneficial interest of a trust? For rules of constructive ownership, see instructions				✓

If "Yes," complete (i) through (iv).

(i) Name of Entity	**(ii)** Employer Identification Number (if any)	**(iii)** Country of Organization	**(iv)** Maximum Percentage Owned in Profit, Loss, or Capital

		Yes	No
6	During this tax year, did the corporation pay dividends (other than stock dividends and distributions in exchange for stock) in excess of the corporation's current and accumulated earnings and profits? (See sections 301 and 316.)		✓

If "Yes," file **Form 5452,** Corporate Report of Nondividend Distributions.

If this is a consolidated return, answer here for the parent corporation and on Form 851 for each subsidiary.

7 At any time during the tax year, did one foreign person own, directly or indirectly, at least 25% of **(a)** the total voting power of all classes of the corporation's stock entitled to vote or **(b)** the total value of all classes of the corporation's stock? . . . .   [No ✓]

For rules of attribution, see section 318. If "Yes," enter:

(i) Percentage owned ▶ _____   and **(ii)** Owner's country ▶ _____

(c) The corporation may have to file **Form 5472,** Information Return of a 25% Foreign-Owned U.S. Corporation or a Foreign Corporation Engaged in a U.S. Trade or Business. Enter the number of Forms 5472 attached ▶ _____

8 Check this box if the corporation issued publicly offered debt instruments with original issue discount . . . . . . ▶ ☐

If checked, the corporation may have to file **Form 8281,** Information Return for Publicly Offered Original Issue Discount Instruments.

9 Enter the amount of tax-exempt interest received or accrued during the tax year ▶ $ _____

10 Enter the number of shareholders at the end of the tax year (if 100 or fewer) ▶ _____

11 If the corporation has an NOL for the tax year and is electing to forego the carryback period, check here . . . . . ▶ ☐

If the corporation is filing a consolidated return, the statement required by Regulations section 1.1502-21(b)(3) must be attached or the election will not be valid.

12 Enter the available NOL carryover from prior tax years (do not reduce it by any deduction on line 29a.) ▶ $ _____

13 Are the corporation's total receipts (line 1a plus lines 4 through 10 on page 1) for the tax year **and** its total assets at the end of the tax year less than $250,000? . . . .   [No ✓]

If "Yes," the corporation is not required to complete Schedules L, M-1, and M-2 on page 5. Instead, enter the total amount of cash distributions and the book value of property distributions (other than cash) made during the tax year. ▶ $ _____

14 Is the corporation required to file Schedule UTP (Form 1120), Uncertain Tax Position Statement (see instructions)? . . . .   [No ✓]

If "Yes," complete and attach Schedule UTP.

Form **1120** (2010)

Form 1120 (2010)   Page **5**

Schedule L	Balance Sheets per Books	Beginning of tax year		End of tax year	
	Assets	**(a)**	**(b)**	**(c)**	**(d)**
1	Cash		454,000		583,000
2a	Trade notes and accounts receivable	21,000		14,000	
b	Less allowance for bad debts	( )	21,000	( )	14,000
3	Inventories		8,426,000		11,114,000
4	U.S. government obligations		42,885,000		36,488,000
5	Tax-exempt securities (see instructions)				
6	Other current assets (attach schedule)				
7	Loans to shareholders				
8	Mortgage and real estate loans				
9	Other investments (attach schedule)		23,000		
10a	Buildings and other depreciable assets	4,623,000		7,297,000	
b	Less accumulated depreciation	(1,953,000)	2,670,000	(2,193,000)	5,104,000
11a	Depletable assets				
b	Less accumulated depletion	( )		( )	
12	Land (net of any amortization)				686,000
13a	Intangible assets (amortizable only)				
b	Less accumulated amortization	( )		( )	
14	Other assets (attach schedule)		3,269,000		5,057,000
15	Total assets		14,840,000		22,558,000
	Liabilities and Shareholders' Equity				
16	Accounts payable		1,121,000		215,000
17	Mortgages, notes, bonds payable in less than 1 year				
18	Other current liabilities (attach schedule)		778,000		6,436,000
19	Loans from shareholders				
20	Mortgages, notes, bonds payable in 1 year or more		6,386,000		7,363,000
21	Other liabilities (attach schedule)				
22	Capital stock: **a** Preferred stock				
	b Common stock	1,000	1,000	1,000	1,000
23	Additional paid-in capital				
24	Retained earnings—Appropriated (attach schedule)				
25	Retained earnings—Unappropriated				
26	Adjustments to shareholders' equity (attach schedule)		6,554,000		8,543,000
27	Less cost of treasury stock		( )		( )
28	Total liabilities and shareholders' equity		14,840,000		22,558,000

Schedule M-1	Reconciliation of Income (Loss) per Books With Income per Return

Note: Schedule M-3 required instead of Schedule M-1 if total assets are $10 million or more—see instructions

1	Net income (loss) per books	1,989,000	7	Income recorded on books this year not included on this return (itemize):	
2	Federal income tax per books				
3	Excess of capital losses over capital gains			Tax-exempt interest $ _____	
4	Income subject to tax not recorded on books this year (itemize): _____			_____	
	_____		8	Deductions on this return not charged against book income this year (itemize):	
5	Expenses recorded on books this year not deducted on this return (itemize):		**a**	Depreciation $ _____	
a	Depreciation $ _____		**b**	Charitable contributions $ _____	
b	Charitable contributions $ _____			_____	
c	Travel and entertainment $ _____			_____	336,000
	_____	248,000	9	Add lines 7 and 8	336,000
6	Add lines 1 through 5	2,237,000	10	Income (page 1, line 28)—line 6 less line 9	1,901,000

Schedule M-2	Analysis of Unappropriated Retained Earnings per Books (Line 25, Schedule L)

1	Balance at beginning of year	6,554,000	5	Distributions: **a** Cash	
2	Net income (loss) per books	1,989,000		**b** Stock	
3	Other increases (itemize): _____			**c** Property	
	_____		6	Other decreases (itemize): _____	
	_____		7	Add lines 5 and 6	
4	Add lines 1, 2, and 3	8,543,000	8	Balance at end of year (line 4 less line 7)	8,543,000

Form **1120** (2010)

Sample Form 5-3

International Boycott Report

Form **5713**

(Rev. December 2010)

Department of the Treasury
Internal Revenue Service

For tax year beginning _____ , 20 __10__ ,
and ending _____ , 20 _____ .

▶ **Controlled groups, see instructions.**

OMB No. 1545-0216

**Attachment
Sequence No. 123**

**Paper filers must file in
duplicate** (see **When and Where
to File** in the instructions)

Name	Identifying number
Joplin Farm Machinery	XX-XXXXXXXXX

Number, street, and room or suite no. If a P.O. box, see instructions.

24 Park Avenue

City or town, state, and ZIP code

Bat Cave, North Carolina

Address of service center where your tax return is filed

Type of filer (check one):

☐ Individual ☐ Partnership ☐ Corporation ☐ Trust ☐ Estate ☐ Other

1 **Individuals**—Enter adjusted gross income from your tax return (see instructions)

2 **Partnerships and corporations:**

a Partnerships—Enter each partner's name and identifying number.

b Corporations—Enter the name and employer identification number of each member of the controlled group (as defined in section 993(a)(3)). Do not list members included in the consolidated return; instead, attach a copy of Form 851. List all other members of the controlled group not included in the consolidated return.

If you list any corporations below or if you attach Form 851, you must designate a common tax year. Enter on line 4b the name and employer identification number of the corporation whose tax year is designated.

Name	Identifying number

If more space is needed, attach additional sheets and check this box . . . . ▶ ☐

	Code	Description
c Enter principal business activity code and description (see instructions)		
d IC-DISCs—Enter principal product or service code and description (see instructions)		

3 **Partnerships**—Each partnership filing Form 5713 must give the following information:

a Partnership's total assets (see instructions) . . . .

b Partnership's ordinary income (see instructions) . . . .

4 **Corporations**—Each corporation filing Form 5713 must give the following information:

a Type of form filed (Form 1120, 1120-FSC, 1120-IC-DISC, 1120-L, 1120-PC, etc.) . . .

b Common tax year election (see instructions)

(1) Name of corporation ▶ _____

(2) Employer identification number . . . .

(3) Common tax year beginning _____ , 20 _____ , and ending _____ , 20 _____ .

c Corporations filing this form enter:

(1) Total assets (see instructions) . . . .

(2) Taxable income before net operating loss and special deductions (see instructions) . .

5 **Estates or trusts**—Enter total income (Form 1041, page 1) . . . .

6 Enter the total amount (before reduction for boycott participation or cooperation) of the following tax benefits (see instructions):

a Foreign tax credit . . . .

b Deferral of earnings of controlled foreign corporations . . . .

c Deferral of IC-DISC income . . . .

d FSC exempt foreign trade income . . . .

e Foreign trade income qualifying for the extraterritorial income exclusion . . . .

**Please
Sign
Here**

Under penalties of perjury, I declare that I have examined this report, including accompanying schedules and statements, and to the best of my knowledge and belief, it is true, correct, and complete.

▶ _____ _____ ▶ _____
Signature   Date   Title

For Paperwork Reduction Act Notice, see separate instructions.

Cat. No. 12030E

Form **5713** (Rev. 12-2010)

Form 5713 (Rev. 12-2010)   Page **2**

		Yes	No
7a	Are you a U.S. shareholder (as defined in section 951(b)) of any foreign corporation (including a FSC that does not use the administrative pricing rules) that had operations reportable under section 999(a)?		✓
b	If the answer to question 7a is "Yes," is any foreign corporation a controlled foreign corporation (as defined in section 957(a))?		✓
c	Do you own any stock of an IC-DISC?		✓
d	Do you claim any foreign tax credit?		✓
e	Do you control (within the meaning of section 304(c)) any corporation (other than a corporation included in this report) that has operations reportable under section 999(a)?		✓
	If "Yes," did that corporation participate in or cooperate with an international boycott at any time during its tax year that ends with or within your tax year?		✓
f	Are you controlled (within the meaning of section 304(c)) by any person (other than a person included in this report) who has operations reportable under section 999(a)?		✓
	If "Yes," did that person participate in or cooperate with an international boycott at any time during its tax year that ends with or within your tax year?		✓
g	Are you treated under section 671 as the owner of a trust that has reportable operations under section 999(a)? .		✓
h	Are you a partner in a partnership that has reportable operations under section 999(a)?		✓
i	Are you a foreign sales corporation (FSC) (as defined in section 922(a), as in effect before its repeal)?		✓
j	Are you excluding extraterritorial income (defined in section 114(e), as in effect before its repeal) from gross income?		✓

Part I **Operations in or Related to a Boycotting Country** (see instructions)

	Yes	No
8 **Boycott of Israel**—Did you have any operations in or related to any country (or with the government, a company, or a national of that country) associated in carrying out the boycott of Israel which is on the list maintained by the Secretary of the Treasury under section 999(a)(3)? (See **Boycotting Countries** in the instructions.)	✓	

If "Yes," complete the following table. If more space is needed, attach additional sheets using the exact format and check this box . . . . ▶ ☐

	Name of country (1)	Identifying number of person having operations (2)	Principal business activity		IC-DISCs only—Enter product code (5)
			Code (3)	Description (4)	
a	Boron	XX-XXXXXXXXX	3520	Sales, Farm Machinery	
b					
c					
d					
e					
f					
g					
h					
i					
j					
k					
l					
m					
n					
o					

Form **5713** (Rev. 12-2010)

Form 5713 (Rev. 12-2010)   Page **3**

		Yes	No
9	**Nonlisted countries boycotting Israel—** Did you have operations in any nonlisted country which you know or have reason to know requires participation in or cooperation with an international boycott directed against Israel?		✓

If "Yes," complete the following table. If more space is needed, attach additional sheets using the exact format and check this box . . . . ▶ ☐

	Name of country (1)	Identifying number of person having operations (2)	Principal business activity		IC-DISCs only—Enter product code (5)
			Code (3)	Description (4)	
a					
b					
c					
d					
e					
f					
g					
h					

		Yes	No
10	**Boycotts other than the boycott of Israel—** Did you have operations in any other country which you know or have reason to know requires participation in or cooperation with an international boycott other than the boycott of Israel?		✓

If "Yes," complete the following table. If more space is needed, attach additional sheets using the exact format and check this box . . . . ▶ ☐

	Name of country (1)	Identifying number of person having operations (2)	Principal business activity		IC-DISCs only—Enter product code (5)
			Code (3)	Description (4)	
a					
b					
c					
d					
e					
f					
g					
h					

		Yes	No
11	Were you requested to participate in or cooperate with an international boycott?		
	If "Yes," attach a copy (in English) of any and all such requests received during your tax year. If the request was in a form other than a written request, attach a separate sheet explaining the nature and form of any and all such requests. (See instructions.)		
12	Did you participate in or cooperate with an international boycott?		
	If "Yes," attach a copy (in English) of any and all boycott clauses agreed to, and attach a general statement of the agreement. If the agreement was in a form other than a written agreement, attach a separate sheet explaining the nature and form of any and all such agreements. (See instructions.)		

Note: *If the answer to either question 11 or 12 is "Yes," you must complete the rest of Form 5713. If you answered "Yes" to question 12, you must complete Schedules A and C or B and C (Form 5713).*

Form **5713** (Rev. 12-2010)

Form 5713 (Rev. 12-2010)

Page **4**

Part II	Requests for and Acts of Participation in or Cooperation With an International Boycott	Requests		Agreements	
		Yes	No	Yes	No

13a Did you receive requests to enter into, or did you enter into, any agreement (see instructions):

(1) As a condition of doing business directly or indirectly within a country or with the government, a company, or a national of a country to—

(a)	Refrain from doing business with or in a country which is the object of an international boycott or with the government, companies, or nationals of that country?		✓		✓
(b)	Refrain from doing business with any U.S. person engaged in trade in a country which is the object of an international boycott or with the government, companies, or nationals of that country?		✓		✓
(c)	Refrain from doing business with any company whose ownership or management is made up, in whole or in part, of individuals of a particular nationality, race, or religion, or to remove (or refrain from selecting) corporate directors who are individuals of a particular nationality, race, or religion?		✓		✓
(d)	Refrain from employing individuals of a particular nationality, race, or religion?		✓		✓
(2)	As a condition of the sale of a product to the government, a company, or a national of a country, to refrain from shipping or insuring products on a carrier owned, leased, or operated by a person who does not participate in or cooperate with an international boycott?		✓		✓

b **Requests and agreements**—if the answer to any part of 13a is "Yes," complete the following table. If more space is needed, attach additional sheets using the exact format and check this box . . . . ▶ ☐

	Name of country (1)	Identifying number of person receiving the request or having the agreement (2)	Principal business activity		IC-DISCs only— Enter product code (5)	Type of cooperation or participation			
			Code (3)	Description (4)		Number of requests		Number of agreements	
						Total (6)	Code (7)	Total (8)	Code (9)
a	Boron	XX-XXXXXXXXX		Sales, Farm Machinery					
b									
c									
d									
e									
f									
g									
h									
i									
j									
k									
l									
m									
n									
o									
p									

Form **5713** (Rev. 12-2010)

Sample Form 5-4

SCHEDULE A
(Form 5713)

(Rev. December 2010)

Department of the Treasury
Internal Revenue Service

International
Boycott Factor (Section 999(c)(1))

*Complete only if you are **not** computing a loss of tax benefits using the specifically attributable taxes and income method on Schedule B (Form 5713)*

▶ **Attach to Form 5713.**   ▶ **See instructions on page 2.**

OMB No. 1545-0216

Name	Identifying number
Joplin Farm Machinery	XX-XXXXXXXXX

Name of country being boycotted (check one): ☐ Israel   ☐ Other (identify) ▶ _____

Important: *If you are involved in more than one boycott, use a separate Schedule A for each boycott and attach to Form 5713.*

Name of Country (1)	Purchases, sales, and payroll attributable to boycotting operations, by operation		
	Boycott purchases (2)	Boycott sales (3)	Boycott payroll (4)
a Boron		$20,000,000	
b			
c			
d			
e			
f			
g			
h			
i			
j			
k			
l			
m			
n			
o			
Total		$20,000,000	

1 Numerator of boycott factor (add totals of columns (2), (3), and (4)) $20,000,000
2 Denominator of boycott factor:
  a Total purchases from countries other than United States . . . . . .
  b Total sales to or from countries other than United States $60,000,000
  c Total payroll paid or accrued for services performed in countries other than United States . . . .
  d Total of lines 2a, b, and c $60,000,000
3 **International boycott factor** (divide line 1 by line 2d). Enter here and on Schedule C (Form 5713) (see instructions) . . . . ▶   .3333

For Paperwork Reduction Act Notice, see the Instructions for Form 5713.   Cat. No. 12050W   **Schedule A (Form 5713) (Rev. 12-2010)**

General Instructions

References are to the Internal Revenue Code.

Who Must File

Complete Schedule A (Form 5713) if:

• You participated in or cooperated with an international boycott and

• You are using the international boycott factor to figure the loss of tax benefits.

You must use the international boycott factor to figure the reduction to foreign trade income qualifying for the extraterritorial income exclusion. To figure the loss of all other applicable tax benefits, you may either use the international boycott factor or you may specifically attribute taxes and income by operation on Schedule B (Form 5713).

Boycott Operations

All your operations in a boycotting country are considered to be boycott operations, unless you rebut the presumption of participating in or cooperating with the boycott (as explained below). In addition, your operations that are not in a boycotting country are boycott operations if they are connected to your participation in or cooperation with the boycott.

Rebutting the presumption of boycott participation or cooperation. One act of participation or cooperation creates the presumption that you participate in or cooperate with the boycott unless you rebut the presumption. The presumption applies to all your operations and those of each member of any controlled groups (defined in section 993(a)(3)) to which you belong, in each country that helps carry out the boycott.

You can rebut the presumption of participation in or cooperation with a boycott for a particular operation by demonstrating that the operation is separate from any participation in or cooperation with an international boycott. The presumption applies only to operations in countries that carry out the boycott. Therefore, you do not need to rebut the presumption for operations that are related to those countries if the operations take place outside of those countries.

International Boycott Factor

Your international boycott factor reflects boycott purchases, boycott sales, and boycott payroll.

Controlled groups. All members of a controlled group generally share one international boycott factor, which reflects all their purchases, sales, and payroll. However, if you belong to two or more controlled groups, your international boycott factor will reflect the purchases, sales, and payroll of all the controlled groups to which you belong.

Partnerships and trusts. You are deemed to have a prorated share of the purchases, sales, and payroll of each partnership in which you are a partner and of each trust of which you are treated as the owner under section 671. As a result, your international boycott factor may also reflect purchases, sales, and payroll of partnerships or trusts.

Specific Instructions

Compute a **separate** boycott factor and a separate schedule for **each** international boycott you participated in or cooperated with. Include your own operations and, if applicable, the operations of partnerships, trusts, and members of your controlled group.

See the instructions for lines 8 through 13, in the Instructions for Form 5713, to determine the years for which you should report purchases, sales, and payroll for partnerships, trusts, and controlled groups.

Columns (1) Through (4)

In completing columns (1) through (4), show all boycott purchases, boycott sales, and boycott payroll from one operation on one line.

Partnerships. Complete **only** lines **a** through **o,** the total of columns (2), (3), and (4), and line 2. Do not complete line 3. Give this information to all partners so they can compute their own international boycott factor.

Column (1). Enter the name of the country that requires participation in or cooperation with an international boycott as a condition of doing business in that country. The country named in column (1) is not necessarily the country in which the operation takes place. For example, if you have an operation in Country Z that is not a boycotting country and the operation relates to Country X that is a boycotting country, enter the name of Country X in column (1). The Secretary maintains a list, under section 999(a)(3), of countries that require participation in or cooperation with an international boycott. See the Instructions for Form 5713 for the current list of boycotting countries.

Column (2). Enter all purchases that are made from boycotting countries that are attributable to the operation reported on each line.

Column (3). Enter the sales that are made to or from boycotting countries and that are attributable to the operation reported on each line.

Column (4). Enter the total payroll that was paid or accrued for services performed in boycotting countries and that are attributable to the operation reported on each line.

Lines 1 Through 3

Line 1. Add the totals of columns (2), (3), and (4). This amount is the numerator of your international boycott factor.

Do not include amounts attributable to operations for which you rebutted the presumption of participating in or cooperating with the boycott.

Line 2. The denominator of the international boycott factor reflects all your purchases, sales, and payroll in or related to all countries other than the United States. If applicable, the denominator also reflects these items for your controlled groups, partnerships, and trusts. Include the amounts that are attributable to operations for which you rebutted the presumption of participating in or cooperating with the boycott.

Line 3. Enter the international boycott factor from line 3 of this form on the appropriate line of Schedule C (Form 5713) as follows.

IF you . . .	THEN enter the international boycott factor on . . .
Are required to reduce your foreign tax credit,	Line 2a(2).
Are denied a tax deferral on subpart F income,	Line 3a(4).
Are denied a tax deferral on IC-DISC income,	Line 4a(2).
Are denied an exemption of foreign trade income of a FSC,	Line 5a(2).
Are required to reduce foreign trade income qualifying for the extraterritorial income exclusion,	Line 6b.

Sample Form 5-5

SCHEDULE B
(Form 5713)

(Rev. December 2010)

Department of the Treasury
Internal Revenue Service

Specifically Attributable Taxes
and Income (Section 999(c)(2))

► Complete only if you are **not** computing a loss of tax benefits
using the international boycott factor on Schedule A (Form 5713).

► **Attach to Form 5713.**   ► **See instructions on page 2.**

OMB No. 1545-0216

Name	Identifying number
Joplin Farm Machinery	XX-XXXXXXXX

Name of country being boycotted (check one)   ☑ Israel   ☐ Other (identify) ►

Important: *If you are involved in more than one international boycott, use a separate Schedule B (Form 5713) to compute the specifically attributable taxes and income for each boycott.*

Specifically Attributable Taxes and Income by Operation (Use a separate line for each operation.)

		Principal business activity		Foreign tax credit	Subpart F income	IC-DISC income	FSC income
Name of country (1)	Code (2)	Description (3)		Foreign taxes attributable to boycott operations (4)	Prorated share of international boycott income (5)	Taxable income attributable to boycott operations (6)	Taxable income attributable to boycott operations (7)
a							
b							
c							
d							
e							
f							
g							
h							
i							
j							
k							
l							
m							
n							
o Total . . . . ►							

For Paperwork Reduction Act Notice, see the instructions for Form 5713.   Cat. No. 12060S   Schedule B (Form 5713) (Rev. 12-2010)

General Instructions

Section references are to the Internal Revenue Code unless otherwise noted.

Who Must File

Complete Schedule B (Form 5713) if:

• You participated in or cooperated with an international boycott and

• You figure the loss of tax benefits by specifically attributing taxes and income.

If you do not specifically attribute taxes and income for this purpose, you must compute the international boycott factor on Schedule A (Form 5713).

Do not use Schedule B (Form 5713) to figure the reduction to foreign trade income qualifying for the extraterritorial income exclusion. Instead, use Schedule A (Form 5713).

Certain shareholders. IC-DISC benefits, certain FSC benefits, the "deemed paid" foreign tax credit under section 902, and the deferral of subpart F income are lost at the shareholder level. Shareholders in an IC-DISC, certain FSCs, or a foreign corporation must report their prorated share of the tax benefits denied. The denial of these benefits is discussed in the specific instructions for columns (4) through (7).

Boycott Operations

All of your operations in a boycotting country are considered to be boycott operations, unless you rebut the presumption of participation in or cooperation with the boycott (as explained below). In addition, your operations that are not in a boycotting country are boycott operations if they are connected to your participation in or cooperation with the boycott.

Rebutting the presumption of boycott participation or cooperation. One act of participation or cooperation creates the presumption that you participate in or cooperate with the boycott unless you rebut the presumption. The presumption applies to all of your operations and those of each member of any controlled groups (defined in section 993(a)(3)) to which you belong, in each country that helps carry out the boycott.

You can rebut the presumption of participation in or cooperation with a boycott for a particular operation by demonstrating that the operation is separate from any participation in or cooperation with an international boycott. The presumption applies only to operations in countries that carry out the boycott. Therefore, you do not need to rebut the presumption for operations that are related to those countries if the operations take place outside of those countries.

Specific Instructions

File Schedule B (Form 5713) for the period covered by your income tax return. Report only your own taxes and income; do not include the taxes and income of other members of any controlled groups to which you belong.

Columns (1) through (7)

In completing columns (1) through (7), show all specifically identifiable taxes and income in each appropriate column from one operation on one line.

Column (1). Enter the name of the country that requires participation in or cooperation with an international boycott as a condition of doing business in that country. The country named in column (1) is not necessarily the country where you have operations. For example, if you have operations in Country Z that is not a boycotting country and the operation relates to Country X that is a boycotting country, enter the name of Country X in column (1). See the Instructions for Form 5713 for a list of boycotting countries.

Column (2). Enter the principal business activity code of the boycott operation from the list in the Instructions for Form 5713.

Column (3). Briefly describe the principal business activity of the boycott operation. For IC-DISCs, enter the major product code and description in parentheses. See the Instructions for Schedule N of Form 1120-IC-DISC for a list of the codes.

Column (4). Enter the foreign taxes paid, accrued, or deemed paid that are attributable to the boycott operation. These taxes are not eligible for the foreign tax credit. Omit foreign taxes otherwise disallowed under sections 901 through 907, 911, and 6038. For more information, see Part N of the Treasury Department's International Boycott Guidelines.

Enter the column (4) total on line 2b, Schedule C (Form 5713).

Column (5). Enter your prorated share of the controlled foreign corporation's income that is attributable to the boycott operation. (This includes your share of the non-exempt income of a FSC. See section 923(a)(2), as in effect before its repeal.) This amount is not eligible for tax deferral. Omit the foreign corporation's income attributable to earnings and profits that are included in gross income under section 951 (except by reason of section 952(a)(3)). Also omit amounts excluded from subpart F income by section 952(b). In figuring the amount to enter in column (5), you are allowed a reasonable amount for deductions (including foreign taxes) allocable to that income.

Enter the column (5) total on line 3b, Schedule C (Form 5713).

Column (6). An IC-DISC's taxable income attributable to boycott participation or cooperation is not eligible for deferral.

If you are a shareholder in an IC-DISC, follow these steps for each boycott operation and enter the result in column (6).

1. Determine the portion of the amount on Form 1120-IC-DISC, Schedule J, Part I, line 7, that is attributable to the boycott operation.

2. Subtract that amount from the IC-DISC's taxable income attributable to the boycott operation for the tax year, before reduction for any distributions.

3. If you are a C corporation, determine your pro rata share of the remainder and multiply that amount by 16/17. If you are not a C corporation, determine your pro rata share of the remainder.

4. Enter the result in column (6).

Enter the column (6) total on line 4b, Schedule C (Form 5713).

Column (7). A FSC's taxable income attributable to boycott participation or cooperation is not eligible for exemption from income tax. Enter in column (7) the taxable income attributable to foreign trade income of a FSC for each boycott operation that would have been exempt had there not been boycott participation or cooperation.

Enter the column (7) total on line 5b, Schedule C (Form 5713).

Sample Form 5-6

SCHEDULE C (Form 5713)	Tax Effect of the International Boycott Provisions	
(Rev. December 2010)	▶ **Attach to Form 5713.**	OMB No. 1545-0216
Department of the Treasury Internal Revenue Service	▶ **See instructions on page 2.**	

Name	Identifying number
Joplin Farm Machinery	XX-XXXXXXXXX

1 Method used to compute loss of tax benefits (check one):

a International boycott factor from Schedule A (Form 5713). See lines 2a, 3a, 4a, and 5a below . . . . ▶ ☑

b Identification of specifically attributable taxes and income from Schedule B (Form 5713). See lines 2b, 3b, 4b, and 5b below . . . . ▶ ☐

2 Reduction of foreign tax credit (section 908(a)):

a **International boycott factor.** Complete if you checked box 1a above and answered "Yes" to the question on line 7d, Form 5713.

    (1) Foreign tax credit before adjustment from Form 1116 or 1118 (see instructions) . . . . . | $933,000

    (2) International boycott factor from Schedule A (Form 5713), line 3 . . . . | .33333

    (3) Reduction of foreign tax credit. Multiply line 2a(1) by line 2a(2). Enter here and on Form 1116 or 1118 (see instructions) . . . . | $307,890

    (4) Adjusted foreign tax credit. Subtract line 2a(3) from line 2a(1) . . . . | $625,110

b **Specifically attributable taxes and income.** Complete if you checked box 1b above and answered "Yes" to the question on line 7d, Form 5713. Enter the amount from line o, column (4), Schedule B (Form 5713) . . . .

Enter the appropriate part of this amount on Form 1116 or 1118 (see instructions).

3 Denial of deferral under subpart F (section 952(a)(3)):

a **International boycott factor.** Complete if you checked box 1a above and answered "Yes" to the question on line 7b, Form 5713.

    (1) Prorated share of total income of controlled foreign corporations (see instructions) . . . . .

    (2) Prorated share of income attributable to earnings and profits of controlled foreign corporations included in income under sections 951(a)(1)(A)(ii), 951(a)(1)(A)(iii), 951(a)(1)(B), 952(a)(1), 952(a)(2), 952(a)(4), 952(a)(5), and 952(b) . . . .

    (3) Subtract line 3a(2) from line 3a(1) . . . .

    (4) International boycott factor from Schedule A (Form 5713), line 3 . . . .

    (5) Prorated share of subpart F international boycott income. Multiply line 3a(3) by line 3a(4). Enter here and on line 22 of Worksheet A in the Form 5471 instructions . . . .

b **Specifically attributable taxes and income.** Complete if you checked box 1b above and answered "Yes" to the question on line 7b, Form 5713. Enter the amount from line o, column (5), Schedule B (Form 5713) here and on line 22 of Worksheet A in the Form 5471 instructions . . . .

4 Denial of IC-DISC benefits (section 995(b)(1)(F)(ii)):

a **International boycott factor.** Complete if you checked box 1a above and answered "Yes" to the question on line 7c, Form 5713.

    (1) Prorated share of section 995(b)(1)(F)(i) amount (see instructions) . . . .

    (2) International boycott factor from Schedule A (Form 5713), line 3 . . . .

    (3) Prorated share of IC-DISC international boycott income. Multiply line 4a(1) by line 4a(2). Enter this amount here and the IC-DISC will include it on line 10, Part I, Schedule J, Form 1120-IC-DISC . .

b **Specifically attributable taxes and income.** Complete if you checked box 1b above and answered "Yes" to the question on line 7c, Form 5713. Enter the amount from line o, column (6), Schedule B (Form 5713) here and the IC-DISC will include it on line 10, Part I, Schedule J, Form 1120-IC-DISC

5 Denial of exemption of foreign trade income (section 927(e)(2), as in effect before its repeal):

a **International boycott factor.** Complete if you checked box 1a above and answered "Yes" to the question on line 7i, Form 5713.

    (1) Add amounts from columns (a) and (b), line 10, Schedule B (Form 1120-FSC) . . . .

    (2) International boycott factor from Schedule A (Form 5713), line 3 . . . .

    (3) Exempt foreign trade income of a FSC attributable to international boycott operations. Multiply line 5a(1) by line 5a(2). Enter here and on line 2, Schedule F, Form 1120-FSC . . . .

b **Specifically attributable taxes and income.** Complete if you checked box 1b above and answered "Yes" to the question on line 7i, Form 5713. Enter the amount from line o, column (7), Schedule B (Form 5713) here and on line 2, Schedule F, Form 1120-FSC . . . .

For Paperwork Reduction Act Notice, see Instructions for Form 5713.   Cat. No. 120700   **Schedule C (Form 5713) (Rev. 12-2010)**

6	Reduction of foreign trade income qualifying for the extraterritorial income exclusion. Complete if you answered "Yes" to the question on line 7j, Form 5713.	
a	Enter amount from line 49 of Form 8873	
b	International boycott factor from Schedule A (Form 5713), line 3	
c	Reduction of qualifying foreign trade income. Multiply line 6a by 6b. Enter here and on Form 8873, line 50	

Instructions

Section references are to the Internal Revenue Code unless otherwise noted.

Purpose of Form

Schedule C (Form 5713) is used to compute the loss of tax benefits attributable to participation in or cooperation with an international boycott.

Who Must File

Complete Schedule C (Form 5713) if you completed either Schedule A or Schedule B of Form 5713.

Partnerships. Each partner must complete a separate Schedule C (Form 5713). Partnerships do not complete Schedule C (Form 5713).

Controlled groups. Unless a controlled group (described in section 993(a)(3)) files a consolidated return, each member may independently choose to either **(a)** apply the international boycott factor under section 999(c)(1) or **(b)** identify specifically attributable taxes and income under section 999(c)(2). Each member must consistently use a single method to figure the loss of tax benefits.

Example. A member that chooses to use the international boycott factor must apply it to determine its loss of the section 902 indirect foreign tax credit on a dividend that another member of the controlled group paid to it, even if the other member determines its own loss of tax benefits

by identifying specifically attributable taxes and income.

Other Requirements

• A person who applies the international boycott factor to one operation must apply the factor to all that tax year's operations under section 908(a), 952(a)(3), 995(b)(1)(F)(ii), or 927(e)(2).

• A person who identifies specifically attributable taxes and income under section 999(c)(2) must use that method for all that tax year's operations under section 908(a), 952(a)(3), 995(b)(1)(F)(ii), or 927(e)(2).

• An IC-DISC whose tax year differs from the common tax year of the controlled group of which it is a member does not need to amend its return to show on Schedule J (Form 1120-IC-DISC) the amount of IC-DISC benefits lost because of boycott participation. Because the IC-DISC benefits are lost at the shareholder level, the shareholder must include in income the prorated share of income attributable to boycott operations shown on line 4a(3).

• A person excluding extraterritorial income must reduce qualifying foreign trade income using the international boycott factor computed on Schedule A.

Lines 2 through 6

Note. *All line references are to 2010 forms unless otherwise noted.*

Line 2a(1). Enter the foreign tax credit before adjustment from Form 1116 or 1118. Individual filers, enter the

amount from line 27, Part IV, of Form 1116. Corporate filers, enter the amount from line 4, Part III, Schedule B, of Form 1118.

Line 2a(3). Enter the reduction of foreign tax credit from this line on either Form 1116 or 1118. Individual filers, enter this amount on line 28, Part IV, of Form 1116. Corporate filers, enter this amount on line 5, Part III, Schedule B, of Form 1118.

Line 2b. Enter the reduction of foreign taxes available for credit from this line on Form 1116 or 1118. Individual filers, include this amount on line 12, Part III, of Form 1116. Corporations, enter this amount on line C, Schedule G, of Form 1118.

Line 3a(1). Enter your share of the income of the controlled foreign corporation on line 3a(1).

Nonexempt foreign trade income of a foreign sales corporation (FSC) that was computed without regard to the administrative pricing rules is subject to the subpart F rules. Include your share of these types of income on line 3a(1).

Line 4a(1). Enter your pro rata share of section 995(b)(1)(F)(i) amount on line 4a(1) as follows:

• **Shareholder that is not a C corporation.** Enter your pro rata share of line 8, Part I, Schedule J, Form 1120-IC-DISC.

• **Shareholder that is a C corporation.** Enter your pro rata share of line 8, Part I, Schedule J, Form 1120-IC-DISC, multiplied by 16/17.

Sample Form 5-7

DEPARTMENT OF THE TREASURY
FINANCIAL CRIMES ENFORCEMENT NETWORK

OMB NO. 1506-0014

FinCEN Form **105**

March 2011
Department of the Treasury
FinCEN

▶ **Please type or print.**

REPORT OF INTERNATIONAL TRANSPORTATION OF CURRENCY OR MONETARY INSTRUMENTS

▶ To be filed with the Bureau of Customs and Border Protection
▶ For Paperwork Reduction Act Notice and Privacy Act Notice, see back of form.

31 U.S.C. 5316; 31 CFR 1010.340 and 1010.306

PART I	FOR A PERSON DEPARTING OR ENTERING THE UNITED STATES, OR A PERSON SHIPPING, MAILING, OR RECEIVING CURRENCY OR MONETARY INSTRUMENTS. (IF ACTING FOR ANYONE ELSE, ALSO COMPLETE PART II BELOW.)

1. NAME *(Last or family, first, and middle)*	2. IDENTIFICATION NO. *(See instructions)*	3. DATE OF BIRTH *(Mo./Day/Yr.)*

4. PERMANENT ADDRESS IN UNITED STATES OR ABROAD	5. YOUR COUNTRY OR COUNTRIES OF CITIZENSHIP

6. ADDRESS WHILE IN THE UNITED STATES	7. PASSPORT NO. & COUNTRY

8. U.S. VISA DATE *(Mo./Day/Yr.)*	9. PLACE UNITED STATES VISA WAS ISSUED	10. IMMIGRATION ALIEN NO.

11. IF CURRENCY OR MONETARY INSTRUMENT IS ACCOMPANIED BY A PERSON, COMPLETE 11a OR 11b, not both

A. EXPORTED FROM THE UNITED STATES	**COMPLETE "A" OR "B" NOT BOTH**		B. IMPORTED INTO THE UNITED STATES
Departed From: *(U.S. Port/City in U.S.)*	Arrived At: *(Foreign City/Country)*	Departed From: *(Foreign City/Country)*	Arrived At: *(City in U.S.)*

12. IF CURRENCY OR MONETARY INSTRUMENT WAS MAILED OR OTHERWISE SHIPPED, COMPLETE 12a THROUGH 12f

12a. DATE SHIPPED *(Mo./Day/Yr.)*	12b. DATE RECEIVED *(Mo./Day/Yr.)*	12c. METHOD OF SHIPMENT *(e.g. u.s. Mail, Public Carrier, etc.)*	12d. NAME OF CARRIER

12e. SHIPPED TO *(Name and Address)*

12f. RECEIVED FROM *(Name and Address)*

PART II	INFORMATION ABOUT PERSON(S) OR BUSINESS ON WHOSE BEHALF IMPORTATION OR EXPORTATION WAS CONDUCTED

13. NAME *(Last or family, first, and middle or Business Name)*

14. PERMANENT ADDRESS IN UNITED STATES OR ABROAD

15. TYPE OF BUSINESS ACTIVITY, OCCUPATION, OR PROFESSION	15a. IS THE BUSINESS A BANK? ☐ Yes ☐ No

PART III	CURRENCY AND MONETARY INSTRUMENT INFORMATION (SEE INSTRUCTIONS ON REVERSE)(To be completed by everyone)

16. TYPE AND AMOUNT OF CURRENCY/MONETARY INSTRUMENTS		17. IF OTHER THAN U.S. CURRENCY IS INVOLVED, PLEASE COMPLETE BLOCKS A AND B.
Currency and Coins	▶ $	A. Currency Name
		Bearer Bonds
Other Monetary Instruments *(Specify type, issuing entity and date, and serial or other identifying number.)*	▶ $ $5,000,000	B. Country
(TOTAL)	▶ $ $5,000,000	Republic of Antigua

PART IV	SIGNATURE OF PERSON COMPLETING THIS REPORT

Under penalties of perjury, I declare that I have examined this report, and to the best of my knowledge and belief it is true, correct and complete.

18. NAME AND TITLE (Print)	19. SIGNATURE	20. DATE OF REPORT *(Mo./Day/Yr.)*

CUSTOMS AND BORDER PROTECTION USE ONLY

THIS SHIPMENT IS ☐ INBOUND ☐ OUTBOUND	PORT CODE	CBP QUERY? Yes ☐ No ☐	COUNT VERIFIED Yes ☐ No ☐	VOLUNTARY REPORT Yes ☐ No ☐
DATE	AIRLINE/FLIGHT/VESSEL	LICENSE PLATE		INSPECTOR *(Name and Badge Number)*
		STATE/COUNTRY NUMBER		

FinCEN FORM 105

GENERAL INSTRUCTIONS

This report is required by 31 U.S.C. 5316 and Treasury Department regulations (31 CFR Chapter X).

WHO MUST FILE:

(1) Each person who physically transports, mails, or ships, or causes to be physically transported, mailed, or shipped currency or other monetary instruments in an aggregate amount exceeding $10,000 at one time from the United States to any place outside the United States or into the United States from any place outside the United States, and

(2) Each person who receives in the United States currency or other monetary instruments In an aggregate amount exceeding $10,000 at one time which have been transported, mailed, or shipped to the person from any place outside the United States.

A TRANSFER OF FUNDS THROUGH NORMAL BANKING PROCEDURES, WHICH DOES NOT INVOL VE THE PHYSICAL TRANSPORTATION OF CURRENCY O R MONETARY INSTRUMENTS, IS NOT REQUIRED TO BE REPORTED.

Exceptions: Reports are not required to be filed by:

(1) a Federal Reserve bank,

(2) a bank, a foreign bank, or a broker or dealer in securities in respect to currency or other monetary instruments mailed or shipped through the postal service or by common carrier,

(3) a commercial bank or trust company organized under the laws of any State or of the United States with respect to overland shipments of currency or monetary instruments shipped to or received from an established customer maintaining a deposit relationship with the bank, in amounts which the bank may reasonably conclude do not exceed amounts commensurate with the customary conduct of the business, industry or profession of the customer concerned,

(4) a person who is not a citizen or resident of the United States in respect to currency or other monetary instruments mailed or shipped from abroad to a bank or broker or dealer in securities through the postal service or by common carrier

(5) a common carrier of passengers in respect to currency or other monetary instruments in the possession of its passengers,

(6) a common carrier of goods in respect to shipments of currency or monetary instruments not declared to be such by the shipper

(7) a travelers' check issuer or its agent in respect to the transportation of travelers' checks prior to their delivery to selling agents for eventual sale to the public,

(8) a person with a restrictively endorsed travele's check that is in the collection and reconciliation process afer the traveler's check has been negotiated, nor by

(9) a person engaged as a business in the transportation of currency, monetary instruments and other commercial papers with respect to the transportation of currency or other monetary instruments overland between established offices of banks or brokers or dealers in securities and foreign persons.

WHEN AND WHERE TO FILE:

A. Recipients—Each person who receives currency or other monetary instruments in the United States shall file FinCEN Form 105, within 15 days after receipt of the currency or monetary instruments, with the Customs officer in charge at any port of entry or departure or by mail with the **Commissioner of Customs, Attention: Currency Transportation Reports, Washington DC 20229.**

B. Shippers or Mailers— If the currency or other monetary instrument does not accompany the person entering or departing the United States, FinCEN Form 105 may be filed by mail on or before the date of entry , departure, mailing, or shipping with the **Commissioner of Customs, Attention: Currency Transportation Reports, Washington DC 20229.**

C. Travelers—Travelers carrying currency or other monetary instruments with them shall file FinCEN Form 105 at the time of entry into the United States or at the time of departure from the United States with the Customs officer in charge at any Customs port of entry or departure.

An additional report of a particular transportation, mailing, or shipping of currency or the monetary instruments is not required if a complete and truthful report has already been filed. However, no person otherwise required to file a report shall be excused from liability for failure to do so if, in fact, a complete and truthful report has not been filed. Forms may be obtained from any Bureau of Customs and Border Protection office.

PENALTIES: Civil and criminal penalties, including under certain circumstances a fine of not more than $500,000 and Imprisonment of not more than ten years, are provided for failure to file a report, filing a report containing a material omission or misstatement, or filing a false or fraudulent report. In addition, the currency or monetary instrument may be subject to seizure and forfeiture. See 31 U.S.C.5321 and 31 CFR 1010.820; 31 U.S.C. 5322 and 31 CFR 1010.840; 31 U.S.C. 5317 and 31 CFR 1010.830, and U.S.C. 5332.

DEFINITIONS:

Bank—Each agent, agency, branch or office within the United States of any person doing business in one or more of the capacities listed: (1) a commercial bank or trust company organized under the laws of any State or of the United States; (2) a private bank; (3) a savings association, savings and loan association, and building and loan

association organized under the laws of any State or of the United States; (4) an insured institution as defined in section 401 of the National Housing Act; (5) a savings bank, industrial bank or other thrift institution; (6) a credit union organized under the laws of any State or of the United States; (7) any other organization chartered under the banking laws of any State and subject to the supervision of the bank supervisory authorities of a State other than a money service business; (8) a bank organized under foreign law; and (9) any national banking association or corporation acting under the provisions of section 25A of the Federal Reserve Act (12 U.S.C. Sections 611-632).

Foreign Bank—A bank organized under foreign law, or an agency, branch or office located outside the United States of a bank. The term does not include an agent, agency, branch or office within the United States of a bank organized under foreign law.

Broker or Dealer in Securities— A broker or dealer in securities, registered or required to be registered with the Securities and Exchange Commission under the Securities Exchange Act of 1934.

Currency: The coin and paper money of the United States or any other country that is (1) designated as legal tender and that (2) circulates and (3) is customarily accepted as a medium of exchange in the country of issuance.

Identification Number—Individuals must enter their social security number if any. However, aliens who do not have a social security number should enter passport or alien registration number. All others should enter their employer identification number

Monetary Instruments— (1) Coin or currency of the United States or of any other country (2) traveler's checks in any form, (3) negotiable instruments (including checks, promissory notes, and money orders) in bearer form, endorsed without restriction, made out to a fictitious payee, or otherwise in such form that title thereto passes upon delivery, (4) incomplete instruments (including checks, promissory notes, and money orders) that are signed but on which the name of the payee has been omitted, and (5) securities or stock in bearer form or otherwise in such form that title thereto passes upon delivery. Monetary instruments do not include (i) checks or money orders made payable to the order of a named person which have not been endorsed or which bear restrictive endorsements, (ii) warehouse receipts, or (iii) bills of lading.

Person—An individual, a corporation, partnership, a trust or estate, a joint stock company, an association, a syndicate, joint venture or other unincorporated organization or group, an Indian Tribe (as that term is defined in the Indian Gaming Regulatory Act), and all entities cognizable as legal personalities.

SPECIAL INSTRUCTIONS:

You should complete each line that applies to you **PART I.** — **Complete 11A or 11B, not both.** Block 12A and 12B; enter the exact date you shipped or received currency or monetary instrument(s). **PART II.** -Block 13; provide the complete name of the shipper or recipient on whose behalf the exportation or importation was conducted. **PART III.** — Specify type of instrument, issuing entity , and date, serial or other identifying number, and payee (if any). Block 17, if currency or monetary instruments of more than one country is involved, attach a list showing each type, country or origin and amount.

PRIVACY ACT AND PAPERWORK REDUCTION ACT NOTICE:

Pursuant to the requirements of Public law 93-579 (Privacy Act of 1974), notice is hereby given that the authority to collect information on Form 105 in accordance with 5 U.S.C. 552a(e)(3) is Public law 91-508; 31 U.S.C. 5316; 5 U.S.C. 301; Reorganization Plan No.1 of 1950; Treasury Department Order No. 165, revised, as amended; 31 CFR Chapter X; and 44 U.S.C. 3501.

The principal purpose for collecting the information is to assure maintenance of reports or records where such reports or records have a high degree of usefulness in criminal, tax, or regulatory investigations or proceedings. The information collected may be provided to those officers and employees of the Bureau of Customs and Border Protection and any other constituent unit of the Department of the Treasury who have a need for the records in the performance of their duties. The records may be referred to any other department or agency of the Federal Government upon the request of the head of such dep artment or agency. The information collected may also be provided to appropriate state, local, and foreign criminal law enforcement and regulatory personnel in the performance of their official duties.

Disclosure of this information is mandatory pursuant to 31 U.S.C. 5316 and 31 CFR Chapter X. Failure to provide all or any part of the requested information may subject the currency or monetary instruments to seizure and forfeiture, as well as subject the individual to civil and criminal liabilities.

Disclosure of the social security number is mandatory . The authority to collect this number is 31 U.S.C. 5316(b) and 31 CFR 1010.306(d). The social security number will be used as a means to identify the individual who files the record.

An agency may not conduct or sponsor, and a person is not required to respond to, a collection of information unless it displays a currently valid OMB control number. The collection of this information is mandatory pursuant to 31 U.S.C. 5316, of Title II of the Bank Secrecy Act, which is administered by Treasury's Financial Crimes Enforcement Network (FINCEN).

Statement required by 5 CFR 1320.8(b)(3)(iii): The estimated average burden associated with this collection of information is 11 minutes per respondent or record keeper depending on individual circumstances. Comments concerning the accuracy of this burden estimate and suggestions for reducing this burden should be directed to the Department of the Treasury, Financial Crimes Enforcement Network, P.O. Box 39 Vienna, Virginia 22183. **DO NOT send completed forms to this office—See When and Where To File above.**

FinCEN FORM 105

Sample Form 5-8

TD F 90-22.1
(Rev. March 2011)
Department of the Treasury

Do not use previous editions of this form

REPORT OF FOREIGN BANK AND FINANCIAL ACCOUNTS

Do NOT file with your Federal Tax Return

OMB No. 1545-2038

1 This Report is for Calendar Year Ended 12/31

2 0 1 0

Amended ☐

Part I   Filer Information

2 Type of Filer

a ☐ Individual   **b** ☐ Partnership   **c** ☐ Corporation   **d** ☐ Consolidated   **e** ☐ Fiduciary or Other—Enter type _____

3 U.S. Taxpayer Identification Number	**4** Foreign identification (Complete only if item 3 is not applicable.)	**5** Individual's Date of Birth MM/DD/YYYY
XX-XXXXXXXX **If filer has no U.S. Identification Number complete Item 4.**	**a** Type: ☐ Passport ☐ Other _____ **b** Number **c** Country of Issue	

6 Last Name or Organization Name	**7** First Name	**8** Middle Initial
The Sessions Group		

9 Address (Number, Street, and Apt. or Suite No.)

956 W. 54th Street

10 City	**11** State	**12** Zip/Postal Code	**13** Country
New York	New York	10007	United States

14 Does the filer have a financial interest in 25 or more financial accounts?

☐ Yes   If "Yes" enter total number of accounts _____

(If "Yes" is checked, do not complete Part II or Part III, but retain records of this information)

☑ No

Part II   Information on Financial Account(s) Owned Separately

15 Maximum value of account during calendar year reported	**16** Type of account **a** ☑ Bank **b** ☐ Securities **c** ☐ Other—Enter type below
$1,000,000	

17 Name of Financial Institution in which account is held

Monetary Trust Company

18 Account number or other designation	**19** Mailing Address (Number, Street, Suite Number) of financial institution in which account is held
	24, av, Juarez, Guadalajara, MEXICO

20 City	**21** State, if known	**22** Zip/Postal Code, if known	**23** Country

Signature

44 Filer Signature	**45** Filer Title, if not reporting a personal account	**46** Date (MM/DD/YYYY)

File this form with: U.S. Department of the Treasury, P.O. Box 32621, Detroit, MI 48232-0621

This form should be used to report a financial interest in, signature authority, or other authority over one or more financial accounts in foreign countries, as required by the Department of the Treasury Regulations 31 CFR 1010.350 (formerly 31 CFR 103.24). No report is required if the aggregate value of the accounts did not exceed $10,000. **See Instructions For Definitions.**

PRIVACY ACT AND PAPERWORK REDUCTION ACT NOTICE

Pursuant to the requirements of Public Law 93-579 (Privacy Act of 1974), notice is hereby given that the authority to collect information on TD F 90-22.1 in accordance with 5 USC 552a (e) is Public Law 91-508; 31 USC 5314; 5 USC 301; 31 CFR 1010.350 (formerly 31 CFR 103.24).

The principal purpose for collecting the information is to assure maintenance of reports where such reports or records have a high degree of usefulness in criminal, tax, or regulatory investigations or proceedings. The information collected may be provided to those officers and employees of any constituent unit of the Department of the Treasury who have a need for the records in the performance of their duties. The records may be referred to any other department or agency of the United States upon the request of the head of such department or agency for use in a criminal, tax, or regulatory investigation or proceeding. The information collected may also be provided to appropriate state, local, and foreign law enforcement and regulatory personnel in the performance of their official duties. Disclosure of this information is mandatory. Civil and criminal penalties, including in certain circumstances a fine of not more than $500,000 and imprisonment of not more than five years, are provided for failure to file a report, supply information, and for filing a false or fraudulent report. Disclosure of the Social Security number is mandatory. The authority to collect is 31 CFR 1010.350 (formerly 31 CFR 103.24) . The Social Security number will be used as a means to identify the individual who files the report.

The estimated average burden associated with this collection of information is 20 minutes per respondent or record keeper, depending on individual circumstances. Comments regarding the accuracy of this burden estimate, and suggestions for reducing the burden should be directed to the Internal Revenue Service, Bank Secrecy Act Policy, 5000 Ellin Road C-3-242, Lanham MD 20706.

Cat. No. 12996D   Form **TD F 90-22.1** (Rev. 3-2011)

Part II *Continued*—Information on Financial Account(s) Owned Separately	Form TD F 90-22.1

Complete a Separate Block for Each Account Owned Separately

This side can be copied as many times as necessary in order to provide information on all accounts.

Page Number

_____ of _____

1 Filing for calendar year	3-4 Check appropriate Identification Number	6 Last Name or Organization Name
___ ___ ___ ___	☐ Taxpayer Identification Number ☐ Foreign Identification Number Enter identification number here:	

15 Maximum value of account during calendar year reported	16 Type of account **a** ☐ Bank **b** ☐ Securities **c** ☐ Other—Enter type below
17 Name of Financial Institution in which account is held	

18 Account number or other designation	19 Mailing Address (Number, Street, Suite Number) of financial institution in which account is held
20 City	21 State, if known	22 Zip/Postal Code, if known	23 Country

15 Maximum value of account during calendar year reported	16 Type of account **a** ☐ Bank **b** ☐ Securities **c** ☐ Other—Enter type below
17 Name of Financial Institution in which account is held	

18 Account number or other designation	19 Mailing Address (Number, Street, Suite Number) of financial institution in which account is held
20 City	21 State, if known	22 Zip/Postal Code, if known	23 Country

15 Maximum value of account during calendar year reported	16 Type of account **a** ☐ Bank **b** ☐ Securities **c** ☐ Other—Enter type below
17 Name of Financial Institution in which account is held	

18 Account number or other designation	19 Mailing Address (Number, Street, Suite Number) of financial institution in which account is held
20 City	21 State, if known	22 Zip/Postal Code, if known	23 Country

15 Maximum value of account during calendar year reported	16 Type of account **a** ☐ Bank **b** ☐ Securities **c** ☐ Other—Enter type below
17 Name of Financial Institution in which account is held	

18 Account number or other designation	19 Mailing Address (Number, Street, Suite Number) of financial institution in which account is held
20 City	21 State, if known	22 Zip/Postal Code, if known	23 Country

15 Maximum value of account during calendar year reported	16 Type of account **a** ☐ Bank **b** ☐ Securities **c** ☐ Other—Enter type below
17 Name of Financial Institution in which account is held	

18 Account number or other designation	19 Mailing Address (Number, Street, Suite Number) of financial institution in which account is held
20 City	21 State, if known	22 Zip/Postal Code, if known	23 Country

15 Maximum value of account during calendar year reported	16 Type of account **a** ☐ Bank **b** ☐ Securities **c** ☐ Other—Enter type below
17 Name of Financial Institution in which account is held	

18 Account number or other designation	19 Mailing Address (Number, Street, Suite Number) of financial institution in which account is held
20 City	21 State, if known	22 Zip/Postal Code, if known	23 Country

Form **TD F 90-22.1** (Rev. 3-2011)

Part III Information on Financial Account(s) Owned Jointly	Form TD F 90-22.1
Complete a Separate Block for Each Account Owned Jointly	Page Number
This side can be copied as many times as necessary in order to provide information on all accounts.	___ of ___

1 Filing for calendar year ___ ___ ___ ___	3–4 Check appropriate Identification Number ☐ Taxpayer Identification Number ☐ Foreign Identification Number Enter identification number here:	6 Last Name or Organization Name

15 Maximum value of account during calendar year reported	16 Type of account **a** ☐ Bank **b** ☐ Securities **c** ☐ Other—Enter type below

17 Name of Financial Institution in which account is held

18 Account number or other designation	19 Mailing Address (Number, Street, Suite Number) of financial institution in which account is held

20 City	21 State, if known	22 Zip/Postal Code, if known	23 Country

24 Number of joint owners for this account	25 Taxpayer Identification Number of principal joint owner, if known. See instructions.

26 Last Name or Organization Name of principal joint owner	27 First Name of principal joint owner, if known	28 Middle initial, if known

29 Address (Number, Street, Suite or Apartment) of principal joint owner, if known

30 City, if known	31 State, if known	32 Zip/Postal Code, if known	33 Country, if known

15 Maximum value of account during calendar year reported	16 Type of account **a** ☐ Bank **b** ☐ Securities **c** ☐ Other—Enter type below

17 Name of Financial Institution in which account is held

18 Account number or other designation	19 Mailing Address (Number, Street, Suite Number) of financial institution in which account is held

20 City	21 State, if known	22 Zip/Postal Code, if known	23 Country

24 Number of joint owners for this account	25 Taxpayer Identification Number of principal joint owner, if known. See instructions.

26 Last Name or Organization Name of principal joint owner	27 First Name of principal joint owner, if known	28 Middle initial, if known

29 Address (Number, Street, Suite or Apartment) of principal joint owner, if known

30 City, if known	31 State, if known	32 Zip/Postal Code, if known	33 Country, if known

15 Maximum value of account during calendar year reported	16 Type of account **a** ☐ Bank **b** ☐ Securities **c** ☐ Other—Enter type below

17 Name of Financial Institution in which account is held

18 Account number or other designation	19 Mailing Address (Number, Street, Suite Number) of financial institution in which account is held

20 City	21 State, if known	22 Zip/Postal Code, if known	23 Country

24 Number of joint owners for this account	25 Taxpayer Identification Number of principal joint owner, if known. See instructions.

26 Last Name or Organization Name of principal joint owner	27 First Name of principal joint owner, if known	28 Middle initial, if known

29 Address (Number, Street, Suite or Apartment) of principal joint owner, if known

30 City, if known	31 State, if known	32 Zip/Postal Code, if known	33 Country, if known

Form **TD F 90-22.1** (Rev. 3-2011)

Part IV **Information on Financial Account(s) Where Filer has Signature Authority but No Financial Interest in the Account(s)**

Form TD F 90-22.1
Page Number
___ of ___

Complete a Separate Block for Each Account

This side can be copied as many times as necessary in order to provide information on all accounts.

1 Filing for calendar year ___ ___ ___ ___	3–4 Check appropriate Identification Number ☐ Taxpayer Identification Number ☐ Foreign Identification Number Enter identification number here:	6 Last Name or Organization Name

15 Maximum value of account during calendar year reported	16 Type of account **a** ☐ Bank **b** ☐ Securities **c** ☐ Other—Enter type below

17 Name of Financial Institution in which account is held

18 Account number or other designation	19 Mailing Address (Number, Street, Suite Number) of financial institution in which account is held		
20 City	21 State, if known	22 Zip/Postal Code, if known	23 Country

34 Last Name or Organization Name of Account Owner	35 Taxpayer Identification Number of Account Owner

36 First Name	37 Middle initial	38 Address (Number, Street, and Apt. or Suite No.)
39 City	40 State	41 Zip/Postal Code	42 Country

43 Filer's Title with this Owner

---

15 Maximum value of account during calendar year reported	16 Type of account **a** ☐ Bank **b** ☐ Securities **c** ☐ Other—Enter type below

17 Name of Financial Institution in which account is held

18 Account number or other designation	19 Mailing Address (Number, Street, Suite Number) of financial institution in which account is held
20 City	21 State, if known	22 Zip/Postal Code, if known	23 Country

34 Last Name or Organization Name of Account Owner	35 Taxpayer Identification Number of Account Owner

36 First Name	37 Middle initial	38 Address (Number, Street, and Apt. or Suite No.)
39 City	40 State	41 Zip/Postal Code	42 Country

43 Filer's Title with this Owner

---

15 Maximum value of account during calendar year reported	16 Type of account **a** ☐ Bank **b** ☐ Securities **c** ☐ Other—Enter type below

17 Name of Financial Institution in which account is held

18 Account number or other designation	19 Mailing Address (Number, Street, Suite Number) of financial institution in which account is held
20 City	21 State, if known	22 Zip/Postal Code, if known	23 Country

34 Last Name or Organization Name of Account Owner	35 Taxpayer Identification Number of Account Owner

36 First Name	37 Middle initial	38 Address (Number, Street, and Apt. or Suite No.)
39 City	40 State	41 Zip/Postal Code	42 Country

43 Filer's Title with this Owner

Form **TD F 90-22.1** (Rev. 3-2011)

Part V	**Information on Financial Account(s) Where the Filer is Filing a Consolidated Report**	**Form TD F 90-22.1** Page Number

Complete a Separate Block for Each Account

This side can be copied as many times as necessary in order to provide information on all accounts.

___ of ___

1 Filing for calendar year ___ ___ ___ ___	3-4 Check appropriate Identification Number ☐ Taxpayer Identification Number ☐ Foreign Identification Number Enter identification number here:	6 Last Name or Organization Name

15 Maximum value of account during calendar year reported	16 Type of account **a** ☐ Bank **b** ☐ Securities **c** ☐ Other—Enter type below

17 Name of Financial Institution in which account is held

18 Account number or other designation	19 Mailing Address (Number, Street, Suite Number) of financial institution in which account is held

20 City	21 State, if known	22 Zip/Postal Code, if known	23 Country

34 Corporate Name of Account Owner	35 Taxpayer Identification Number of Account Owner

38 Address (Number, Street, and Apt. or Suite No.)

39 City	40 State	41 Zip/Postal Code	42 Country

15 Maximum value of account during calendar year reported	16 Type of account **a** ☐ Bank **b** ☐ Securities **c** ☐ Other—Enter type below

17 Name of Financial Institution in which account is held

18 Account number or other designation	19 Mailing Address (Number, Street, Suite Number) of financial institution in which account is held

20 City	21 State, if known	22 Zip/Postal Code, if known	23 Country

34 Corporate Name of Account Owner	35 Taxpayer Identification Number of Account Owner

38 Address (Number, Street, and Apt. or Suite No.)

39 City	40 State	41 Zip/Postal Code	42 Country

15 Maximum value of account during calendar year reported	16 Type of account **a** ☐ Bank **b** ☐ Securities **c** ☐ Other—Enter type below

17 Name of Financial Institution in which account is held

18 Account number or other designation	19 Mailing Address (Number, Street, Suite Number) of financial institution in which account is held

20 City	21 State, if known	22 Zip/Postal Code, if known	23 Country

34 Corporate Name of Account Owner	35 Taxpayer Identification Number of Account Owner

38 Address (Number, Street, and Apt. or Suite No.)

39 City	40 State	41 Zip/Postal Code	42 Country

Form **TD F 90-22.1** (Rev. 3-2011)

General Instructions

Form TD F 90-22.1, Report of Foreign Bank and Financial Accounts (the "FBAR"), is used to report a financial interest in or signature authority over a foreign financial account. The FBAR must be **received** by the Department of the Treasury on or before **June 30th** of the year immediately following the calendar year being reported. The June 30th filing date may not be extended.

Who Must File an FBAR. A United States person that has a financial interest in or signature authority over foreign financial accounts must file an FBAR if the aggregate value of the foreign financial accounts exceeds $10,000 at any time during the calendar year. See General Definitions, to determine who is a United States person.

General Definitions

Financial Account. A financial account includes, but is not limited to, a securities, brokerage, savings, demand, checking, deposit, time deposit, or other account maintained with a financial institution (or other person performing the services of a financial institution). A financial account also includes a commodity futures or options account, an insurance policy with a cash value (such as a whole life insurance policy), an annuity policy with a cash value, and shares in a mutual fund or similar pooled fund (i.e., a fund that is available to the general public with a regular net asset value determination and regular redemptions).

Foreign Financial Account. A foreign financial account is a financial account located outside of the United States. For example, an account maintained with a branch of a United States bank that is physically located outside of the United States is a foreign financial account. An account maintained with a branch of a foreign bank that is physically located in the United States is not a foreign financial account.

Financial Interest. A United States person has a financial interest in a foreign financial account for which:

(1) the United States person is the owner of record or holder of legal title, regardless of whether the account is maintained for the benefit of the United States person or for the benefit of another person; or

(2) the owner of record or holder of legal title is one of the following:

(a) An agent, nominee, attorney, or a person acting in some other capacity on behalf of the United States person with respect to the account;

(b) A corporation in which the United States person owns directly or indirectly: (i) more than 50 percent of the total value of shares of stock or (ii) more than 50 percent of the voting power of all shares of stock;

(c) A partnership in which the United States person owns directly or indirectly: (i) an interest in more than 50 percent of the partnership's profits (e.g., distributive share of partnership income taking into account any special allocation agreement) or (ii) an interest in more than 50 percent of the partnership capital;

(d) A trust of which the United States person: (i) is the trust grantor and (ii) has an ownership interest in the trust for United States federal tax purposes. See 26 U.S.C. sections 671-679 to determine if a grantor has an ownership interest in a trust;

(e) A trust in which the United States person has a greater than 50 percent present beneficial interest in the assets or income of the trust for the calendar year; or

(f) Any other entity in which the United States person owns directly or indirectly more than 50 percent of the voting power, total value of equity interest or assets, or interest in profits.

Person. A person means an individual and legal entities including, but not limited to, a limited liability company, corporation, partnership, trust, and estate.

Signature Authority. Signature authority is the authority of an individual (alone or in conjunction with another individual) to control the disposition of assets held in a foreign financial account by direct communication (whether in writing or otherwise) to the bank or other financial institution that maintains the financial account. See Exceptions, Signature Authority.

United States. For FBAR purposes, the United States includes the States, the District of Columbia, all United States territories and possessions (e.g., American Samoa, the Commonwealth of the Northern Mariana Islands, the Commonwealth of Puerto Rico, Guam, and the United States Virgin Islands), and the Indian lands as defined in the Indian Gaming Regulatory Act. References to the laws of the United States include the laws of the United States federal government and the laws of all places listed in this definition.

United States Person. United States person means United States citizens; United States residents; entities, including but not limited to, corporations, partnerships, or limited liability companies created or organized in the United States or under the laws of the United States; and trusts or estates formed under the laws of the United States.

Note. The federal tax treatment of an entity does not determine whether the entity has an FBAR filing requirement. For example, an entity that is disregarded for purposes of Title 26 of the United States Code must file an FBAR, if otherwise required to do so. Similarly, a trust for which the trust income, deductions, or credits are taken into account by another person for purposes of Title 26 of the United States Code must file an FBAR, if otherwise required to do so.

United States Resident. A United States resident is an alien residing in the United States. To determine if the filer is a resident of the United States apply the residency tests in 26 U.S.C. section 7701(b). When applying the residency tests, use the definition of United States in these instructions.

Exceptions

Certain Accounts Jointly Owned by Spouses. The spouse of an individual who files an FBAR is not required to file a separate FBAR if the following conditions are met: (1) all the financial accounts that the non-filing spouse is required to report are jointly owned with the filing spouse; (2) the filing spouse reports the jointly owned accounts on a timely filed FBAR; and (3) both spouses sign the FBAR in Item 44. See Explanations for Specific Items, Part III, Items 25-33. Otherwise, both spouses are required to file separate FBARs, and each spouse must report the entire value of the jointly owned accounts.

Consolidated FBAR. If a United States person that is an entity is named in a consolidated FBAR filed by a greater than 50 percent owner, such entity is not required to file a separate FBAR. See Explanations for Specific Items, Part V.

Correspondent/Nostro Account. Correspondent or nostro accounts (which are maintained by banks and used solely for bank-to-bank settlements) are not required to be reported.

Governmental Entity. A foreign financial account of any governmental entity of the United States (as defined above) is not required to be reported by any person. For purposes of this form, governmental entity includes a college or university that is an agency of, an instrumentality of, owned by, or operated by a governmental entity. For purposes of this form, governmental entity also includes an employee retirement or welfare benefit plan of a governmental entity.

International Financial Institution. A foreign financial account of any international financial institution (if the United States government is a member) is not required to be reported by any person.

IRA Owners and Beneficiaries. An owner or beneficiary of an IRA is not required to report a foreign financial account held in the IRA.

Participants in and Beneficiaries of Tax-Qualified Retirement Plans. A participant in or beneficiary of a retirement plan described in Internal Revenue Code section 401(a), 403(a), or 403(b) is not required to report a foreign financial account held by or on behalf of the retirement plan.

Signature Authority. Individuals who have signature authority over, but no financial interest in, a foreign financial account are not required to report the account in the following situations:

(1) An officer or employee of a bank that is examined by the Office of the Comptroller of the Currency, the Board of Governors of the Federal Reserve System, the Federal Deposit Insurance Corporation, the Office of Thrift Supervision, or the National Credit Union Administration is not required to report signature authority over a foreign financial account owned or maintained by the bank.

(2) An officer or employee of a financial institution that is registered with and examined by the Securities and Exchange Commission or Commodity Futures Trading Commission is not required to report signature authority over a foreign financial account owned or maintained by the financial institution.

U.S. Taxation of International Operations: Key Knowledge

(3) An officer or employee of an Authorized Service Provider is not required to report signature authority over a foreign financial account that is owned or maintained by an investment company that is registered with the Securities and Exchange Commission. Authorized Service Provider means an entity that is registered with and examined by the Securities and Exchange Commission and provides services to an investment company registered under the Investment Company Act of 1940.

(4) An officer or employee of an entity that has a class of equity securities listed (or American depository receipts listed) on any United States national securities exchange is not required to report signature authority over a foreign financial account of such entity.

(5) An officer or employee of a United States subsidiary is not required to report signature authority over a foreign financial account of the subsidiary if its United States parent has a class of equity securities listed on any United States national securities exchange and the subsidiary is included in a consolidated FBAR report of the United States parent.

(6) An officer or employee of an entity that has a class of equity securities registered (or American depository receipts in respect of equity securities registered) under section 12(g) of the Securities Exchange Act is not required to report signature authority over a foreign financial account of such entity.

Trust Beneficiaries. A trust beneficiary with a financial interest described in section (2)(e) of the financial interest definition is not required to report the trust's foreign financial accounts on an FBAR if the trust, trustee of the trust, or agent of the trust: **(1)** is a United States person and **(2)** files an FBAR disclosing the trust's foreign financial accounts.

United States Military Banking Facility. A financial account maintained with a financial institution located on a United States military installation is not required to be reported, even if that military installation is outside of the United States.

Filing Information

When and Where to File. The FBAR is an annual report and must be **received** by the Department of the Treasury **on or before June 30th** of the year following the calendar year being reported. **Do Not file with federal income tax return.**

File by mailing to:

Department of the Treasury
Post Office Box 32621
Detroit, MI 48232-0621

If an express delivery service is used, file by mailing to:

IRS Enterprise Computing Center
ATTN: CTR Operations Mailroom, 4th Floor
985 Michigan Avenue
Detroit, MI 48226

The FBAR may be hand delivered to any local office of the Internal Revenue Service for forwarding to the Department of the Treasury, Detroit, MI. The FBAR may also be delivered to the Internal Revenue Service's tax attaches located in United States embassies and consulates for forwarding to the Department of the Treasury, Detroit, MI. The FBAR is not considered filed until it is received by the Department of the Treasury in Detroit, MI.

No Extension of Time to File. There is no extension of time available for filing an FBAR. Extensions of time to file federal tax returns do NOT extend the time for filing an FBAR. If a delinquent FBAR is filed, attach a statement explaining the reason for the late filing.

Amending a Previously Filed FBAR. To amend a filed FBAR, check the "Amended" box in the upper right hand corner of the first page of the FBAR, make the needed additions or corrections, attach a statement explaining the additions or corrections, and staple a copy of the original FBAR to the amendment. An amendment should not be made until at least 90 calendar days after the original FBAR is filed. Follow the instructions in "When and Where to File" to file an amendment.

Record Keeping Requirements. Persons required to file an FBAR must retain records that contain the name in which each account is maintained, the number or other designation of the account, the name and address of the foreign financial institution that maintains the account, the type of account, and the maximum account value of each account during the reporting period. The records must be retained for a

period of 5 years from June 30th of the year following the calendar year reported and must be available for inspection as provided by law. Retaining a copy of the filed FBAR can help to satisfy the record keeping requirements.

An officer or employee who files an FBAR to report signature authority over an employer's foreign financial account is not required to personally retain records regarding these accounts.

Questions. For questions regarding the FBAR, contact the Detroit Computing Center Hotline at 1-800-800-2877, option 2.

Explanations for Specific Items

Part I — Filer Information

Item 1. The FBAR is an annual report. Enter the calendar year being reported. If amending a previously filed FBAR, check the "Amended" box.

Item 2. Check the box that describes the filer. Check only one box. Individuals reporting only signature authority, check box "a". If filing a consolidated FBAR, check box "d". To determine if a consolidated FBAR can be filed, see Part V. If the type of filer is not listed in boxes "a" through "c", check box "e", and enter the type of filer. Persons that should check box "e" include, but are not limited to, trusts, estates, limited liability companies, and tax-exempt entities (even if the entity is organized as a corporation). A disregarded entity must check box "e", and enter the type of entity followed by "(D.E.)". For example, a limited liability company that is disregarded for United States federal tax purposes would enter "limited liability company (D.E.)".

Item 3. Provide the filer's United States taxpayer identification number. Generally, this is the filer's United States social security number (SSN), United States individual taxpayer identification number (ITIN), or employer identification number (EIN). Throughout the FBAR, numbers should be entered with no spaces, dashes, or other punctuation. If the filer does NOT have a United States taxpayer identification number, complete Item 4.

Item 4. Complete Item 4 only if the filer does NOT have a United States taxpayer identification number. Item 4 requires the filer to provide information from an official foreign government document to verify the filer's nationality or residence. Enter the document number followed by the country of issuance, check the appropriate type of document, and if "other" is checked, provide the type of document.

Item 5. If the filer is an individual, enter the filer's date of birth, using the month, day, and year convention.

Items 9, 10, 11, 12, and 13. Enter the filer's address. An individual residing in the United States must enter the street address of the individual's United States residence, not a post office box. An individual residing outside the United States must enter the individual's United States mailing address. If the individual does not have a United States mailing address, the individual must enter a foreign residence address. An entity must enter its United States mailing address. If the entity does not have a United States mailing address, the entity must enter its foreign mailing address.

Item 14. If the filer has a financial interest in 25 or more foreign financial accounts, check "Yes" and enter the number of accounts. Do not complete Part II or Part III of the FBAR. If filing a consolidated FBAR, only complete Part V, Items 34-42, for each United States entity included in the consolidated FBAR.

Note. If the filer has signature authority over 25 or more foreign financial accounts, only complete Part IV, Items 34-43, for each person for which the filer has signature authority, and check "No" in Part I, Item 14.

Filers must comply with applicable recording keeping requirements. See Record Keeping Requirements.

Part II — Information on Financial Account(s) Owned Separately

Enter information in the applicable parts of the form only. Number the pages used, and mail only those pages. If there is not enough space to provide all account information, copy and complete additional pages of the required Part as necessary. Do not use any attachments unless otherwise specified in the instructions.

Item 15. Determining Maximum Account Value.

Step 1. Determine the maximum value of each account (in the currency of that account) during the calendar year being reported. The maximum value of an account is a reasonable approximation of the greatest value of currency or nonmonetary assets in the account during the calendar year. Periodic account statements may be relied on to determine the maximum value of the account, provided that the statements fairly reflect the maximum account value during the calendar year. For Item 15, if the filer had a financial interest in more than one account, each account must be valued separately.

Step 2. In the case of non-United States currency, convert the maximum account value for each account into United States dollars. Convert foreign currency by using the Treasury's Financial Management Service rate (this rate may be found at www.fms.treas.gov) from the last day of the calendar year. If no Treasury Financial Management Service rate is available, use another verifiable exchange rate and provide the source of that rate. In valuing currency of a country that uses multiple exchange rates, use the rate that would apply if the currency in the account were converted into United States dollars on the last day of the calendar year.

If the aggregate of the maximum account values exceeds $10,000, an FBAR must be filed. An FBAR is not required to be filed if the person did not have $10,000 of aggregate value in foreign financial accounts at any time during the calendar year.

For United States persons with a financial interest in or signature authority over fewer than 25 accounts that are unable to determine if the aggregate maximum account values of the accounts exceeded $10,000 at any time during the calendar year, complete Part II, III, IV, or V, as appropriate, for each of these accounts and enter "value unknown" in Item 15.

Item 16. Indicate the type of account. Check only one box. If "Other" is selected, describe the account.

Item 17. Provide the name of the financial institution with which the account is held.

Item 18. Provide the account number that the financial institution uses to designate the account.

Items 19-23. Provide the complete mailing address of the financial institution where the account is located. If the foreign address does not include a state (e.g., province) or postal code, leave the box(es) blank.

Part III — Information on Financial Account(s) Owned Jointly

Enter information in the applicable parts of the form only. Number the pages used, and mail only those pages. If there is not enough space to provide all account information, copy and complete additional pages of the required Part as necessary. Do not use any attachments unless otherwise specified in the instructions.

For Items 15-23, see Part II. Each joint owner must report the entire value of the account as determined under Item 15.

Item 24. Enter the number of joint owners for the account. If the exact number is not known, provide an estimate. Do not count the filer when determining the number of joint owners.

Items 25-33. Use the identifying information of the principal joint owner (excluding the filer) to complete Items 25-33. Leave blank items for which no information is available. If the filer's spouse has an interest in a jointly owned account, the filer's spouse is the principal joint owner. Enter "(spouse)" on line 26 after the last name of the joint spousal owner. See Exceptions, Certain Accounts Jointly Owned by Spouses, to determine if the filer's spouse is required to independently report the jointly owned accounts.

Part IV — Information on Financial Account(s) Where Filer has Signature Authority but No Financial Interest in the Account(s)

Enter information in the applicable parts of the form only. Number the pages used, and mail only those pages. If there is not enough space to provide all account information, copy and complete additional pages of the required Part as necessary. Do not use any attachments unless otherwise specified in the instructions.

25 or More Foreign Financial Accounts. Filers with signature authority over 25 or more foreign financial accounts must complete only Items 34-43 for each person on whose behalf the filer has signature authority.

Modified Reporting for United States Persons Residing and Employed Outside of the United States. A United States person who (1) resides outside of the United States, (2) is an officer or employee of an employer who is physically located outside of the United States, and (3) has signature authority over a foreign financial account that is owned or maintained by the individual's employer should only complete Part I and Part IV, Items 34-43 of the FBAR. Part IV, Items 34-43 should only be completed one time with information about the individual's employer.

For Items 15-23, see Part II.

Items 34-42. Provide the name, address, and identifying number of the owner of the foreign financial account for which the individual has signature authority over but no financial interest in the account. If there is more than one owner of the account for which the individual has signature authority, provide the information in Items 34-42 for the principal joint owner (excluding the filer). If account information is completed for more than one account of the same owner, identify the owner only once and write "Same Owner" in Item 34 for the succeeding accounts with the same owner.

Item 43. Enter filer's title for the position that provides signature authority (e.g., treasurer).

Part V — Information on Financial Account(s) Where Corporate Filer Is Filing a Consolidated Report

Enter information in the applicable parts of the form only. Number the pages used, and mail only those pages. If there is not enough space to provide all account information, copy and complete additional pages of the required Part as necessary. Do not use any attachments unless otherwise specified in the instructions.

Who Can File a Consolidated FBAR. An entity that is a United States person that owns directly or indirectly a greater than 50 percent interest in another entity that is required to file an FBAR is permitted to file a consolidated FBAR on behalf of itself and such other entity. Check box "d" in Part I, Item 2 and complete Part V. If filing a consolidated FBAR and reporting 25 or more foreign financial accounts, complete only Items 34-42 for each entity included in the consolidated FBAR.

For Items 15-23, see Part II.

Items 34-42. Provide the name, United States taxpayer identification number, and address of the owner of the foreign financial account as shown on the books of the financial institution. If account information is completed for more than one account of the same owner, identify the owner only once and write "Same Owner" in Item 34 for the succeeding accounts of the same owner.

Signatures

Items 44-46. The FBAR must be signed by the filer named in Part I. If the FBAR is being filed on behalf of a partnership, corporation, limited liability company, trust, estate, or other entity, it must be signed by an authorized individual. Enter the authorized individual's title in Item 45.

An individual must leave "Filer's Title" blank, unless the individual is filing an FBAR due to the individual's signature authority. If an individual is filing because the individual has signature authority over a foreign financial account, the individual should enter the title upon which his or her authority is based in Item 45.

A spouse included as a joint owner, who does not file a separate FBAR in accordance with the instructions in Part III, must also sign the FBAR (in Item 44) for the jointly owned accounts. See the instructions for Part III.

Penalties

A person who is required to file an FBAR and fails to properly file may be subject to a civil penalty not to exceed $10,000. If there is reasonable cause for the failure and the balance in the account is properly reported, no penalty will be imposed. A person who willfully fails to report an account or account identifying information may be subject to a civil monetary penalty equal to the greater of $100,000 or 50 percent of the balance in the account at the time of the violation. See 31 U.S.C. section 5321(a)(5). Willful violations may also be subject to criminal penalties under 31 U.S.C. section 5322(a), 31 U.S.C. section 5322(b), or 18 U.S.C. section 1001.

Chapter 6

Foreign Branches and Affiliated Companies

Operating Through a Foreign Branch

Introduction

After exporting goods, the next step for a U.S. business is conducting direct business operations overseas, either through foreign branch operations or through affiliated corporations. A foreign business operation may manufacture goods, provide services, or perform special functions (for example, advertising, financing, and sales). Frequently a foreign business operation requires a significant number of full-time personnel, including people who are transferred from the United States to the foreign country.

General Considerations

The term "branch" describes a complete, distinct business operation of a U.S. corporation. Although a branch may be separate in terms of function, personnel, or location, it is part of the same U.S. corporation. All of a branch's items of income and expense are combined on U.S. Form 1120 with the income and expense of the business's U.S. operations.

Whether an Operation Is a Branch or a Corporation

Choosing to operate in a foreign country either as a branch or a corporation has significant tax consequences. For example, determining whether a foreign business operation constitutes a separate corporation for U.S. tax purposes will affect the amount and the timing of available foreign tax credits, the applicability of the pass-through rules of Subpart F, applicability of other deferral rules of Subchapter C, as well as a number of other Internal Revenue Code provisions.

Example 6-1

Brubeck Boilerplate Corp., a U.S. corporation, manufactures electric heaters in its domestic plant. It manufactures 220-volt heaters for the central European market in its branch in the Grand Duchy of Aukum. Aukum law requires every foreign-owned plant to adopt a fixed opening amount of capital investment and to compute its taxable income as if it were incorporated under Aukum law. Remittances from the branch to the home office are treated as if they were dividends and are subject to a withholding tax of 12 percent.

Brubeck also manufactures heaters for the Middle Eastern market in the Emirate of Jamul. Local business custom has impelled Brubeck to place its Jamul branch into a legal entity called an enterprise. Under Jamul law, and by the terms of the formation documents, the enterprise creates an entity with separate legal personality, a separate balance sheet, and separate local tax liability. Ownership of

> the enterprise is evidenced by share certificates. The duration of any enterprise is limited by law to ten years, the shareholders are fully liable for any debts of the enterprise, and the share certificates are not transferable without permission of the Jamul Foreign Investment Board.

The following discussion reviews the law as it applies to the facts presented in Example 6-1.

Regulations published in 1996 permit an unincorporated business organization to elect to be treated as a corporation or as a partnership. Under prior law, the determination of whether the Aukum and Jamal entities constitute branch operations or affiliated corporations is an analysis of whether each entity possesses sufficient corporate characteristics. Corporate characteristics include the following:

- Associates,

- An objective to carry on a business and divided gains therefrom,

- Continuity of life,

- Centralized management,

- Limited liability, and

- Free transferability of ownership interests.

Under prior law an organization must possess a majority of these characteristics to be classified as a corporation. Prior law is based on historical differences under local (U.S. state) law between partnerships and corporations.

Many states have revised statutes to provide that partnerships and other unincorporated organizations may possess characteristics traditionally associated with corporations. Some state partnership statutes now provide that no partnership is unconditionally liable for all debts of the partnership. Similarly almost all states have enacted statutes allowing the formation of limited liability companies. These entities provide protection of all members from liability, but may qualify as partnerships for federal tax purposes under prior law.

Per Se Corporations

The 1996 regulations apply to any "business entity"—defined as an organization that is recognized as an entity for federal tax purposes and is not classified as a trust or other special entity for federal tax purposes. Several types of business entities are always treated as corporations for federal tax purposes, including the entities listed below.

- A business entity organized under a federal or state law that describes the entity as "incorporated as a corporation, body corporate, or body politic [or] as a joint-stock company or joint-stock association…"

- A business entity organized under any one of several dozen foreign laws specifically identified in the 1996 regulations as analogous to state incorporation laws.

- An entity subject to tax as an insurance company.

- A business entity wholly owned by a foreign government.

- A business entity that is required to be taxed as a corporation, for example, a publicly traded partnership.

Assume that neither Aukum nor Jamal statutes applicable to Brubeck Boilerplate's plant operations in Aukum and Jamal are foreign statutes specifically identified in the 1996 regulations as analogous to state incorporation laws. Therefore, neither of Brubeck Boilerplate's plant operations constitutes a *per se* corporation.

Form 8832 Election

A business entity that is not a *per se* corporation can elect to be taxed as a corporation or as a partnership (if it has two or more owners) or to be disregarded as an entity separate from its owner if it has only one owner. The election is made or changed by filing Form 8832 with the appropriate IRS Center. The election is effective as of the date stated on the Form 8832 provided that date is not more than 75 days before or 12 months after the election is filed. If no effective date is specified on Form 8832, the election is effective when filed. For example, a newly organized entity may make an election effective as of the date of organization if the election is filed within 75 days of the organization date.

No Election Made

If no election is made, an entity organized under the laws of the United States or any U.S. state or the District of Columbia after December 31, 1996 is treated as a partnership if the newly organized entity has two or more owners or is disregarded if the newly organized entity has one owner. Any other entity (any entity organized under laws other than those of the United States or any state or the District of Columbia) organized after December 31, 1996 is

- Treated as a partnership if the entity has two or more owners, at least one of whom has unlimited liability,

- Disregarded if the entity has one owner and the owner has unlimited liability, or

- Treated as a corporation if none of its owners has unlimited liability.

Under these rules, if no election is made, Brubeck Boilerplate's Aukum plant operation will be treated as a corporation because its owner, Brubeck Boilerplate, does not have unlimited liability under Aukum law. Brubeck Boilerplate's Jamal plant operation will be disregarded because the owner of the Jamal plant operation, Brubeck Boilerplate, has unlimited liability under Jamal law.

Unlimited liability is personal liability for the debts of or for the claims against the entity by reason of being an owner. An owner has personal liability if creditors of the entity may seek satisfaction of all or any portion of the debts or claims against the entity from the owner.

An entity in existence on January 1, 1997, retains the status claimed under prior law until that entity elects a different status under the 1996 regulations.

Effect of Designations under Foreign Law

Although the analysis of whether a corporation has a branch or an affiliated corporation is made under U.S. principles, foreign law must also be considered to determine the legal relationships of the entity, the shareholders and the general public. A U.S. taxpayer generally does not rely on the designation or labeling of the entity by that foreign jurisdiction. However, in the case of the Jamul entity in Example 6-1, it is Jamul law that tells us that there is no free transferability of interests, no continuity of life, and no limitation of liability of the shareholders.

Threshold of Liability to Foreign Tax

The basis on which a foreign country taxes a branch of a U.S. company is generally a function of the level and quality of business activity carried out by that branch. In the case of most of the U.S. trading partners with which there are income tax treaties, the liability of the branch to local tax depends on whether the branch constitutes a permanent establishment within that country and whether the income in question derives from that permanent establishment.

The Corporate Shell Issue

In some circumstances, the existence of a foreign corporation organized under local law may be ignored either by foreign authorities or by the Internal Revenue Service if that corporation does not maintain even the trappings of normal corporate existence. In addition, a foreign operation that is recognized as a corporation may nevertheless be "looked through" with respect to specific transactions. In other words, foreign authorities or the IRS may treat the corporation as an agent or straw corporation for another, related business.

> **Note:** Remember that characterizing an entity as a corporation or as a partnership turns on the legal rights and liabilities governing the entity under local law, as analyzed according to U.S. tax principles. The analysis, however, observes the legal rights and obligations as stated in the documents of formation (partnership agreement or articles of incorporation), not whether the interest holders in the entity are "likely" to act in one manner or another. In other words, a wholly owned subsidiary that elects to be taxed as a corporation and that maintains minimal corporate formalities will be treated as a separate corporation for most tax purposes even though there is absolutely no separation or interest between the subsidiary and its parent corporation. Similarly, businesses that form six or seven overlapping or stacked partnerships involving the same partners will be treated as separate entities for purposes of reporting taxable income on Form 1065.

Calculating Income of a Foreign Branch

Pre-1986 Rules

Until the Tax Reform Act of 1986, foreign-branch profits were computed either by the net worth method or the net profit method. Under the net worth method, the profit of a foreign branch, in U.S. dollars, was determined by comparing the difference between the opening and closing balance sheets of the branch. Fixed assets and liabilities were translated at the exchange rate prevailing at the time that the item was acquired or created. Current assets and liabilities were translated at the year-end exchange rate. Remittances were converted at the exchange rate prevailing on the date of the remittance. Under this method, a U.S. business recognized, in addition to actual remittances, changes in the U.S. dollar value of current assets or liabilities. Thus, any income of a foreign branch that was not remitted was picked up only insofar as it represented an increase in current assets at year-end.

Under the net profit method, a foreign branch first computed its net income as if it had a closed balance sheet like that of a separate corporation. This income was translated at the year-end exchange rate. Any remittances during the year were translated at the exchange rate prevailing at the time of the remittance. Thus, any gain or loss due to changes in the dollar value of current assets or liabilities was deferred.

Classifications under Current Law

In a manner similar to the net profit method, foreign branches that are qualified business units (QBUs) must compute their net income as if the branch had a closed balance sheet like that of a separate corporation. Also, certain QBUs must keep their books on the basis of the U.S. dollar. However, some QBUs, meeting certain qualifications, may keep their books on the basis of a foreign currency and must follow specific rules for computing taxable income on that basis.

Qualified Business Units

Only a QBU is entitled to elect to keep its books in terms of a foreign currency. A QBU is a business operation that is a "separate and clearly identified" unit of a company. The regulations provide that a QBU must be a complete business, including every operation that ordinarily forms a part of that particular business. A QBU may not perform one or more functions that merely are a part of another business. A corporation may have more than one QBU.

Functional Currency

The currency in which a foreign branch keeps its books is called its functional currency. Although the functional currency of a foreign branch is generally the U.S. dollar, a QBU may elect to use foreign currency as its functional currency if a significant part of its operations takes place in a commercial environment in which the foreign currency is used. Analysis of the commercial environment is based on the following:

1. The currency of the country in which a QBU is formed;

2. The currency of a QBU's cash flows;

3. The currency in which a QBU typically borrows and lends;

4. The currency received by a QBU from the sale of goods;

5. The currency of a QBU's principal items of income and expense;

6. The duration of a QBU's business operations; and

7. The size and nature of a QBU's independent operations.

Notwithstanding qualifying to use a foreign currency as its functional currency, a QBU may elect to use the U.S. dollar as its functional currency if it keeps its books in U.S. dollars and if it uses a separate transaction method of accounting. This U.S. dollar election is made on Form 8819, which is attached to the annual tax return for the first tax year in which the choice is available.

Computation of Net Earnings

A foreign branch that maintains its books in terms of a foreign currency must compute its net income in terms of that foreign currency. This amount is then translated into U.S. dollars at the "appropriate" exchange rate, which is generally the weighted average of the exchange rates during the tax year. Remittances are recognized only insofar as the dollar value thereof, as of the date of the remittance, generates an exchange gain or loss.

Example 6-2

Oliver Organization, Inc. maintains a foreign branch in the Commonwealth of Oxnard that qualifies as a QBU. The currency of Oxnard is the omega, which was traded ten omegas to one U.S. dollar on January 1, 2010, eight omegas to one U.S. dollar on January 1, 2009, and six omegas to one U.S. dollar on January 1, 2008. The weighted average of the exchange rates was nine omegas to one U.S. dollar for calendar year 2010 and seven omegas to one U.S. dollar for calendar year 2009. In 2009, the branch net profit was 921,000. In 2010, the branch net profit was 921,500. Taxable income of the branch may be computed as follows:

	Earnings	Weighted Average Exchange Rate	Taxable Net Income
2009	921,000	7:1	$131,571
2010	921,500	9:1	102,389
Total	1,842,500		$233,960

Payment of Foreign Taxes

If a QBU pays or accrues foreign taxes during a tax year, the amount of the payment is translated into U.S. dollars at the exchange rate prevailing at the time of payment. If the QBU pays additional foreign taxes or receives a refund of foreign taxes as a result of a redetermination of its tax liability, those amounts are translated at the weighted average exchange rate for the year to which the tax relates.

Adjustments for Remittances

Although the net income of a QBU is computed as if it were a separate business with its own balance sheet, legally the foreign QBU remains a part of a U.S. corporation and its income or loss is included in the calculation of taxable income in the U.S. tax return. Remittances from the QBU to the head office are not taxed again, with one exception. To the extent that the exchange rate prevailing on the date of the remittance differs from the weighted average exchange rate for the tax year, a taxpayer will recognize a currency exchange gain or loss.

Foreign currency gain or loss, called "Section 987 gain or loss," is recognized whenever property of a QBU branch is transferred to another branch of a subsidiary of the U.S. business or when the branch terminates.

The Section 987 proposed regulations utilize two pools—an equity pool and a basis pool—as tools for determining Section 987 gain or loss. Both pools essentially represent the business's investment in the branch including accumulated income. The equity pool states this investment in the branch's functional currency while the basis pool states the investment in the business' overall functional currency. Section 987 gain or loss is the difference between a branch remittance, translated into the overall functional currency at the spot rate at the remittance date, and the portion of the basis pool that is allocated to the remittance.

All transfers from a branch to other units of the business are remittances if the aggregate of these transfers during the tax year do not exceed the equity pool determined at year-end without regard to transfers from the branch during the year. If the branch's transfers during the year exceed the equity pool, the pool is allocated among the transfers by any reasonable method applied consistently for all of the business' QBU branches and each transfer is a remittance to the extent of the equity pool allocated to it.

Equity and Basis Pools

The opening balance in the equity pool is the sum of the adjusted bases of the branch's property, less branch liabilities, on the first date the branch begins business. This balance is stated in the branch's functional currency. Annually the equity pool is increased or decreased by adjustments shown below.

- Increased or decreased by taxable income or loss for the year as determined in the branch's functional currency under the profit or loss method.

- Increased by amounts transferred by the business to the branch during the year and decreased by transfers from the branch to other branches or the business's head office.

Borrowings and principal repayments of borrowings generally have no effect on the pool because borrowing and repayments neither create nor reduce basis.

The basis pool is determined in the same way as the equity pool, except for the adjustments shown below.

- The opening balance is translated into the business's overall functional currency (U.S. dollars) at the spot rate for the date on which the profit and loss method is first used.

- Branch profit or loss is translated into the overall functional currency at the average exchange rate over the tax year.

- Transfers to the branch from other branches of the business are translated into the overall functional currency at the spot on the transfer date, as are transfers from the branch that are not remittances because the transfers exceed the equity pool.

Section 987 Gain or Loss—Remittances

Section 987 gain or loss is recognized on remittances to the extent of the difference between the amounts of the remittance and the portion of the basis pool allocated to the remittance. The gain or loss is treated as income or loss of the business apart from the operating results of the branch and is not reported on the branch's profit or loss statement. The amount of a remittance is generally the remitted property basis, in the branch's functional currency, translated into the business's overall functional currency at the spot rate on the remittance date. The portion of the basis pool allocated to a remittance is the amount of the pool, multiplied the amount of the remittance in the branch's functional currency and divided by the basis pool.

Example 6-3

Assume, as in Example 6-2, that during the first year of branch operations in Oxnard (Year One), Oliver Organization and its Oxnard branch engage in the transactions listed below:

- Oliver Organization transfers 1,000 omegas to its Oxnard branch when 1 omega = $1

- Oliver Organization transfers $1,000 to the branch when 1 omega = $2

- The Oxnard branch has profits of 1,000 omegas, which are translated at the average exchange rate during Year One of 1 omega = $2

- The Oxnard branch transfers 1,000 omegas to Oliver Organization when 1 omega = $2

Before considering the fourth transaction, the Oxnard branch's equity and basis pools as of Year One year-end are calculated as shown below.

	Equity	**Basis**
Opening Balance	0	0
Increased by profits	1,000 omegas	$2,000
Transfers		
1,000 omegas	1,000 omegas	1,000
$1,000	500 omegas	1,000
	2,500 omegas	$4,000

The Oxnard branch's 1,000 omega transfer to Oliver Organization is a remittance because the transfer does not exceed the year-end balance in the equity pool, determined without regard to the remittance. The portion of the basis pool allocated to the remittance is calculated as shown below:

$$\frac{1,000 \text{ omegas}}{2,500 \text{ omegas}} \times \$4,000 = \$1,600$$

Section 987 gain is $400: The excess of (1) the dollar value of the 1,000 omega remittance, translated at the spot rate at the transfer date (1 omega = $2), which is $2,000 over (2) the basis allocated to the distribution ($1,600). The remitted 1,000 omegas is no longer functional currency, because Oliver Organization's overall functional currency is the dollar. The omegas are treated as property other than money with a basis of $2,000 (1,000 × $2).

The U.S. Dollar Election

A QBU that would ordinarily use a foreign currency as its functional currency may elect to use the U.S. dollar for this purpose, but only if it is an "eligible QBU." An eligible QBU is one for which the appropriate functional currency would otherwise be a hyperinflationary currency (that is, one that has experienced inflation of at least 100 percent annually over the three preceding years).

A QBU that makes the U.S. dollar election computes its earnings on the basis of a four-step process called the dollar approximate separate transactions method. This four-step method is as follows:

1. The QBU computes its net earnings in a foreign currency.

2. The QBU makes necessary adjustments to conform the income statement to U.S. tax accounting principles.

3. The QBU translates items of income and expense on the basis of the weighted average exchange rate prevailing for the reported period.

4. The QBU computes its currency gain or loss for the year as follows:

   a. The net worth of the QBU in historical U.S. dollars for the current tax year; plus

   b. The dollar amount of any item that decreased the net worth of the QBU for the year but does not affect the net income of the QBU; minus

   c. The net worth of the QBU in historical U.S. dollars for the preceding tax year; minus

   d. The amount of net income of the QBU, if any, earned in U.S. dollars; minus

   e. The U.S. dollar amount of any item that increased the net worth of the QBU for the year but does not affect the net income of the QBU.

With respect to step 3, allowances for depreciation, depletion, or amortization are translated on the basis of the weighted average exchange rate for the reported period. Inventory items are translated on the basis of the weighted average exchange rate for the reported period, except that items written down to a lower market rate are translated on the basis of the year-end exchange rate. Prepaid expenses are translated at the weighted average exchange rate for the reported period.

The election consists of identifying the taxpayer and stating the election on Form 8819.

Transfers of Property

Pre-Section 367 Rules

Early U.S. tax statutes provided exceptions from the usual recognition rules for transfers of property among members of the same controlled corporate group. A U.S. business was able to contribute appreciated property to a corporation controlled by the U.S. business without recognition of gain whether the controlled corporation was domestic or foreign.

The Revenue Act of 1932 provided that if a U.S. business sought to qualify for non-recognition any transaction that involved a foreign corporation, the U.S. business would first have to obtain a ruling that the proposed transaction was not in pursuance of a plan having as one of its principal purposes the avoidance of federal income taxes.

Logically, a clearance statute of the type contained in the Revenue Act of 1932 requires substantive administrative guidelines in order to be effective. However, the statute remained virtually unchanged for thirty-six years, and the body of law created by the ruling practices of the Internal Revenue Service was sparse. The first comprehensive administrative guidelines were issued in Revenue Procedure 68-23. This revenue procedure set forth a set of circumstances that allowed U.S. businesses to benefit from the non-recognition provisions. For example, a transfer of business property by a U.S. business to a foreign corporation that intended to use the property to generate active business income was generally given favorable treatment under Revenue Procedure 68-23. The revenue procedure, however, also established circumstances in which taxpayers could not defer gain. For example, property that could be exploited by a foreign corporation in order to earn passive income could not be transferred without recognition of income.

Section 367 Rules

Three years after Revenue Procedure 68-23 was issued, Section 367 finally became a substantive statute, eliminating the advance ruling requirement and providing that certain transactions were taxable and that other transactions were not. Later, extensive regulations were issued that elaborated on Section 367. Section 367 was again substantially reworked in the Tax Reform Act of 1986.

General Provisions

The first group of transactions regulated by Section 367 is comprised of transfers of property by a U.S. business to a foreign corporation. The general rule is that any gain realized by the transferor will be recognized as income. However, "gain," for this purpose, does not mean net gain. Realized losses will still be deferred as if the transfer of property were made to a domestic corporation.

The Internal Contradiction of Section 367

Originally, recognition of gain by the transferor of property to a foreign corporation was the last chance to tax any appreciated gain, unless the transfer was made to a foreign personal holding company. With the enactment of Subpart F in 1962, however, the IRS effectively extended its tax net to cover many more transactions. It might have been reasonable to think, therefore, that the Service would be willing to permit non-recognition treatment for the transfer of appreciated assets to controlled foreign corporations, since any subsequent disposition would be subject to U.S. tax. Although the 1968 administrative guidelines reflect some of this "tax net" thinking, for the most part Section 367 would tax transfers of property likely to generate Subpart F income. This duality remains under current law.

THE "ACTIVE BUSINESS" EXCEPTION

Section 367(a) provides that if a U.S. person transfers property to a foreign corporation in connection with certain types of exchanges, then the foreign corporation is generally not considered to be a corporation for purposes of determining the extent to which gain is recognized on the transfer. There are several exceptions to this general rule, including the transfer of tangible property for use by the foreign transferee in the active conduct of a trade or business outside the United States, as indicated in Example 6-4.

Example 6-4

CD Co., a U.S.-based manufacturer of compact disks (CDs) for data storage, performs its research and development and manufacturing and warehousing in the United States. CD Co. has been approached by a compact disk distributor (Distco) located in Foronia. DistCo wants to contract with CD Co. for the manufacture of a line of compact disks with the DistCo brand name to be resold by DistCo in Foronia.

CD Co.'s business with DistCo develops well, and CD Co. management determines that the market potential in Foronia justifies a CD Co. physical presence there. CD Co. establishes an office in Foronia by renting office space, employing local personnel, and sending sales technicians from the United States to reside in Foronia and work for the local office there.

Sales continue to develop to the point that CD Co. management decides to establish a manufacturing operation in Foronia. Sales and net profit projections indicate that the manufacturing operation is likely to incur losses for a time, which CD Co. would like to deduct against income reported on its U.S. income tax return. Therefore, CD Co. conducts the manufacturing and sales operation as a branch of the U.S. company.

The activities of the CD Co. branch in Foronia continue to expand. Eventually, CD Co. management decides that operations in Foronia would be best conducted through a Foronia subsidiary in order to segregate activities there for legal, tax, and other purposes. Accordingly, CD Co. forms a Foronia corporation (ForCo) and transfers all of the assets and liabilities of the branch to ForCo.

This transaction will be treated as a tax-free incorporation for U.S. tax purposes under Section 351(a). Since the transfer by CD Co. is a cross-border transaction, the general rule of Section 367(a) would provide that ForCo is not a corporation for purposes of this transaction. However, the general rule will not be applicable here because the transferee is conducting an active trade or business.

Within the limits of Section 367, a business may be able to transfer appreciated property to a foreign affiliate that intends to use the property for active business operations. The ground rules for such transfers are as follows:

1. The foreign affiliate must be conducting an active business.

2. The transferred property must be used in the foreign affiliate's trade or business.

3. The transferor must report this transfer of assets on Form 926, together with its annual income tax return.

For this purpose, the term "active business" is substantially the same as in the QBU regulations. The Section 367 regulations also separate the concepts of a trade or business and active conduct of that trade or business. This separation is achieved by providing that certain investment types of activity (for example, licensing of intangibles) might be a business but not one that requires active conduct. The apparent purpose of this distinction is to deny non-recognition for transfers of property that (1) could be used by the transferee in its business and (2) could also be licensed by the transferee to other foreign affiliates.

Using the Active Business Exception

Some general guidelines on the use of the active business exception can be found in a number of revenue rulings:

1. Foreign currency is considered property to a U.S. corporation, and its transfer to a foreign affiliate would be subject to the Section 367 rules.

2. On the other hand, U.S. currency cannot appreciate, and its transfer is not ordinarily subject to Section 367.

3. A U.S. business may not offset its depreciated assets against its appreciated assets.

Exceptions to the Active Business Exception

Section 367 grants non-recognition treatment to transfers of property but not to transfers of whole businesses. Moreover, certain types of property will not be given nonrecognition treatment even if used both by the transferor and by the transferee in an active business. These types of property are as follows:

- Inventory;

- Copyrights or other rights to literary or artistic property, within the limits of Section 1221(3);

- Accounts receivable and similar property;

- Foreign currency or rights to foreign currency;

- Intangible property; and

- Leased property (unless the lessee is the transferee).

Reporting Transfers of Property

Transfers of appreciated property to a foreign corporation are reported on Form 926. Transfers to noncorporate entities were generally not covered by Section 367 and its predecessors; that role was fulfilled by Section 1491, which levied an excise tax on the value of the property transferred. Form 926 must be filed whenever a U.S. person transfers appreciated property to a noncorporate foreign legal entity.

Form 926 basically provides a check on certain types of transfers of property. If the transfer of property is governed by Section 367, then the form is merely a record. If the transfer of property is not subject to Section 367, then the return becomes the means by which the excise tax is computed and paid. The form is filed at least by the date on which the transfer of property is made.

Transfers of Certain Intangible Property

Section 367(d) provides that if a U.S. business transfers any intangible property to a foreign corporation in a non-recognition transaction, the U.S. business will be treated as having sold the property in exchange for payments which are contingent upon the productivity, use, or disposition of such property, and as receiving amounts that would have been received

- Annually in the form of such payments over the useful life of such property, or

- In the case of a disposition following such transfer (whether direct or indirect), at the time of the disposition.

The amounts recognized as income have to be commensurate with the income attributable to the intangible transferred.

The U.S. business is deemed to have sold the intangible for its fair market value. If the disposition is to a related party, then the deemed payments are received over the useful life of the intangible. In the case of a subsequent disposition of the intangible property by the foreign corporation, the U.S. business is treated as if it sold the intangible property for its fair market value. For these purposes, the term fair market value is defined as the single payment arm's-length price that would be paid for the property by an unrelated purchaser.

If a U.S. business transfers intangible property to a U.S. corporation with a principal purpose of avoiding U.S. tax and thereafter transfers the stock of that U.S. corporation to a related foreign corporation, the U.S. business will be treated as having transferred the intangible property directly to the foreign corporation. A U.S. business will be presumed to have transferred intangible property for a principal purpose of avoiding U.S. tax if the property is transferred to the U.S. corporation less than two years prior to the transfer of the stock of that U.S. corporation to a foreign corporation. This presumption may be rebutted by clear evidence that the subsequent transfer of the stock of the U.S. corporation was not contemplated at the time the intangible property was transferred to that corporation and that avoidance of U.S. tax was not a principal purpose of the transaction. A transfer may have more than one principal purpose.

The provisions of Section 367(d) are applicable only where there has been a transfer of the intangible itself, as in a contribution to capital or other form of outright transfer, as opposed to a licensing where the transferor retains significant ownership in the intangible.

> **Example 6-5**
>
> Assume the same situation as in Example 6-4, except that following the formation of ForCo, CD Co. decides that a patent it has received on manufacturing technology could more appropriately be exploited by ForCo and so transfers the patent to ForCo in a transaction that would qualify for non-recognition if it were between U.S. corporations.
>
> In this situation, Section 367(d) is applicable. CD Co. would be deemed to have sold the patent to ForCo in exchange for payments contingent upon the productivity, use or disposition of the patent and would be entitled to receive payments over the useful life of the patent, or upon its disposition, that are commensurate with the income attributable to the patent.

On the other hand, if the intangible is not transferred but instead is licensed to the foreign operation, Section 367(d) does not apply but the transfer pricing rules under Section 482 will apply, as illustrated in Example 6-6.

> **Example 6-6**
>
> Assume the same situation as in Example 6-4, except that the transfer by CD Co. to ForCo is a license arrangement, whereby CD Co. allows ForCo to use the patent for a period in a specified territory in exchange for a stated royalty rate.

Effective for amounts treated as received on or after August 5, 1997, deemed payments under Section 367(d) in exchange for outbound transfers of intangible property by means of a contribution and other nonrecognition transactions are treated as royalties for purposes of applying the separate limitation categories of the foreign tax credit.

In this situation, Section 482 would apply.

Incorporating a Foreign Branch

As foreign country branch operations expand, or as the initial step is taken in establishing operations in a foreign country, it will be appropriate to address the formation of a foreign subsidiary corporation to conduct business locally for the U.S. parent company.

> **Example 6-7**
>
> Assume the same situation as in Example 6-4, except that the business of the CD Co. branch in Foronia has continued to expand to the point that it is necessary to maintain inventories of goods and initiate manufacturing activities closer to the Foronia market. CD Co. management is analyzing whether it is appropriate to form a corporation in Foronia to continue the business of the branch.

The United States generally taxes U.S. businesses on their world-wide incomes. If U.S. businesses own foreign corporations, the United States generally taxes the foreign corporation only on income from U.S. sources or an income from a U.S. trade or business.

Overall Loss Recapture

Section 367 imposes a tax designed to recapture foreign branch losses previously deducted by a U.S. business. Even if a transfer of property by a U.S. business to a newly-incorporated foreign subsidiary qualifies for the active business exception to Section 367, the foreign-branch recapture rule will impose a tax to the extent of foreign-branch losses previously deducted by a U.S. business. The foreign-branch recapture rule may also apply to incorporations of foreign branch operations that do not qualify for the active business exception.

Definition of "Foreign Branch"

The definition of "foreign branch," for purposes of the recapture rule, is broader than that for a QBU. It includes any foreign operation, regardless of whether or not it constitutes an integral business unit. The regulations state that "foreign branch" includes any operation that might constitute a permanent establishment under the relevant tax treaty provision, but there is no guarantee that a determination that an operation does not constitute a permanent establishment will prevent the application of the loss recapture rule.

Computing the Loss Recapture Amount

One benefit of conducting initial foreign operations as a branch is the ability of the U.S. company to include start-up losses in its U.S. income tax return. These losses can then be used to offset other U.S. income, and conducting initial foreign operations as a branch avoids the existence and accumulation of losses in the foreign country, as indicated by Example 6-8.

Example 6-8

Assume the same situation as in Example 6-4, except that the Foronia branch of CD Co. has a current loss of U.S. $1,000.

If this loss is used to offset U.S. income, the current after-tax cost would be the net amount. For example if the U.S. tax rate were 40 percent, the net after-tax cost to CD Co. of the Foronia branch would be U.S. $600 and there would be no foreign earnings and profits. On the other hand, if the loss had been incurred in a Fornia corporation, with no prior profits that could be offset, the current after-tax cost would be U.S. $1,000. There would also be a deficit in the earnings and profits of the Foronia corporation.

In the event that in the next year CD Co.'s Foronia branch has a profit of U.S. $1,000, this would be taxable in Foronia at the local effective rate (for example, 50 percent); it would also be included in CD Co.'s U.S. return with normal tax liability and availability of a foreign tax credit. In this simple example, the U.S. tax liability would be U.S. $40 (40 percent rate) and the tax credit would be U.S. $50, so that there will be an excess credit carryback or carryforward. Over the two years, the net U.S. tax result is a wash ($1,000 loss in year 1, and $1,000 income in year 2), but the U.S fiscal base has actually lost revenue because of the loss in year one and profit with tax paid in Foronia and a U.S. foreign tax credit.

An "overall foreign loss" is an excess of deductions allocated and apportioned to gross income from foreign sources over that gross income. An overall foreign loss is recaptured by recharacterizing subsequent foreign source income as U.S. income. Generally, recapture of overall foreign losses has priority over recapture within the separate foreign tax credit limitation baskets except that not more than 50 percent of foreign source taxable income may be recharacterized as U.S. source income unless the U.S. business elects a higher percentage.

The 50 percent limitation is subject to two modifications.

1. *Dispositions of Foreign Business Assets*—Overall foreign loss recapture applies without the 50 percent ceiling to gain recognized on disposition of property used in a foreign business. Moreover, if property used in a foreign business is transferred in a nonrecognition transaction under Section 367 while an overall foreign loss awaits recapture, gain is recognized up to the amount of the unrecaptured loss.

> **Example 6-9**
>
> In January 2009, the William Fry Corporation opened a foreign branch (a QBU) in the Republic of Ocotillo. During calendar year 2009, the QBU realized a $1,000,000 loss. Fry Corporation's foreign branch uses equipment with a basis of $500 and a fair market value of $2,500,000. On January 1, 2010, Fry Corporation transfers the branch assets to a newly formed Ocotillo corporation.
>
> Fry Corporation recognizes $1,000,000 gain on the transfer of equipment to the Ocotillo corporation, even though Section 367 would otherwise preclude recognition. These rules apply to any transfer of property used predominantly outside the United States in a trade or business. The predominant use test is applied taking into account only use during the three years preceding the disposition, or, if less, the period the U.S. business has held the property.

The foreign loss recapture rules apply to unrecaptured overall foreign losses for all years before the disposition of foreign business assets. The unrecaptured amount of an overall foreign loss is the amount of the loss, less amounts recaptured in prior years and the amount recaptured in the current year from foreign source income other than gains on dispositions of foreign business assets. Up to the amount of unrecaptured loss, gain on disposition of foreign business assets is initially considered foreign source income, regardless of how the income would be classified under the general rules. Gain on disposition of foreign business assets is then reclassified as U.S. income by the recapture rule.

2. *Recapture Limited to Same Basket*—Overall foreign loss is recaptured only from foreign source income from the same basket or baskets as the overall foreign loss.

Section 987 Gain or Loss on Termination

Section 987 gain or loss is recognized upon termination of a QBU branch. Generally, a QBU branch terminates when its activities cease, whether as a result of the transfer of its assets to another branch of the business or a sale or other disposition of substantially all of the assets or for any other reason. A transfer of branch assets to a wholly owned, newly incorporated, foreign subsidiary of a U.S. business terminates a QBU branch.

The Section 987 gain or loss recognized upon termination of the QBU branch under the general rules for remittances made by a branch discussed above and calculated as shown below.

1. The branch's profit or loss is computed for the portion of the tax year ending with the termination date.

2. The equity and basis pools are adjusted for this profit or loss and for transfers to and by the branch during the year preceding the termination.

3. If the equity pool exceeds zero after these adjustments, Section 987 gain or loss on termination is the difference between (1) the equity pool, translated into the business' overall functional currency at the spot rate for the termination date, and (2) the basis pool.

4. If the equity is less than zero (1) the business is deemed to make a transfer to the branch immediately before the termination sufficient to bring the pool to zero; (2) this transfer increases the basis pool by the amount of the deemed transfer, translated into the overall functional currency at the spot rate on the termination date; and (3) a negative balance in the basis pool after this increase is Section 987 gain, and a positive balance is Section 987 loss.

Example 6-10

Assume, as in Example 6-3, that Oliver Organization terminates its Oxnard branch at the end of Year 10. As of the beginning of Year 10, the Oxnard branch's equity and basis pools were 200 omegas and $200, the Oxnard branch has profits of 120 omegas for the portion of the tax year ending with the termination, the average exchange rate for Year 10 is 2 omega = $1, at which rate the profits are translated as $60, and the spot rate for the termination date is 4 omegas to $1. If there are no transfers to or by the branch during the year, the equity pool at termination is 320 omegas (200 omegas at the beginning of the year plus current profit of 120 omegas), and the basis pool is $260 ($200 plus $60). Translated into dollars at the spot rate on the date of termination, the equity pool is $80 (320 omegas / 4). The difference between the translated equity pool ($80) and the basis pool ($260) is Section 987 loss ($180).

If the Oxnard branch's equity and basis pools were negative 160 omegas and negative $50 at the beginning of Year 10, the pools, after adjustment for Year 10 profit, are negative 40 omegas (negative 160 omegas plus 120 omegas) and positive $10 (negative $50 plus $60). Because the adjusted equity pool is less than zero, Oliver Organization is deemed to make a transfer to the Oxnard branch equal to the deficit (40 omegas), bringing the pool to zero. The corresponding increase to the basis pool, translated at the spot rate for the date of termination, is $10 (4 omegas / 4), bringing the basis pool to $20. This $20 is Section 987 loss.

Overall Foreign Loss Recapture on Sale of CFC Stock

Effective for dispositions after October 22, 2004, gain on dispositions of controlled foreign corporation stock in which a taxpayer owns more than 50 percent by vote or value are recognized as U.S.-source income for foreign tax credit limitation purposes in an amount equal to the lesser of the fair market value of the stock over adjusted basis or the amount of prior unrecaptured overall foreign losses without regard to the 50 percent limit.

Gains realized in Section 351 contributions to corporations, Section 721 contributions to partnerships, Section 332 liquidations and other reorganizations are not recaptured as U.S.-source income if, after the transaction, the transferor owns the same percentage of stock in the controlled foreign corporation that the transferor owned prior to the transaction.

Recharacterization of Overall Domestic Loss

U.S.-source income earned in tax years beginning after 2008 will be recharacterized as foreign-source income in an amount equal to the lesser of (1) the amount of U.S.-source loss or (2) 50 percent of U.S.-source income. U.S.-source income so recharacterized will be allocated among and increases foreign tax credit limitation categories in the same proportion that the separate limitation categories were reduced by previous U.S.-source losses.

Reporting Requirements for Foreign Branches and Affiliates

Corporate Foreign Tax Credit—Form 1118

In addition to claiming foreign tax credits on Form 1118 for taxes actually paid or accrued, a U.S. business receiving dividends from foreign affiliates may also claim a credit for foreign taxes deemed paid by the affiliate on the earnings from which dividends are paid. This is the "deemed paid" credit for foreign taxes.

Example 6-11

Kolb Industries owns 100 percent of the only class of stock of two corporations in two foreign countries, Phelan and Piru. The subsidiary in Piru, in turn, owns 100 percent of the only class of stock of a corporation in Pixley. At the end of 2010, Kolb-Phelan paid a dividend of $372,750 to Kolb-U.S.; Kolb-Piru paid a dividend of $203,435 to Kolb-U.S.; and Kolb-Pixley paid a dividend of $645,000 to Kolb-Piru. For 2010, the relevant financial data are as follows:

	Kolb-Phelan Owned by: Kolb-U.S.	**Kolb-Piru** Kolb-U.S.	**Kolb-Pixley** Kolb-Piru
E&P:	$2,500,000	$2,000,000	$600,000
Income	2,250,000	450,000	1,650,000
Expenses	1,375,000	116,500	575,000
Profits	875,000	333,500	1,075,000
For. tax rate	29%	39%	25%
Tax paid	253,750	130,065	268,750
Profits	621,250	203,435	806,250

Based on the facts in Example 6-11:

Kolb-U.S. must report its dividend income on Form 1118. Kolb-U.S. begins completing the form first by checking the box for "All Other Income From Sources Outside the U.S. (General Limitation Income)" at the top of the form. Now, Kolb-U.S. is ready to complete Schedule A.

Schedule A

Kolb-U.S. completes Schedule A, Column 1, Lines A and B, listing its limitation income from Phelan and Piru. The dividends are listed in Columns 3a and 3b, Lines A and B. The amounts in Column 3a, Lines A and B are the dividends paid without taking into account any foreign taxes paid, and the amounts in Column 3b, Lines A and B are the foreign taxes attributable to the dividends paid. The amounts in Column 3b, Lines A and B, are arrived at by grossing up the dividends by the tax rate of each foreign country (29 percent and 39 percent for Phelan and Piru, respectively), and then adding those amounts to the withholding taxes actually paid.

With respect to the dividend income paid to Kolb-U.S. by the Phelan subsidiary, the tax rate of Phelan, expressed as a decimal, is subtracted from 1.00 (1.00 – 0.29 = 0.71). The dividend paid to Kolb-U.S. is then divided by the difference ($372,750 / 0.71 = $525,000), resulting in the pretax earnings amount that is entered in Column 8, Line A, and again in Column 12, Line A. Now Kolb-U.S. computes the first part of the gross-up by subtracting the dividend paid to it from the pretax earnings listed in Column 8, Line A ($525,000 – $372,750 = $152,250). Then, Kolb-U.S. computes the second part of the gross-up. It does so by multiplying the dividend paid to it by the Phelan subsidiary by the withholding tax, which is assumed to be 5 percent ($372,750 × .05 = $18,638). The sum of the two parts of the gross-up is entered in Column 3b, Line A ($170,888). The actual cash dividend excluding gross-up on Line 3a is similarly reduced by the 5 percent withholding. The actual dividend received is $354,112 ($372,750 – $18,638).

Schedule B

Kolb-U.S. must also complete Schedule B. First, Kolb-U.S. checks the Paid Box in Column 1, because it is claiming a credit for taxes paid, and Kolb-U.S. lists the dates it paid taxes to Phelan and Piru, respectively, on Lines A and B. Having completed the foreign withholding taxes paid to Phelan and Piru, respectively, in Part I, Columns 2a and 2h, Lines A and B, Kolb-U.S. sums the total foreign taxes paid at the base of Columns 2a and 2h ($18,638 + $20,344 = $38,982). Also, having entered the taxes deemed paid on Lines A and B of Column 3 (which was carried over from Schedule C, Part I, Column 10), Kolb-U.S. computes the total tax deemed paid at the base of Column 3 ($108,098 + $86,641 = $194,739). The total foreign taxes paid is entered in Part II, Line 1 ($38,982) and the total tax deemed paid is entered on Line 2 ($194,739). Lines 1 and 2 are then totaled, and the result, which represents total foreign taxes paid, is entered on Line 5 ($233,721). The total of Column 12 on Schedule A, $858,000, is entered on Line 6. Kolb-U.S. now enters its total taxable income from all sources on Line 7a ($2,500,000). Line 7b is blank because Kolb-U.S. has no adjustments to its income. Thus, Line 7c is the same as line 7a ($2,500,000). Now, Kolb-U.S. determines the ratio of its taxable foreign-source income, $858,000, calculated as shown on Column 12 of Schedule A, to Kolb-U.S.'s taxable Worldwide income, $2,500,000, by dividing Line 6 by Line 7c and enters the result, .3434, on Line 8. The total U.S. income tax on Worldwide taxable income, $875,000, and against which the foreign tax credit is allowed is entered on Line 9. Then, Line 9 is multiplied by the ratio of taxable foreign-source income to taxable Worldwide income on Line 8 and the result is entered on Line 10. The lesser of foreign taxes actually and deemed to have been paid, calculated as shown on Line 5 on the general limitation category limitation calculated as shown on Line 10 is entered on Line 11, $233,721.

The amount on Line 11 represents the foreign tax credit available to Kolb-U.S. and normally would be placed in Part III of Schedule B. However, the author has created a Master Schedule that replaces Schedule B, Part III. It is on this Master Schedule that the summary of all foreign tax credits is placed. While Example 6-11 involves only one statutory grouping of income (that is, general limitation income), most taxpayers will typically have foreign-source income from more than one grouping.

Schedule C

The effective tax rate on income to the Piru subsidiary is not 39 percent because part of its income has also been taxed in Pixley. The next step for Kolb-U.S. is to complete Schedule C, Part 1. Kolb-U.S. enters the name of the Kolb-Phelan subsidiary in Column 1 and the country of incorporation in Column 3. Next, the sum of the undistributed earnings and profits at the beginning of 2009 and the accumulated profits for 2010 is entered in Column 4 ($2,500,000 + $875,000 = $3,375,000). The total foreign corporate taxes paid on the total earnings is placed in Column 6a ($3,375,000 × 0.29 = $978,750). Column 6b is zero because there are no taxes deemed paid from Schedule D, Part 1, Column 9. Now Kolb-U.S. adds the amounts in Columns 4 and 6, and the total is entered in Column 7 ($978,750). Kolb-U.S. lists the gross amount of the dividends paid in the functional currency, which is assumed to be U.S. dollars ($372,750) in Column 8a. The same figure is entered in Column 8b. Now, the amount in Column 8a is divided by the amount in Column 4 ($372,750 /$3,375,000 = .1104), and the result, which represents the ratio of the dividends paid to the total earnings, is entered in Column 9. Next, the ratio in Column 9 is multiplied by the foreign taxes paid on all earnings of Kolb-Phelan in Column 6a, and the result, which represents the tax deemed paid, is entered in Column 10. This figure is then carried over to Schedule B and entered in Column 3, Line A. Also, on Schedule B, Part 1, Columns 2a and 2h, Line A, the foreign withholding taxes paid to each country, are listed.

The process just described is repeated for the Kolb-Piru subsidiary. The name of the subsidiary and the country of incorporation are listed in Columns 1 and 2, respectively. The sum of the undistributed earnings and profits at the beginning of 2009 and the accumulated profits for 2010 is entered in Column 4 ($2,000,000 + $333,500 = $2,333,500). The total foreign corporate taxes paid on the total earnings is placed in Column 6a ($2,333,500 × 0.39 = $910,065). In the case of Kolb-Piru there are taxes deemed paid, the amount of which is taken from Schedule D, Part I, Column 10 ($83,750). Now Kolb-U.S. adds the amounts in Columns 6a and 6b, and the total is entered in Column 7 ($910,065 + $83,750 = $993,815). In Column 8a, Kolb-U.S. lists the gross amount of the dividends paid in the functional currency, which is assumed to be U.S. dollars ($203,435). The same figure is entered in Column 8b. Now, the amount in Column 8a is divided by the amount in Column 3 ($203,435 / $2,333,500 =.0872), and the result, which represents the ratio of the dividends paid to the total earnings, is entered in Column 9. Next, the ratio in Column 9 is multiplied by the foreign taxes paid on all earnings of Kolb-Piru in Column 7, and the result, which represents the tax deemed paid is entered in Column 10. This figure is then carried over to Schedule B and entered in Column 3, Line B. Also, on Schedule B, Part I, Columns 2a and 2h, Line B, the foreign withholding taxes paid to each country are listed.

Schedule D—Second-Tier Tax

Because Kolb-Pixley, a second-tier corporation that is owned by Kolb-Piru, paid a dividend ($645,000) to Kolb-Piru, Schedule D, Part I, must be completed to determine the tax deemed paid on that dividend. Kolb-U.S. begins completing Schedule D, Part 1, by listing the names of the second-tier foreign corporation and its related first-tier corporation, Kolb-Pixley and Kolb-Piru respectively, in Column 1. The undistributed earnings and profits amount is entered in Column 4 ($1,625,000). In Column 5, Kolb-U.S. enters the foreign taxes paid on the earnings and profits ($418,750). Columns 6a and 6b are zero because Kolb-Pixley has not actually, or been deemed to have, paid any taxes on the dividend paid to Kolb-Piru. Now, Kolb-U.S. adds Columns 5 and 6, and the result is entered in Column 7 ($418,750 + $0 = $418,750). In Column 8a, Kolb-U.S. lists the dividends paid by Kolb-Pixley, $335,000, in the functional currency, which is assumed to be U.S. dollars. Thus, the same figure is entered in Column 8b. Now, Column 8a is divided by Column 4 ($335,000/$1,625,000 = 0.2), and the result is entered in Column 9. Column 7 is then multiplied by Column 9 ($418,750 × 0.2 = $83,750), and the result, which represents the tax deemed paid, is entered in Column 10. This amount is then carried over to Schedule C, Column 6b, on the line for Kolb-Piru, which received the dividend and which is deemed to have paid the Pixley tax.

Reporting Requirements for Foreign Affiliates—Form 5471

Purpose of the Form

Form 5471 is designed to provide a worksheet for an IRS auditor to examine transactions involving every foreign corporation in which U.S. taxpayers have a direct or indirect interest. A separate Form 5471 must be filed for each foreign corporation.

Filing Responsibility

Form 5471 is filed annually, together with the income tax return of the U.S. business. Several different types of U.S. businesses are responsible for filing Form 5471, in different permutations and combinations. These types are denominated in Categories (1) through (5). These categories are as follows:

1. Officers, directors, and 10 percent-or-more (of value) shareholders of a foreign corporation if that corporation is a foreign personal holding company. These businesses must complete the front page of Form 5471, Schedule A, Parts I and II, Schedule B and Schedule N.

2. Any officers or directors of any foreign corporation if, since the prior filing, any U.S. person has acquired either a 10 percent-or-more (of value) equity interest in the foreign corporation or an amount of stock that results in that person owning 10 percent-or-more equity interest. These businesses must complete the front page of Form 5471and Part I of Schedule O. For transactions that occurred prior to January 1, 1998, the stock ownership requirement was 5 percent (of value).

3. Any person that acquires a 10 percent-or-more (of value) equity interest in a foreign corporation; a U.S. person that has acquired an additional 10 percent-or-more equity interest in a foreign corporation since the last filing; a U.S. person that ends up owning a 10 percent-or-more equity interest in a foreign corporation at the time when that corporation undergoes a "tax-deferred reorganization," within the meaning of Section 361; a U.S. person that reduces its equity interest in a foreign corporation below 10 percent; and a person that becomes a U.S. person while owning a 10

percent-or-more equity interest in a foreign corporation. These businesses must complete the identifying information on page one of Form 5471 (the information above Schedule A), Schedule A Part I, Schedule B, Schedules C, E and F and Part II of Schedule O.

4.   This category includes U.S. citizens or residents, electing nonresident aliens, domestic partnerships, domestic corporations and domestic estates and trusts which owned, for an uninterrupted period of at least 30 days, more than 50 percent of the total value of all classes of stock in the foreign corporation. For this purpose if any of these entities owns more than 50 percent of the combined voting power or value of all classes of stock in a foreign corporation that, in turn, owns more than 50 percent of the voting power or value of another foreign corporation, that entity is also treated as owning more than 50 percent of the voting power or value of the second foreign corporation. Businesses in this category must complete the identifying information on page 1 (the information above Schedule A), Schedule A Part I, Schedule B, Schedules C, E and F and Schedules H, I, J and M of Form 5471.

5.   Citizens or residents of the United States, domestic partnerships, corporations and estates and trusts owning directly, indirectly or constructively 10 percent or more of the total combined voting power or value of a controlled foreign corporation or any shares of a controlled foreign corporation that is a captive insurance company. A controlled foreign corporation is a foreign corporation owned by U.S. shareholders that own directly, indirectly or constructively more than 50 percent of the total combined voting power or value of the stock of the corporation. Businesses in this category must complete the identifying information on page 1 (the information above Schedule A), Schedules H, I and Separate Schedule J of Form 5471.

Sample Form 6-1

| Form **1118** (Rev. December 2009) Department of the Treasury Internal Revenue Service | **Foreign Tax Credit—Corporations** ▶ See separate instructions. ▶ Attach to the corporation's tax return. | OMB No. 1545-0122 |

For calendar year 20 **10**, or other tax year beginning _____, 20 _____, and ending _____, 20 _____

Name of corporation: **Kolb Industries, Inc.**   Employer identification number: **XX-XXXXXXX**

Use a **separate** Form 1118 for each applicable category of income listed below. See **Categories of Income** in the instructions. Also, see **Specific Instructions.** Check only one box on each form.

☐ Passive Category Income

☑ General Category Income

☐ Section 901(j) Income: Name of Sanctioned Country ▶ _____

☐ Income Re-sourced by Treaty: Name of Country ▶ _____

Schedule A **Income or (Loss) Before Adjustments** *(Report all amounts in U.S. dollars. See Specific Instructions.)*

Gross Income or (Loss) From Sources Outside the United States (*INCLUDE* Foreign Branch Gross Income here *and* on Schedule F)

1. Foreign Country or U.S. Possession (Enter two-letter code; see instructions. Use a separate line for each.)*	2. Deemed Dividends (see instructions)		3. Other Dividends		4. Interest	5. Gross Rents, Royalties, and License Fees	6. Gross Income From Performance of Services	7. Other (attach schedule)	8. Total (add columns 2(a) through 7)
	(a) Exclude gross-up	(b) Gross-up (sec. 78)	(a) Exclude gross-up	(b) Gross-up (sec. 78)					
A Phelan			$354,112	$170,888					$525,000
B Piru			$181,294	$152,206					$333,500
C									
D									
E									
F									
Totals (add lines A through F)									$858,500

* For section 863(b) income, NOLs, income from RICs, and high-taxed income, use a single line (see instructions).

Deductions (*INCLUDE* Foreign Branch Deductions here *and* on Schedule F)

9. Definitely Allocable Deductions					10. Apportioned Share of Deductions Not Definitely Allocable (enter amount from applicable line of Schedule H, Part II, column (d))	11. Net Operating Loss Deduction	12. Total Deductions (add columns 9(e) through 11)	13. Total Income or (Loss) Before Adjustments (subtract column 12 from column 8)
Rental, Royalty, and Licensing Expenses		(c) Expenses Related to Gross Income From Performance of Services	(d) Other Definitely Allocable Deductions	(e) Total Definitely Allocable Deductions (add columns 9(a) through 9(d))				
(a) Depreciation, Depletion, and Amortization	(b) Other Expenses							
A								$525,000
B								$333,500
C								
D								
E								
F								
Totals								$858,500

For Paperwork Reduction Act Notice, see separate instructions.   Cat. No. 10900F   Form **1118** (Rev. 12-2009)

Form 1118 (Rev. 12-2009)

Schedule B Foreign Tax Credit (*Report all foreign tax amounts in U.S. dollars.*)

Part I—Foreign Taxes Paid, Accrued, and Deemed Paid (*see instructions*)

1. Credit is Claimed for Taxes:		2. Foreign Taxes Paid or Accrued (attach schedule showing amounts in foreign currency and conversion rate(s) used)							(h) Total Foreign Taxes Paid or Accrued (add columns 2(a) through 2(g))	3. Tax Deemed Paid (from Schedule C—Part I, column 10, Part II, column 8(b), and Part III, column 8)
☑ Paid ☐ Accrued		Tax Withheld at Source on:			Other Foreign Taxes Paid or Accrued on:					
Date Paid	Date Accrued	(a) Dividends	(b) Interest	(c) Rents, Royalties, and License Fees	(d) Section 863(b) Income	(e) Foreign Branch Income	(f) Services Income	(g) Other		
A 3/1/10										
B 3/31/10									$86,641	
C										
D										
E										
F										
Totals (add lines A through F)		$38,982							$38,982	$194,739

Part II—Separate Foreign Tax Credit (*Complete a separate Part II for each applicable category of income.*)

1	Total foreign taxes paid or accrued (total from Part I, column 2(h))	$38,982
2	Total taxes deemed paid (total from Part I, column 3)	$194,739
3	Reductions of taxes paid, accrued, or deemed paid (enter total from Schedule G)	( )
4	Taxes reclassified under high-tax kickout	
5	Enter the sum of any carryover of foreign taxes (from Schedule K, line 3, column (xiv)) plus any carrybacks to the current tax year	
6	Total foreign taxes (combine lines 1 through 5)	$233,721
7	Enter the amount from the applicable column of Schedule J, Part I, line 11 (see instructions). If Schedule J is **not** required to be completed, enter the result from the "Totals" line of column 13 of the applicable Schedule A	$858,000
8a	Total taxable income from all sources (enter taxable income from the corporation's tax return)	$2,500,000
b	Adjustments to line 8a (see instructions)	
c	Subtract line 8b from line 8a	$2,500,000
9	Divide line 7 by line 8c. Enter the resulting fraction as a decimal (see instructions)	.3434
10	Total U.S. income tax against which credit is allowed (regular tax liability (see section 26(b)) minus American Samoa economic development credit)	$875,000
11	Credit limitation (multiply line 9 by line 10) (see instructions)	$291,890
12	**Separate foreign tax credit** (enter the smaller of line 6 or line 11 here and on the appropriate line of Part III)	$233,721

Part III—Summary of Separate Credits (Enter amounts from Part II, line 12 for **each** applicable category of income. **Do not** include taxes paid to sanctioned countries.)

1	Credit for taxes on passive category income	
2	Credit for taxes on general category income	
3	Credit for taxes on income re-sourced by treaty (combine all such credits on this line)	
4	Total (add lines 1 through 3)	
5	Reduction in credit for international boycott operations (see instructions)	
6	**Total foreign tax credit** (subtract line 5 from line 4). Enter here and on the appropriate line of the corporation's tax return	

Form **1118** (Rev. 12-2009)

Form 1118 (Rev. 12-2009) — Page **3**

Schedule C — Tax Deemed Paid by Domestic Corporation Filing Return

Use this schedule to figure the tax deemed paid by the corporation with respect to dividends from a first-tier foreign corporation under section 902(a), and deemed inclusions of earnings from a first- or lower-tier foreign corporation under section 960(a). **Report all amounts in U.S. dollars unless otherwise specified.**

Part I—Dividends and Deemed Inclusions From Post-1986 Undistributed Earnings

1. Name of Foreign Corporation (identify DISCs and former DISCs)	2. Tax Year End (Yr-Mo) (see instructions)	3. Country of Incorporation (enter country code from instructions)	4. Post-1986 Undistributed Earnings (in functional currency—attach schedule)	5. Opening Balance in Post-1986 Foreign Income Taxes	6. Foreign Taxes Paid and Deemed Paid for Tax Year Indicated (a) Taxes Paid	(b) Taxes Deemed Paid (from Schedule D, Part I—see instructions)	7. Post-1986 Foreign Income Taxes (add columns 5, 6(a), and 6(b))	8. Dividends and Deemed Inclusions (a) Functional Currency	(b) U.S. Dollars	9. Divide Column 8(a) by Column 4	10. Tax Deemed Paid (multiply column 7 by column 9)
Kolb-Phelan	12/10	Phelan	$3,375,000		$978,750	-0-	$978,750	$372,750	$372,750	.1104	$108,098
Kolb-Piru	12/10	Piru	$2,333,500		$910,065	$83,750	$993,815	$203,435	$203,435	.0872	$86,641

Total (Add amounts in column 10. Enter the result here and include on "Totals" line of Schedule B, Part I, column 3.) . . . . ▶ $194,739

Part II—Dividends Paid Out of Pre-1987 Accumulated Profits

1. Name of Foreign Corporation (identify DISCs and former DISCs)	2. Tax Year End (Yr-Mo) (see instructions)	3. Country of Incorporation (enter country code from instructions)	4. Accumulated Profits for Tax Year Indicated (in functional currency computed under section 902) (attach schedule)	5. Foreign Taxes Paid and Deemed Paid on Earnings and Profits (E&P) for Tax Year Indicated (in functional currency) (see instructions)	6. Dividends Paid (a) Functional Currency	(b) U.S. Dollars	7. Divide Column 6(a) by Column 4	8. Tax Deemed Paid (see instructions) (a) Functional Currency	(b) U.S. Dollars

Total (Add amounts in column 8b. Enter the result here and include on "Totals" line of Schedule B, Part I, column 3.) . . . . ▶

Part III—Deemed Inclusions From Pre-1987 Earnings and Profits

1. Name of Foreign Corporation (identify DISCs and former DISCs)	2. Tax Year End (Yr-Mo) (see instructions)	3. Country of Incorporation (enter country code from instructions)	4. E&P for Tax Year Indicated (in functional currency translated from U.S. dollars, computed under section 964) (attach schedule)	5. Foreign Taxes Paid and Deemed Paid for Tax Year Indicated (see instructions)	6. Deemed Inclusions (a) Functional Currency	(b) U.S. Dollars	7. Divide Column 6(a) by Column 4	8. Tax Deemed Paid (multiply column 5 by column 7)

Total (Add amounts in column 8. Enter the result here and include on "Totals" line of Schedule B, Part I, column 3.) . . . . ▶

Form **1118** (Rev. 12-2009)

Form 1118 (Rev. 12-2009)

Schedule D   Tax Deemed Paid by First- and Second-Tier Foreign Corporations under Section 902(b)

Use Part I to compute the tax deemed paid by a first-tier foreign corporation with respect to dividends from a second-tier foreign corporation. Use Part II to compute the tax deemed paid by a second-tier foreign corporation with respect to dividends from a third-tier foreign corporation. **Report all amounts in U.S. dollars unless otherwise specified.**

Part I—Tax Deemed Paid by First-Tier Foreign Corporations

Section A—Dividends Paid Out of Post-1986 Undistributed Earnings (Include the column 10 results in Schedule C, Part I, column 6(b).)

1. Name of Second-Tier Foreign Corporation and Its Related First-Tier Foreign Corporation	2. Tax Year End (Yr-Mo) (see instructions)	3. Country of Incorporation (enter country code from instructions)	4. Post-1986 Undistributed Earnings (in functional currency—attach schedule)	5. Opening Balance in Post-1986 Foreign Income Taxes	6. Foreign Taxes Paid and Deemed Paid for Tax Year Indicated		7. Post-1986 Foreign Income Taxes (add columns 5, 6(a), and 6(b))	8. Dividends Paid (in functional currency)		9. Divide Column 8(a) by Column 4	10. Tax Deemed Paid (multiply column 7 by column 9)
					(a) Taxes Paid	(b) Taxes Deemed Paid (see instructions)		(a) of Second-tier Corporation	(b) of First-tier Corporation		
Kolb-Pixley / Kolb-Piru	2010	Pixley	$1,625,000	$418,750	-0-		$418,750	$335,000	$335,000	.2	$83,750

Section B—Dividends Paid Out of Pre-1987 Accumulated Profits (Include the column 8(b) results in Schedule C, Part I, column 6(b).)

1. Name of Second-Tier Foreign Corporation and Its Related First-Tier Foreign Corporation	2. Tax Year End (Yr-Mo) (see instructions)	3. Country of Incorporation (enter country code from instructions)	4. Accumulated Profits for Tax Year Indicated (in functional currency—attach schedule)	5. Foreign Taxes Paid and Deemed Paid for Tax Year Indicated (in functional currency—see instructions)	6. Dividends Paid (in functional currency)		7. Divide Column 6(a) by Column 4	8. Tax Deemed Paid (see instructions)	
					(a) of Second-tier Corporation	(b) of First-tier Corporation		(a) Functional Currency of Second-tier Corporation	(b) U.S. Dollars

Part II—Tax Deemed Paid by Second-Tier Foreign Corporations

Section A—Dividends Paid Out of Post-1986 Undistributed Earnings (Include the column 10 results in Section A, column 6(b), of Part I above.)

1. Name of Third-Tier Foreign Corporation and Its Related Second-Tier Foreign Corporation	2. Tax Year End (Yr-Mo) (see instructions)	3. Country of Incorporation (enter country code from instructions)	4. Post-1986 Undistributed Earnings (in functional currency—attach schedule)	5. Opening Balance in Post-1986 Foreign Income Taxes	6. Foreign Taxes Paid and Deemed Paid for Tax Year Indicated		7. Post-1986 Foreign Income Taxes (add columns 5, 6(a), and 6(b))	8. Dividends Paid (in functional currency)		9. Divide Column 8(a) by Column 4	10. Tax Deemed Paid (multiply column 7 by column 9)
					(a) Taxes Paid	(b) Taxes Deemed Paid (from Schedule E, Part I, column 10)		(a) of Third-tier Corporation	(b) of Second-tier Corporation		

Section B—Dividends Paid Out of Pre-1987 Accumulated Profits (Include the column 8(b) results in Section A, column 6(b), of Part I above.)

1. Name of Third-Tier Foreign Corporation and Its Related Second-Tier Foreign Corporation	2. Tax Year End (Yr-Mo) (see instructions)	3. Country of Incorporation (enter country code from instructions)	4. Accumulated Profits for Tax Year Indicated (in functional currency—attach schedule)	5. Foreign Taxes Paid and Deemed Paid for Tax Year Indicated (in functional currency—see instructions)	6. Dividends Paid (in functional currency)		7. Divide Column 6(a) by Column 4	8. Tax Deemed Paid (see instructions)	
					(a) of Third-tier Corporation	(b) of Second-tier Corporation		(a) In Functional Currency of Third-tier Corporation	(b) U.S. Dollars

Form **1118** (Rev. 12-2009)

Form 1118 (Rev. 12-2009)

Schedule E — Tax Deemed Paid by Certain Third-, Fourth-, and Fifth-Tier Foreign Corporations Under Section 902(b)

Use this schedule to report taxes deemed paid with respect to dividends paid with respect to dividends from eligible post-1986 undistributed earnings of fourth-, fifth- and sixth-tier controlled foreign corporations. **Report all amounts in U.S. dollars unless otherwise specified.**

Part I — Tax Deemed Paid by Third-Tier Foreign Corporations (Include the column 10 results in Schedule D, Part II, Section A, column 6(b).)

1. Name of Fourth-Tier Foreign Corporation and Its Related Third-Tier Foreign Corporation	2. Tax Year End (Yr-Mo) (see instructions)	3. Country of Incorporation (enter country code from instructions)	4. Post-1986 Undistributed Earnings (in functional currency—attach schedule)	5. Opening Balance in Post-1986 Foreign Income Taxes	6. Foreign Taxes Paid and Deemed Paid for Tax Year Indicated		7. Post-1986 Foreign Income Taxes (add columns 5, 6(a), and 6(b))	8. Dividends Paid (in functional currency)		9. Divide Column 8(a) by Column 4	10. Tax Deemed Paid (multiply column 7 by column 9)
					(a) Taxes Paid	(b) Taxes Deemed Paid (from Part II, column 10)		(a) Of Fourth-tier CFC	(b) Of Third-tier CFC		

Part II — Tax Deemed Paid by Fourth-Tier Foreign Corporations (Include the column 10 results in column 6(b) of Part I above.)

1. Name of Fifth-Tier Foreign Corporation and Its Related Fourth-Tier Foreign Corporation	2. Tax Year End (Yr-Mo) (see instructions)	3. Country of Incorporation (enter country code from instructions)	4. Post-1986 Undistributed Earnings (in functional currency—attach schedule)	5. Opening Balance in Post-1986 Foreign Income Taxes	6. Foreign Taxes Paid and Deemed Paid for Tax Year Indicated		7. Post-1986 Foreign Income Taxes (add columns 5, 6(a), and 6(b))	8. Dividends Paid (in functional currency)		9. Divide Column 8(a) by Column 4	10. Tax Deemed Paid (multiply column 7 by column 9)
					(a) Taxes Paid	(b) Taxes Deemed Paid (from Part III, column 10)		(a) Of Fifth-tier CFC	(b) Of Fourth-tier CFC		

Part III — Tax Deemed Paid by Fifth-Tier Foreign Corporations (Include the column 10 results in column 6(b) of Part II above.)

1. Name of Sixth-Tier Foreign Corporation and Its Related Fifth-Tier Foreign Corporation	2. Tax Year End (Yr-Mo) (see instructions)	3. Country of Incorporation (enter country code from instructions)	4. Post-1986 Undistributed Earnings (in functional currency—attach schedule)	5. Opening Balance in Post-1986 Foreign Income Taxes	6. Foreign Taxes Paid For Tax Year Indicated	7. Post-1986 Foreign Income Taxes (add columns 5 and 6)	8. Dividends Paid (in functional currency)		9. Divide Column 8(a) by Column 4	10. Tax Deemed Paid (multiply column 7 by column 9)
							(a) Of Sixth-tier CFC	(b) Of Fifth-tier CFC		

Form **1118** (Rev. 12-2009)

Form 1118 (Rev. 12-2009)

Schedule F — Gross Income and Definitely Allocable Deductions for Foreign Branches

1. Foreign Country or U.S. Possession (Enter two-letter code from Schedule A, column 1. Use a separate line for each.)	2. Gross Income	3. Definitely Allocable Deductions
A		
B		
C		
D		
E		
F		
Totals (add lines A through F)* ▶		

* Note: *The Schedule F totals are not carried over to any other Form 1118 Schedule. (These totals were already included in Schedule A.) However, the IRS requires the corporation to complete Schedule F under the authority of section 905(b).*

Schedule G — Reductions of Taxes Paid, Accrued, or Deemed Paid

A	Reduction of Taxes Under Section 901(e)—Attach separate schedule
B	Reduction of Foreign Oil and Gas Taxes—Enter amount from Schedule I, Part II, line 6
C	Reduction of Taxes Due to International Boycott Provisions—Enter appropriate portion of Schedule C (Form 5713), line 2b. **Important:** Enter only "specifically attributable taxes" here.
D	Reduction of Taxes for Section 6038(c) Penalty—Attach separate schedule
E	Other Reductions of Taxes—Attach schedule(s)
	Total (add lines A through E). Enter here and on Schedule B, Part II, line 3 . . . . ▶

Form **1118** (Rev. 12-2009)

Form 1118 (Rev. 12-2009)

Schedule H   Apportionment of Deductions Not Definitely Allocable (complete only once)

Part I—Research and Development Deductions

	(a) Sales Method					(b) Gross Income Method—Check method used: ☐ Option 1 ☐ Option 2 (See instructions)		(c) Total R&D Deductions Not Definitely Allocable (enter all amounts from column (a)(v) or all amounts from column (b)(vii).)
	Product line #1 (SIC Code: _____)*		Product line #2 (SIC Code: _____)*		(v) Total R&D Deductions Under Sales Method (add columns (ii) and (iv))			
	(i) Gross Sales	(ii) R&D Deductions	(iii) Gross Sales	(iv) R&D Deductions		(vi) Gross Income	(vii) Total R&D Deductions Under Gross Income Method	
1 Totals (see instructions)								
2 Total to be apportioned								
3 Apportionment among statutory groupings:								
a General category income								
b Passive category income								
c Section 901(j) income*								
d Income re-sourced by treaty*								
4 Total foreign (add lines 3a through 3d)								

* Important: See *Computer-Generated Schedule H* in *instructions*.

Form **1118** (Rev. 12-2009)

Form 1118 (Rev. 12-2009)

Schedule H Apportionment of Deductions Not Definitely Allocable *(continued)*

Part II—Interest Deductions, All Other Deductions, and Total Deductions

	(a) Average Value of Assets—Check method used: [ ] Fair market value [ ] Tax book value [ ] Alternative tax book value		(b) Interest Deductions		(c) All Other Deductions Not Definitely Allocable	(d) Totals (add the corresponding amounts from column (c), Part I; columns (b)(iii) and (b)(iv), Part II; and column (c), Part II). Enter each amount from lines 3a through 3d below in column 10 of the corresponding Schedule A.
	(i) Nonfinancial Corporations	(ii) Financial Corporations	(iii) Nonfinancial Corporations	(iv) Financial Corporations		
1a Totals (see instructions)						
b Amounts specifically allocable under Temp. Regs. 1.861-10T(e)						
c Other specific allocations under Temp. Regs. 1.861-10T						
d Assets excluded from apportionment formula						
2 Total to be apportioned (subtract the sum of lines 1b, 1c, and 1d from line 1a)						
3 Apportionment among statutory groupings:						
a General category income						
b Passive category income						
c Section 901(j) income*						
d Income re-sourced by treaty*						
4 Total foreign (add lines 3a through 3d)						

* **Important:** See *Computer-Generated Schedule H* in *instructions.*

Form **1118** (Rev. 12-2009)

Chapter 7

Indirect Sale or Use of Tangible Property

Determining the Transfer Price

General Considerations

Section 482 provides that in any case of two or more organizations, trades, or businesses (whether or not incorporated, whether or not organized in the United States, and whether or not affiliated) owned or controlled directly or indirectly by the same interests, the Internal Revenue Service may distribute, apportion, or allocate gross income, deductions, credits, or allowances between or among these organizations, trades, or businesses if considered necessary in order "to prevent evasion of taxes or clearly to reflect the income of any of such organizations, trades, or businesses." In the case of any transfer or license of intangible property, the income with respect to such transfer or license must be commensurate with the income attributable to the intangible.

The language of Section 482 authorizes the IRS to make allocations where necessary to prevent evasion of taxes or to clearly reflect income. The touchstone for evaluating the propriety of prices paid in transactions between controlled organizations is the arm's-length standard. This standard provides that pricing in controlled transactions should reflect the price that an uncontrolled party would have paid under identical circumstances.

Example 7-1

Copland Corp. manufactures sensor devices for waste treatment plants and sells the devices to its wholly owned sales company, Copland Sales Co. (SaleCo), incorporated in the Netherlands. SaleCo sells the sensors to customers in the European Union. Copland's costs, direct and indirect, to manufacture the sensors total $75,000 per sensor. Copland's usual sales price to unrelated U.S. customers is $260,000 per sensor.

SaleCo has one small office and employs two administrative clerks. The office's only functions are paying Copland for the sensors purchased, arranging the transshipment of sensors from the United States to the customer's plant, and collecting the purchase price from the customer. In 2010, Copland sold sensors to SaleCo for $260,000 per sensor.

This arrangement would appear to satisfy the arm's-length standard, since the price charged by Copland for the sensors provided to SaleCo, a controlled party, reflects the same price that it charges for the same or similar goods to uncontrolled parties.

Pricing under the Regulations

If the Service challenges the correctness of a price set by a U.S. business exporting goods, the U.S. exporter may defend the price under one or more of five specific methods. These are as follows:

1. The comparable uncontrolled price method

2. The resale price method

3. The cost plus method

4. The comparable profits method

5. Other methods

The Comparable Uncontrolled Price Method (CUP)

An uncontrolled price is the price charged between an unrelated buyer and seller. A comparable uncontrolled price is one for a transaction that is, but for the relationship to between the parties, like the controlled transaction being tested. There are two general exceptions to the requirement of comparability: (1) where the differences between the two sales are too small to have an effect on price and (2) where any differences in price between the controlled and uncontrolled transactions can be identified.

Transfer pricing regulations provide that whether a controlled transaction produces an arm's-length result is evaluated by comparing the results of that transaction to results realized by uncontrolled businesses engaged in comparable transactions under comparable circumstances. The comparability of transactions and circumstances must be evaluated considering all factors that could affect prices or profits in arm's-length dealings (comparability factors). Such factors include the following:

1. Functions

2. Contractual terms

3. Risks

4. Economic conditions

5. Property or services

To be considered comparable to a controlled transaction, an uncontrolled transaction need not be identical to the controlled transaction, but must be sufficiently similar that it provides a reliable measure of an arm's-length result. If there are material differences between the controlled and uncontrolled transactions, adjustments must be made if the effect of such differences on prices or profits can be ascertained with sufficient accuracy.

For this purpose, a material difference is one that would materially affect the measure of an arm's-length result under the method being applied. If adjustments for material differences cannot be made, an uncontrolled transaction may be used as a measure of an arm's-length result, but the reliability of the analysis will be reduced.

For the comparable uncontrolled price method, similarity of products generally will have the greatest effect on comparability. In addition, because even minor differences in contractual terms or economic conditions could materially affect the amount charged in an uncontrolled transaction, comparability under this method depends on close similarity with respect to these factors, or adjustments to account for any differences.

Example 7-2

Assume the same facts as in Example 7-1 except that Copland decides to sell its sensor devices to customers in the European Union through SaleCo and an unrelated distributor (DistCo). The circumstances surrounding the controlled and uncontrolled transactions are substantially similar, except that the controlled sales prices to SaleCo is a delivered price and the uncontrolled sales to the unrelated distributor are made FOB Copland's manufacturing facility in the United States.

Differences in the contractual terms of transportation and insurance generally have a definite and reasonably ascertainable effect on price, and adjustments are made to the results of the uncontrolled transaction with DistCo to account for these differences.

If there are differences between the controlled and uncontrolled transactions that would affect price, adjustments should be made to the price of the uncontrolled transaction. Specific examples of the factors that may be particularly relevant to this method include the following:

1. Quality of the product

2. Contractual terms (for example, scope and terms of warranties provided, sales or purchase volume, credit terms, transport terms)

3. Level of the market (that is, wholesale, retail, and so on)

4. Geographic market in which the transaction takes place

5. Date of the transaction

6. Intangible property associated with the sale

7. Foreign currency risks

8. Alternatives realistically available to the buyer and seller.

Example 7-3

Assume that the facts are the same as in Example 7-2, except that Copland affixes its valuable trademark to the sensor devices sold in the controlled transactions to SaleCo but does not affix its trademark to the sensor devices sold in the uncontrolled transactions to the unrelated distributor.

Under these facts, the effect on price of the trademark is material and cannot reasonably be estimated. Since there are material product differences for which reliable adjustments cannot be made, the comparable uncontrolled price method is unlikely to provide a reliable measure of the arm's-length result.

The Resale Price Method

Under the resale price method, the component sought to be tested is the percentage markup earned by an entity that acts as the purchaser and the reseller of tangible property. Basically, the method envisions a situation in which a U.S. exporter sells tangible property to a foreign subsidiary, which then resells the tangible property to unrelated customers.

A reseller's gross profit provides compensation for the performance of resale functions related to the product or products under review, including an operating profit in return for the reseller's investment of capital and assumption of risks. Therefore, although all of the general comparability factors must be considered, comparability under the resale price method is particularly dependent on similarity of functions performed, risks borne, and contractual terms, or adjustments to account for the effects of any such differences. If possible, appropriate gross profit margins should be derived from comparable uncontrolled purchases and resales of the reseller involved in the controlled sale, because similar characteristics are more likely to be found among different resales of property made by the same reseller than among sales made by other resellers. In the absence of comparable uncontrolled transactions involving the same reseller, an appropriate gross profit margin may be derived from comparable uncontrolled transactions of other resellers.

If there are material differences between the controlled and uncontrolled transactions that would affect the gross profit margin, adjustments should be made to the gross profit margin earned with respect to the uncontrolled transaction. Consideration of operating expenses associated with the functions performed and risks assumed may be necessary, because differences in functions performed are often reflected in operating expenses. Specific examples of the factors may be particularly relevant to this method include the following:

1. Inventory levels and turnover rates, and corresponding risks, including any price programs offered by the manufacturer

2. Contractual terms (for example, scope and terms of warranties provided, sales or purchase volume, credit terms, transport terms)

3. Sales, marketing and advertising programs and services (including promotional programs, rebates and co-op advertising)

4. The level of the market (for example, wholesale, retail, and so on)

5. Foreign currency risks

If the controlled business is comparable to a sales agent that does not take title to tangible property or otherwise assume risk with respect to ownership of such goods, the commission earned by such sales agent, expressed as a percentage of the uncontrolled sales price of the goods involved, may be used as the comparable gross profit margin.

Consistency in accounting practices between the controlled transaction and the uncontrolled comparables affects the reliability of the result. The controlled transaction and the uncontrolled comparable should be consistent in the reporting of items (such as discounts, returns and allowances, rebates of transportation costs, insurance, and packaging) as between cost of goods and operating expenses.

Example 7-4

Assume that Copland is manufacturing one unbranded line of sensor devices and selling the same to SaleCo. SaleCo personnel make minor modifications to the sensor devices and supply packaging to meet requirements of European consumer protection legislation. SaleCo then sells the modified and repackaged sensor devices to several unrelated European distributors, UT1, UT2, and UT3. UT1, UT2, and UT3 also sell a competing line of sensor devices. All of the products are unbranded.

Relatively complete data are available regarding the functions performed and risks borne by the uncontrolled distributors and the contractual terms under which they operate in the uncontrolled transactions. In addition, data is available to ensure accounting consistency between UT1, UT2, and UT3 and SaleCo.

Since available data is sufficiently complete and accurate to conclude that all material differences between the controlled and uncontrolled transactions have been identified, that such differences have a definite and reasonably ascertainable effect, and that reliable adjustments are made to account for such differences, the results of each of the uncontrolled distributors may be used to establish an arm's-length range.

Example 7-5

The facts are the same as in Example 7-4, except that the Copland sensor devices are branded, in the European market only, with a valuable trademark that is owned by an unrelated third party. UT1, UT2, and UT3 also distribute unbranded sensor devices, while two other uncontrolled distributors distribute sensor devices branded with other trademarks. The value of the sensor devices sold under a competing trademark is similar to the value of the Copland sensor devices sold by SaleCo. The value of the unbranded sensor devices sold by UT1, UT2, and UT3 is not similar to the Copland line sold by SaleCo.

Although close product similarity is not as important for a reliable application of the resale price method as for the comparable uncontrolled price method, significant differences in the value of the products involved in the controlled and uncontrolled transactions may affect the reliability of the results. Because in this situation it is difficult to determine the effect the trademark will have on price and profits, reliable adjustments for the differences cannot be made. Therefore, the unbranded line of waste treatment sensors sold by UT1, UT2, and UT3 has a higher level of comparability than does the branded line sold by the other two uncontrolled distributors.

The Cost Plus Method

The cost plus method is analytically the same as the resale price method, except that the computation of the sales price is determined at the front end of the transaction. First, the direct and indirect costs to manufacture the tangible property are calculated. Then, an appropriate profit figure is added on the basis of industry standards, in order to arrive at a fair transfer price to a sales affiliate.

The regulations adopt the same comparability language for the cost plus method as for the resale price method, substituting the term "producer" for "reseller" and "production functions" for "resale functions."

Example 7-6

Assume, in Example 7-4, that UT1, UT2, and UT3 are U.S. manufacturers of sensor devices and also compete with Copland in foreign markets. All three manufacturers sell to uncontrolled foreign purchasers.

Relatively complete data is available regarding the functions performed and risks assumed by UT1, UT2, UT3 and the contractual terms in the uncontrolled transactions. In addition, data is available to ensure accounting consistency between UT1, UT2, UT3, and Copland.

Since data is sufficiently complete to conclude that all material differences between the controlled and uncontrolled transactions have been identified and reliable adjustments are made to account for those differences, an arm's-length range can be established.

Example 7-7

Assume, in Example 7-6, that Copland accounts for supervisory, general, and administrative costs as operating expenses and does not allocate any of these expenses to SaleCo sales. The gross profit markups of UT1, UT2, and UT3, however, reflect supervisory, general and administrative expenses because they are accounted for as costs of goods sold. Therefore, the gross profit markups of UT1, UT2, and UT3 must be adjusted to provide accounting consistency.

If data are not sufficient to determine whether such accounting differences exist between the controlled and uncontrolled transactions, the reliability of the results will be decreased.

Example 7-8

The facts are the same as in Example 7-6, except that under its contract with SaleCo, Copland uses materials consigned by SaleCo. UT1, UT2, and UT3, on the other hand, purchase their own materials, and their gross profit markups are determined by including the costs of materials.

The fact that Copland does not carry an inventory risk by purchasing its own materials while the uncontrolled producers carry inventory is a significant difference that may require an adjustment if the difference has a material effect on the gross profit markups of the uncontrolled producers. Inability to reasonably ascertain the effect of the difference on the gross profit markups will affect the reliability of the results of UTI, UT2, and UT3.

The Comparable Profits Method

This method does not, as such, rely on comparable uncontrolled transactions as do the CUP, resale price, and cost plus methods. Rather, it is premised on the idea that similarly situated businesses conducting a similar economic activity will tend to earn similar returns over a reasonable period. Accordingly, if those returns can adequately be demonstrated, it should be possible to establish a range which can be used to evaluate the returns of the controlled business. If the margins of the controlled business fall within this range, then it may appear that it has an arm's-length return.

Example 7-9

Assume, in Example 7-4, that SaleCo earns a gross margin to operating expense ratio of 120 percent. SaleCo prepares a list of uncontrolled distributors of waste treatment sensors including UT1, UT2, and UT3, which are believed to perform similar economic functions and to achieve similar economic results. The range of the same ratio of uncontrolled distributors is from 101 to 132 percent.

The comparable profits method determines the arm's-length consideration for a controlled transfer of tangible property by referring to objective measures of profitability (profit level indicators) derived from uncontrolled taxpayers that engage in similar business activities with other uncontrolled taxpayers under comparable circumstances.

The determination of an arm's-length result is based on the amount of operating profit that the tested party would have earned on related party transactions if its profit level indicators were equal to that of an uncontrolled comparable operating profit. The term "comparable operating profit" is calculated by determining a profit level indicator for an uncontrolled comparable, and applying the profit level indicator to the financial data related to the tested party's most narrowly identifiable business activity. Profit level indicators are applied solely to the tested party's financial data that is related to controlled transactions. The tested party's reported operating profit is compared to the comparable operating profits derived from the profit level indicators of uncontrolled comparables to determine whether the reported operating profit represents an arm's-length result.

The tested party will be the participant in the controlled transaction whose operating profit attributable to the controlled transactions can be certified using the most reliable data and requiring the fewest and most reliable adjustments, and for which reliable data regarding uncontrolled comparables can be located. In most cases the tested party will be the least complex of the controlled taxpayers and will not own valuable intangible property or unique assets that distinguish it from potential uncontrolled comparables.

For purposes of the comparable profits method, the arm's-length range will be established using comparable operating profits derived from a single profit level indicator. A variety of profit level indicators can be calculated. Whether use of a particular profit level indicator is appropriate depends upon a number of factors, including the nature of the activities of the tested party, the reliability of the available data with respect to uncontrolled comparables and the extent to which the profit level indicator is likely to produce a reliable measure of the income that the tested party would have earned had it dealt with controlled taxpayers at arm's-length. The profit level indicators should be derived from a sufficient number of years of data to reasonably measure returns that accrue to uncontrolled comparables. Generally, such a period should encompass at least the tax year under review and the preceding two tax years.

Profit level indicators that provide a reliable basis for comparing operating profits of the tested party and uncontrolled comparables include the following:

1. *Rate of return on capital employed*—The rate of return on capital employed is the ratio of operating profit to operating assets. The reliability of this profit level indicator increases as operating assets play a greater role in generating operating profits for both the tested party and the uncontrolled comparable. In addition, reliability under this profit level indicator depends on the extent to which the composition of the tested party's assets is similar to the assets of the uncontrolled comparable. Difficulties in properly valuing operating assets will diminish the reliability of this profit level indicator.

2. *Financial ratios*—Financial ratios measure relationships between profit and costs or sales revenue. Since functional differences generally have a greater effect on the relationship between profit and costs or sales revenue than the relationship between profit and operating assets, financial ratios are more sensitive to functional differences than the rate of return on capital employed. Therefore, closer functional comparability normally is required under a financial ratio than under the rate of return on capital employed to achieve a similarly reliable arm's-length result. Financial ratios that may be appropriate include the following:

   a. Ratio of operating profit to sales and

   b. Ratio of gross profit to operating expenses.

   Reliability under this profit level indicator also depends on the extent to which the composition of the tested party's operating expenses is similar to that of the uncontrolled comparables.

3. *Other profit level indicators*—Other profit level indicators may be used if they provide reliable measures of the income that the tested party would have earned had it dealt with controlled businesses at arm's-length.

   Other comparability factors may also be particularly relevant under the comparable profits method. The regulations provide that because operating profit usually is less sensitive than gross profit to product differences, reliability under the comparable profits method is not as dependent on product similarity as the resale price or cost plus method.

   If there are differences between the tested party and an uncontrolled comparable that would materially affect the profits determined under the relevant profit level indicator, adjustments should be made according to the general comparability provisions. In some cases, the assets of an uncontrolled comparable may need to be adjusted to achieve greater comparability between the tested party and the uncontrolled comparable. In addition, the degree of consistency in accounting practices between the controlled transaction and the uncontrolled comparables that materially affect operating profit can influence the reliability of the result.

Example 7-10

Assume, in Example 7-4, that Copland and SaleCo are under audit for the 2010 tax year. Copland does not allow uncontrolled distributors to sell its sensor devices. Similar sensor devices are sold by other companies, but none are sold to uncontrolled distributors.

The district director determines that the comparable profits method will provide the most reliable measure of an arm's-length result. SaleCo is selected as the tested party because it engages in activities that are less complex than those undertaken by Copland.

There is data from a number of independent operators of wholesale distribution businesses. These potential comparables are further narrowed to select companies in the same industry segment that perform similar functions and bear similar risks to SaleCo. An analysis of the information available on these taxpayers shows that the ratio of operating profit to sales is the most appropriate profit level indicator, and this ratio is relatively stable where at least three years are included in the average. For the years 2008 through 2010, SaleCo shows the following results:

	2008	**2009**	**2010**	**Average**
Sales	$500,000	$560,000	$500,000	$520,000
Cost of Goods Sold	393,000	412,400	400,000	401,800
Operating Exp.	80,000	110,000	104,600	98,200
Operating Profit	$27,000	$37,600	($4,600)	$20,000

After adjustments have been made to account for identified material differences between Copland and the uncontrolled distributors, the average ratio of operating profit to sales is calculated for each of the uncontrolled distributors. Applying each ratio to SaleCo would lead to the following comparable operating profit (COP) for SaleCo:

Uncontrolled Distributors	**Operating Profit/Sales**	**SaleCo COP**
A	1.7%	$8,840
B	3.1%	16,120
C	3.8%	19,760
D	4.5%	23,400
E	4.7%	24,440
F	4.8%	24,960
G	4.9%	25,480
H	6.7%	34,840
I	9.9%	51,480
J	10.5%	54,600

The district director measures the arm's-length range by the interquartile range of results, which consists of the results ranging from $19,760 to $34,840. Although SaleCo's operating income for 2010 shows a loss of $4,600, the district director determines that no allocation should be made because SaleCo's average reported operating profit of $20,000 is within this range.

Example 7-11

The facts are the same as in Example 7-10, except that SaleCo reported the following income and expenses:

	2008	2009	2010	Average
Sales	$500,000	$560,000	$500,000	$520,000
Cost of Goods Sold	370,000	460,000	400,000	410,000
Operating Expenses	110,000	110,000	110,000	110,000
Operating Profit	$20,000	$(10,000)	$(10,000)	$0

The interquartile range of comparable operating profits remains the same as derived in Example 7-10: $19,760 to $34,840. SaleCo's average operating profit for the years 2008 through 2010 ($0) falls outside this range. Therefore, the district director determines that an allocation may be appropriate.

To determine the amount of the allocation, the district director compares SaleCo's reported operating profit for 2010 to comparable operating profits derived from the uncontrolled distributors' results for 2010. The ratio of operating profit to sales in 2010 is calculated for each of the uncontrolled comparables and applied to SaleCo's 2010 sales to derive the following results:

Uncontrolled Distributors	Operating Profit/Sales	SaleCo COP
C	.5%	$2,500
D	1.5%	7,500
E	2.0%	10,000
A	2.6%	13,000
F	2.8%	14,000
B	2.9%	14,500
J	3.0%	15,000
I	4.4%	22,000
H	6.9%	34,500
G	7.4%	37,000

Based on these results, the median of the comparable operating profits for 2010 is $14,250. Therefore, SaleCo's income for 2010 is increased by $14,250, the difference between SaleCo's reported operating profit for 2010 and the median of the comparable operating profits for 2010.

Other Methods

The regulations provide that if a pricing determination cannot be made by applying the CUP method, the resale price method, the cost plus method, or the comparable profits method because there are not sufficient comparable data on which to base the pertinent determinations, then the pricing determination can be made by applying some other, appropriate method. The regulations provide little further guidance. The application of such other methods has been referred to as fourth method analysis, reflecting that the method is pertinent where none of the specified methods is applicable.

For example, the comparable uncontrolled price method compares a controlled transaction to similar uncontrolled transactions to provide a direct estimate of the price to which the parties would have agreed had they resorted directly to a market alternative to the controlled transaction. Therefore, in establishing whether a controlled transaction achieved an arm's-length result, an unspecified method would provide information on the prices or profits that the controlled taxpayer could have realized by choosing a realistic alternative to the controlled transaction.

Example 7-12

Assume, in Example 7-4, that Copland manufactures a unique line of sensor devices utilizing laser and holographic technology for industrial use at its U.S. manufacturing facility. Copland agrees by contract to supply SaleCo with 1,000 units per year to serve the European industrial market for laser and holographic optical equipment. Prior to entering into a contract with SaleCo, Copland had received a bona fide offer from an independent European industrial optical equipment company, Optico, to serve as the European distributor for laser and holographic industrial optical equipment at a price of $5,000 per unit.

If the circumstances and terms of the SaleCo supply contract are sufficiently similar to those of the OptiCo offer, or sufficiently reliable adjustments can be made for differences between them, then the OptiCo offer price of $5,000 may indicate that an arm's-length consideration under the SaleCo contract will not be less than $5,000 per unit.

Best Method Rule

There is no strict priority of methods, and no method will be considered to be more reliable than others. An arm's-length result may be determined under any method without establishing the inapplicability of another method, but if another method subsequently is shown to produce a more reliable measure of an arm's-length result, the other method must be used. Similarly, if two or more applications of a single method provide inconsistent results, the arm's-length result must be determined under the application that, under the facts and circumstances, provides the most reliable measure of an arm's-length result.

Confirmation of Results by Another Method

If two or more methods produce inconsistent results, the best method rule is applied to select the method that provides the most reliable measure of an arm's-length result. If the best method rule does not clearly indicate which method should be selected, an additional factor that may be taken into account in selecting a method is whether any of the competing methods produce results that are consistent with the results obtained from the appropriate application of another method. Further, in evaluating different applications of the same method, the fact that a second method (or another application of the first method) produces results that are consistent with one of the competing applications may be taken into account.

Range Concept

The flexibility that is intended to be spawned by the best method rule is supported by the "range" concept for purposes of determining the transfer price.

As in negotiations between unrelated parties over the purchase for an item of property, the right price is generally within a range of potential results, and the parties negotiate to find the point where both are comfortable given their respective points of view. This is the "right" price between unrelated parties. A similar approach is appropriate in international transfer pricing matters.

For this purpose, the arm's-length range will be derived only from those uncontrolled comparables that have, or through adjustments can be brought to, a similar level of comparability and reliability, and uncontrolled comparables that have a significantly lower level of comparability and reliability will not be used in establishing the arm's-length range.

Example 7-13

Assume, in Example 7-10, that the district director considers applying the resale price method to evaluate the arm's-length result of a controlled transaction between Copland and SaleCo. The district director identifies ten potential uncontrolled transactions. The distributors in all ten uncontrolled transactions purchase and resell similar sensor devices and perform similar functions to those of SaleCo.

Data with respect to three of the uncontrolled transactions is very limited, and although some material differences can be identified and adjusted for, the level of comparability of three of these comparables is significantly lower than that of the other seven. Further, of those seven, adjustments for the identified material differences can be reliably made for only four of the uncontrolled transactions.

The arm's-length range will consist of the results of all of the uncontrolled comparables that meet the following conditions:

1. The information on the controlled transaction and the uncontrolled comparables is sufficiently complete that it is likely that all material differences have been identified;

2. Each such difference has a definite and reasonably ascertainable effect on price or profit; and

3. Adjustment is made to eliminate the effect of each such difference.

Example 7-14

The facts are the same as in Example 7-13. Applying the resale price method to the four uncontrolled comparables and making adjustments to the uncontrolled comparables, the district director derives the following results:

Comparable	Result ($ Price)
1	44.00
2	45.00
3	45.00
4	45.00

The district director determines that data regarding the four uncontrolled transactions are sufficiently complete and accurate so that it is likely that all material differences between the controlled and uncontrolled transactions have

---

been identified and appropriate adjustments were made for these differences. Accordingly, if the resale price method is determined to be the best method, the arm's-length range for the controlled transaction will consist of the results of all the uncontrolled comparables and the arm's-length range in this case would be the range from $44.00 to $45.00.

The reliability of the analysis must be increased, where possible, by adjusting the range through application of a "valid statistical method to the results of all of the uncontrolled comparables so selected." For this purpose, the reliability of the analysis is increased when statistical methods are used to establish a range of results in which the limits of the range will be determined in such a way that there is a 75 percent probability of a result falling above the lower end of the range and a 75 percent probability of a result falling below the upper end of the range. The interquartile range ordinarily provides an acceptable measure of this range; however, a different statistical method may be applied if it provides a more reliable measure.

If the interquartile range is used to determine the arm's-length range, such adjustment will ordinarily be to the median of all the results (the fiftieth percentile of the results). In other cases, an adjustment will normally be made to the arithmetic mean of all the results.

Example 7-15

The facts are the same as in Example 7-14, except in this case there are some product and functional differences between the four uncontrolled comparables and SaleCo. However, the data are insufficiently complete to determine the effect of the differences. Applying the resale price method to the four uncontrolled comparables and making adjustments to the uncontrolled comparables, the district director derives the following results:

Comparable	Result ($ Price)
1	42.00
2	44.00
3	45.00
4	47.50

It cannot be established in this case that all material differences are likely to have been identified and reliable adjustments made for those differences. Accordingly, if the resale price method is determined to be the best method, the arm's-length range for the controlled transaction must be established. In this case, the district director uses the interquartile range to determine the arm's-length range, which is the range from $43.00 to $46.25. If SaleCo's price falls outside this range, the district director may make an allocation. In this case, that allocation would be to the median of the results, or $44.50.

Controlled Foreign Corporations

General Considerations

Because U.S. corporations are subject to U.S. income tax on their worldwide income, the income of a foreign branch of a U.S. corporation will be subject to U.S. income tax. The income of foreign corporations, on the other hand, is not subject to U.S. income tax, unless it is effectively connected with the conduct of a trade or business in the United States or is from sources within the United States.

Normally, a foreign corporation's income that is not effectively connected with a U.S. trade or business and not U.S.-source income will not be taxed by the United States until it is distributed to U.S. shareholders, at which time it will be taxed as dividend income. Subpart F of the Code is a critical exception to this general rule. Under Subpart F, certain U.S. shareholders of a foreign corporation are taxed directly on certain categories of the corporation's income.

The Subpart F provisions (Sections 951 through 954) were enacted to discourage U.S. investment in foreign corporations that are structured primarily to avoid taxes. Consequently, the Subpart F provisions tax only those U.S. shareholders whose ownership is considered sufficient to control and influence the foreign corporation, and the Subpart F provisions apply only to income and assets manipulated, without economic substance, among low tax jurisdictions to avoid taxes.

Determining Control

Subpart F applies to any foreign corporation that is a controlled foreign corporation (CFC) for at least thirty consecutive days in the corporation's taxable year. A foreign corporation is a CFC if more than 50 percent of the voting power or value of the foreign corporation is owned by U.S. shareholders. For purposes of calculating the more than 50 percent ownership requirement, only U.S. shareholders who own 10 percent or more of the corporation's voting power will be considered. If a foreign corporation is a CFC, every U.S. shareholder who owns at least 10 percent of the corporation's voting stock on the last day of the corporation's taxable year must include in his gross income his pro rata share of the corporation's Subpart F income and earnings and profits invested in passive assets.

Foreign Base Company Sales Income

Foreign base company sales income is derived from personal property that is (1) produced outside the country where the CFC is organized; (2) purchased from or sold to a related person or on behalf of a related person and (3) sold for use outside the country where the CFC is organized. Agricultural commodities that are not grown in the United States in commercially marketable quantities are not considered personal property. A related person is an individual, corporation, partnership, trust, or estate that controls or is controlled by the CFC, or is controlled by the same person that controls the CFC. A related person does not have to be a U.S. person. If the property is produced or substantially transformed prior to sale in the country where the CFC is organized, the income from that property is not foreign base company sales income.

The IRS has written regulations to determine foreign base company sales income where a CFC conducts business outside the country of incorporation through a branch or similar establishment and the branch activities have…"substantially the same tax effect as if… [the branch or similar establishment]… was a wholly owned subsidiary of the CFC." The "branch rule" regulations define the term substantially the same tax effect as if the branch or similar establishment was a subsidiary of the CFC by reference to a mechanical tax rate test. Under these regulations, the prohibited tax result is present if income allocated to the remainder of the CFC (that is, CFC activities carried on in the country of incorporation) is taxed in the year earned at an effective rate that is less than 90 percent of, and at least 5 percentage points less than, the effective rate of tax that would apply to such income under the laws of the country in which the branch or similar establishment is located.

Example 7-16

MafCo is a U.S. based manufacturer of cameras, doing research and development, manufacturing, and warehousing in the United States. Anticipating an opportunity to expand sales, MafCo forms a sales subsidiary (SubCo) in the country of Euronia. MafCo begins manufacturing an unbranded line of cameras and accessory equipment and sells the same to SubCo. Subsequently, MafCo decides to develop a complete manufacturing capability in Euronia and does so by expanding the SubCo minor assembly and supply packaging office there. MafCo opens a separate sales subsidiary, FSO, in nearby Foronia on December 15, 2009. There are no synergies—geographic or otherwise—to the MafCo business in Foronia. There is a potential market for the cameras and accessory equipment to be manufactured in Euronia, but this market is easily accessed by Euronia personnel. The primary reason for incorporating the sales subsidiary in Foronia is the marginal statutory tax rate for corporations of 8 percent.

All three companies—MafCo, SubCo, and FSO—have a calendar taxable year.

In 2010, SubCo manufactures a line of cameras and accessory equipment and sells these products to FSO which markets the cameras and accessory equipment to unrelated customers in Foronia and beyond.

In 2010, SubCo is a CFC because (1) more than 50 percent of its stock is owned by a U.S. shareholder, MafCo, and (2) MafCo owns at least 10 percent of the combined voting power of SubCo's stock. Subpart F also applies to FSO in 2009 because FSO is a CFC for at least thirty consecutive days in that tax year. The income earned by FSO is foreign base company sales income, taxed directly to MafCo, because this income is derived in connection with (1) the purchase of cameras and accessory equipment from a related person, SubCo; (2) the cameras and accessory equipment are produced outside of Foronia; and (3) the cameras and accessory equipment are sold for use outside Foronia. Any income that FSO earns on the sale of cameras and accessory equipment for use in Foronia is not foreign base company sales income. However, if at least 70 percent of FSO's income is foreign base company sales income, all of the income including income from sales to Foronia customers, will be taxed directly to MafCo as foreign base company sales income.

This result is consistent with the policy underlying the Subpart F rules. The income earned by FSO is easily moved to a low tax jurisdiction. Moreover, there is no apparent reason other than tax avoidance for placing a marketing subsidiary in Foronia rather than in Euronia where the cameras and accessory equipment are manufactured. This example is precisely the type of situation that Congress had in mind when it enacted Subpart F.

Subpart F applies to SubCo in 2009, because SubCo is a CFC for at least thirty consecutive days in 2009. The income earned by SubCo is not foreign base company sales income, however, because the cameras and accessory equipment are manufactured in Euronia.

Example 7-17

Assume, in Example 7-16, that MafCo initially develops its overseas manufacturing capability in Foronia through FSO. MafCo has identified a number of raw material sourcing and finished product sales opportunities in Foronia that are most efficiently exploited through the FSO subsidiary in Foronia.

However, certain raw materials and component parts are available only in Euronia. MafCo determines that it is economically most efficient to establish a subsidiary of FSO in Euronia, SubCo, to source these raw materials and component parts and resell the same to FSO and to perform minor assembly and packaging functions and to provide after-sales technical support to customers in Euronia, Foronia and other countries. SubCo is formed in Euronia and commences operations December 15, 2009.

The tax rate in Euronia is 35 percent.

In 2010, FSO manufactures a line of cameras and accessory equipment and sells these products to customers in Foronia, Euronia, and other countries. SubCo performs sourcing services for certain raw materials and component parts and resells the same to FSO and performs minor assembly and packaging functions and after-sale technical support services to customers in Foronia, Euronia, and other countries.

In 2010, FSO is a CFC because (1) more than 50 percent of its stock is owned by a U.S. shareholder, MafCo, and (2) MafCo owns at least 10 percent of the combined voting power of FSO's stock. The income earned by FSO is not foreign base company sales income, however, because the cameras and accessory equipment are manufactured in Foronia. This result is consistent with the policy underlying the Subpart F rules, which were not intended to prohibit deferral of U.S. income tax on the income earned from substantive economic activity, even when that economic activity takes place in a low-tax jurisdiction.

In 2009, SubCo is a CFC because more than 50 percent of its stock is constructively owned by a U.S. shareholder, MafCo. Since MafCo is the direct owner of FSO, FSO's ownership of SubCo is attributed to MafCo. Also MafCo constructively owns at least 10 percent of the combined voting power of SubCo's stock.

SubCo has earned income from (1) sourcing raw materials and components parts and reselling the same to FSO, a related party, for use outside and inside Euronia; (2) performing minor assembly and packaging services on cameras and accessory equipment manufactured by FSO, a related party, for use outside and inside

Euronia; and (3) providing after-sales technical support for cameras and accessory equipment manufactured by FSO and sold for use inside and outside Euronia.

More than 70 percent of the income earned from all three economic functions is income derived from personal property produced outside Euronia and sold to a related party for use outside Euronia. However, since the tax rate in Euronia is at least 90 percent of the U.S. tax rate, the income earned by SubCo is excluded from the foreign base company sales income provisions.

Example 7-18

Assume, in Example 7-16, that MafCo management determines that there are compelling business reasons to create a sales subsidiary in Foronia. Specifically, marketing surveys in Foronia and other non-Euronia countries indicate an overwhelming bias or prejudice among non-Euronia consumers against Euronia labeled products. Management determines that the most efficient way to overcome this obstacle is to establish an assembly, labeling, packaging, and resale operation in Foronia for the cameras and accessory equipment manufactured in Euronia.

Management determines that the assembly, labeling, and packaging operation in Foronia should be a separate subsidiary, incorporated in Foronia. The additional entity is important to management's objective not to reveal the country of manufacture to non-Euronia consumers and also serves to place an additional layer of protection between MafCo's manufacturing assets in Euronia and potential plaintiffs in the markets served by the Euronia manufacturing operation. Accordingly, MafCo establishes FSO as an assembly, labeling, and packaging subsidiary in Foronia. In 2010, SubCo manufactures a line of cameras and accessory equipment and sells the same to FSO for assembly, packaging, labeling, and resale to customers in Euronia, Foronia, and other countries.

In 2010, SubCo and FSO are CFC's because (1) more than 50 percent of the stock of each entity is owned by a U.S. shareholder, MafCo, and (2) MafCo owns at least 10 percent of the combined voting power of SubCo and FSO stock. SubCo has earned income from manufacturing cameras and accessory equipment and resale of same to FSO, a related party, for use outside and inside Euronia. This income is not foreign base company sales income, however, because the cameras and accessory equipment are manufactured in Euronia.

FSO has earned income from assembly, packaging, labeling and resale of cameras and accessory equipment, purchased from a related party, produced outside the country of incorporation and of which more than 70 percent will be used outside the country of incorporation. However in these circumstances FSO's income is not foreign base company sales income. In this situation, FSO was incorporated in Foronia for compelling business reasons other than deferral of U.S. taxes—specifically Foronia labeling and packaging is critical to success in the target markets and performance of these functions through a Foronia corporation is the most practical means of accomplishing this objective. Also, the Foronia subsidiary will limit legal liability and thereby protect MafCo's investment in Euronia manufacturing operations. Foreign base company sales income is created from the purchase and sale of property where the selling corporation does not add appreciable value. Here, however, the selling corporation adds significant value. The fact that the selling corporation is incorporated in a low-tax jurisdiction is a fortunate circumstance for the taxpayer but does not, standing alone, create foreign base company sales income.

Goods Manufactured, Produced, or Assembled by CFC

The legislative history to Subpart F states that Congress intended that foreign base company sales income include only income from the purchase and sale of property, without any appreciable value being added to the product by the selling corporation, and that foreign base company sales income exclude sales income attributable to manufacturing, major assembling, or construction activity carried on with respect to the product by the selling business. According to regulations effective in 2009, a CFC manufactures, produces, or constructs personal property only if the CFC's employees substantially transform, substantially assemble, or substantially contribute to transformation or assembly.

The regulations, amended in 2008, are the culmination of a long-standing debate over the treatment of contract manufacturing under the foreign base company sales rules. In a controversial 1997 ruling, the IRS argued that a CFC is not a manufacturer of goods produced by a separate manufacturer under contract with the CFC. The 1997 ruling revoked a contrary ruling issued in 1975 in which the IRS treated a contract manufacturer's activities as activities of its CFC-principal, and characterized these activities as a branch of the CFC in the country in which the contract manufacturer did its work. The Tax Court rejected the branch characterization soon after, and the IRS concluded that it could not regard the contract manufacturer's activities as activities of the CFC after the Tax Court had blocked attribution of the contract manufacturer's activities to the CFC.

Under the 2008 regulations, a CFC is not a contract manufacturer merely because a contract manufacturer substantially transforms materials or performs substantial assembly on the CFC's behalf, and, in so providing, follows the IRS 1997 ruling. More importantly, however, the 2008 regulations offer a "substantial contribution" possibility under which a CFC can qualify as a manufacturer, for purposes of analyzing foreign base company sales income, even though the physical manufacturing work is performed by a contract manufacturer, as long as the CFC's employees are actively involved in substantial transformation or assembly of personal property.

1. *Substantial Transformation.* A CFC is considered to have manufactured goods that it sells if personal property that the CFC purchases and incorporates into goods is substantially transformed by the CFC prior to sale. Under the 2008 regulations, examples of substantial transformation include producing paper from wood pulp, making screws and bolts from steel rods, and canning fish. A CFC is considered to have manufactured goods only if the CFC's employees accomplish the substantial transformation.

2. *Substantial assembly.* A CFC is likewise considered to have manufactured property if the CFC purchases components and incorporates the purchased components into

property through activities of its employees. These activities must be substantial in nature and generally considered to constitute production, construction, or manufacture of property. Under a safe harbor rule, a CFC is considered engaged in substantial assembly with respect to particular goods if conversion costs (direct labor and factory burden) are at least 20 percent of the cost of goods sold. The 20 percent threshold is a safe harbor and a CFC may satisfy the substantial assembly test where its conversion costs are less than 20 percent of the cost of goods sold, if the CFC's activities are otherwise substantial in nature and generally considered to constitute production, construction, or manufacture of property.

3. *Substantial contribution.* If a CFC would be considered to have manufactured goods under the substantial transformation or assembly test, except that the CFC's employees did perform all of the substantial transformation or assembly operations, the CFC may nevertheless be deemed to have manufactured the goods if, through the activities of its employees, the CFC makes a substantial contribution to the manufacture, production, or construction of the goods. Whether a CFC's employees make a substantial contribution depends on all relevant facts and circumstances, and the regulations provide a nonexclusive list of CFC employees' activities that are considered:

    a. Oversight and direction of the activities or process by which goods are produced

    b. Activities of the CFC's employees that are considered in, but are insufficient to satisfy, the substantial transformation and assembly tests

    c. Material selection, vendor selection or control of raw materials, work-in-process or finished goods

    d. Management of manufacturing costs or capacities

    e. Control of manufacturing related logistics

    f. Quality control

    g. Developing, or directing the use or development of, intellectual property used in producing the property, including product design, design specifications, trade secrets and technology

All CFC employee activities in these categories are considered, but performance or lack of performance of any particular activity or group of activities is not dispositive. Also, the weight accorded to any one activity or group of activities will depend on the facts and circumstances of the business. There is no minimum performance threshold.

Example 7-19

Assume CFC, a CFC, purchases raw materials from a related person and hires CM, an unrelated business, to produce goods from the raw materials in a process that is generally considered to be substantially transformative. Throughout the manufacturing process, CFC owns the raw materials, works-in-process, finished

---

goods, and manufacturing intangibles. CFC has a right to oversee and direct CM's activities, but CFC does not regularly exercise this right through CFC's employees. CFC does not satisfy the substantial transformation or assembly tests because CFC's employees do not perform activities by which the materials are transformed or assembled. CFC could satisfy the substantial contribution test because CM substantially transforms raw materials that CFC owns, but CFC's employees' activities do not rise to a substantial contribution.

Ownership of raw materials, manufacturing intangibles, or the right to direct and control are not, standing alone, sufficient. CFC does not qualify as a manufacturer on these facts.

Example 7-20

Assume the same facts as Example 7-19 except that CFC, through its employees, designs the finished product, performs quality control, and regularly exercises its right to oversee and direct CM's activities.

On these facts, CFC satisfies the substantial contribution test and, therefore, does qualify as the manufacturer of the goods produced. Income resulting from sale of these goods is not foreign base company sales income, with respect to CFC.

A CFC's contribution to manufacture of goods by a contact manufacturer may be substantial, even if another business (other than the contract manufacturer) also contributes substantially.

Example 7-21

Assume unrelated CFCs, CFC1, and CFC2, contract with CM to manufacture Product X in a process that will substantially transform all materials used in production. CFC1's employees design Product X, direct CM in its application of the design, design specifications and other intellectual property, and select the materials that CM will use and the vendors to provide the materials. CFC2's employees design the manufacturing process for Product X and manage manufacturing costs and capacities. CFC1 and CFC2 each provide quality control, oversight, and direction with respect to different aspects of CM's activities. The substantial contribution test is potentially applicable because CFC1 and CFC2 would each satisfy the substantial transformation or assembly test, if CFC1 and CFC2 performed all of CM's activities.

That CFC1 makes a substantial contribution to the manufacturing process does not preclude a finding that CFC2 also makes a substantial contribution, and vice versa. The activities of each CFC's employees are separately analyzed, and no minimum activity level is required. On these facts, CFC1 and CFC2 both satisfy the substantial contribution test, because each independently makes a substantial contribution to the manufacture of Product X through CFC1's and CFC2's employees' activities.

Branch Rule

The Subpart F branch rule was enacted to prevent CFCs from avoiding the foreign base company sales income rules by using branch operations.

> **Example 7-22**
>
> Assume, in Example 7-16, that MafCo forms a sales subsidiary in Foronia and that FSO forms a branch operation in Euronia to manufacture the cameras and accessory equipment. The effective tax rate of MafCo in the United States is 35 percent. The effective tax rates in Foronia and Euronia are 8 percent and 35 percent, respectively. In this situation, FSO could take the position that it conducts same country operations in Foronia, even though the cameras and accessory equipment are actually manufactured in Euronia.

Congress responded to this concern by enacting Section 954(d)(2) as follows:

> (2) CERTAIN BRANCH INCOME. For purposes of determining foreign base company sales income in situations in which the carrying on of activities by a controlled foreign corporation through a branch or similar establishment outside the country of incorporation of the controlled foreign corporation has substantially the same effect as if such branch or similar establishment were a wholly owned subsidiary corporation deriving such income, under regulations prescribed by the Secretary the income attributable to the carrying on of such activities of such branch or similar establishment shall be treated as income derived by a wholly owned subsidiary of the controlled foreign corporation and shall constitute foreign base company sales income of the controlled foreign corporation.

Branch rule regulations define the term "substantially the same tax effect as if it were a subsidiary corporation" by reference to a mechanical tax rate test. These regulations state that the tax effect is present if income allocated to the remainder of the CFC is taxed in the year earned at an effective rate that is "less than 90 [percent] of, and at least 5 percentage points less than, the effective rate of tax that would apply to such income under the laws of the country in which the branch or similar establishment is located."

The regulations focus on the relationship of the manufacturing rate (which is assumed to be the rate of the branch in a higher tax country) as opposed to the sales rate (which is assumed to be the rate of the CFC in a lower tax country). The apparent logic of this approach is a presumed intent of U.S. shareholders to avoid U.S. income taxes by separating manufacturing and sales activities. In GCM 35961, the General Counsel discussed the purpose of the branch rule:

> The branch rule, like the foreign base company sales rules generally, was established to prevent a foreign corporation from separating its manufacturing activities in order to obtain a lower rate of tax with respect to the sales income.

To date, the Tax Court has interpreted the branch rule narrowly in light of legislative history indicating that Congress enacted the branch rule simply to modify the foreign base company sales income provisions to cover situations in which separate sales subsidiaries are created for the sole purpose of separating taxation of manufacturing and sales activities.

Read together, the legislative history of the foreign base company sales income provisions and the related branch rule and GCM 35961 teach that the underlying purpose of the foreign base company sales income provisions and the related branch rule is to curtail deferral of U.S. income taxes attributable to tax haven activities without economic substance. Tax rate disparities among countries in which different economic functions are performed do not, alone, attract applicability of these provisions. Another statement of this policy is that the objective of these provisions is to prevent the separation of sales functions from manufacturing functions merely to obtain a lower rate of tax with respect to the sales income. An additional statement of this policy is that the purpose of these rules is to capture income from the purchase and sale of property that is earned without appreciable value being added to the product by the selling corporation. Taken together, it is clear that the foreign base company sales income provisions and the related branch rule are intended to capture income that has no economic basis and is positioned in a tax haven by a U.S. shareholder merely to avoid U.S. income tax.

Example 7-23

Assume, in Example 7-18, that rules governing foreign corporate ownership in Foronia are not receptive to foreign investment. Specifically, these rules require that nonresident shareholders of a Foronia corporation must own and vote shares beneficially through a trust administered by a Foronia resident. MafCo management is not willing to place MafCo assets and operations under control of a third party. Moreover, MafCo is unwilling to operate a U.S. branch in Foronia because of concern that substantial Mafco assets in the United States will be exposed to attachment by potential Foronia claimants. To overcome these obstacles, MafCo decides to operate in Foronia as a branch of SubCo, MafCo's Euronia subsidiary.

In 2010, SubCo is a CFC because (1) more than 50 percent of the stock is owned by a U.S. shareholder, MafCo, and (2) MafCo owns at least 10 percent of the combined voting power of SubCo's stock. SubCo has earned income from manufacturing cameras and accessory equipment and resale of same to its branch operation in Foronia, for use outside and inside Euronia. This income is not foreign base company sales income, however, because the cameras and accessory equipment are manufactured in Euronia.

The SubCo branch operation in Foronia has earned income from assembly, packaging, labeling, and resale of cameras and accessory equipment, purchased from a related party, produced outside the country of incorporation and more than 70 percent of which will be used outside the country of incorporation. The SubCo branch operates outside Euronia, SubCo's country of incorporation. The tax rate in Foronia is 8 percent which is less than 90 percent of, and more than 5 percentage points less than, the 35 percent tax rate in Euronia.

It would appear that SubCo is a CFC carrying on activities through a branch or similar establishment outside the country of incorporation under a tax rate that has substantially the same tax effect as if the branch is a wholly owned subsidiary corporation. Because the tax effect is present, income earned by the branch operation appears to constitute foreign base company sales income.

However, in these circumstances, the income earned by the Foronia branch operation is not foreign base company sales income. The foreign base company sales income provisions and the related branch rule were enacted to prevent separation of sales and manufacturing income merely to obtain a lower rate of tax for the sales income. Similarly, the branch rule was established to prevent a foreign corporation from separating manufacturing activities from sales activities by conducting the former or the latter through a branch operation merely to obtain a lower rate of tax with respect to the sales income.

In this situation SubCo is operating a packaging, labeling, and distribution operation through a branch in Foronia for business reasons other than avoidance of U.S. taxes. Specifically, Foronia corporate provisions make ownership of corporate shares in a subsidiary incorporated in Foronia cumbersome at best and at worst could leave significant MafCo assets under control of a third party. Also, some form of operation other than a U.S. branch in Foronia is necessary to protect significant MafCo U.S. assets from attachment by potential Foronia claimants. Operating in Foronia through a branch of SubCo, the Euronia subsidiary, is a practical solution to these problems. Although the literal terms of the tax rate test in the branch rule regulations are applicable, the presumed intent by U.S. shareholders to avoid U.S. taxes that follows is not present here.

The Concept of Economic Risk and Attributed Activities—Revenue Ruling 75-7

In Revenue Ruling 75-7, the Service ruled that a CFC's income from the sale to foreign unrelated persons of a product derived from raw material purchased from related persons in the United States and Canada and converted for a fee by an unrelated corporation in a country with a lower effective tax rate than the CFC's country was not foreign base company sales income.

Most importantly, however, the Service concluded from all of the terms of the contractual arrangement between the CFC and the third party raw material converter that conversion by the unrelated third party is considered for U.S. tax purposes a performance by the CFC and ruled, therefore, that the CFC would be treated as having "substantially transformed personal property."

Further the Service concluded that the CFC "substantially transformed personal property" through a branch or similar establishment outside the CFC's country of incorporation. However, the Service concluded that the branch or similar establishment did not have substantially the same tax effect as if it were a subsidiary corporation because the tax rate in the CFC's country of incorporation was higher than the tax rate in the branch country.

The terms of the contractual arrangement recited in the revenue ruling included the following:

> X [the CFC] paid Y [the third party converter] a conversion fee. The ore concentrate, [raw material subject of the contract] before and during processing and the finished product remained the sole property of X at all times. X alone purchased all raw material and other ingredients necessary for the processing operation and X bore the risk of loss at all times in connection with the operations. Complete control of the quality of the product was also vested in X, and Y was at all times required to use such processes as were directed by X. X could, when the occasion warranted, send engineers or technicians to

> Y's plant to inspect, correct, or advise with regard to the processing of the ore concentrate into the finished product.

The Service treated the performance by Y as a performance by X largely because X alone bore the risk of loss at all times in connection with the iron ore conversion operation. In GCM 35961, the General Counsel remarked on then proposed Revenue Ruling 75-7:

> Since X "substantially transforms" property in foreign country N and presumably sells such property through a sales office in foreign country M, the situation outlined in the proposed revenue ruling is within the scope of the branch rule. We are not bothered by the fact that in the typical case involving an application of the branch rule the manufacturing activity is conducted by a permanent establishment of the CFC rather than by an unrelated corporation on behalf of the CFC. In either case, the CFC will be incurring a separate tax on the manufacturer, either directly or indirectly, as a cost of the manufacturing and thereby separating the taxation of its manufacturing and selling activities.

Ashland Oil *and* Vetco *Decisions and Revenue Ruling 97-48*

In *Ashland Oil*, the Tax Court partially rejected Revenue Ruling 75-7, holding that a Liberian CFC's control of an unrelated Belgian contract manufacturer through assumed economic risk, ownership of raw materials under manufacture and the right to supervise the manufacturing process does not create a "branch or similar establishment" as the term is defined in the branch rule regulations and, therefore, does not create foreign base company sales income. The court noted that the unrelated party operated under an arm's-length, contractual relationship with the CFC and that the statutory term "branch" should be given its normal and customary meaning in the absence of a specific technical definition.

Although *Ashland Oil* limits the terms "branch" and "similar establishment" to their customary meanings and thereby prevents unrelated corporations from being treated as "branches or similar establishment[s]" for purposes of the branch rule, the decision does not negate the reasoning that substantial economic performance, actually or by assumed economic risk, renders a CFC's income outside the intended scope of foreign base company sales income provisions. Rather, the *Ashland Oil* holding is entirely consistent with the legislative policy objective of the foreign base company sales provisions and the related branch rule—because the CFC shouldered responsibility for economic loss. Similarly, income earned by the CFC from the sale of products acquired from an unrelated manufacturing corporation for arm's-length compensation should not be treated as foreign base company sales income if these rules are intended to capture only income for which there is no substantive economic value added. The Tax Court reached the same conclusion in *Vetco, Inc.*, where the contract manufacturer was a foreign subsidiary of the CFC.

The IRS response to *Ashland Oil* and *Vetco* was to revoke Revenue Ruling 75-7 in Revenue Ruling 97-48, which concluded that a contract manufacturer's activities cannot be attributed to a CFC to determine whether the income of a CFC is foreign base company sales income. The IRS concluded that a contract manufacturer's activities could not be regarded as CFC activities for the purpose of determining whether the CFC was a manufacturer after the Tax Court had blocked attribution of a contract manufacturer's activities to a CFC for purposes of determining whether the attributed activities constitute a CFC branch in *Ashland Oil* and *Vetco*.

RATE COMPARISONS

Under the branch rules, a branch is treated as a separate corporation for purposes of calculating foreign base company sales income if the branch has substantially the same tax effect as if the branch or similar establishment was a subsidiary corporation. A branch's tax effect is calculated by comparing the actual effective rate of tax on income attributable to the CFC's selling activities to a hypothetical rate at which the income would have been taxed in the country in which the CFC is organized (in the case of a selling branch) or the country in which the CFC manufactures goods (in the case of a manufacturing branch). A branch is treated as a separate corporation if the actual rate is less than 90 percent of, and at least five percentage points below, the hypothetical rate. This calculation is made under the rules listed below.

1. A branch is treated as a subsidiary corporation of the CFC, organized in the country in which the branch does business for the purposes of determining whether the branch should be treated as a separate subsidiary in calculating foreign base company sales income.

2. Purchasing or selling activities performed through the branch with respect to goods produced, purchased, or sold to the remainder of the CFC are considered performed on behalf the remainder of the CFC.

3. If the branch is engaged in production activities (manufacturing, producing, constructing, growing or extracting personal property), purchasing or selling activities performed by the remainder of the corporation with respect to those goods are treated as performed on behalf of the branch.

An effective tax rate is the amount of tax divided by the amount of income, as determined for U.S. income tax purposes. If the statutory tax rate in a country is 30 percent, but that country only taxes one third of income attributable to a branch under U.S. rules, the effective tax rate on the branch's income is 10 percent.

Example 7-24

Assume CFC, a CFC organized in country M, has a branch (Branch A) in country A that manufactures Product X from raw materials purchased from unrelated businesses. CFC, through activities of its employees located in country M, sells Product X to a related business for use outside country M. The effective rate of country M tax on sales of Product X is 10 percent. Although country A generally taxes corporate income at 20 percent, country A taxes manufacturing income and related sales income at a uniformly applicable incentive rate of 10 percent. The hypothetical country A rate is 10 percent.

CFC's use of Branch A to manufacture Product X does not have substantially the same tax effect as if the branch were a subsidiary because the effective rate of country M tax on the sales income (10 percent) is not less than 90 percent, and at least five percentage points less than, the effective rate of tax that would apply to such income in the country in which Branch A is located (10 percent). Branch A is therefore not treated as a separate subsidiary in determining foreign base company sales income.

SALES OR PURCHASING BRANCHES

A branch engaged in selling or purchasing goods is treated as a separate corporation for purposes of applying the definition of foreign base company sales income if

a. The branch is located outside the country in which the CFC is incorporated, and

b. The effective rate at which the CFC is taxed on the branch's income falls below a threshold rate, which is the lesser of (1) 90 percent of the rate at which the country of incorporation would tax the same income or (2) a rate five percentage points below the country of incorporation rate.

The country of incorporation rate is the rate at which that country would tax the income if (1) the income were from sources within the country, (2) the income were attributable to a permanent establishment in the country, and (3) the branch were a subsidiary managed or controlled in the country. The threshold rate is only applied to the portion of the subsidiary's income from each transaction that is attributable to the branch's activities and only to income that is foreign base company sales income if the branch is treated as a separate subsidiary.

If the actual tax on the branch's income is less than the threshold rate, the branch is treated as a separate subsidiary, organized in the country in which the branch does business. Its income is tested under the general definition of foreign base company sales income, as though the branch functioned as a sales agent for the remainder of the corporation.

Example 7-25

Assume a CFC manufactures goods in foreign country X, in which the CFC is organized and sells the goods through a branch in country Y. Country X taxes corporate income at an effective rate of 30 percent, but exempts all income of country X corporations from business operations in other countries, including the income of the CFC's country Y branch. Country Y imposes a 10 percent tax on the branch's income. The branch is treated as a separate country Y corporation because (1) it is located outside the country in which the CFC is incorporated, and (2) the 10 percent tax rate in country Y is less than 90 percent of, and more than five percentage points below, the 30 percent rate of country X.

The income of this hypothetical corporation may be foreign base company sales income because its sales are deemed made on behalf of the CFC (the hypothetical corporation's parent) and the goods sold are produced in a country (X) other than the country of the hypothetical corporation's incorporation (Y). However, because sales for use, consumption, or disposition in the country of incorporation does not generate foreign base company sales income, the branch's foreign base company sales income is limited to the income allocable to the branch from sales made for use, consumption, or disposition in countries other than Y. The income from these sales must be apportioned between the manufacturing and sales functions because the portion allocable to manufacturing is not foreign base company sales income.

MANUFACTURING BRANCHES

If a CFC has a branch outside the country of its incorporation through which the CFC engages in production activities (manufacturing, production, construction, growing, or extraction of personal property), the branch and the remainder of the CFC are treated as separate corporations if use of the branch for these activities with respect to personal property purchased or sold by or through the remainder of the CFC has substantially the same tax effect as if the branch were a wholly owned subsidiary of the CFC. The threshold rate test described above is applied to income of the remainder of the corporation, not the branch. This income only includes income that would be foreign base company sales income (apart from the exceptions for goods produced or sold for use, consumption, or disposition in the CFC's country of incorporation) if the remainder of the CFC is treated as a separate corporation. The effective rate at which the CFC is actually taxed on this income is compared with the effective rate that would apply in the country of the manufacturing branch if the income were from sources within that country and attributable to a permanent establishment in the country, and the CFC was organized and taxed there. Foreign base company sales income is determined treating the manufacturing branch and the remainder of the CFC as separate corporations, unless the actual effective rate is at least 90 percent of, and not more than five percentage points less than, the hypothetical effective rate in the country of manufacture. If a CFC fails this threshold test, the definition of foreign base company sales income is applied to the income of the remainder of the CFC as though its sales or purchasing activities were performed as agent for the branch (the hypothetical manufacturing corporation).

Example 7-26

Assume a CFC incorporated in foreign country X manufactures goods in foreign country X. Country Y taxes corporate income at 30 percent, but the CFC is only subject to country Y tax on its manufacturing profits. Country X has no income tax, and the CFC pays no income taxes to any country on the portion of its income that Y does not tax as manufacturing profits. The manufacturing branch is treated as a separate corporation because (1) it is not located in the country in which the CFC is organized, and (2) the zero rate of tax on income not allocable to manufacturing (the income of the remainder of the corporation) is less than 90 percent of, and more than five percentage points below, the 30 percent rate at which country Y would tax the income.

The hypothetical subsidiary has no foreign base company sales income because it is a manufacturer. However, income of the remainder of the CFC can be foreign base company sales income because it is earned on sales on behalf of a related business (the hypothetical manufacturing corporation) and the goods are not produced in the country of incorporation (produced in Y, incorporated in X). None of the income from sales for use, consumption or disposition in country X is foreign base company sales income because income from sales in the country of incorporation is always excepted. The nonmanufacturing portion of the income from sales for use, consumption, or disposition in countries other than X is foreign base company sales income because the goods are sold on behalf of a related business and are neither produced nor sold in the country of incorporation (X).

Foreign Personal Holding Company Income

Dividends and Interest

Foreign personal holding income ("FPHCI") generally consists of a CFC's dividend, interest, annuities, rents, royalties as well as net gains on dispositions of property generating these types of income and net gains from foreign currency transactions.

Dividend or interest income is excluded from FPHCI if received from a related corporation organized under the laws of the same foreign country as the CFC and the payor corporation uses a substantial part of its assets in a trade or business in the same country.

However this "same country" FPHCI exception does not apply to interest paid by a CFC that reduces the payor's subpart F income or the payment of interest that creates or increases a deficit that reduces the subpart F income of either the payor or another CFC, presently or in the future.

Rents and Royalties

FPHCI includes rents and royalties. Subject to two exceptions described below, rents are included in FPHCI whether the property rented is real or personal.

1. *Active Business Income.* Rents and royalties received from unrelated, third parties and earned from the active conduct of a trade or business are not FPHCI.

2. *Income From Related Persons.* Rents or royalties received from a related person are usually excluded if paid for the use of or the right to use property within the foreign country in which the CFC is incorporated. This exclusion is lost, however, if the rents or royalties reduce the payor's Subpart F income or create or increase a deficit that may reduce the Subpart F income of the payor or another CFC.

LOOK-THROUGH RULE FOR DIVIDENDS, INTEREST, RENTS AND ROYALTIES

Dividends, interest, rents and royalties are not FPHC income if (1) received from a related CFC and (2) attributable or allocable to income of the related CFC that is neither CFC income nor income effectively connected with a US trade or business.

If a CFC has or has had income effectively connected with a US trade or business, the pass-through rule does not apply to dividends from earnings and profits consisting of this income. Similarly, the look-through does not apply to dividends from earnings and profits attributable to Subpart F income.

Interest is considered paid from effectively connected income to the extent the payor's deduction for interest is allocated and apportioned to gross income effectively connected or is attributable to a US taxable permanent establishment.

Generally, interest is considered paid from Subpart F income or effectively connected income only to the extent that the payor CFC's interest is allocated and apportioned to current Subpart F income or effectively connected income. However, interest is also considered paid from Subpart F income or effectively connected income to the extent that the payor's deduction becomes part of an earnings and profits deficit that reduces or may reduce Subpart F income or effectively connected income of the payor CFC or another CFC.

Transactions That Reduce U.S. Tax Base

A transaction that yields income otherwise eligible for the look-through exception from FPHCI is considered abusive if the transaction reduces the US income tax base by creating a deduction in the form of a payment, accrual, or loss for a person subject to US tax without a corresponding inclusion in the Subpart F income of a CFC also party to the transaction.

GAINS ON SALES OF INVESTMENT PROPERTY

FPHC includes the excess of gains over losses from sales or exchanges of (1) property that creates FPHC dividend, interest, royalty and rent income and as well as property that produces no income. However, FPHC income does not include:

1. net gains over losses of inventory or other property held for sale to customers in the ordinary course of business,

2. depreciable property held for a purpose other than rental or license,

3. real property used in a non-rental business of the CFC and

4. goodwill or and other intangibles used in the CFC's business and sold in a sale of the entire business.

Characterization of gain or loss as FPHCI-included or excluded depends on the CFC's purpose in holding the property. Where the CFC's holding purpose changes and a principal purpose of the change is to avoid including gain or loss on the sale or exchange in FPHC income, the gain or loss is fully included in FPHC income.

NET GAINS IN FOREIGN CURRENCY TRANSACTIONS

FPHC income includes gains over losses from transactions in non-functional currencies.

However, gain or loss from foreign currency transactions directly related to a CFC's business needs is not FPHCI. A gain or loss is directly related to a CFC's business needs if (1) it arises from a transaction entered into, or property held for use, in the normal course of its trade or business; (2) it is clearly determinable from the CFC's records as derived from such transaction and (3) the transaction or property does not itself yield Subpart F income other than foreign currency gain or loss. Gain or loss on a bona fide hedging transaction with respect to such a transaction or such property is also directly related to business needs.

Similarly, if a CFC elects to treat exchange gain or loss on a forward, futures, or option contract as capital gain or loss, the gain or loss is treated as gain or loss on a sale of property, subject to the FPHCI rules for investment property sales, rather than as foreign currency gain or loss. If foreign currency gain or loss arises from an activity or investment generating Subpart F income in a category other than FPHC income, an election may be made to include the gain or loss in that category and exclude it from FPHC income.

EXCEPTION FOR ACTIVE BANKING, FINANCING AND SIMILAR BUSINESSES

The exclusion from FPHCI income for banking, financing or similar businesses applies to qualified banking or financing income of an eligible CFC. To be eligible, a CFC must be predominantly engaged in the active conduct of a banking, financing or similar business and must conduct substantial activity with respect to such business. A CFC is predominantly engaged in a banking, financing or similar business if the CFC conducts substantial activity with respect to such business and satisfies one of three tests described below.

1. *More than 70 percent of the CFC's gross income is derived directly for active and regular conduct of a lending or finance business from transactions with customers who are not related persons.* If a CFC satisfies only this test, none of its income is qualified active financing income unless more than 30 percent of the income of the CFC derived directly from conduct of a lending or finance business from transactions with customers who are not related customers and who are located in the country that the CFC is incorporated in.

2. *A CFC actively conducts a banking business and is licensed to do business as a bank in the United States or any other country.*

3. *A CFC is actively engaged as a securities business and is (1) registered as a securities broker or dealer or (2) qualified as such under criteria established by regulations.* A CFC actively engaged in a securities business but not registered as a broker or dealer in the United States should qualify for the FPHCI active financing exception if the CFC is licensed or authorized in the country in which it is organized to conduct securities activities and is subject to bona fide regulation by a regulatory authority in that country.

Qualified banking or financing income is determined separately for a CFC and each of its QBUs. The CFC's qualified banking or financing income is determined by taking into account only items of income, deduction, gain, or loss and activities not properly allocable or attributable to a QBU. Similarly only income, deduction, gain, loss and activities properly allocable or attributable to a QBU are considered in determining the QBU's qualified banking or financing income.

Exceptions from Subpart F Treatment

A U.S. exporter will not be subject to tax on the income of its CFC unless the total base company income (foreign base company sales income, foreign base company services income, foreign personal holding company income, foreign base company shipping income and foreign base company oil-related income) and gross insurance income constitute at least 5 percent of the CFC's total gross income and totals at least $1 million. Except in the case of foreign base company oil-related income, base company income and insurance income do not include any income of a CFC that is taxed by a foreign country at an effective rate of more than 90 percent of the highest U.S. marginal corporate tax rate. This exception, however, is not granted automatically. Businesses must make an election to claim it.

Exception for Income Subject to High Foreign Tax

The election of the exception for income subject to high foreign taxes is to be made by the controlling shareholders of the CFC by attaching a statement to that effect to original or amended income tax returns. This election is binding on all U.S. shareholders of the CFC.

Example 7-27

Assume, in Example 7-16, that the effective tax rate in Foronia is 33 percent. At 33 percent, the effective tax rate in Foronia is greater than 90 percent of the marginal U.S. income tax rate on corporate income of 35 percent. The income earned by FSO on sales of cameras and accessory equipment to customers outside Foronia will not be foreign base company services income if MafCo attaches a statement to its original or amended U.S. corporate income tax return for 2010 stating that MafCo is electing to claim the exception for income subject to high foreign taxes.

Accounting Elections in Computing Taxable Income of a Controlled Foreign Corporation

The regulations provide that computing taxable income of a CFC is done according to the accounting provisions of Internal Revenue Code Section 446. Thus, a CFC has the option of making all the accounting elections that are available for a U.S. corporation.

Election to Exclude Net Foreign Currency Gains from Personal Holding Company Income

The excess of foreign currency gains over foreign currency losses may be considered foreign personal holding company income and therefore foreign base company income, unless the foreign currency transactions are clearly identified on the records of the CFC as derived from qualified business [or] hedging transactions.

A qualified business transaction

- Does not have investment or speculation as a significant purpose,

- Is not attributable to property that would otherwise create subpart F income, and

- Is otherwise integrally related to the purchase or sale of property that would be considered inventory and similar property as owned by the CFC.

The term "inventory and similar property" means property that is stock in trade of the CFC or other property of a kind which would properly be included in the inventory of the CFC if on hand at the close of the taxable year (if the CFC was a U.S. corporation), or property held by the CFC primarily for sale to customers in the ordinary course of its trade or business. Rights to property that reduce the risk of price changes in the cost of inventory and similar property are included in the definition of that term if such rights to property are an integral part of the system by which a CFC purchases such property.

A qualified hedging transaction means a bona fide hedging transaction that

- Is reasonably necessary to the conduct of regular business operations in the manner in which such business operations are customarily and usually conducted by others, and

- Is entered into primarily to reduce the risk of price fluctuations with respect to property or services sold or to be sold or expenses incurred or to be incurred in transactions that are qualified business transactions.

Qualified business or hedging transactions must be identified on the books of the CFC before the close of the fifth day after the day during which the hedging transaction is entered into and at a time during which there is a reasonable risk of currency loss. If the CFC is unable to specifically identify qualified business or hedging transactions and the foreign currency gain or loss derived therefrom, the IRS district director in his sole discretion may determine which transactions of the corporation giving rise to foreign currency gains and losses are attributable to qualified business or hedging transactions.

Election to Include Foreign Currency Gains and Losses in Foreign Personal Holding Company Income

A CFC may elect a method of accounting under which all foreign currency gains and losses are included in foreign personal holding company income. The election is made by filing a statement with the CFC's original or amended income tax return for the year for which the election is made. Alternatively, the controlling U.S. shareholders of the CFC may make the election on behalf of the CFC and related corporations by filing a statement to with their original or amended income tax returns for the tax year during which the taxable year of the CFC for which the election is made ends. The election is effective for the taxable year of the CFC for which the election is made, for the taxable year of all related CFC's ending within such taxable year, and for all subsequent years of those corporations.

Example 7-28

Assume, in Example 7-16, that SubCo, incident to its manufacturing function, is required to maintain a significant inventory of raw material A, the price of which fluctuates broadly on commodities markets.

To hedge this exposure, SubCo enters a series of forward contracts with unrelated parties under which SubCo is obligated to deliver or accept delivery of, at different future dates, varying quantities of raw material A. The dates of delivery and acceptance and the respective quantities of raw material coincide with Subco's planned manufacturing requirements.

Use of similar forward contracts to hedge raw material price fluctuation risk is widespread in the industry.

SubCo clearly identifies each forward contract as a qualified hedging contract within five days of executing each contract.

Immediately prior to the maturity of each forward contract, SubCo settles the contract for cash with an unrelated party. Frequently, SubCo accepts settlement of

---

the contract in Euronian native currency, but occasionally SubCo accepts settlement in other currencies, including U.S. dollars.

Any foreign currency gain or loss realized with respect to cash settlement of each forward contract will not be foreign personal holding company income because the forward contracts executed by SubCo are reasonably necessary to the conduct of its business operations, are customary and usually conducted in the industry and are entered primarily to reduce the risk of price fluctuations with respect to raw material A.

Example 7-29

Assume, in Example 7-28, that MafCo files a statement with its 2010 income tax return electing to treat all foreign currency gains and losses as foreign personal holding company income.

Any foreign currency gain or loss realized with respect to the cash settlement of each forward contract will be foreign personal holding company income.

Deducting Interest Expense

In computing and deducting its interest expenses, a CFC must choose between the asset method and the modified gross income method in making its allocations and apportionments. However, the gross income method may not be elected if a U.S. corporate shareholder elects the fair market value method of apportioning its interest expenses.

Election by Individual Shareholders of a Controlled Foreign Corporation

An individual shareholder of a CFC, including a trust or estate, may elect to be treated as a corporate taxpayer. If this election is made, the income of the CFC is taxable to the shareholder at corporate rates. More important, the shareholder is given the benefit of the second-level foreign tax credit available under Internal Revenue Code Section 960. A shareholder makes the election in the form of a statement on his annual tax return. The statement should include the CFC's name, gross income, earnings and profits, and distributions. Once the election is made, it can be revoked only with the permission of the IRS.

Distributions by Controlled Foreign Corporations

The gross income of a U.S. shareholder in a controlled foreign corporation does not include the distribution of earnings and profits attributable to amounts previously taxed to the shareholders as Subpart F income.

Example 7-30

MafCo, a U.S. person, owns all the stock of SubCo, a controlled foreign corporation. During 2010, SubCo earns $100,000 of foreign base company sales income which is taxed to MafCo. During 2009, SubCo distributes $50,000 to MafCo.

> Under Code Sec. 959(a)(1), MafCo can exclude the $50,000 distribution from income, even if, in 2010, SubCo has some earnings that are not Subpart F income. If, instead, SubCo had earned $100,000 of Subpart F income in 2010, MafCo would still have been able to exclude from income the $50,000 distribution in 2010.

Allocation of Distributions among Different Types of Earnings and Profits

Section 959(a) excludes a distribution only if it is allocable to earnings and profits that are attributable to amounts that have been included in income as Subpart F income. Therefore, Section 959(a)(1) requires some method to allocate distributions to earnings and profits and some method to attribute earnings and profits to income that has been previously taxed to U.S. shareholders as Subpart F income or as amounts invested in U.S. property. Section 959(c) provides the allocation rules.

Section 959(c) treats a distribution as first being attributable to earnings and profits of the first priority, if any, then to earnings and profits of the second priority, if any, and finally to earnings and profits of the third priority.

FIRST-PRIORITY EARNINGS AND PROFITS

The earnings and profits with the highest priority are those attributable to amounts invested in U.S. property.

SECOND-PRIORITY EARNINGS AND PROFITS

The earnings and profits with the next priority are those attributable to amounts constituting Subpart F income.

THIRD-PRIORITY EARNINGS AND PROFITS

The earnings and profits with the third and lowest priority are all other earnings and profits. These earnings have not been taxed to U.S. shareholders previously as amounts invested in U.S. property or as Subpart F income. Section 959 does not exclude from income any distribution that comes from these earnings and profits.

Current and Accumulated Earnings and Profits

Within each of the three types of earnings and profits, Section 959(c) allocates distributions first to current earnings and profits and then to earnings and profits from prior years. When dealing with earnings and profits from prior years, Section 959(c) starts with the most recent prior year and continues backward in order.

Effect of Deficit in Earnings and Profits

If a controlled foreign corporation has a deficit in earnings and profits for a particular year, that deficit reduces only the earnings and profits of the third priority. This rule favors U.S. shareholders, since no exclusion under Section 959(a) results from earnings and profits of the third type.

Example 7-31

MafCo, a U.S. entity, owns all the stock of SubCo, a controlled foreign corporation. Three significant tax events occur in 2010.

First, SubCo has $100,000 of Subpart F income and total earnings and profits of $200,000. MafCo must report $100,000 of Subpart F income.

Second, SubCo invests $50,000 in U.S. property. MafCo need not report this income because it is already reporting $100,000 of Subpart F income.

Third, SubCo distributes $20,000 cash to MafCo. Section 959(c)(1) allocates that distribution to earnings and profits of the first and second priorities. Since Mafco has already reported $100,000 of Subpart F income, MafCo does not include the $20,000 distribution.

Following these events, MafCo has the following interest in the earnings and profits of SubCo:

1. Amounts invested in U.S. property: $30,000 ($50,000 invested by SubCo in U.S. property less $20,000 cash distribution allocated to first priority earnings and profits).

2. Subpart F income: $50,000 ($100,000 of Subpart F income less $50,000 invested in U.S. property and thereby shifted to first priority earnings and profits).

3. Other earnings and profits: $100,000 (total earnings and profits of $200,000 less $20,000 distribution, and less earnings and profits allocated to first and second priority earnings and profits).

In 2010, SubCo has earnings and profits of $300,000 and $90,000 of Subpart F income. MafCo includes $90,000 in income. Also in 2010, SubCo distributes $250,000 in cash to MafCo. Since distributions are allocated first to current earnings and profits and second to accumulated earnings and profits, the $250,000 distribution has the following sources:

Amounts invested in U.S. property:	$30,000 (from 2010)
Subpart F income:	$90,000 (from 2010)
First priority earnings and profits	$50,000 (from 2010)
Other earnings and profits:	$80,000 (from 2010)

MafCo excludes from income all of the distributions allocated to the first and second priorities. Therefore, MafCo excludes $170,000 from income ($30,000 plus $90,000 plus $50,000).

At the end of 2010, after taking into account SubCo's distribution of $250,000, the remaining earnings and profits fall in the following categories:

1. Amounts invested in U.S. property: 0 (beginning balance of $30,000 less a distribution of $30,000).

2. Subpart F income: 0 (beginning balance of $50,000 increased by Subpart F income of $90,000 less distributions of $140,000).

> 3. Other earnings and profits: $230,000 (beginning balance of $100,000 increased by 2010 earnings and profits of $300,000 less $90,000 of 2010 earnings and profits allocated to second priority earnings and profits, less $80,000 of distributions allocated to third priority earnings and profits).

Adjustments to Basis

U.S. shareholders of a controlled foreign corporation are taxed on undistributed income and earnings of the corporation. The amount of undistributed earnings reported by a U.S. shareholder generally increases the shareholder's basis in the stock of the controlled foreign corporation. The regulations provide that the increase occurs as of the last day in the taxable year of the foreign corporation in which it is a controlled foreign corporation. The basis increase takes place separately with respect to each share of stock.

Where a U.S. shareholder receives a distribution from a foreign corporation and does not have to include that distribution in income, basis is reduced by the amount of the distribution excluded from income. The basis reduction occurs separately with respect to each share of stock. Section 959(a)(2) may exclude an amount from the income of a U.S. shareholder when a controlled foreign corporation invests its earnings in U.S. property.

If a person receives a distribution that is excluded from income under Section 959(a) and that exceeds the basis of the property with respect to which it is distributed, the excess is taxed as gain from the sale or exchange of property.

Example 7-32

Assume MafCo owns all 1,000 shares of the one class of stock in SubCo, a controlled foreign corporation. Assume that each share of MafCo's stock in Subco has a basis of $200. MafCo and SubCo have a calendar taxable year. In 2009, SubCo has $100,000 in earnings and profits after payment of $50,000 Euronia income taxes. MafCo includes $100,000 foreign base company income in its 2009 tax return with respect to SubCo.

MafCo will increase the basis of each of its 1,000 shares of SubCo to $300 ($200 + $100,000/1,000) as of December 31, 2009.

On July 31, 2010, MafCo sells 250 of its shares of stock in SubCo to U.S. corporation N for $350 per share. On September 30, 2010, the earnings and profits attributable to the $100,000 foreign base company income included in Mafco's taxable income in 2008 is distributed to MafCo and N corporation, net of a 10 percent or $10,000 Euronia withholding tax. MafCo receives $67,500 (750/1,000 × $90,000) and excludes the distribution from taxable income. Corporation N receives $22,500 (250/1,000 × $90,000) and excludes this amount from taxable income.

As of September 30, 2010, MafCo must reduce the adjusted basis of each of its 750 shares of stock in SubCo to $232.50 ($300 minus ($67,500/1,000)) and N corporation must reduce the basis of each of its 250 shares of stock in MafCo to $260 ($350 minus ($22,500/250)).

Repatriation

Effective for a U.S. corporate shareholder's last tax year beginning before October 22, 2004 or the corporate shareholder's first tax year beginning during the one-year period beginning October 22, 2004, U.S. shareholders of controlled foreign corporations may elect to claim a deduction equal to 85 percent of cash dividends received in excess of base-period cash dividends.

The cash dividend must be invested in the United States under a domestic reinvestment plan for funding worker hiring and training, infrastructure, research and development, capital investments and financial stabilization of the corporation for the purpose of job retention or creation. The domestic reinvestment plan must be approved by a top officer and the board of directors of the U.S. corporate shareholder.

The dividend amount eligible for the 85 percent deduction is limited to the greater of $500 million or the amount disclosed as earnings permanently reinvested outside the United States on a published financial statement. The base-period amount is the average annual repatriations over three of the most recent five years ending on or before June 30, 2003, disregarding the high and low years.

The dividend amount eligible for the deduction is also reduced by any related-party indebtedness of the controlled foreign corporation occurring between October 3, 2004, and the close of the tax year in which the deduction is claimed. No foreign tax credit (or deduction) is allowed for foreign taxes attributable to the deductible portion of any dividend. Additionally, expenses appropriately allocated and apportioned to the deductible portion of the dividend will be disallowed.

Overall Foreign Loss Recapture on Sale of CFC Stock

Effective for dispositions after October 22, 2004, gain or dispositions of controlled foreign corporation stock in which a taxpayer owns more than 50 percent by vote or value are recognized as U.S.-source income for foreign tax credit limitation purposes in an amount equal to the lesser of the fair market value of the stock over adjusted basis or the amount of prior unrecaptured overall foreign losses without regard to the 50 percent limit.

Gains realized in Section 351 contributions to corporations, Section 721 contributions to partnerships, Section 332 liquidations and other reorganizations are not recaptured as U.S.-source income, if after the transaction, the transferor owns the same percentage of stock in the controlled foreign corporation that the transferor owned prior to the transaction.

Passive Assets

Subpart F applies to income and assets that are manipulated among low tax jurisdictions, without economic substance, in order to avoid taxes. Passive assets are taxed directly to 10 percent U.S. shareholders under Sections 956 and 956A of the Internal Revenue Code.

Section 956 Amount

In general, each U.S. shareholder who owns at least 10 percent of the combined voting power of a CFC must include in gross income his pro rata share of the amount of U.S. property held directly or indirectly by the CFC. The amount of U.S. property that is included in gross income is determined by looking at the average amount of U.S. property held directly or indirectly by the CFC at the end of each quarter of its taxable year.

Subject to certain exceptions, U.S. property includes tangible property located in the United States, obligations of a U.S. person, intellectual property rights, and stock of a U.S. corporation. Short-term debts arising from the performance of services, if ordinary and necessary in amount and paid within sixty days, are excluded from the term "obligation."

Ordinary and Necessary Exception

U.S. property does not include the obligations of a U.S. person arising in connection with the sale or processing of property. The amount of the outstanding obligation must not exceed at any time during the taxable year the amount that would be ordinary and necessary to carry on the trade or business of both the other party to the sale or processing transaction and the U.S. person if the transaction occurred between unrelated persons.

The legislative history of this exception indicates that Congress intended to prohibit CFCs from investing in the United States except where the investment is ordinary and necessary to the active conduct of the foreign corporation's business and without any intention to permit the funds to remain in the United States indefinitely.

In reported cases to date, taxpayers have failed to establish that intercompany obligations resulting from investment of CFC funds in the United States were ordinary and necessary to the business of both companies. However, the Service has ruled that a U.S. obligation outstanding for four years is not currently taxable U.S. property.

The obligation in question arose out of a transaction between N, a U.S. parent corporation, and R, a CFC. N produced and marketed alcoholic beverages. One of the alcohols N produced was a blend of "base" alcohol and various other alcohols that required at least three years to mature before sale. The Service ruled that the obligation was ordinary and necessary because the payment schedule on the obligation was tied to maturity and sale of the blended alcohol. This ruling teaches that the critical inquiry in determining the current taxability of U.S. investment is not limited to how long an obligation is outstanding but rather is a broader analysis of all factors surrounding the obligation including amount, time outstanding and all other factors germane to the businesses of both the U.S. parent and the CFC.

The U.S. property held by a CFC will be taken into account only to the extent of the CFC's earnings. For purposes of Section 956, earnings in a given taxable year are the sum of (1) earnings and profits for such taxable year plus (2) accumulated earnings and profits.

Earnings and Profits

The concept of "earnings and profits" plays a pivotal role in the Code provisions governing CFCs. In general, rules substantially similar to the provisions that apply to a U.S. corporation determine the earnings and profits (or deficit in earnings and profits) of a foreign corporation for purposes of Subpart F. Regulations under Section 964 describe the preparation of a profit-and-loss statement computed substantially as if the CFC were a U.S. corporation reporting income under accounting principles generally accepted in the United States and adjusted to conform to U.S. tax accounting standards.

All tangible assets, including inventory when reflected at cost, is taken into account at historical cost computed either for individual assets or groups of assets. The historical cost of an asset does not reflect any appreciation or depreciation in its value or in the relative value of the currency in which its cost was incurred. Depreciation and amortization allowances shall be based on the historical cost of underlying assets and no effect shall be given to any such allowance determined on the basis of a factor other than historical cost.

Example 7-33

Assume, in Example 7-16, that MafCo forms a sales subsidiary (SubCo) in the country of Euronia. MafCo begins manufacturing an unbranded line of cameras and accessory equipment and sells the same to SubCo.

Initially, SubCo personnel make minor modifications to the cameras and accessory equipment and supply packaging to meet Euronia consumer product legislation requirements. SubCo then sells the modified and repackaged cameras and accessory equipment to unrelated Euronia distributors.

In 2008, MafCo management decides to develop a complete manufacturing capability in Euronia and proceeds to do so by expanding the SubCo minor assembly and supply packaging office there. Both companies—MafCo and SubCo—have a calendar taxable year. In 2009, SubCo manufactures a line of cameras and accessory equipment and sells these cameras and accessory equipment to unrelated distributors.

SubCo maintains books of account in accordance with generally accepted accounting practice in Euronia. Consequently, the profit and loss statement prepared from these books of account reflects an allocation to an arbitrary reserve of current income and depreciation allowances based on replacement values of assets, which values exceed historical cost. Adjustments are necessary to conform the Euronia financial statements to accounting principles generally accepted in the United States. Assuming these adjustments are material, the unacceptable replacement of reserves (from a U.S. accounting standards perspective) must be eliminated from the Euronia financial statements, and an increase in the amount of profit (or a decrease in the amount of loss) will result.

Relation to CFC's Earnings and Profits

A key concept is that a CFC's U.S. shareholders will not be taxed on a CFC's investment in U.S. property unless the CFC has sufficient earnings and profits to cover the amount of the investment. Examples 7-34 through 7-36 illustrate this concept.

Example 7-34

Amount invested in U.S. property for the year	$100
Previously taxed amount	0
Excess of line 1 over line 2	$100
Earnings and profits	$1,000
Gross income to U.S. shareholders	
Lesser of line 3 or line 4	$100

In this example, there are sufficient earnings and profits in the CFC to absorb the investment in U.S. property, which is taxed to the U.S. shareholders because they have not been previously taxed. If the CFC does not have sufficient earnings and profits to cover the amount of investment in U.S. property, the lesser amount will be taxed for the current year to the U.S. shareholders.

Example 7-35

Amount invested in U.S. property for the year	$100
Previously taxed amount	0
Excess of fine 1 over line 2	$100
Earnings and profits	0
Amount taxed to U.S. shareholders	
Lesser of line 3 or line 4	0

However, if in the following year the investment in U.S. property remains in place and the CFC has current earnings and profits, the amount of the investment in U.S. property will be taxed to the U.S. shareholders to the extent of the lesser of current earnings and profits or the amount of the investment in U.S. property. Assume that the amount of the CFC's current earnings and profits in the following year is $100.

Example 7-36

Amount invested in U.S. property for the year	$100
Previously taxed amount	0
Excess of line 1 over line 2	$100
Earnings and profits	$100
Amount taxed to U.S. shareholders	
Lesser of line 3 or line 4	$100

If the amount of earnings and profits was less than $100 for the year—say, $50—then only $50 would be shown on Line 4 and the amount taxed to U.S. shareholders for the year would be only $50. At the same time, if the current earnings and profits shown on line 4 were $200, only $100 would be taxed to the U.S. shareholders, because the amount taxed to U.S. shareholders is the lesser of the amount of the investment in U.S. property or the amount of the CFC s current and accumulated earnings and profits.

Effect of Previously Taxed Investment in U.S. Property

Where there has been an investment in U.S. property taxed to U.S. shareholders in a prior year, an additional adjustment must be made. In Example 7-36, assume that the CFC's investment in U.S. property is $200 and its accumulated earnings and profits at the end of the year are also $200.

Example 7-37

Amount invested in U.S. property	$200
Previously taxed investment in U.S. property	$100
Excess of line 1 over line 2	$100
Earnings and profits	$100
Income taxed to U.S. shareholders	
Lesser of line 3 or line 4	$100

If there were not sufficient additional earnings and profits to cover the additional investment by the CFC in U.S. property, the additional investment would be taxed only to the extent of the additional earnings and profits with the balance of the additional investment taxed in any subsequent year when there are sufficient earnings and profits.

Passive Foreign Investment Companies

Passive foreign investment companies (PFICs) are foreign corporations that satisfy either of two tests. The first test is an income test. Under the income test, 75 percent or more of the gross income for the taxable year is passive income. The second test is the asset test. Under the asset test, 50 percent of the assets (by value or adjusted basis, if the corporation is a CFC or if the taxpayer so elects) held by the foreign corporation during the taxable year must be held to produce passive income. Passive income is essentially the same as foreign personal holding income under Section 954(c), although some exceptions do apply. However, when the PFIC rules and Subpart F rules are both applicable, the Subpart F rules preempt the PFIC rules.

PFIC shareholders can be taxed under either of two sets of taxation rules for PFICs. One set of rules allows tax to be deferred but requires payment of interest. The other set of tax rules, which must be elected, taxes shareholders on undistributed PFIC income as the income is earned by the PFIC.

Under the first, or non-elective, set of tax rules for PFICs, an interest charge is imposed when a PFIC shareholder recognizes gain on the sale of stock or receives a distribution from the PFIC. Interest is calculated as if the gain or distribution had been reported in taxable income by the PFIC shareholder ratably over the stock ownership period. The interest rate is the rate for underpayments of tax. Under this set of PFIC tax rules, gain realized from sale of the PFIC stock is ordinary income as opposed to capital gain.

The alternative set of tax rules applies to shareholders who elect to treat the PFIC as a qualified electing fund (QEF) and provide the IRS with information necessary to administer the QEF rules. QEF shareholders pay tax on their pro rata share of PFIC income as earned.

The election is made by a shareholder of a PFIC, not by the PFIC itself. The QEF election is made by attaching a "Shareholder Election Statement," a "PFIC Annual Statement," and a Form 8621 to the shareholder's income tax return for the first year in which the election is to be effective. The shareholder election statement should include (1) the shareholder's name, address, and tax identification number; (2) the total of the shareholder's equity in the PFIC; (3) the name, address, tax identification number (if any), and the date and place of incorporation of the PFIC and (4) a statement similar to the following: The shareholder of [name of corporation], a PFIC within the meaning of IRC Section 1296, elects under IRC Section 1295(b) to treat said PFIC as a qualified electing fund.

The QEF annual information statement must include the PFIC's fiscal year designation, the shareholder's pro rata share of PFIC earnings and profits, an analysis of all distributions made by the PFIC during the tax year, and a statement by the PFIC similar to the following: [Name of corporation], which is a PFIC within the meaning of IRC Section 1296, hereby agrees to permit [name of shareholder] to inspect and copy any and all books and records of [name of corporation] which are necessary and sufficient for determination of income for any purposes of U.S. taxation and according to the principles of U.S. taxation.

The most important effect of the QEF election is that a U.S. shareholder agrees to include in income its ratable share of the earnings and profits of a QEF, which is subject to a deferral that is available for certain types of QEF income. A QEF agrees to maintain complete books and records and agrees to keep a copy of them in the United States, where they are available to the IRS.

Example 7-38

Assume in Example 7-37 SubCo has $100,000 in assets, of which $55,000 are passive. SubCo earns $15,000 income in 2009, of which $11,250 is from passive sources. SubCo elects to pay tax currently as a QEF.

SubCo is a PFIC because (1) more than 50 percent of the assets held to produce income are passive and (2) 75 percent of the income is passive income. Since SubCo is a PFIC, MafCo (and any other shareholders, if applicable) is currently taxed on the passive income regardless of its individual or combined ownership interest in SubCo.

Ordinary and Necessary Exception

The Service has ruled that a controlled foreign corporation's trade receivables from the sale of its products to related and unrelated customers in the ordinary course of business are non-passive assets for purposes of Sections 1296(a).

Example 7-39

Y and Z are CFCs indirectly owned by X, a U.S. corporation. Y conducts its business only within country S, and Z conducts its business only within country C. Y manufactures products or purchases the products from related companies. Y then sells the products to Z or to unrelated customers. If a customer in country C requests a product manufactured by Y, the customer must purchase the product through Z. Sales to Z are a necessary part of Y's business and form the link for

---

the efficient transfer of products from Y to the end customer in country C. Z adds value to the product purchased from Y through further manufacturing, marketing, sales, and support.

As a part of some transactions, Y takes back obligations in exchange for the product. In the case of sales to Z, Z pays Y interest on the obligations. Generally, those obligations are outstanding for sixty days. However, obligations arising from sales to unrelated customers may be outstanding for up to five years. The obligations are interest bearing; the rate of interest is dependent on market conditions and may be different from the rate charged to Z.

The Service's conclusion that the trade receivables are non-passive is conditioned on the assumptions that (1) the transactions are sales, (2) no part of the payments are royalties for use of intangibles, (3) the income from the product sales is non passive, (4) the sales terms are standard in relation to the industry and (5) the interest on the trade receivables is incidental.

QEF Regulations

Regulation Section 1.1291-1(b)(2) provides the following classification scheme for PFICs:

(1) A pedigreed QEF is a PFIC that has elected under Section 1295 to be a QEF with respect to a particular shareholder for all PFIC taxable years during that shareholder's holding period.

(2) An unpedigreed QEF is a PFIC (a) for which a QEF election is in effect; (b) which has not [emphasis added] been a QEF with respect to a particular shareholder for all [emphasis added] PFIC taxable years during the shareholder's holding period; and (c) for which the shareholder has not made an election to purge the prior PFIC years from the shareholder's holding period.

(3) A nonqualified fund is a PFIC for which a shareholder has not made a QEF election.

(4) A Section 1291 fund is (a) an unpedigreed QEF, or (b) a non-qualified fund.

According to this classification scheme, a PFIC shareholder owns an interest in either a Section 1291 fund or a pedigreed QEF. Both the proposed indirect ownership rules and the expanded definitions of PFIC stock "disposition" and "excess distribution" increase the exposure to taxation of a shareholder of a Section 1291 fund. The increased taxation exposure should encourage shareholders of Section 1291 funds to purge the Section 1291 fund taint through proposed qualified election procedures.

Ownership through a PFIC

If a U.S. person directly or indirectly owns stock in a corporation that is a PFIC (PFIC No. 1), he or she is considered to own a *pro rata* share of any stock owned directly or indirectly by PFIC No. 1. If PFIC No. 1 owns stock in another PFIC (for example, PFIC No. 2), the shareholder of PFIC No. 1 indirectly owns a *pro rata* interest in PFIC No. 2.

If a U.S. person directly or indirectly owns at least 50 percent of the value of the stock of a non-PFIC foreign corporation (FC), he or she is treated as owning a proportionate amount (by value) of any stock directly or indirectly owned by the FC. In other words, if FC owns stock in a PFIC (that is, it has a lower-tier subsidiary that is a PFIC), the shareholder of FC will be an indirect owner of the PFIC if he or she owns at least 50 percent of FC. This result may be a surprise to the shareholder who intended to purchase an interest in a domestic entity.

Ownership through a Partnership or an S Corporation

If a partnership or an S corporation directly or indirectly owns stock, each partner or shareholder is considered to own a proportion of such stock in accordance with his or her ownership interest in the partnership or S corporation. For example, if a domestic corporation is a joint-venture partner in a foreign partnership, the domestic corporation is treated as owning a proportionate amount of any PFIC stock owned by the partnership.

Planning Considerations

The acquisition of an interest in virtually any type of entity involves the potential for indirect ownership of a PFIC. A careful examination to identify the existence of PFICs within the entity structures should become a routine part of structuring any sale of goods transaction. Additionally, there is a facts and circumstances test to consider in determining indirect ownership in a PFIC.

It is possible that taxpayers can rely on an arrangement's language to mitigate the extensive reach of the indirect ownership rules.

Dispositions of PFIC Stock

The regulations reflect an all-inclusive view of dispositions: unless otherwise provided, any direct or indirect disposition of PFIC stock is a taxable transaction. Gain, which is computed on a per-share basis, is taxed as an excess distribution. Loss is not recognized on the disposition of PFIC stock unless some other provision allows recognition.

A "disposition" is defined as any transaction that constitutes an actual or deemed transfer or property. The term "disposition" includes, but is not limited to, the following:

1.   Sales,

2.   Exchanges,

3.   Gifts or transfers at death,

4.   Exchanges in connection with liquidations or redemptions, and

5.   Other distributions.

Furthermore, the term "disposition" includes a PFIC shareholder who becomes a nonresident alien for U.S. tax purposes. The disposition occurs on the last day that the shareholder is a U.S. person. Additionally, the disposition rules extend to indirect shareholders using PFIC stock as collateral in a disposition of the stock or as security for performance of an obligation where the principal purpose of the security arrangement is to avoid the effect of the proposed regulations.

Indirect Dispositions

An indirect shareholder of a PFIC is subject to tax when an indirect disposition of the fund stock occurs. An indirect disposition is any of the following transactions:

1. A disposition of PFIC stock by its actual owner if the proposed regulations attribute ownership to an indirect shareholder (even if the indirect shareholder's ownership of the PFIC is unchanged by the disposition).

2. A disposition of PFIC stock by an indirect shareholder.

3. Any transaction that results in a reduction or termination of the indirect shareholder's ownership in the PFIC.

Distributions by PFICs

The proposed regulations define a "distribution" as any actual or constructive transfer of money or property by a PFIC with respect to its stock. The proposed regulations also introduce the concept of indirect distributions. A distribution by a PFIC to the actual owner of PFIC stock is an indirect distribution to a U.S. person who is treated as an owner of that stock under the proposed regulations.

Example 7-40

S, a U.S. corporation, owns 1,000 shares of PFIC. U, U.S. person, purchases 20 percent of S, thus becoming an indirect shareholder of 200 shares of PFIC. PFIC distributes a $10 per share dividend to its shareholders, constituting a $10,000 distribution to S. U is treated as receiving a distribution from PFIC of $2,000. The $2,000 is included with any other distributions received by U in determining if U received an excess distribution for the taxable year.

Elections to Purge PFIC Taint

Two mechanisms are available to a shareholder of a PFIC to purge the stock of its PFIC taint— that is, to escape future applications of the PFIC rules.

Using the first mechanism, a shareholder who elects the QEF regime and can establish the fair market value of the PFIC stock on the first day of the taxable year of the QEF election can further elect to recognize the untaxed gain in the stock as if he had sold the stock at its fair market value on the first day of the QEF election year. This election permits a shareholder of an unpedigreed QEF to convert the investment into a pedigreed QEF. The price of the conversion is current recognition of gain.

The deemed sale is taxed as a disposition under the PFIC rules; that is, the tax and interest are currently payable. The electing shareholder increases the basis of the QEF stock by the amount of gain recognized on the deemed sale. Furthermore, the shareholder is given a fresh-start holding period for the QEF stock that begins on the date of the deemed sale.

If a QEF is also a CFC, a shareholder can also purge the PFIC taint by electing to include in gross income his proportionate share of the post-1986 earnings and profits as of the first day that the QEF election is effective. Clearly, this election is advisable when the PFIC has relatively little post-1986 earnings and profits. The deemed dividend is treated as an excess distribution on the deemed dividend day. The shareholder's holding period in the stock is treated as beginning on the day of the deemed dividend.

Final Regulations

Final regulations provide rules for making a deemed sale or deemed dividend election to purge a shareholder's holding period of stock of a PFIC for those taxable years during which the PFIC was not a QEF.

The regulations provide two methods to purge the non-QEF years from a shareholder's holding period of PFIC stock. A shareholder may elect to be treated as having sold the stock of the PFIC. The gain on the deemed sale is subject to interest and is taxed as an excess distribution. Alternatively, if the PFIC is a CFC, any U.S. person that is a shareholder of the PFIC may elect to be treated as receiving a dividend in the amount of its pro rata share of the post-1986 undistributed earnings and profits of the PFIC. The deemed dividend is taxed to the shareholder as an excess distribution. If either election is made, the shareholder's holding period is treated, for purposes of the PFIC rules, as beginning on the date of the deemed sale or dividend.

Time for Making the Elections

In response to comments, the final regulations clarify the time for making the deemed sale and dividend elections. The regulations provide that if the shareholder and the PFIC have the same taxable year and therefore the first day of the shareholder's election year and the qualification date are the same, the shareholder may make the election on the same tax return on which it makes the QEF election or on an amended tax return. The regulations also provide that if the shareholder and the PFIC have different taxable years and therefore the qualification date precedes the first day of the shareholder's election year, the shareholder must make the deemed sale or deemed dividend election on an amended tax return. If the shareholder is making the election on an amended tax return, the amended tax return must be filed within three years of the due date for the return for the taxable year that includes the qualification date.

PFIC Reporting and Disclosure Requirements

The Hiring Incentives to Restore Employment of 2010 (HIRE Act) was signed by President Obama March 18, 2010, and as its name suggests, provides businesses with tax incentives to hire and retain new employees. The Foreign Account Tax Compliance Act (FATCA) was added to the HIRE Act to raise tax revenues to finance the HIRE Act tax incentives. FATCA's purpose is to "detect, deter and discourage offshore tax evasion through use of financial institutions outside the US" and to close "certain information reporting loopholes" that permitted US taxpayers to avoid reporting offshore assets and income.

Prior to FATCA, a US taxpayer with a PFIC interest was required only to file information regarding the PFIC when an event occurred that would trigger a tax liability with respect to the PFIC (for example when the PFIC paid a dividend or the investor sold the PFIC stock). FATCA authorizes the IRS to require an annual report disclosing PFIC investment without regard to tax incidence during the filing year.

The HIRE Act does not specify the form or content of the report, only that the report should contain "such information as the Secretary [of the Treasury] may require."

Chapter 8

Foreign Business Operations in the United States

Transactions with Unrelated U.S. Customers

The initial activity of a foreign-based business in the United States is frequently to sell its tangible property or license its intangible property to unrelated customers in the United States.

Example 8-1

ForCo is a manufacturer of cameras based in Foronia, and performs research and development, manufacturing and warehousing in Foronia. ForCo is contacted by a camera retailer located in the United States (RetCo) that wants to contract with ForCo to manufacture a line of cameras to be resold by RetCo in the United States. The camera will bear the ForCo brand name.

Because ForCo is merely selling tangible property directly to a U.S. customer, ForCo is unlikely to have any U.S. tax filing or reporting obligations.

Another common start-up phase of business activity for a foreign-based company in the United States is for the business to license its intangible property for use in the United States.

Example 8-2

The situation is the same as in Example 8-1, except that RetCo wants to manufacture the line of cameras that ForCo produces. RetCo will sell the cameras in the United States, and the cameras will bear the brand name of ForCo (which is well known throughout the world). RetCo does not seek to purchase cameras that ForCo manufactures.

The principal U.S. international tax issue in this situation concerns the treatment of the U.S. source royalty income that RetCo will pay ForCo for manufacturing know-how including the U.S. withholding on same.

U.S. Branch Operations

If a foreign-based business determines that expansion of its U.S. activities requires a presence in the United States, the next step may be the establishment of an office in the United States. The purpose of the U.S. office is frequently to facilitate the flow of business between the foreign business and its U.S. customers, licensees, or suppliers. Such an office is frequently referred to as a "branch" operation, in the sense that the foreign office is merely a branch of the foreign company conducting business in the United States. The purpose of a branch operation is indicated by Example 8-3.

Example 8-3

The situation is the same as in Example 8-1, except that ForCo's business with RetCo has developed so well that ForCo has been sending foreign-based marketing personnel to the United States to help RetCo market the line of cameras. ForCo determines that a physical presence in the United States would better serve and expand Retco's customer base. Accordingly, ForCo has established an office in the United States by renting office space, employing local staff and sending two sales technicians from its Foronia operation to reside in the United States and staff the office.

This office is a branch or a division of ForCo. The branch may or may not be taxable in the United States. If it is, the U.S. source income or loss is included in the U.S. return of the foreign business.

A branch operation is usually the way to establish a U.S. presence that poses the fewest risks to the foreign business in terms of cost, legal and tax complexity and related matters. The establishment of a branch operation may allow the foreign company to include any start-up losses incurred in the United States in its home country return. A branch operation may also be expanded to conduct a full range of business activities, such as manufacturing and marketing of the products produced in the United States.

Example 8-4

The situation is the same as in Example 8-3, except that the sales technicians in the U.S. branch are successful in developing the camera business in the United States. The branch has received a large volume of orders for a variety of different camera and optical products manufactured by ForCo that ForCo does not have the capacity to manufacture in its Foronia plants. Accordingly, the branch leases a manufacturing facility, starts to manufacture certain ForCo products and establishes a sales force in the United States to sell the products.

In this situation, ForCo will certainly have a taxable presence in the United States and will need to file a U.S. return (IRS Form 112OF), which will include all income or deductions effectively connected to ForCo's U.S. trade or business.

Buying Office

Frequently, an office is established to buy goods for the account of the foreign business.

Example 8-5

ForCo has been purchasing optical and semiconductor components from U.S. sources for its Foronia camera manufacturing processes. ForCo has typically relied on U.S. companies to arrange for the manufacture, inspection, and transportation of these components, but has recently determined that it needs to have its representatives on site in order to reduce cost and increase efficiency. Accordingly, ForCo has established an office in the United States by renting office space and employing local staff knowledgeable about the component

---

production and related activities. ForCo does not send any Foronia employees to staff this operation.

The office established in the United States is a branch of ForCo and is not organized as a U.S. corporation.

Manufacturing Branch

Manufacturing operations are frequently conducted through a branch.

> **Example 8-6**
>
> ForCo determines that the sales in the United States have developed to the point that it is appropriate to establish a manufacturing operation in the United States. In making financial and market evaluations of such a manufacturing operation, ForCo determines that the manufacturing operation is likely to incur losses for a period of time as its U.S. sales expand. USCo also determines that it will be advantageous to report such initial losses in its home country income tax return.
>
> Accordingly, ForCo forms a branch in the United States to develop a plant to manufacture one of its lines of cameras for the U.S. market.

Branch vs. Subsidiary Corporation

An initial issue is whether the branch will be treated as a division or as a separate corporation for U.S. tax purposes. The issue is important because the U.S. tax consequences to the foreign company and to the branch can be quite different if what is intended to be treated as a branch (division) of the foreign company is actually treated as a subsidiary corporation.

> **Example 8-7**
>
> The situation is the same as in Example 8-6, except that the U.S. branch is treated as a corporation for U.S. tax purposes.
>
> If the branch is treated as a corporation (the U.S. branch corporation), presumably the branch is a domestic U.S. corporation for U.S. tax purposes, with its own U.S. return filing obligations (IRS Form 1120). In this scenario, the start-up losses may not be deducted against home country and other non-U.S. income reported on the foreign company's home country tax return. In addition, the U.S. branch corporation is no longer subject to the branch profits tax with respect to deemed repatriations. Rather, the U.S. branch corporation is subject to the normal withholding provisions of the U.S. Internal Revenue Code relating to the payment of U.S. source income to foreign persons. U.S. transfer pricing issues are the same for a branch or a subsidiary.

Regulations published in 1996 permit an unincorporated business organization to elect to be treated as a corporation or as a partnership. Under prior law, the determination of whether an unincorporated business organization constitutes a branch operation or an affiliated corporation is an analysis of whether the organization possesses sufficient corporate characteristics.

Corporate characteristics include the following:

- Associates

- An objective to carry on a business and divide gains therefrom

- Continuity of life

- Centralized management

- Limited liability, and

- Free transferability of ownership interests.

Under prior law an organization must possess a majority of these characteristics to be classified as a corporation. Prior law is based on historical differences under local (U.S. state) law between partnerships and corporations.

Many states have revised statutes to provide that partnerships and other unincorporated organizations may possess characteristics traditionally associated with corporations. Some state partnership statutes now provide that no partnership is unconditionally liable for all debts of the partnership. Similarly, almost all states have enacted statutes allowing the formation of limited liability companies. These entities provide protection of all members from liability but may qualify as partnerships for federal tax purposes under prior law.

Per Se Corporations

The 1996 regulations apply to any "business entity"—defined as an organization that is recognized as an entity for federal tax purposes and is not classified as a trust or other special entity for federal tax purposes. Several types of business entities are always treated as corporations for federal tax purposes, including the entities listed below.

- A business entity organized under a federal or state law that describes the entity as "incorporated as a corporation, body corporate, or body politic [or] as a joint-stock company or joint-stock association…"

- A business entity organized under any one of several dozen foreign laws specifically identified in the 1996 regulations as analogous to state incorporation laws.

- An entity subject to tax as an insurance company.

- A business entity wholly owned by a foreign government.

- A business entity that is required to be taxed as a corporation, for example, a publicly traded partnership.

Form 8832 Election

A business entity that is not a *per se* corporation can elect to be taxed as a corporation or as a partnership (if it has two or more owners) or to be disregarded as an entity separate from its owner if it has only one owner. The election is made or changed by filing Form 8832 with the appropriate IRS Center. The election is effective as of the date stated on the Form 8832 provided that date is not more than 75 days before or 12 months after the election is filed. If no effective date is specified on Form 8832, the election is effective when filed. For example, a newly organized entity may make an election effective as of the date of organization if the election is filed within 75 days of the organization date.

No Election Made

If no election is made, an entity organized under the laws of the United States or any U.S. state or the District of Columbia after December 31, 1996, is treated as a partnership if the newly organized entity has two or more owners or is disregarded if the newly organized entity has one owner. Any other entity (any entity organized under laws other than the United States or any state or the District of Columbia) organized after December 31, 1996, is

- Treated as a partnership if the entity has two or more owners, at least one of whom has unlimited liability,

- Disregarded if the entity has one owner and the owner has unlimited liability, or

- Treated as a corporation if none of its owners has unlimited liability.

Unlimited liability is personal liability for the debts of or for the claims against the entity by reason of being an owner. An owner has personal liability if creditors of the entity may seek satisfaction of all or any portion of the debts or claims against the entity from the owner.

An entity in existence on January 1, 1997, retains the status claimed under prior law until that entity elects a different status under the 1996 regulations.

U.S. Taxation of Branch Operations

A U.S. branch operation is a distinct business activity of a foreign-based company, but is treated as a part of the legal entity of the foreign company for U.S. income tax purposes. Accordingly, the income or loss of the branch is included on the U.S. return filed by the foreign company (Form 1120F).

Example 8-8

The situation is the same as in Example 8-3, except that during the first year of operation, the U.S. branch of ForCo incurs a loss of U.S. $1,000x, reflecting the significant costs of starting up the office.

The U.S. $1,000x loss will be included in ForCo's Form 1120F for the tax year in question. ForCo will have a net operating loss carryover.

A foreign business is taxable in the same manner as a U.S. corporation on income that is "effectively connected" with the conduct of a U.S. trade or business. Certain non-effectively connected U.S.-source income is subject to a 30 percent withholding tax. The U.S. Internal Revenue Code also asserts U.S. taxing jurisdiction over certain foreign source income that is effectively connected with a U.S. trade or business if the foreign business has an office or other fixed place of business in the United States to which the foreign source income is attributable.

Threshold for Taxation

The gross income of a foreign business for U.S. income tax purposes includes only (1) gross income from sources in the United States that is not effectively connected with a U.S. trade or business and (2) gross income that is effectively connected with a U.S. trade or business.

In the case of income that is not effectively connected, U.S.-source fixed, determinable annual or periodical income (dividends, interest, rents, royalties, salaries, wages, and certain related items) is subject to tax at a flat 30 percent rate, without allowance for deductions, subject to reduction in the rate if the United States has a tax treaty with the foreign country in question. U.S.-source gains from the sale of intangible property, to the extent contingent on the productivity or use of the property, are also subject to the 30 percent tax. The 30 percent flat rate tax applies, however, only if the items of income are not effectively connected with the conduct of a trade or business in the United States. Other non-effectively connected U.S.-source income (including U.S.-source capital gains) is generally not subject to taxation in the United States, except in the case of certain U.S. real property transactions.

With respect to income that is effectively connected with a U.S. trade or business, U.S. tax is imposed on a net income basis at the same rates applicable to U.S corporations. There are four principal definitions that determine U.S. taxation of a foreign business:

1. The source rules;

2. The U.S. trade or business concept;

3. The "effectively connected" concept; and

4. The branch profits tax.

Sourcing of Income

Generally, interest and dividends are sourced by reference to the residence of the payor. Rents are sourced by reference to the location of the property. Royalties are considered to have a U.S. source if the royalty is for the privilege of using the intangible in the United States, so a license of U.S. rights by a foreign business gives rise to U.S.-source royalty income. Conversely, royalties paid by a U.S. person for the right to use intangibles in a foreign jurisdiction gives rise to non-U.S source royalties, even though paid by a U.S. person.

Gains from the sale of real property are also sourced by reference to the location of the property. Subject to certain exceptions, most gains from the sale of real property are sourced by reference to the residence of the seller. Exceptions are provided for inventory property (still sourced from the place of sale), intangibles (sourced under the general rule only to the extent that gain is not contingent on productivity), depreciable property and stock of foreign affiliates sold by a U.S. person.

Special treatment is applied in the sale of personal property (including inventory) by a foreign corporation. To the extent the sale is attributable to a U.S. office, regardless of where the title to the property passes, the income derived therefrom will be sourced in the United States. An exception to this special rule applies if the property sold is destined for use in a foreign jurisdiction and a foreign office materially participates in the sale.

For sales of intangibles by a foreign business, the residency sourcing rule applies only to the extent that the gain from the sale is not contingent on productivity. If the gain is so measured, the income is sourced by reference to the rules governing royalties. These source rules apply only to the extent that the income from the sale of the intangible is not attributable to an office or other fixed place of business maintained by the foreign business in the United States. If the sale can be so attributed, the gain is considered U.S.-source income, unless the property is destined for use outside of the United States.

Finally, for sales of property manufactured in one country but sold in another, Section 863 of the U.S. Internal Revenue Code provides that such income is generally sourced by treating the sale activities as a separate business when comparable factory sales are present. Otherwise, a mechanism is provided in the regulations to allocate the income between U.S. and foreign sources based on sales and assets.

Engaged in a U.S. Trade or Business Requirement

A foreign business not resident in a country that has an income tax treaty with the United States is subject to tax only on income that is effectively connected to a U.S. trade or business. The Code provides that the term "trade or business within the United States" includes the performance of personal services within the United States at any time within the taxable year, but does not include performance of personal services by a nonresident alien individual in certain circumstances or trading in securities or commodities under certain circumstances.

Case law provides guidance for determining when a trade or business is carried on in the United States. In general, the courts have held that before a taxpayer can be found to have engaged in a trade or business within the United States it must, during some substantial portion of the tax year, have been regularly and continuously transacting a substantial portion of its ordinary business in this country.

These cases clearly require activity that exceeds sporadic sales or maintenance of an office and certainly require some physical presence within the United States. For example, an investment company with U.S. shareholders and U.S. brokers, but no U.S. office and investments restricted to Canadian securities, was held not to be engaged in a trade or business in the United States. The Service has also ruled that a foreign corporation is deemed engaged in a U.S. trade or business if it carries on considerable, continuous, and regular business activities in the United States.

Generally, the mere sale of goods in the United States by a foreign corporation, without additional activity such as an office or agent or employees in the United States, does not constitute a U.S. trade or business. However, the activities of a direct employee or agent may result in engaging in a U.S. trade or business. The courts or the Service must decide whether an agency relationship exists between the foreign entity and the U.S. person or corporation, and, if an agency relationship exists, whether the U.S. agent's activities are sufficient to constitute a U.S. trade or business. The scope of an agent's authority to bind its foreign principal is an important factor in imputing the activities of the agent to the foreign corporation. If a broad power of attorney is given to a U.S. agent, then a court is more likely to conclude that the foreign individual or corporation is engaged in a U.S. trade or business. Consignment sales in which the U.S. seller is an agent of the foreign manufacturer may result in a U.S. trade or business.

U.S. income tax treaties generally exempt from U.S. tax the industrial and commercial profits of a foreign corporation that does not maintain a permanent establishment in the United States. The term "permanent establishment" is ordinarily defined to include an office, branch or other fixed place of business. An employee or other dependent agent who regularly makes contracts in the United States on behalf of his foreign principal will cause the principal to have a permanent establishment. An advantage of the permanent establishment treaty standard over the statutory "trade or business" standard is that wider use of agents may be allowed. An independent agent's activities ordinarily will not be attributed to his foreign principal for purposes of the permanent establishment standard.

Effectively Connected Requirement

If a U.S. trade or business is found to exist, all U.S.-source, non-effectively connected, non-capital gain income is deemed to be effectively connected. This principle is illustrated in an example in the regulations in which a foreign corporation has a branch selling electronic equipment in the United States, which constitutes a U.S. trade or business, and is also engaged in business activities through a foreign home office in the wine business. Sales of wine in the United States, although entirely unrelated to the electronics business conducted in the United States, were deemed to be effectively connected.

U.S.-source fixed or determinable annual or periodic (FDAP) income and capital gains income can be deemed effectively connected based on the application of one of three tests:

1. The asset use test,

2. The business activities test, or

3. The method of accounting test.

Under the asset use test, these types of income are deemed to be effectively connected if the income arises from the investment of assets directly used in the U.S. trade or business. Temporary investments of working capital required in a seasonal business are considered to be effectively connected. Other examples include gains or losses from the disposition of assets, such as stock acquired to ensure a constant source of supply and interest received on accounts receivable acquired in the ordinary course of the business. The asset use test is presumed to be satisfied if

- The asset giving rise to the FDAP income was acquired with funds generated by the U.S. trade or business,

- The income from the asset is retained or reinvested in the U.S. business, and

- U.S. personnel actively involved in the trade or business exercise significant management and control over the asset.

This presumption can be overcome by showing that the assets were held for future expansion or for other activities that are deemed not to have a current connection with the U.S. business.

The business activities test focuses on whether the otherwise passive income is derived directly from the active conduct of a U.S. trade or business. For example, dividends and gains derived by a dealer in stocks and securities meet the business activities test, as do royalties derived in the active conduct of a U.S. licensing business. The Code also notes that if the FDAP or capital gain income is accounted for on books separately kept for the U.S. business, it is considered a factor demonstrating that the income is effectively connected.

Certain items of foreign-source income may also be treated as effectively-connected with a U.S. trade or business. As a threshold matter, the foreign-source income must be attributable to an office or fixed place of business in the United States, defined as a place through which trade or business activities are regularly carried on. In order for foreign-source income to be considered attributable, the U.S. office must be a material factor in the production of the income and must regularly carry on these activities. Royalties from the use of intangibles offshore may be implicated by these rules, when the recipient's income is derived from the active conduct of a U.S. licensing business.

Branch Profits Tax

A foreign corporation having a U.S. trade or business may also be subject to the branch profits tax. This tax is applicable to a foreign corporation if it operates its assets as an unincorporated "branch" operation.

Prior to enactment of the BPT, there was a distinct advantage given to foreign corporations that operated in the United States through a branch as opposed to a domestic subsidiary. Earnings of the branch could be withdrawn from the branch and remitted to the home office for redeployment elsewhere in the world without incurring U.S. withholding tax, whereas a domestic subsidiary would have to pay a dividend to its foreign parent and thereby incur a 30 percent (or treaty-reduced) withholding tax. Dividends paid by a foreign corporation operating as a branch often escaped U.S. tax entirely because if less than 50 percent of its gross income consisted of income effectively connected with its U.S. business, the foreign corporation's dividend was considered foreign-source income.

In addition, tax treaties frequently offered protection from U.S. withholding on tax dividends paid by foreign corporations even when the dividends were funded out of income earned from a U.S. business. Similar disparities existed for payments of interest. A U.S. subsidiary could deduct interest payments to foreign lenders only at the cost of a withholding tax, whereas foreign corporations operating in the U.S. as a branch were allowed interest deductions for U.S. tax purposes. The recipient of the interest escaped U.S. withholding tax, because the interest was not considered to be from U.S. sources. It was often possible for third-country residents to "treaty shop"—establishing corporations in countries that had treaties protecting dividend and interest payments from U.S. tax.

The BPT attempts to level the playing field by imposing a 30 percent tax (or lower treaty rate) on the "dividend equivalent amount" of foreign corporations that carry on a U.S business. The BPT is imposed when earnings and profits derived from a U.S. trade or business are withdrawn from the business, either to be used outside of the U.S. business or to fund dividends to the foreign shareholders. The BPT is intended to operate comparably to a tax on dividends. Therefore, if a U.S. branch is terminated and the foreign corporation is liquidated, no BPT is imposed.

The BPT also applies to foreign corporations that have effectively connected income through an interest in a partnership that is engaged in a U.S. trade or business. A foreign corporation that is a partner in a partnership is treated as having a U.S. asset in an amount equal to the product of the foreign corporation's adjusted basis in the partnership interest multiplied by the ratio of its distributive share of partnership gross income for the taxable year that is effectively connected with the conduct of a trade or business in the United States to its distributive share of all partnership gross income for the taxable year.

In order to determine whether any earnings and profits have been withdrawn from the branch, the branch's "U.S. net equity" at the beginning of the year is added to its effectively connected earnings and profits for the year and then compared with the branch's "U.S. net equity" at the end of the year. "U.S. net equity" is determined by subtracting the amount of liabilities connected with the branch's U.S. business from the amount of assets connected with the business. If all of the earnings and profits for the year are reinvested in the business carried on by the U.S. branch, the "U.S. net equity" should increase over the prior year's net equity. In such a situation, there should be no "dividend equivalent amount" for the year and therefore no BPT.

A number of tax treaties contain nondiscrimination provisions that prevent imposition of the BPT on corporations resident in the treaty country. Under statutory anti-treaty shopping rules, however, a foreign corporation generally is entitled to claim treaty benefits in avoiding the BPT if the foreign corporation is a "qualified resident" (that is, its stock is at least 50 percent owned (directly or indirectly) by individuals who are residents of the treaty country or the United States, and no more than 50 percent of its income is used to meet liabilities to persons who are residents of a country other than the treaty country or the United States). If a corporation resident in a treaty country that does not allow imposition of the BPT is not treaty shopping, the corporation is not subject to the BPT and can continue to withdraw funds for use outside the U.S. business free of U.S. tax.

A portion of a dividend paid by a foreign corporation generally is considered to be income from United States sources if 25 percent or more of the foreign corporation's income for the immediately preceding three years was effectively connected with the conduct of a U.S. trade or business if the effectively connected income was not subject to the U.S. branch profits tax.

This rule imposes, in effect, a secondary withholding tax on dividends paid to foreign persons by foreign corporations that earn U.S. effectively connected income.

Effective for foreign corporation dividend distributions after 2004, U.S.-source dividends paid by a foreign corporation are exempt from U.S. withholding tax without regard to whether the earnings funding the dividend are subject to the U.S. branch profits tax.

Currency

The taxable income of a U.S. branch is generally calculated in the same manner as income from any other source, subject to the translation of income denominated in a foreign currency.

The currency in which a branch keeps its books is called its functional currency. U.S. branches generally conduct their business in U.S. dollars, so the U.S. dollar is considered the functional currency.

Incorporation of U.S. Branch Operation

As the activities of branch operations in the United States expand, or as the initial step in establishing operations in the United States, it may be appropriate for the foreign parent company to form a subsidiary corporation to conduct business in the United States.

Example 8-9

The business of the ForCo branch in the United States has continued to expand to the point that it is necessary to maintain inventories of goods and initiate manufacturing activities closer to the U.S. market. ForCo is considering whether it should form a corporation in the United States to continue the business of the branch.

The incorporation of a U.S. branch office is typically straightforward. The procedure first involves the selection and reservation of the name of the subsidiary. The second step is preparation of the pertinent documents to appropriately record the relationship between the parties, controlled or uncontrolled. Generally, the necessary documents are similar to a corporate charter, bylaws, and resolutions of the board of directors, or the equivalent body under local corporate law. The specific documents required depend on the corporate law and administrative practice in the appropriate state of the United States.

Transfer of Assets to a U.S. Subsidiary

Once a U.S. subsidiary corporation is formed, it is appropriate to transfer to the subsidiary any assets that are necessary in its trade or business. The assets required by a foreign subsidiary of a U.S. corporation may involve tangible assets, assumption of leasehold or other obligations, intangible assets, or financial assets.

Tax Concerns of Assets Transfers

The principal U.S. tax issue that typically arises at the formation of a U.S. subsidiary corporation relates to the inbound transfer of assets.

Example 8-10

The activities of ForCo's branch in the United States have continued to increase, and ForCo has determined that it needs to establish a U.S. subsidiary. Accordingly, ForCo forms a U.S. corporation (USSub), and transfers all of the assets and liabilities of the branch to USSub.

This transaction generally is treated as a tax-free incorporation for U.S. tax purposes under Section 351 of the U.S. Internal Revenue Code.

In general, Section 351 provides that gain or loss is not recognized by the transferor upon the transfer of tangible property to a controlled corporation, or to the transferee corporation. The adjusted basis of the property transferred will carry over to the transferee corporation and be substituted as the basis of the stock or securities received by the transferor from the transferee. The transfer of intangible property to the U.S. subsidiary is tax free and the payment of royalties and other periodic charges is subject to normal transfer pricing guidelines.

> **Example 8-11**
>
> Following the formation of USSub, ForCo determines that a patent that it has received on manufacturing technology can be appropriately exploited by USSub and transfers the patent to USSub. This is a transaction that would qualify for nonrecognition under Section 351 of the Code if it is between domestic corporations.

Effective for transactions completed after October 22, 2004, built-in losses (adjusted basis in excess of fair market value) in property imported into the United States in a tax-free incorporation or reorganization is limited to the fair market value of the property transferred. Any required basis reduction is allocated among transferred assets proportionately, according to the built-in loss immediately preceding the transaction.

Use of Interim Holding Company

In structuring a U.S. subsidiary corporation arrangement, an initial question that is often important is whether a holding company should be formed to hold the stock of the U.S. subsidiary. A holding company arrangement is often used in international corporate structures to perform a variety of functions, such as coordinating and stewardship, finance, and intangibles.

> **Example 8-12**
>
> ForCo has determined to form a holding company (HoldCo) under the laws of Treana, which has advantageous treaty arrangements with Foronia and the United States, for purposes of supervising its investments in the United States.

The principal function of a holding company is often to perform the stewardship functions of supervising investment in its subsidiaries, such as USSub in Example 8-12. In performing this function, HoldCo personnel will engage in the full range of activities that are necessary to supervise the active operations of the subsidiaries, including review of operations results, budgeting, financial needs, personnel and expansion, establishment of performance measurement criteria and related matters. HoldCo may not itself conduct an active trade or business; activities are typically conducted through operating subsidiaries.

HoldCo often may serve as a central source of borrowing to meet the needs of its subsidiaries, especially when favorable terms with lenders can be achieved through the use of a central finance center and adverse withholding or other local tax consequences may be avoided. This might include HoldCo borrowing from unrelated lenders and reloaning the proceeds to operating subsidiaries, as well as performing other controlled finance functions.

HoldCo might serve an intangibles function, whereby it acquires or develops intangible property rights and licenses these rights to its operating subsidiaries or third parties. In this connection, activities might include negotiations for the purchase or license of property rights from the developer and re-licensing of the rights, as well as acquisition of intangibles from unrelated parties for the international use of the group and entering research and development agreements with related or unrelated parties.

Other functions can also be conducted through HoldCo, depending on the needs of the particular situation.

U.S. Tax Implications

The principal U.S. tax question posed by HoldCo's activities in Example 8-12 is whether HoldCo could be deemed to have a U.S. trade or business, so that it is taxable on its effectively connected income in the United States. The regulations explicitly recognize that activities of a holding company do not rise to the level of a U.S. trade or business, even if the foreign holding company maintains a U.S. office, as long as the U.S. operating companies have the staffing to conduct their own operational trade or business activities.

In other words, the mere supervision of long-term investments in subsidiaries, even if conducted in large part in the United States, is not considered to give rise to a U.S. trade or business. This statement is consistent with prior case law principles that maintained the distinction between active business operations and the mere receipt of passive income.

It is important to contrast true holding company activities (essentially, the collection, accounting for, and reinvestment of income from passive sources) with activities constituting "trading," which can give rise to a U.S. trade or business. Several cases have identified "trading activities" as being engaged in market transactions designed to give rise to short-term profit (for example, margin trading, puts and calls, short sales and related matters). These activities have been distinguished from mere investment activities designed to result in profit from the collection of dividends and interest and long-term appreciation in the value of securities bought and sold.

The typical holding company function of primarily making and supervising investments in wholly owned corporations in the United States and abroad, which is inherently investment in character, should not give rise to a U.S. trade or business. Certain other functions (such as use of finance companies and use of technology companies) may not produce such a clear answer. It is important that activities relating to the production of royalty, interest, inventory, and other types of income not be considered as attributable to a U.S. trade or business. For this reason, neither the holding company's sole nor its principal office should be located in the United States.

Transfer Pricing of Holding Company

The performance of coordination and stewardship functions in an offshore holding company, as in Example 8-12, may raise transfer pricing issues in terms of services provided by HoldCo to its U.S. subsidiaries. If the stewardship activities are performed for the benefit of HoldCo, there may be no benefit to the affiliates being supervised, and the service charge regulations under Section 482 may not require any payment by the affiliates. If a benefit is provided, then the normal service charge requirements are applicable.

HoldCo also may provide broader ranges of services to its affiliates, including technical and support services, which do provide benefit to the affiliates. In this event, the normal service charge provisions of the Section 482 regulations are applicable to determine arm's-length compensation requirements, including when intangible property is provided in conjunction with the services.

Tax Issues of Financing the U.S. Subsidiary

An important issue in establishing a U.S. subsidiary is the financing of the activities of the subsidiary. In Example 8-13, which follows, the question is how the required capitalization should be provided to the U.S. subsidiary and how such capitalization should be documented.

Example 8-13

As plans for the new U.S. corporation, USSub, are finalized, the finance executives of ForCo determine that the U.S. subsidiary will require working capital of U.S. $5,000 to initiate operations.

In general, the U.S. subsidiary will be capitalized with all equity with guarantee by the foreign U.S. parent of the borrowings by the U.S. subsidiary from local financial institutions (or creditors in some cases), with a loan from the foreign parent or other affiliates, with the provision of goods or services, or with some combination of these basic approaches.

Equity

The most straightforward approach to the capitalization of a U.S. subsidiary is to contribute cash or property to the subsidiary as a capital contribution.

Example 8-14

ForCo determines that the capital required by USSub should be provided via the transfer of additional property and cash.

A contribution of cash has no U.S. tax consequence in terms of income or loss recognition. The contribution simply provides basis to ForCo in its stock in USSub for U.S. tax purposes. The use of equity capitalization means that any return to ForCo is not provided via payment of interest or principal as in the case of a loan. Rather, a return to ForCo may be received as a dividend from future earnings and profits of USSub, which would not be deductible by USSub for U.S. tax purposes and may be subject to a withholding tax upon payment.

Guarantee of U.S. Borrowing

A second means of indirectly providing working capital to a U.S. subsidiary corporation is to guarantee loans that the U.S. subsidiary arranges from local financial institutions (or trade creditors).

Example 8-15

USSub borrows the working capital from a U.S. financial institution, with a guarantee from ForCo.

The guarantee eliminates the need for ForCo to immediately provide the funds and transfers the borrowing costs to the U.S. subsidiary. The guarantee could have U.S. tax consequences with respect to the so-called earnings stripping provisions. In addition, it is possible that ForCo could be deemed to have received an arm's-length guarantee fee.

Loan

A frequent means of providing capital to a U.S. subsidiary is for the foreign parent to simply make a loan of the funds.

Example 8-16

ForCo loans the working capital directly to USSub.

ForCo will be deemed to receive interest at an arm's-length rate, whether paid or not. The interest payment is currently deductible for U.S. tax purposes by USSub, subject to certain limitations, and may be subject to U.S. withholding upon payment unless there is a reduction by treaty between Foronia and the United States. A repayment of principal is not taxable to ForCo in the United States, assuming that the lean is treated as debt and not equity for U.S. tax purposes.

Debt or Equity Characterization

In evaluating the method of financing provided to a U.S. entity formed by foreign persons, it is important to determine whether the financing will be characterized as debt or equity for U.S. tax purposes. The characterization is significant in determining terms of the U.S. tax consequences of payments for the use of money. The following are the tax results of different characterizations:

1. Payment of interest is deductible by the U.S. payor, subject to certain limitations. The payment of dividends (on equity) will not be deductible.

2. Payment of interest or dividends to foreign persons is subject to U.S. withholding.

3. Repayment of a debt obligation is not subject to withholding. Redemption of stock may be subject to withholding, if it is treated as a dividend.

Provision of Goods, Services, and Support

Another means of providing a U.S. subsidiary with working capital is through the provision of goods, services and support.

Example 8-17

ForCo determines that the U.S. $5,000 of working capital reflects expenses that need to be incurred by USSub to develop the market for ForCo product in the United States, as well as purchase inventory and arrange for the provision of services. ForCo decides to provide these directly, with payment to be made as the goods, services or intangibles are provided.

To the extent that market development expenses need to be incurred, ForCo, as the manufacturer, may incur these expenses directly. Such expenses may be deductible currently by ForCo in its home country. The provision of goods and services by ForCo creates an account receivable and intercompany debt. ForCo and USSub will have to arrange arm's-length compensation for the provision of intangibles through the purchase price of branded goods or through royalty payments.

Use of Noncorporate Entities

A foreign-based multinational may choose to expand its U.S. activities by forming or participating in a U.S. legal entity other than a wholly owned subsidiary U.S. corporation. Such entities typically include partnerships, limited liability companies, or other "pass-through" entities. It may also be appropriate to use a noncorporate entity as the organizational vehicle in a U.S. joint venture.

U.S. Partnerships

The tax consequences of participation by a foreign person in a U.S. partnership are not fundamentally different from the consequences that arise when a U.S. person participates in a U.S. partnership.

Example 8-18

USCo and 3PCo have decided to form a U.S. partnership (USPS) to develop a synthetic optical lens. It is determined that each partner will contribute U.S. $100,000. ForCo will also license certain intangibles to USPS.

One of the critical elements of a partnership, as opposed to a corporation, for U.S. tax purposes, is a single level of tax on partnership income imposed at the partner level. A partner must include in income its distributive share of partnership income for its taxable year ending within or with the taxable year of the partnership. A U.S. partner acquires a basis in its interest in the partnership equal to the amount of cash or adjusted basis of property contributed to the partnership in exchange for the partnership interest. Liabilities assumed or transferred are reflected in adjustments to basis in the partnership interest. Allocated items of income, gain, deduction, loss, or credit are taken into account by the partner on its U.S. income tax return together with appropriate partnership interest basis adjustments. Distributions of property receive an allocation of basis in the partner's hands and a termination of the partner's interest results in gain or loss depending on the nature of the property and cash distributed.

In addition, the partners may agree to allocate profits, or other items of income, gain, loss, deduction, or credit, among themselves, subject to the economic effect provisions of the U.S. Internal Revenue Code. Such allocations are important tax planning vehicles in the international context, in which specific partners may have significantly different effective tax rate situations in their respective countries. In order to plan for special allocations in a U.S. partnership with foreign partners, it will be necessary to consider the effect of the allocations in the United States and the home country of any foreign partner. For example, there are a variety of restrictions on the use of such allocated losses or deductions in the case of a U.S. partner.

The sourcing of the items of income, gain, loss, deduction, or credit is also important with respect to the operations of a foreign partnership. Sourcing issues generally are determined as if the partner realized the profits items directly. Specific allocations are provided with respect to some types of items, including interest, currency gain or loss, and source-based allocations in the partnership agreement.

Upon the disposition of an interest in a U.S. partnership, the foreign partner will be concerned about the same sourcing and characterization issues as upon the contribution of property to a

U.S. partnership. In general, the Service has taken the position that the international sourcing provisions of the Code are to be applied to characterize the gain or loss from the disposition of a partnership interest. If the partnership has a U.S. trade or business, the source of gain or loss is determined by reference to the pertinent provisions of the sourcing rules.

U.S. Limited Liability Company

A second type of noncorporate entity that may be attractive for a foreign-based multinational seeking to expand its U.S. activities is an entity that achieves corporate status for local law purposes, but pass-through tax results of a partnership for U.S. tax purposes. Such hybrid benefits can often be achieved in the United States through a U.S. corporation that "checks-the-box" to be taxed on a pass-through basis for U.S. tax purposes.

A domestic hybrid entity that has received considerable attention in recent years is the limited liability company (LLC). This entity is intended to be treated as a corporation for corporate and other legal purposes and as a partnership for U.S. tax purposes. An LLC may be desirable as an organizational vehicle for foreign activities in certain situations, including a joint venture. If the foreign-based multinationals wish to conduct business in the United States through a U.S. or foreign corporation, but also desire to have limited liability in their home country, they may choose to form a LLC.

The typical reasons for a foreign person participating in a U.S. LLC include

- Obtaining pass-through benefits (deduct losses on the home country tax returns of the LLC members);

- Avoiding U.S. entity level tax; and

- Meeting other objectives unique to the specific business situation.

An LLC is treated as a partnership for U.S. tax purposes, so the substantive matters discussed with respect to the use of partnerships to conduct U.S. operations or joint ventures are applicable in the LLC context.

U.S. Joint Venture

One of the most frequent means of conducting international business, especially when establishing a new operation, is to form a "joint venture" between one or more uncontrolled companies. A joint venture is a good way to share the risk of the enterprise and to take advantage of the relative skills or assets of the joint venturers.

> **Example 8-19**
>
> ForCo and US3PCO have decided to enter a joint venture (JVCo) for the purpose of exploiting their respective technologies to develop a new synthetic optical lens for use in the United States.
>
> The economic activity of a joint venture typically reflects the business, intangibles, skills, or related attributes of the respective venturers in a context that shares certain advantageous characteristics of the venturers. This joint venture resembles a controlled situation to the extent that ForCo has an interest in JVCo.

> On the other hand, it also reflects an uncontrolled arrangement to the extent that US3PCo has an interest.

Substantive Tax Issues of U.S. Joint Venture

The substantive U.S. tax matters that flow from participation by a foreign party in a U.S. joint venture arrangement mainly depend on the type of organization that is chosen to conduct the business activities of the venture.

A joint venture formed for the purpose of conducting business in the United States can be conducted through a foreign corporation (as a branch activity) or through a U.S. corporation.

The joint venture can also be conducted as a partnership. There are also other means of conducting what are, in effect, joint venture arrangements, depending on the nature of the relationship between the parties. For example, a joint venture arrangement relating to research and development that produces intangible property can be formed as a cost-sharing arrangement or as a patent pooling arrangement.

U.S. Tax Reporting

The U.S. tax reporting for branch operations of foreign corporations is accomplished via filing of a Form 1120F (U.S. Income Tax Return of a Foreign Corporation), which has sections for income effectively connected with a U.S. trade or business, income not effectively connected with a U.S. trade or business and determination of the branch profits tax. The transactions between a U.S. branch and its foreign home office, or other related foreign entities, are governed by U.S. Internal Revenue Code Section 6038C and Form 5472 attached to the Form 1120F of the foreign home office, as discussed previously in connection with tax documentation.

The U.S. tax reporting for the formation of a U.S. corporation by a foreign person is accomplished by the filing of IRS Form 1120 for the taxable period in question as well. Transactions between a U.S. corporation that is 25 percent or more owned by foreign persons and related foreign entities are governed by Section 6038A and Form 5472 attached to the Form 1120 of the U.S. corporation.

A foreign person that is a partner in a U.S. partnership is considered engaged in the trade or business within the United States if the partnership of which the foreign person is a member is so engaged. This means that the foreign partner must file Form 1120F. There is no special form that must be filed with respect to capital contributions to a U.S. partnership.

The transactions between a foreign partner and a U.S. partnership must be reported under U.S. Internal Revenue Code Section 6038C, which is similar in requirement to U.S. Internal Revenue Code Section 6038A in the case of foreign shareholders of certain U.S. corporations. The reporting of transactions when the foreign person is considered to be engaged in a U.S. trade or business (as in the case of a foreign partner in a U.S. partnership conducting a U.S. trade or business) is accomplished via Form 5472.

Chapter 9

Foreign Business Sales of Tangible Property in the United States

Taxation of Foreign Business in the United States

Characterization of the Transaction

From a tax standpoint, the fundamental issue in a sale of goods transaction is whether the transaction's form will be respected as a sale or whether it will be recharacterized as another form of transaction with different U.S. tax consequences.

Example 9-1

ForCo is a Foronia-based manufacturer of cameras performing research and development, manufacturing and warehousing in Foronia. DistCo is an unrelated U.S. corporation wholesale distributing cameras and related optical products through retailers in the United States. DistCo purchases a line of cameras manufactured by ForCo in Foronia.

In this example, the U.S. tax issues to ForCo's way of thinking are the familiar domestic questions of when the sales income accrues for U.S. income tax purposes.

However, because ForCo is a foreign entity, the U.S. tax issues become considerably more complex. We must determine whether the terms of the sale of goods to a U.S. purchaser (DistCo) cause ForCo's income to become U.S.-source income. If so, payment remitted to ForCo may be subject to U.S. withholding tax. ForCo may have a U.S. trade or business (or permanent establishment under a treaty). If ForCo is related to DistCo, there will be a question as to whether the purchase price is arm's length for U.S. Internal Revenue Code transfer pricing purposes.

In the inbound context, the characterization of the transaction may also be important for U.S. withholding purposes under Sections 1441 and 1442 of the Code.

Source of Income

The source of income received by a foreign seller of goods to a U.S. person is important in determining the U.S. tax consequences of the payment. The provisions relating to the sourcing of income from the sale of goods in the inbound context are the same as those discussed in the outbound context. In general, income from the sale of tangible property manufactured outside the

Yt6

United States by a non-U.S. business will be sourced by reference to where the economic rights, risks, and obligations are transferred.

Example 9-2

The situation is the same as in Example 9-1. ForCo sells the cameras to DistCo and provides DistCo with no other services or property. Title to the cameras passes outside the United States.

The source of the sales income that ForCo earns is foreign-source and not U.S. source. The cameras are manufactured in Foronia, outside the United States, and title to the cameras passes outside the United States. If, however, ForCo personnel provide assistance to DistCo or DistCo customers in the United States with respect to the sale or resale of the cameras, then there could be other U.S. sourcing issues as to any compensation paid to ForCo for these services.

The sourcing provisions of the U.S. Internal Revenue Code also allocate and apportion related expenses among U.S. and foreign-source income so that the purpose of the sourcing provisions cannot be thwarted by the allocation or apportionment of expenses. For inbound sales of tangible property, these provisions would likely be important only if the seller had a U.S. trade or business. In the absence of a U.S. trade or business, a foreign seller of tangible property should not be subject to U.S. tax and its related expenses would not be relevant.

If income from the sale of goods is treated as sourced in the U.S., the seller may be subject to U.S. tax on this income on a net basis.

Example 9-3

The situation is the same as in Example 9-2, and DistCo pays ForCo U.S. $5,000.

There appears to be no basis for concluding that ForCo has a sufficient presence in the United States to have a trade or business or permanent establishment under a treaty. The U.S.-source sales income should not be subject to U.S. withholding tax when DistCo pays ForCo. If ForCo does more than merely sell the goods, it may at some point have a sufficient presence to constitute a U.S. trade or business, which could raise "effectively connected" and branch profits tax issues.

Withholding on U.S.-Source Sales Income

If a foreign person sells goods for resale in the United States, there should be no question as to whether the sales income is subject to taxation in the United States. Income derived from the sale of goods generally is not subject to withholding, regardless of whether the character of the gain is ordinary or capital.

Conducting a U.S. Trade or Business

If a foreign seller of tangible property has employees or other activities in the United States for more than a *de minimis* period of time, there may be a question as to whether the foreign seller has a U.S. trade or business.

Example 9-4

The situation is the same as in Example 9-3, except that ForCo sends two marketing experts to the United States to assist DistCo. The experts remain in the United States for several months providing assistance to DistCo in distributing ForCo cameras.

ForCo has employees who are conducting business for a period of time in the United States. Depending on the nature and extent of their time in the United States, this could rise to the level of a taxable presence in the United States—a "trade or business" or "permanent establishment" under a treaty. The facts here, however, are unlikely to constitute a U.S. trade or business.

Example 9-5

The situation is the same as in Example 9-4, except that the ForCo employees are so effective that ForCo decides that there is a market for their professional services in the United States independent of the DistCo transaction. ForCo directs the two employees to remain in the United States indefinitely to seek business from U.S. entities that do not compete with DistCo. The two employees rent a small office and successfully find customers for their services and remain in the United States for several years.

The income that ForCo earns from these employees is likely to be U.S.-source income, and this arrangement may also create a U.S. trade or business (or permanent establishment under a treaty). It appears regular and continuous activity may be present.

A foreign corporation residing in a country that does not have an income tax treaty with the United States will be subject only to tax on income that is effectively connected with a U.S. trade or business. Although neither the U.S. Internal Revenue Code nor the regulations define when a trade or business is deemed to be carried on in the United States, case law provides guidance. In general, the courts have held that before a taxpayer can be found to have engaged in a trade or business within the United States, it must, during some substantial portion of the taxable year, have been regularly and continuously transacting a substantial portion of its ordinary business in this country.

These cases clearly require activity that exceeds sporadic sales or maintenance of an office and certainly require some physical presence within the United States.

Effectively Connected Income

Unlike the definition of a U.S. trade or business, the definition of effectively connected income is spelled out in considerable detail in the U.S. Internal Revenue Code and regulations. When a U.S. trade or business is found to exist, all U.S.-source, non-effectively connected, non-capital gain income is deemed to be effectively connected. This principle is illustrated in an example in the regulations in which a foreign corporation has a branch selling electronic equipment in the United States, which constitutes a U.S. trade or business, and is engaged in the wine business in its country of incorporation through the home office. Sales of wine in the United States, although unrelated to the electronics business conducted in the United States, is deemed to be effectively connected.

Effective October 22, 2004, foreign-source income that is economically equivalent to foreign-source rents, royalties, interest, dividends, and gains can be U.S. effectively connected income if the foreign-source income is attributable to an office or other fixed place of business in the United States and would otherwise be considered to be effectively connected.

Branch Profits Tax

If the foreign seller of goods has a U.S. trade or business (or permanent establishment) in the United States it may also be subject to the branch profits tax.

Transfer Pricing of Inbound Tangible Property

Inbound Distribution Activity

The distinction between research and development (R&D) manufacturing and distribution has been one of the core issues in many of the principal transfer pricing cases, both outbound and inbound.

In applying the tangible property transfer pricing provisions, the courts have expressed a preference for the comparable uncontrolled price (CUP) method where comparables can be identified. When the pricing arrangements can be justified by CUP methodology, the pricing analysis with respect to the sale of tangible property should be complete. The resale price method is frequently used, and the regulations indicate the resale price method is often the best method to use with distribution activities. The resale price method also requires comparable transaction data in order to determine the appropriate discount factor, and such information is frequently unavailable.

In the absence of comparable data to facilitate use of the CUP or resale price methods, the courts have turned to other types of financial margin analysis. The distributor cases reflect the importance of isolating the economic function and risk performed by a distributor in order to apply appropriate pricing methodology to its controlled relationships. Also reflected is the role that documentation can play in establishing function and risk. The regulations deal with distributor issues at a variety of points in a manner that is largely consistent with the cases discussed. The cases and the regulations illustrate the need for a distributor to assume, in fact and economic substance, economic function and risk.

Example 9-6

The situation is the same as in Example 9-2, except that DistCo has become the exclusive distributor in the United States. DistCo handles only cameras manufactured by ForCo and is responsible for the expenses of the U.S. distribution operation, including bad debts and all inventory costs. If goods do not sell, DistCo is responsible for disposing of the slow-moving inventory. Historically, the bad debt and inventory risks have been minimal. ForCo is

---

responsible for quality control, warranty, servicing and related costs. For the most recent period, the essential financial information of DistCo is as follows:

Gross profit margin	26%
Operating expenses	24%
Net income (before tax)	2%

The only pricing relationship between ForCo and DistCo concerns the pricing of the cameras, and related products, as there are no services provided by ForCo for DistCo.

In many cases, the economic function performed by a distributor may involve limited economic risk. The only exposure borne by DistCo relates to inventory and bad debts, which are stated to be minimal, and the expenses of conducting its business operations.

Market Share Development or Market Penetration

A frequent transfer pricing question raised by the Internal Revenue Service in inbound distributor situations is whether the foreign seller has sold goods to a related buyer at a price that results in a margin deemed inadequate by the Service. The U.S. distributor's defense may be that its low margins reflect the cost of establishing market share as opposed to a transfer pricing abuse.

Example 9-7

The situation is the same as in Example 9-6 except that DistCo has recently entered the U.S. market and desires to establish its market share. Accordingly, DistCo incurs significant losses.

In order to establish a market share development strategy, the U.S. Internal Revenue Code regulations require that the taxpayer provide documentation that substantiates the factors listed below.

1. The costs incurred to implement the market share strategy are borne by the controlled taxpayer that will obtain the future profits that result from the strategy, and there is a reasonable likelihood that the strategy will result in future profits that reflect an appropriate return in relation to the costs incurred to implement it;

2. The market share strategy is pursued only for a period that is reasonable, taking into consideration the industry and product in question; and

3. The market share strategy, the related costs and expected returns, and any agreement between the controlled taxpayers to share the related costs, were established before the strategy was implemented.

The market share strategy provisions in the regulations purport to limit the strategy to the establishment of market share, as opposed to market share maintenance in the face of competition or uncompetitive products. The rationale for this limitation is briefly described in the preamble to the regulations, which state that if competitors are also adjusting their prices, the lower price level should be reflected in comparable company data.

Chapter 10

Foreign Business Provision of Services in the United States

Taxation of Foreign Service Provider in the United States

> **Example 10-1**
>
> ForCo is a Foronia-based manufacturer of cameras that does its research and development, manufacturing and warehousing in Foronia. DistCo is an unrelated U.S. corporation engaged in the distribution of cameras and other optical products to retailers in the United States. DistCo desires ForCo's assistance in developing and executing a marketing plan for the product lines that Distco handles.
>
> If ForCo is a U.S. business, the U.S. tax issue for DistCo is the familiar question of when the expense for the service charges is deductible for U.S. income tax purposes.
>
> On the other hand, if ForCo is a foreign entity, the question is whether the foreign status of the service provider (ForCo) alters the generally applicable provisions of the U.S. Internal Revenue Code that relate to the timing of the deduction for payment by the payor (DistCo). There is also the issue of whether ForCo's provision of services to a domestic recipient (DistCo) causes ForCo's compensation to be U.S.-source income. If ForCo's compensation is U.S.-source, ForCo's compensation could be subject to U.S. withholding or income tax, depending upon whether ForCo is considered to have a U.S. trade or business (or permanent establishment under a treaty).

If the foreign service provider is related to the U.S. recipient, then the question is whether the payment for the services rendered is an arm's-length consideration for transfer pricing purposes under Section 482 of the U.S. Internal Revenue Code.

Expense for Service Payments

The U.S. income tax deductibility of the expense incurred by the U.S. recipient of services provided by a foreign service provider, as in Example 10-1, depends on whether the recipient (ForCo) is on the cash or accrual method of accounting. In addition, the payment must satisfy the ordinary and necessary expense requirements of Section 162 of the U.S. Internal Revenue Code. The typical issue in this regard is whether the services rendered were provided for the benefit of the U.S. recipient or another party. If the parties are not related, there is generally no question that the services are provided for the benefit of the recipient.

However, if the parties are related, significant questions are raised.

> **Example 10-2**
>
> The situation is the same as in Example 10-1, except that DistCo is a U.S. subsidiary of ForCo and ForCo provides assistance through executives based in Foronia.
>
> The provision of services by the parent to the subsidiary, located in a different country, may raise a question as to whether the services were provided for the benefit of the provider (parent) or recipient (subsidiary).

The Internal Revenue Service and the courts have broadly indicated that services provided for the benefit of the parent or shareholder of a controlled entity that are in the nature of stewardship services generally do not satisfy the ordinary and necessary standard of Section 162 as to the recipient subsidiary and are not deductible.

For this purpose, the term "stewardship" includes services that are in the nature of overseeing functions undertaken for the renderer's own benefit as an investor in the related corporation. The Service has indicated that such services or expenses include the following:

1. The cost of duplicative review or performance of activities already undertaken by the subsidiary;

2. The cost of periodic visitations and general review of the subsidiary's performance;

3. The cost of meeting reporting requirements or other legal requirements of the parent-shareholder that the subsidiary would not incur but for being part of the parent's affiliated group; or

4. The cost of financing or refinancing the parent's ownership participation in the subsidiary.

The distinction between stewardship expenses and other expenses for which deductions may be appropriate has developed principally from challenges by the Commissioner of Internal Revenue to business expense deductions under Internal Revenue Code Section 162 by a parent corporation for salaries paid to employees arguably performing services not for the benefit of the parent but for a subsidiary. The courts have indicated that a deduction is generally allowed only if the services performed are for the direct and proximate benefit of the entity incurring the salary expense and seeking the deduction.

For example, in *Columbian Rope Co. v. Commissioner*, a U.S. hemp rope manufacturer with principal offices in the United States (the U.S. parent) had formed a wholly owned Philippines subsidiary to purchase raw fiber for what were found to be valid business reasons. Many members of the managerial staff of the Philippines subsidiary were employees of the U.S. parent, provided by the U.S. parent on a rotating basis to perform services clearly for the immediate benefit of the subsidiary.

A deduction, by the U.S. parent, was permitted for salaries paid to these employees. Certain clerical employees and executives of the U.S. parent at its U.S. office also spent some of their time attending to the Philippine subsidiary. In regard to these activities, the court observed that it was obviously within the scope of the duties of the U.S. parent's top executives to give some attention to its significant investment in its Philippine subsidiary. The record indicated that the

Philippine subsidiary was adequately staffed, so that any time that the executives devoted to the Philippine subsidiary was simply in the nature of general supervision, which would be an ordinary and necessary part of their duties in conducting and managing the U.S. parent's business. The court further concluded that no part of the services of purchasing clerks of the U.S. parent could be said to have been performed for the Philippine subsidiary's benefit.

The essential distinction drawn by *Columbian Rope* is between services performed by the parent-renderer for its own benefit (supervisory or stewardship activities) and those performed for the benefit of the offshore subsidiary (operational support). A Section 162 deduction by the parent would be allowed for services performed for its own benefit, because the services are ordinary and necessary for the conduct of its trade or business, but not for services performed for the benefit of the subsidiary because these services are not ordinary and necessary to the parent's business. Conversely, from a recipient U.S. subsidiaries' standpoint, as in Example 10-2, a deduction under Section 162 is likely for the latter (operational) expenses and not the former (supervisory) expenses.

The same distinction has been drawn in Internal Revenue Code Section 482 cases, in which the issue is whether an allocation can be made to the parent with respect to services provided by it to a subsidiary, as in Example 10-2. For example, in *Young & Rubicam, Inc. v. United States*, a U.S. advertising agency provided the services of a number of employees to foreign subsidiaries and the Service sought to make Section 482 allocations to the U.S. parent with respect to these services. The services of several of the executives were found to have been performed for the benefit of the foreign affiliates, and allocation of an arm's-length charge was appropriate regarding these services. On the other hand, another executive was responsible for international operations and spent time with several subsidiaries to assist in solving certain local problems in the rendering of services to clients of foreign subsidiaries (and the U.S. parent). The court found that these services were in the nature of supervisory controls or other general activities of the U.S. parent and not management services for the business of a particular subsidiary, as to which a Section 482 allocation was not appropriate because there was no benefit provided to the foreign subsidiaries.

The distinction between stewardship or supervisory services that benefit the renderer of services and operational services that benefit the recipient is a clear bright line. In Example 10-2, DistCo had requested services for the purpose of expanding its distribution capability.

The result may be much different if the services provided are for the benefit of the provider and not the recipient.

Example 10-3

The situation is the same as in Example 10-2, except that the services provided by ForCo relate to the review of management and operations results of DistCo. DistCo has adequate staffing to perform such functions as required for its own benefit.

Here, the services seem to be for the benefit of the foreign parent (ForCo) in its capacity as a shareholder (stewardship expenses) for which a deduction may not be appropriate under Section 162, as indicated by *Columbian Rope*.

Source of Income

The source of the income provided to a U.S. person by a foreign provider can be important in determining the U.S. tax consequences of the payment for the provision of these services.

Example 10-4

The situation is the same as in Example 10-1. In order to provide marketing assistance, ForCo assigns two marketing executives in its Foronian headquarters to advise DistCo. This advice is provided by telephone, facsimile, and electronic mail communication, as well as visits by DistCo personnel to the Foronian offices of ForCo. The ForCo marketing executives do not make any visits to the United States.

There should be no question that the source of the income earned by ForCo for the services provided is foreign, because no services were performed in the United States. This eliminates the potentially troublesome issues that are present if the services are performed in the United States and produce U.S. source income.

However, if income from services provided by a foreign provider to a U.S. recipient is treated as U.S. source, the provider may be subject to U.S. tax on this income on a net or gross basis.

Example 10-5

The situation is the same as in Example 10-4, except that the two ForCo marketing executives come to the U.S. offices of DistCo for the period during which the services are rendered.

In this example, ForCo has employees who are conducting business for a period of time in the United States. Depending on the nature of these employees' time in the United States, such activities could rise to the level of a taxable presence in the United States, a "trade or business" or "permanent establishment" under a treaty. A taxable presence could, in turn, be subject to the branch profits tax (BPT) as ForCo earns income in the United States and is deemed to have repatriations from the U.S. branch to the home office in Foronia. Even if the presence is not sufficient to establish a taxable presence in the United States, the income earned from the services of the ForCo employees could be U.S.-source income that is subject to U.S. withholding tax when paid by DistCo to ForCo. Finally, the employees who come to the United States could be present for a sufficient period to become "residents" and incur a U.S. tax liability.

Withholding on U.S-Source Service Income

If a foreign corporation provides services through employees located in the United States, the service income may be subject to U.S. withholding taxation.

Example 10-6

The situation is the same as in Example 10-5, except that the ForCo employees spend six months of continuous time in the United States in order to render the

---

support services that DistCo requests. For these services, ForCo charges DistCo U.S. $100,000.

In this example, the income is likely to be U.S.-source income under the U.S. tax law because the services were performed in the United States. Payments made by the U.S. recipient of services (DistCo) that are U.S. source may be subject to U.S. withholding tax when the U.S. recipient (DistCo) pays them to a foreign provider (ForCo).

U.S. Trade or Business or Permanent Establishment

If a foreign corporation provides services through employees located in the United States and the service income is determined to be U.S. source, there is also a question as to whether the service activities are sufficient to constitute a trade or business or permanent establishment in the United States.

Example 10-7

The situation is the same as in Example 10-6. The ForCo employees spend six months of continuous time in the United States in order to render the support services that DistCo requests. For these services, ForCo charges DistCo U.S. $100,000, which is determined to be U.S.-source income.

In this example, the service activity may at some point become sufficiently regular and continuous as to constitute a U.S. trade or business or permanent establishment.

A foreign corporation resident in a country that does not have an income tax treaty with the United States will only be subject to tax on income that is effectively connected to a U.S. trade or business. The U.S. Internal Revenue Code provides that the term "trade or business within the United States" includes performance of personal services within the United States at any time within the taxable year but does not include performance of personal services in limited circumstances by a nonresident alien individual.

Although the Code and the regulations do not affirmatively define when a trade or business is deemed to be carried on in the United States, the case law provides guidance. In general, the courts have held that before a taxpayer can be found to have engaged in a trade or business within the United States it must, during some substantial portion of the taxable year, have been regularly and continuously transacting a substantial portion of its ordinary business in this country.

These cases clearly require activity that exceeds sporadic sales or maintenance of an office and certainly require some physical presence within the United States. The Service has ruled that a foreign corporation is deemed engaged in a U.S. trade or business if it carries on "considerable, continuous, and regular" business activities in the United States. Generally, the mere sale of goods in the United States by a foreign corporation, without additional activity such as an office or agent or employees in the United States, does not constitute a U.S. trade or business. However, the activities of a direct employee or agent may result in a U.S. trade or business.

U.S. income tax treaties generally exempt from U.S. tax the industrial and commercial profits of a foreign corporation that does not maintain a "permanent establishment" in the United States. Although the concepts of "U.S. trade or business" and "permanent establishment" are not synonymous, they are related, and precedents under one concept are often useful in analyzing issues under the other concept.

In Example 10-7, two employees of ForCo are present in the United States for the limited purpose of performing a specific task for the benefit of DistCo. This limited activity is probably not sufficiently regular and consistent to constitute a U.S. trade or business.

If a foreign service provider has employees or other activities in the United States for more than a *de minimis* period of time, it is more likely to be considered as having a U.S. trade or business (or permanent establishment in the United States under a treaty).

Example 10-8

The situation is the same as in Example 10-7, except that the ForCo employees are so effective that ForCo decides that there is a market for such professional services in the United States beyond the needs of its own U.S. subsidiary, DistCo. Accordingly, ForCo directs the two employees to remain in the United States indefinitely and to seek opportunities to provide their expertise to U.S. entities that do not compete with DistCo. The two employees rent a small office, successfully find customers for their services, and remain in the United States for several years.

The income earned by ForCo from these employees is likely to rise to the level of a U.S. trade or business (or permanent establishment under a treaty). The activities of the employees are regular and continuous and are provided from a fixed place of business (the rented office space).

When a U.S. trade or business is found to exist, the question arises as to the scope of activities of the foreign taxpayer that are effectively connected with such trade or business. There will also be a question as to the applicability of the BPT.

If it is likely that a U.S. trade or business will be deemed to exist, the foreign corporation should consider whether it is appropriate to simply form a U.S. subsidiary to conduct the U.S. activities.

Branch Profits Tax

If the foreign service provider has a U.S. trade or business (or permanent establishment in the United States), the income may also be subject to the BPT.

Example 10-9

The situation is the same as in Example 10-8, except that the ForCo employees are successful, and their efforts produce U.S. $100,000 of net income after U.S. tax during 2006. It is determined that their activities constitute a U.S. trade or business and an appropriate U.S. income tax return (IRS Form 1120F) is filed.

The BPT imposes a 30 percent tax (or lower treaty rate) on the "dividend equivalent amount" of foreign corporations that carry on a U.S. business. The BPT is imposed when earnings and profits derived from a U.S. trade or business are withdrawn from the business, either to be used outside of the U.S. business or to fund dividends to the foreign corporation's shareholders.

A number of tax treaties contain nondiscrimination provisions that prevent imposition of the BPT on corporations resident in a treaty country. If a corporation is not found to be simply treaty shopping, the corporation will not be subject to the BPT and can continue to withdraw funds for use outside the U.S. business free of U.S. tax.

In Example 10-9, the BPT could apply to the U.S. income of ForCo, depending on how the profits are deployed.

Foreign Corporation Employees as U.S. Residents

When a foreign corporation assigns foreign individuals (nonresident aliens) to an assignment in the United States, the nonresident aliens need to consider at what point they individually become subject to tax in the United States, as U.S. residents.

U.S. Tax Reporting

The U.S. tax reporting by a U.S. payor of fees for the performance of services by a foreign person principally involves consideration of U.S. withholding obligations if the service fees are deemed to have a U.S. source. If the provider and recipient of the services are commonly controlled entities, reporting under Section 6038A as well as the determination of an arm's-length fee for transfer pricing purposes is required.

Chapter 11

Exploitation of Business Assets Outside the United States

Taxation of Foreign Source Income

Sale of Property

Sale or other disposition of property differs from exploitation by usage in that a taxpayer gives up all rights and interests in the property. As long as the seller disposes of all of the ordinary attributes of ownership, it may retain a security interest or bare legal title as insurance for installment payments of the purchase price. The purchase price may be payable over a period of years; it may even be measured, like a royalty, as a function of the income earned by the purchaser in exploiting the property.

Generally income from the sale of personal property is U.S.-source if sold by a U.S. resident and foreign-source if sold by a nonresident. Gain from the sale of depreciable personal property is allocated between U.S. and foreign sources. Generally, the portion of gain from the sale of depreciable property that is allocated to U.S. sources is equal to the gain on depreciable property multiplied by U.S. depreciation adjustments divided by total depreciation adjustments. The source of income from the sale of inventory property is generally the place where the right, title, and interest to the inventory are transferred to the purchaser.

Example 11-1

Diamond Travel, Inc., operates bus tours for U.S. residents to Canada and Mexico and bus tours of the United States for Canadian and Mexican tourists. Diamond maintains offices in the United States, Canada, and Mexico. At any given time, Diamond owns between 20 and 25 large touring buses. In 2010, Diamond sells a bus that it purchased in 2004 to Lully Limousine Travel, which is incorporated in the Republic of Lebec. The allocation of the gain is computed as follows:

Sale price of bus	$75,000
Purchase price of bus	$100,000
Depreciation rate: 2004-2010 (10 percent per annum)	× 60%
Depreciation: 2004-2010	60,000
Adjusted basis of bus ($100,000 – $60,000)	(40,000)
Gain on sale	$35,000
Percentage of depreciation previously deducted against foreign-source income	× 35%
Foreign-source gain	$12,250
U.S.-source gain ($35,000 – $12,250)	$22,750

Income from licensing an intangible asset takes its source from the place where the asset is exploited; income from a sale of rights takes its source from the place where property is sold. A sale of rights by an individual for consideration that is contingent on use or production is treated in the same manner as a license.

Example 11-2

Calabro Corp. owns a valuable patent for technology used in the production of sugar-free sweetening agents. In 2010, Calabro grants a nonexclusive license to use the technology for four years in the Kingdom of Thermal; the consideration is a royalty of 8 percent of gross income. In the same year, Calabro sells all right, title, and interest to the technology with respect to the territory of the Kingdom of Tagus; the consideration is 8 percent of gross income realized by the buyer. Under current law, the royalty for the license is treated as foreign-source income to Calabro, since that is where the intangible asset is exploited. The receipts from the sale, however, may be treated as U.S.-source income if the sale is considered to have taken place in the United States.

Note: The treatment would be different if Calabro, in Example 11-2 above, were an individual. In that case, both types of receipts, the royalties and the contingent sale proceeds, would be treated as royalties for purposes of determining their source.

Interest

The source of interest income usually depends on the residence or place of incorporation of the payor. It generally makes no difference where or how the actual payment of interest is made; nor does it matter whether there is an actual payment or a deemed payment. A payment on a guarantee of a loan obligation by a borrower will assume the character that the borrower's payment would have had. A pass-through payment, such as a pledge and loan through an unrelated bank, will be treated as if the depositor made the loan directly.

Interest income from a foreign government is considered foreign-source income. Interest received from a nonresident of the United States is also foreign-source income. For purposes of determining the source of interest income, a "nonresident" includes individuals as well as foreign partnerships and foreign corporations. However, interest received from a foreign corporation or foreign partnership that is engaged in a U.S. trade or business at any time during the taxable year is considered U.S.-source income. In the case of a guaranteed interest payment, the source of income is determined by the residence of the primary lender.

Example 11-3

Debussy, Inc. is a French corporation that borrows money from Ives, a U.S. resident. The loan is guaranteed by Debussy, Inc.'s Hungarian affiliate, Brahms Corp., which is engaged in a U.S. trade or business. Brahms Corp. also has a primary loan from Ives.

The interest paid by Debussy, Inc., is foreign-source income, because Debussy is a French corporation. The interest paid by Brahms Corp. to Ives on the loan to Brahms Corp. is U.S.-source income, because Brahms Corp. is engaged in a U.S. trade or business. If Debussy, Inc., defaults on the loan and Brahms Corp. pays

---

> the remaining interest and principal, that interest paid by Brahms, Inc. is foreign-source income, because its source is determined by the residency of the primary borrower, Debussy, Inc.

Interest from a resident individual or domestic corporation is deemed foreign-source income if it is established to the satisfaction of the Secretary that at least 80 percent of the gross income of the resident individual or domestic corporation is active foreign business income for the three-year period ending with the close of the taxable year in which the interest is paid. For this purpose, "active foreign business income" means gross income that (1) is derived from sources outside the United States (or, in the case of a domestic corporation, is attributable to foreign-source income derived by a subsidiary) and (2) is attributable to the active conduct of a trade or business in a foreign country (or possession) by the corporation (or subsidiary).

License or Sale

Determining whether a transaction constitutes a sale or a license may be difficult. The language of agreements granting rights in technology may be misleading. Contracts that are clearly agreements of sale are frequently labeled "License." A quick indicator of whether the agreement is a license or a sale is whether it transfers "all substantial rights" in the technology for its entire economic useful life for a defined geographic area. If it does, it is generally a sale.

Example 11-4

The Chadwick Corp. processes and sells packaged food products in the United States and abroad. In the course of its operations, Chadwick develops many techniques for improving growing techniques and preserving food. The same research yields hundreds of patents that are not immediately useful to the company and that are simply retained.

Occasionally, Chadwick finds an opportunity to exploit one of these patented technologies in a manner that will generate some revenue without creating the risk of assisting a potential competitor. One such process, which breaks down peach pits into a certain chemical mix, was not considered useful to the company until Busoni Chemicals, Ltd., incorporated in the Republic of Chowchilia, offered to acquire it for purposes of attempting to synthesize Taxol.

In a contract negotiated and executed in the United States, Chadwick granted Busoni the exclusive right in the Eastern Hemisphere to use and to sublicense the process for the life of the patents. Busoni agreed to compensate Chadwick by paying 5 percent of any gross income earned from exploitation of the patented technology. Chadwick retained the right to recover the patent rights if Busoni became insolvent or if Busoni exploited the technology outside the Eastern Hemisphere.

Based on these facts, the income earned by Chadwick should be characterized as deriving from the sale of personal property and the source of the income would be the United States. If, however, the agreement granted Busoni only a nonexclusive right to the patents, the income would probably be characterized as a royalty, and

---

> the source would be Chowchilla and any other countries in which Busoni exploited the process.

More Than One Agreement

In some cases, the owner of the technology may grant both a license and an option to acquire the technology outright. Whether these two agreements, taken together, could constitute a purchase is usually a close call. Before the option is exercised, the operative agreement is a license. The licensee still has the power, at any time, to cause all right, title, and interest in the technology to pass from the licensor.

Lump-Sum Payments

The method of payment for a grant of rights to technology does not generally determine, even in part, whether the grant is a sale or a license. Thus, percentage payments are quite acceptable in sales, and a one-time, lump-sum payment is acceptable in a license.

Rental of Know-How or Provision of Services

Income from the provision of services and income from the sale of intangible property are treated differently for purposes of determining the source of income. Sometimes it is difficult, however, to know whether the income was earned from the sale of property or the provision of services. This is an old problem, originating in cases of authors exploiting rights in their written work. Currently, the problem exists where services are provided in areas involving technical know-how, such as computer programming.

Example 11-5

Paine Petroleum Corp., a U.S. corporation, designs and operates oil refineries that yield unusually clean petroleum products. When Paine is hired by petroleum producers or refiners, its general practice is to grant a client a license to modify or to redesign a portion of the client's refining capacity and to apply to the redesigned part a number of specialized production techniques that Paine has developed over the years.

In addition, because the techniques are based in part on secret know-how and because there are few other companies operating in quite the same manner, Paine sends a team of engineers to the client's plant to oversee the changeover to Paine's innovative process. Once the physical changes have been completed, some of Paine's engineers remain indefinitely, on a part-time basis, to train the client's personnel and to monitor (and troubleshoot) the new configuration of equipment.

Clients are the beneficiaries of new research and development by Paine. Paine has contracted with Azusa Associates, incorporated in the Caribbean nation of Soboda, to convert part of its refinery capacity. All of Azusa's crude oil comes from Venezuela and, once refined, is sold to purchasers in the United States. Azusa pays a substantial lump-sum amount up front and then pays an annual fee based on production of clean oil products and on time spent by Paine personnel at Azusa's facility.

> Based on the facts in this example, it is unclear whether the payments to Paine are for the provision of services or for the license of Paine's know-how, or both. If the payments are for services provided by Paine personnel, Paine's income would be foreign-source income, following the place where the services are performed. If the payments are for the license of Paine's processes, Paine's income would be U.S.-source income, following the place where the lump sum payment was received. The answer in this circumstance may be to make an allocation between where the services are performed and where the rights are exploited.

Determining the Allocation

Once it is determined that there is more than one type of income generated by the agreement, the next question is which of the types constitutes the essential element of the transaction. Based on the facts in Example 11-5, would the skills of Paine's engineers be of little value without the use of the special process or would the process be of little value without the supervision of the skilled engineers?

Finally, it should be determined whether the agreement and the surrounding circumstances suggest how the parties intended to allocate between the provision of services and the sale or license of technology. If there is no allocation recited in the contract, then an allocation must be made on the basis of a good-faith estimate of the relative value of the two elements. The exercise is similar to that of a buyer and seller of a business allocating amounts of the purchase price to specific assets.

Royalties or Business Income

What is probably the most difficult definitional issue arises in distinguishing between income from the rental of property and general business income. The distinction frequently turns not on the transaction itself but on the general business operations of a taxpayer. However, the terms of the transaction involving the use of property will often determine whether the taxpayer realizes income from royalties, from occasional sales, or from current business operations.

> **Example 11-6**
>
> The Carter Corp., a one-man research firm owned by George Carter, has developed a strong, lightweight metal that will be valuable in the manufacturing of engine blocks. He agrees to provide this process to Salieri, S.A., a company incorporated in the Republic of Soboda. Carter will disclose to Salieri his secret process and will provide consulting services for at least three months each year for the first five years of the agreement. Salieri agrees to pay an annual fee plus a percentage of the sales of engine blocks employing the Carter process.
>
> These facts are incomplete. If Carter retains ownership of the secret process, there is an argument that at least part of the money received from Salieri should be treated as royalty income. If Carter does not retain ownership of the process, then the transaction could be described as a sale. Each case has its own rules for determining the source of income.

> Assume that Carter did transfer all right, title, and interest in the process, at least for the country of Soboda, to Salieri. The question now is whether Carter's regular and substantial personal services to Salieri's business raise his level of involvement to that of a co-venturer. Where the licensor makes a complete disposition of intangible property in exchange for a percentage payment and where the licensor, at the same time, provides substantial services to the licensee to exploit the intangible asset, either the United States or the Soboda Revenue Department, or both, could treat the arrangement as an active business.

Reporting Foreign-Source Royalty Income

Depending on the transaction and the taxpayer, a royalty may constitute income that may be described generally either as passive income or as active income. The distinction is more important in the context of international transactions, since the two types of income are generally taxed in different ways. A passive item of royalty income that is earned from foreign sources is usually taxed by the host country by applying a percentage rate to gross receipts. A royalty that derives from an active business in the host country will generally be combined with other business income and then taxed.

The United States has tried to respond to the distinction by treating the two kinds of royalties differently for purposes of the U.S. foreign tax credit. The foreign tax credit draws not on foreign law but on U.S. law for determining whether royalty income should be treated as active or passive income.

> **Example 11-7**
>
> Creston Consolidated Chemical Corp. (Creston) is the holding company of a group of U.S. corporations engaged in a variety of businesses involving chemical processes. The group sells products made substantially from its chemical technology. Creston continually develops new techniques and refines existing ones. Many of these processes are patented. A number of the chemical technologies, both patented and unpatented, are used not to manufacture products but are exploited directly through licenses to unrelated companies. All rights to such technologies are first transferred to Creston's U.S. licensing corporation, located in the city of Metacomet. Metacomet then issues a nonexclusive license to the customer. Metacomet has no plant but maintains a U.S. office with a small clerical staff. In addition, Metacomet employs a team of traveling salesmen who seek licensees for its technologies. For 2010, Metacomet's information regarding the royalty income it received was
>
> | Country | Royalty | Tax Rate | Tax Paid | Expenses |
> |---------|---------|----------|----------|----------|
> | Arvin | $453,000 | 24% | $108,720 | $235,000 |
> | Alpaugh | 553,450 | 38 | 210,311 | 135,000 |
> | Aukus | 27,133 | 12 | 3,256 | 9,000 |
> | Aguanga | 654,325 | 25 | 163,581 | 225,000 |
> | Azusa | 75,650 | 22 | 16,643 | 500 |
> | U.S. | 3,500,000 | – | – | 2,050,000 |
> | Total | $5,263,558 | | | $2,654,500 |

Based on the facts in Example 11-7:

Creston reports the royalty income on its Form 1118 first by completing Schedule A. The five foreign countries of source are listed in Column 1. Next, for each source country, the amount of income is listed in Column 5 and totaled in Column 8. Then, directly allocable expenses for each country are listed in Columns 9, 9e, and 11. The directly allocable expenses are subtracted from the royalty income and the differences are entered in Column 12 and totaled.

Now, Creston fills out Schedule B, Part 1. The foreign taxes paid to each country are listed in Columns 2c and 2h and are totaled at the base of Column 2h. This total is entered on Part II, Lines 1 and 5. The total from Schedule A, Column 12, is entered on Line 6. The overall taxable income of the Creston Group, which would come from Form 1120, Line 20, is entered on Lines 7a and 7c. This amount is $301,200. Then, Line 6 is divided by Line 7c, and the quotient is entered on Line 8. The tentative U.S. tax liability (that is, before figuring any foreign tax credit) is entered on Line 9. The product of Lines 8 and 9 is entered on Line 10, and the lesser of Lines 5 and 10 is entered on Line 11. The amount on Line 11 is the net amount of foreign tax that is currently creditable. This amount is then entered on Master Form 1118, Line 9 (that is, Schedule B, Part III, Line 10), which is then combined with any other creditable foreign taxes available to the Creston Group for 2010.

More than $100,000 of foreign taxes are unavailable for credit on a current basis, even though the effective foreign tax rate appears to be no more than the U.S. tax rate. The reason is that the foreign taxes in all cases in Example 11-7 are imposed on gross royalty income, whereas the computations for U.S. purposes, including the foreign tax credit, deal with net or taxable income.

Chapter 12

Use of Foreign Tangible Property in the United States

Agreements for the Inbound Use of Tangible Property

Agreements for U.S. persons' use of tangible property owned by foreign persons is a common international transaction.

Example 12-1

ForCo is a Foronia-based manufacturer of cameras that does its research and development, manufacturing and warehousing in Foronia. DistCo is an unrelated U.S. corporation engaged in the distribution of cameras and other optical products to retailers in the United States. DistCo desires to lease an optical grinding machine developed by ForCo.

Tangible property can be divided into two categories—real and personal. Broadly speaking, real property includes land and structures permanently affixed to land, the latter being commonly referred to as "fixtures." Personal property is movable property. The distinction between real and personal property is fundamental and has significant tax and legal ramifications. Usually, the distinction is obvious. For example, if a company builds a manufacturing facility, the land and building are real property, whereas the machinery and office equipment (desks, computers, furniture, and the like) are personalty. Sometimes, however, property that is initially movable in nature may become part of the real property by virtue of its having been affixed to the land or structure.

A lease of personal property should document

- A description of the property;

- The specific period of use, including any renewal term;

- The rental rate;

- Any warranties by the lessor as to condition of the property at the commencement of the lease;

- Any obligations on the part of the lessee to maintain the property and provide for the redelivery of the property at lease-end;

- A stipulation as to the governing law;

- Dispute resolution arrangements; and

- Rights, if any, of the lessee to assign its rights under the agreement to a third party.

From an economic standpoint, the tenor of the agreement will be determined in large part by the intended function of the transaction (that is, as an operating lease or a finance lease).

Leases as a Financing Technique

The decision to transfer property by way of a lease, as opposed to a sale, may be driven by commercial reasons, tax planning, or a combination of both. A lease also is appropriate when the transferee of the property requires its use only for a temporary period, and then returns the property to the possession of the owner. This type of agreement is often referred to as an operating lease or "true lease."

The popularity of leasing as a financing technique is largely attributable to the generous tax incentives (accelerated depreciation, investment tax credits, and related matters) afforded by many governments to stimulate investment in a new plant and equipment.

These benefits are an incentive only, however, if the person acquiring the property is in a position to utilize them fully. For property users with little or no tax liability, such as start-up companies or companies with significant net operating loss carryovers, accelerated depreciation and tax credits are of no immediate benefit.

However, if a third party in a position to utilize such benefits purchases the property and leases it to the end-user, the purchaser or lessor can pass part of the value of the tax benefit on to the lessee in the form of lower rentals. Through the finance lease, tax benefits incidental to the ownership of property can be converted into the cash equivalent for the benefit of persons not otherwise able to utilize them.

Leases are especially popular in cross-border transactions. By exploiting differences in national tax laws, it may be possible to structure the arrangement so that it qualifies as a lease in the transferor's country and as a sale in the transferee's, thereby giving rise to tax benefits in both jurisdictions. This process is known as "double dipping." A lease may provide the only feasible financing tool when currency exchange laws prohibit the export of capital.

Over the years, many innovative types of finance leases have developed, tailored to the criteria of local tax laws. Some transactions have featured "evergreen" clauses, under which the lessee has the right to renew the lease indefinitely at a nominal rental upon the conclusion of the initial term. Other agreements provide for fluctuating rentals, intended to offset the difference in the tax treatment of loan repayments and rental payments. Frequently, the lease accords the lessee an option to purchase the property upon termination of the lease for a nominal amount, unrelated to the fair value of the leased asset.

Leasing not only offers an alternative to conventional financing in the acquisition of new equipment, but also a means by which corporations can refinance existing assets by selling them to a party who in turn leases the equipment back to the original owner at a rental reflecting part of the tax benefits derived by the purchaser or lessor. If tax benefits are limited by restrictions on tax-exempt use property, such sale or leaseback transactions may be used by municipalities and other tax-free entities that are not able to make use of depreciation allowances.

Lease financing is frequently structured as a "leveraged lease." Under a typical leveraged lease, the purchaser or lessor invests only a small portion—maybe 20 percent—of the capital required to buy the asset. The balance is provided by a third-party lender. In addition to the benefits of depreciation, a leveraged lease generates current interest expense deductions to the lessor. Generally, the lease is arranged in such a manner that the rental paid by the lessee can cover the debt service obligations of the lessor to the third-party lender.

Although a finance lease may be viewed as the functional equivalent of a secured financing, there are significant tax and legal differences, apart from the question of which party is entitled to underlying tax benefits from the transaction. For example, in a secured financing, the debtor makes payments of both principal and interest. The interest is deductible by the debtor (and taxable in the hands of the lender), whereas the amount corresponding to principal is tax neutral. Typically, the interest expenses decline over the term of the loan as the principal is amortized, even if the loan payments themselves remain constant (as in a direct reduction loan). In a loan, the tax benefits are often front loaded.

Under a lease, the entire rental payment is deductible by the lessee as a business expense and taxable in the hands of the lessor, providing for an even distribution of tax deductions. In cross-border transactions, the foreign law may provide for differential rates of withholding tax on rentals and interest. Similarly, if a double taxation treaty exists, the benefits accorded rental payments and interest, such as limitations on the maximum rate of withholding tax, may differ. Under a secured financing, the debtor has the risk or benefit of the asset's residual value.

This has both tax and economic implications. Any shortfall in residual value will decrease the lessor's return on its investment (unless this risk is hedged through insurance or put options) and the disposal of the asset may result in taxable gain being recognized.

Taxation of Foreign Lessor in the United States

The inbound use of tangible property involves a variety of U.S. tax issues, which vary depending on whether the parties, lessor and lessee, are unrelated or controlled.

When the U.S. party is the lessee of tangible property from an unrelated person in an inbound transaction, the U.S. tax issues concern how the international elements of the transaction alter the generally applicable provisions of the U.S. Internal Revenue Code to the user of the tangible property.

> **Example 12-2**
>
> The situation is the same as in Example 12-1 except that ForCo is an unrelated U.S. entity leasing the machine to DistCo for use in the United States.

In this example, the U.S. tax issue to DistCo is the familiar domestic question of when the rental expense may be deducted.

On the other hand, if ForCo is a foreign entity, it is necessary to determine whether the foreign status of the lessor (ForCo) alters the U.S. Internal Revenue Code's general provisions relating to the timing of the deduction of the rental payment by the payor (DistCo). It also must be determined whether the lessee of tangible property to a domestic recipient (DistCo) causes the income of ForCo to become U.S. source income, which could subject the payment to U.S. withholding tax, result in ForCo having a U.S. trade or business (or permanent establishment under a treaty), or related other taxes. If the foreign lessor is related to the U.S. lessee, there is the question of whether the rental payment is arm's length for transfer pricing purposes under U.S. Internal Revenue Code Section 482.

Sale vs. Lease Characterization

From a tax standpoint, the fundamental question in any leasing transaction is whether the transaction will be respected as a lease or whether it will be recharacterized as a sale. This issue affects the extent to which the lessee may deduct rental payments made under the lease and the tax treatment of these payments in the hands of the lessor. In a sale, only the portion of the payment representing interest is deductible by the lessee and taxable to the lessor. More significantly, the characterization of the lease determines whether the lessor or lessee will be entitled to depreciation benefits on the property. The sale versus lease issue for U.S. tax purposes is discussed in detail in the outbound context.

In the inbound use of tangible property context, the characterization of the transaction may also be important for purposes of U.S. withholding under Sections 1441 and 1442 of the U.S. Internal Revenue Code. If the transaction is a sale, there should be no U.S. withholding on payments of principal (as opposed to rent), though there may be an interest component that could be subject to withholding.

Expense for Rental Payments

Tax treatment of the expense incurred by the U.S. lessee in leasing personal property from a foreign lessor is subject to the normal provisions of the Code, depending on whether the recipient is on the cash or accrual method of accounting. In addition, the payment must satisfy the ordinary and necessary business expense requirements of Internal Revenue Code Section 162.

Source of Income

The source of rental income received from a U.S. person by a foreign lessor is important for purposes of determining the U.S. tax consequences of the rental payment.

Example 12-3

The situation is the same as in Example 12-1. To provide DistCo with the use of the machine, ForCo leases it to DistCo. ForCo provides no other services or property to DistCo, and ForCo employees do not make any visits to the United States.

In general, the location where the tangible property is used defines the source of the income. In this example, there should be no question that the source of the rental income earned by ForCo for the use of the machine is the United States, because the machine is used in the United States.

In addition to designating categories of income, the sourcing provisions of the Code also allocate and apportion related expenses to the income to insure that the purposes of the sourcing provisions cannot be thwarted. For inbound tangible property transactions, these provisions would be important only if the lessor has a U.S. trade or business. In the absence of a U.S. trade or business, the foreign lessor is subject to U.S. tax on a gross basis, and its related expenses are not pertinent.

If income from the use of tangible property paid to a foreign lessor by a U.S. lessee is treated as U.S.-source, the lessor may be subject to U.S. tax on this income on a net or gross basis.

Example 12-4

The situation is the same as in Example 12-3, and DistCo pays ForCo U.S. $50,000 under the terms of the lease agreement.

In this example, there does not seem to be a basis for concluding that ForCo has a sufficient presence in the United States to have a "trade or business" or "permanent establishment" under a treaty. However, the U.S. source rental payment could be subject to U.S. withholding tax when DistCo pays the rental payment to ForCo.

If ForCo does more than merely lease the property, it may at some point have a sufficient presence to constitute a U.S. trade or business, which could raise "effectively connected" and branch profits tax issues.

Withholding on U.S.-Source Rental Income

If a foreign corporation leases tangible property for use in the United States, there is a question as to whether the rental income is subject to taxation in the United States. The initial question is whether the payment is U.S. source income.

Referring to Example 12-3, the income is likely to be U.S.-source income under the U.S. tax law, because the tangible property (the ForCo machine) will be used in the United States. Payments made by DistCo that are U.S. source may be subject to U.S. withholding tax when the U.S. licensee (DistCo) pays same to a foreign provider (ForCo).

The anti-conduit financing provisions of Section 7701(l) of the U.S. Internal Revenue Code may be applicable to inbound transfers of tangible property if the effect of a financing arrangement is to reduce the amount of U.S. withholding tax (under U.S. Internal Revenue Code Section 881).

U.S. Trade or Business—Permanent Establishment

If a foreign lessor of tangible property has employees or other activities in the United States for more than a *de minimis* period of time, there may be a question as to whether it has a U.S. trade or business (or permanent establishment in the United States under a treaty).

Example 12-5

The situation is the same as in Example 12-3, except that in order to assist DistCo, ForCo sends two process manufacturing engineers to the United States. The engineers remain for several months as the DistCo manufacturing operation becomes operational and the machine is properly installed.

In this example, ForCo has employees who are conducting business for a period of time in the United States. Depending on the nature and extent of their time in the United States, their presence could rise to the level of a taxable presence for ForCo.

However, given these facts, it is unlikely that there could be a sufficient ForCo presence to constitute a U.S. trade or business.

The result could be much different with a greater presence in the United States.

Example 12-6

The situation is the same as in Example 12-5, except that the ForCo employees are so effective that ForCo decides that there is a market for such professional services in the United States beyond the needs of its own U.S. subsidiary, DistCo. ForCo directs the two employees to remain in the United States indefinitely and to seek opportunities to provide their expertise to U.S. entities that do not compete with DistCo. The two employees rent a small office and successfully find customers for their services, remaining in the United States for several years.

The income that ForCo earns from these employees is likely to be U.S.-source income, and it may also rise to the level of a U.S. trade or business (or permanent establishment under a treaty). This is necessary to establish because a foreign corporation resident in a country that does not have an income tax treaty with the United States is subject to tax only on income that is effectively connected with a U.S. trade or business.

Although the Code and regulations do not affirmatively define when a trade or business is deemed to be carried on in the United States, the case law provides guidance. In general, the courts have held that before a taxpayer can be found to have engaged in a trade or business within the United States it must, during some substantial portion of the taxable year, have been regularly and continuously transacting a substantial portion of its ordinary business in this country.

These cases clearly require activity that exceeds sporadic sales or maintenance of an office and certainly require some physical presence within the United States. In this example, it seems that such regular and continuous activity may be present.

Effectively Connected

Unlike the definition of conducting a U.S. trade or business, the definition of effectively connected income is spelled out in considerable detail in the Code and regulations. When a U.S.

trade or business is found to exist, all U.S. source, non-effectively connected, non-capital gain income is deemed to be effectively connected.

This principle is illustrated by an example in the regulations in which a foreign corporation has a branch selling electronic equipment in the United States, which constitutes a U.S. trade or business, and also is engaged in business activities through a foreign home office in the wine business. Sales of wine in the United States, although entirely unrelated to the electronics business conducted in the United States, is deemed to effectively connected.

For U.S.-source fixed or determinable annual or periodical (FDAP) income and capital gains, such income can deemed to be effectively connected by applying one of three tests: (1) the asset use test, (2) the business activities test, or (3) the method of accounting test.

Branch Profits Tax

If the foreign lessor of tangible property has a U.S. trade or business (or permanent establishment) in the United States, the lessor may also be subject to the branch profits tax.

Transfer Pricing

The Internal Revenue Service (the Service) has indicated that it will apply U.S. Internal Revenue Code Section 482 to so-called "lease strips" and "stripping transactions," which involve, in essence, the separation of income from expenses with respect to specific types of transactions. The Service expressed its concern that this separation of income and expense reflect arm's-length dealing between related parties. In Notice 95-53, the Service indicated that it intends to exercise its authority under Section 482 to assure arm's-length dealing in such transactions.

The anti-conduit financing provisions of Section 7701(1) of the Code could be applicable to inbound transfers of tangible property, if the effect of a financing arrangement is to reduce the amount of U.S. withholding tax under U.S. Internal Revenue Code Section 881 from that which would have been paid in the absence of the financing arrangement.

U.S. Tax Reporting

The U.S. tax reporting requirements by a U.S. payor of rent to a foreign person for the use of tangible property principally involve consideration of U.S. withholding obligations, if the rent is deemed to have a U.S. source. If the lessor and lessee of the property are commonly controlled entities, there also is a reporting requirement under Section 6038A, as well as the determination of arm's-length fees for transfer pricing purposes.

Chapter 13

Use of Foreign Intangible Property in the United States

Taxation of Foreign Licensor in the United States

If the foreign licensor is related to the U.S. recipient, there is the question of whether the payment for the use of the intangible property is an arm's-length consideration for transfer pricing purposes under U.S. Internal Revenue Code Section 482.

Example 13-1

ForCo is a Foronia-based manufacturer of cameras that does its research and development, manufacturing and warehousing in Foronia. DistCo is an unrelated U.S. corporation engaged in the distribution of cameras and other optical products to retailers in the United States. DistCo wants to use a trademark of ForCo in the United States.

If ForCo is an unrelated U.S. entity that licenses the intangible to DistCo for use in the United States, the U.S. tax question for DistCo is when the royalty expense is deductible for U.S. income tax purposes.

On the other hand, if ForCo is a foreign entity, then the U.S. tax questions are considerably more complex. It must then be determined whether the foreign status of the licensor (ForCo) alters the general provisions of the U.S. Internal Revenue Code relating to the timing of the deduction for the royalty payment by the payor (DistCo). It also must be determined whether the licensing of intangible property to a domestic recipient (DistCo) causes the income of ForCo to become U.S.-source income, which could subject the payment to U.S. withholding tax, result in ForCo having a U.S. trade or business (or permanent establishment under a treaty), or be subject to other taxes.

Timing of Expense for Royalty Payments

The treatment of expenses incurred by the U.S. licensee of intangibles is subject to provisions, depends on whether the recipient uses the cash or accrual method of accounting. In addition payments need to satisfy the ordinary and necessary expense requirements of U.S. Internal Revenue Code Section 162.

Source of Income

The source of royalty income received from a U.S. person by a foreign licensor is important for purposes of determining the U.S. tax consequences of the royalty payment.

> **Example 13-2**
>
> The situation is the same as in Example 13-1. In order to provide the trademark to DistCo, ForCo licenses the mark to DistCo. ForCo provides no other services or property to DistCo, and ForCo marketing executives do not make any visits to the United States.
>
> There is no doubt that the royalty income that ForCo earns for the use of the intangible is U.S. source, because the intangible is used in the United States. If ForCo personnel provided assistance in the United States with respect to the development of the DistCo marketing intangibles, there could be other sourcing issues.

In general, the place where the intangible is used determines the source of the income. To apply the source rule to royalties, the place of use of the property for which the royalties are paid must be known. In the case of a trademark, the place of use generally should be the country in which the property covered by the trademark is sold and whose laws protect the intangible (not the place where the property is produced).

In Revenue Ruling 80-362, the Internal Revenue Service applied the intangible sourcing rules to a nonresident alien's license of a patent to an unrelated foreign corporation, which, in turn, relicensed the patent to a domestic corporation for use in the United States. The Service ruled that the royalties on both the license and the relicense were U.S.-source income, because the royalties were based on the use of property in the United States. The Service reasoned that the foreign licensor's royalties on the original license had a U.S. source, because those royalties were paid in consideration for the foreign licensee's privilege of using the patent in the United States by relicensing the patent to the domestic corporation for use in the United States. The result was that the royalties received by the licensor were U.S.-source fixed or determinable annual or periodic (FDAP) income subject to withholding under Internal Revenue Code Sections 1441 or 1442.

When an intangible is used in more than one country, the transferor must make an appropriate allocation between the different uses for source determination purposes. In applying the royalty sourcing rule, royalty income must often be distinguished from other types of income.

In addition to distinguishing the categories of income, the sourcing provisions of the Code also allocate and apportion related expenses to the specific income so that the purpose of the sourcing provisions cannot be thwarted by the allocation or apportionment of expenses. For inbound intangible transactions, these provisions are important principally if the licensor has a U.S. trade or business. In the absence of a U.S. trade or business, the licensor would be subject to U.S. tax on a gross basis, and its related expenses would not be pertinent.

> **Example 13-3**
>
> The situation is the same as in Example 13-2, and DistCo pays ForCo U.S. $5,000x under the terms of the license agreement.
>
> In this example, the income is U.S. source, but there does not appear to be a basis for concluding that ForCo has a sufficient presence in the United States to have a trade or business or permanent establishment under a treaty. But the U.S. source

royalty payment could be subject to U.S. withholding tax when DistCo pays the royalty payment to ForCo.

If ForCo does more than merely license the right to use certain intangibles, it may at some point have a sufficient presence to constitute a U.S. trade or business, which could raise effectively connected and branch profits tax issues. Finally, any foreign employees who come to the United States to provide services to a U.S. licensee could be present for a sufficient period to become residents and have personal U.S. tax liability.

Withholding on U.S.-Source Royalty Income

If a foreign corporation licenses intangible property for use in the United States, the initial question for purposes of determining whether the royalty income is subject to taxation in the United States is whether the payment is U.S.-source income.

> **Example 13-4**
>
> The situation is the same as in Example 13-3, in which ForCo licenses its trademark to DistCo for use in the United States.
>
> In this example, the income is likely to be U.S.-source income under the U.S. tax law, because the intangible property (the ForCo trademark) will be used in the United States. Payment made by the U.S. licensee (DistCo) that is U.S. source may be subject to U.S. withholding tax when DistCo pays them to a foreign licensor (ForCo).

The anti-conduit financing provisions of Section 7701(l) of the U.S. Internal Revenue Code may be applicable to inbound transfers of intangible property, if the effect of a financing arrangement is to reduce the amount of U.S. withholding tax under U.S. Internal Revenue Code Section 881 from the amount that would have been owed in the absence of the financing arrangement.

U.S. Trade or Business—Permanent Establishment

If a foreign licensor of intangible property has employees or other activities in the United States for more than a *de minimis* period of time, there may be a question as to whether it has a U.S. trade or business (or permanent establishment in the United States under a treaty).

> **Example 13-5**
>
> The situation is same as in Example 13-4 except that DistCo also licenses manufacturing intangibles from ForCo so that it can manufacture a new line of cameras. In order to assist DistCo, ForCo sends two process manufacturing engineers to the United States who remain here for several months as the DistCo manufacturing operation becomes operational.
>
> ForCo will have employees conducting business for a period of time in the United States. Depending on the nature and extent of the Forco employees' time in the United States, their presence could rise to the level of a taxable presence in the United States, a trade or business or permanent establishment under a treaty.

However, in this instance, it is unlikely that the ForCo presence is sufficient to constitute a U.S. trade or business.

Example 13-6

The facts are the same as in Example 13-5, except that the ForCo employees are so effective that ForCo decides that there is a market for their professional services in the United States beyond the needs of its own U.S. subsidiary, DistCo. Accordingly, ForCo directs the two employees to remain in the United States indefinitely and to seek opportunities to provide their expertise to U.S. entities that do not compete with DistCo. The two employees rent a small office and successfully find customers for their services, remaining in the United States for several years.

The income earned by ForCo from these employees is likely to be U.S.-source income, and this greater presence is likely to rise to the level of a U.S. trade or business (or permanent establishment under a treaty).

A foreign corporation that is not a resident in a country that has an income tax treaty with the United States will only be subject to tax on income that is effectively connected to a U.S. trade or business. Although the Code and regulations do not affirmatively define when a trade or business is deemed to be carried on in the United States, the case law provides guidance. In general, the courts have held that before a taxpayer can be found to have engaged in a trade or business within the United States it must, during some substantial portion of the taxable year, have been regularly and continuously transacting a substantial portion of its ordinary business in this country.

These cases clearly require activity that exceeds sporadic sales or maintenance of an office and certainly require some physical presence within the United States.

Effectively Connected

When a U.S. trade or business is found to exist, all U.S. source, non-effectively connected, non-capital gain income is deemed to be effectively connected. This principle is illustrated by an example in the regulations in which a foreign corporation with a branch selling electronic equipment in the United States, which constituted a U.S. trade or business, also engaged in business activities through a foreign home office in the wine business. The sales of wine in the United States, although entirely unrelated to the electronics business conducted in the United States, are deemed to be effectively connected.

U.S.-source FDAP and capital gains income can be deemed to be effectively connected based on the application of three tests: (1) the asset use test, (2) the business activities test, or (3) the method of accounting test.

Example 13-7

The facts are the same as in Example 13-6, except that ForCo seeks to acquire TarCo, which conducts a related business to that of ForCo worldwide. TarCo's

---

operating subsidiaries have a variety of intangibles that could be quite beneficial to the ForCo group. ForCo plans to acquire TarCo and continue the TarCo business as a unit of the ForCo group.

ForCo has established an international technology company located in Finora (TechCorp), which is the owner of incremental technology of the ForCo group. TechCorp is located in a country where it can amortize the cost of acquired technology over a short period.

This example demonstrates the potential applicability of the effectively connected provisions. TechCorp could acquire the intangible property of the TarCo group separately from the acquisition of the remainder of the TarCo group by ForCo. TechCorp could then license the intangibles to its affiliates or unrelated parties as appropriate. The royalty income is subject to tax in Finora (unless Finora exempts such income, TechCorp has a tax holiday, or Finora does not impose an income tax). The amortization of the TarCo intangible acquisition, continuing research and development, or related costs may offset the income. TechCorp could also arrange for the development of incremental generations of technology by contracting with related or unrelated parties to conduct the development projects.

The regulations take the position that a corporation can be engaged in a trade or business of licensing and that royalties or gains from the sale of intangibles can be effectively connected with the conduct of that trade or business. However, as long as the actual activities relating to the licensing business are conducted by employees who have no connection with the United States, the mere fact that the intangibles are licenses for use in the United States should not give rise to effectively connected income, even if another U.S. business is being conducted.

The regulations provide some further guidance in discussing the business activities test for effectively connected purposes. In an example, foreign corporation N was engaged in a U.S. trade or business through a U.S. branch that acted as an importer of goods. N was also engaged in licensing patents to unrelated U.S. persons for use in the United States, which the example assumes constituted a business. Several factors indicated that U.S.-source royalty income was not effectively connected with the U.S. branch, including the fact that the licensee's business had no connection with the business of the U.S. branch, even though the products marketed by the branch were similar in type to the licensed products. Additionally, negotiations and other activities leading up to the consummation of licenses were concluded by employees of N, who had no connection with the U.S. marketing branch, and the branch did not otherwise participate in arranging for the licenses. The example concludes that royalties that N received from the licenses are not effectively connected with the conduct of the branch business in the United States because the activities of [the branch] business were not a material factor in the realization of such [royalty] income.

The principal activities of TechCorp, in Example 13-7, could consist of acquiring intangible property, negotiation of licenses for the use of the property, and the collection of income therefrom. To the extent that these operational activities are handled by TechCorp personnel having no U.S. connection, the income from licensing of intangible rights for use in the United States should not, standing alone, be considered to be effectively connected to a U.S. trade or business. On the other hand, if TechCorp were engaged in the active conduct of a U.S. licensing business through the use of a U.S. office or other fixed place of business, even foreign-source royalties or gains from the sale of intangibles may be considered effectively connected, and thus subject to full U.S. taxation, if the royalty or sale income is attributable to the U.S. office.

In this regard, the regulations provide guidance as to when a U.S. office is considered to be a material factor in the production of the foreign-source royalty income. Specifically, a U.S. office is not considered a material factor when the U.S. office merely conducts one or more of the following activities:

1. Develops, creates, produces, or acquires and adds substantial value to the intangible in the United States;

2. Collects or accounts for the income in the United States;

3. Exercises supervisory activities over the persons directly involved in time negotiation, solicitation, or performance of obligations under the license;

4. Performs clerical functions incident to the sale or license; or

5. Exercises final approval over license or sale.

It should be noted that the performance of all these activities in the United States could result in an active licensing business, so that any U.S.-source royalty income derived in conjunction with these activities would be considered effectively connected income. The prudent course of action may be to conduct as few of these activities as possible in a U.S office.

With regard to licenses for the use of intangible property outside the United States, the income from this use is considered effectively connected only if the foreign-source income is attributable to a U.S. office, which constitutes a material factor in the production of the income and the U.S. office must regularly be engaged in the activities giving rise production of the income. Creation or acquisition of the intangible in the United States, collection of royalties, general supervisory activity over the activities of those employees negotiating, soliciting, or arranging for the license, clerical functions, and exercise of final approval are apparently disregarded in determining whether the U.S. office is a material factor in the production of the foreign-source royalty income.

There should be no U.S. trade or business income for TechCorp in Example 13-7, if the activities connected with the negotiation, servicing, and collection of royalties from licensing activities are conducted in TechCorp's offices in Finora, or otherwise outside the United States. General supervisory activities conducted in the United States, not directly associated with the negotiation of these licensing arrangements, should not give rise to income attributable to the U.S. office.

Branch Profits Tax

If the foreign licensor of intangible property has a U.S. trade or business (or permanent establishment in the United States), it may also be subject to the branch profits tax.

Transfer Pricing

The discussion of transfer pricing for inbound intangible property arrangements under Section 482 of the U.S. Internal Revenue Code is the same as discussed for services and sales and use of tangible property.

U.S. Tax Reporting

The required U.S. tax reporting by a U.S. person paying royalties for the use of intangible property owned by a foreign person principally involves the U.S. withholding obligations, if the royalties are deemed to have a U.S. source. If the licensor and licensee of the property are commonly controlled entities, there is also required reporting under Internal Revenue Code Section 6038A, as well as the determination of arm's-length fees for transfer pricing purposes. This is included on IRS Form 5472.

Chapter 14

U.S. Withholding Taxes on Foreign Businesses

U.S. Tax Withholding Requirements

U.S. withholding taxes are an important consideration in structuring inbound investments or business activities.

A nonresident alien individual or a foreign corporation (a foreign payee) is subject to tax in the United States under two tax systems, according to the U.S. Internal Revenue Code. There is one tax system on income and expense effectively connected with the conduct of a trade or business within the United States (or permanent establishment in a treaty country context). A foreign payee is subject to U.S. tax on the effectively connected income of a U.S. trade or business at the same rates as U.S. persons. The U.S. tax liability of a foreign corporation conducting a U.S. trade or business is reported on IRS Form 1120F and the tax is paid in accordance with normal U.S. requirements.

The second system for taxing a foreign payee in the United States applies to income that is not effectively connected with the conduct of a U.S. trade or business. A foreign payee not conducting a U.S. trade or business does not have a tax presence in the United States. Generally, there are three situations that give rise to non-effectively connected U.S.-source income of foreign payees.

The first situation relates to investment (or portfolio) income.

Example 14-1

ForCo is a Foronia-based multinational engaged in the business of developing, manufacturing, and marketing cameras and other optical products on a worldwide basis. ForCo has no business operations of any kind in the United States, and it has significant investment assets that, from time to time, are not currently required as working capital in its core businesses. In order to invest such funds in a stable environment, ForCo invests in securities of U.S. government units or issuers. ForCo's accounts are credited with the income earned from these investments.

In this example, ForCo has no U.S. trade or business and no income effectively connected therewith. ForCo only has portfolio (investment) income from U.S. sources.

A second type of non-effectively connected income is U.S.-source income from business transactions that do not rise to the level of a U.S. trade or business.

> **Example 14-2**
>
> The situation is the same as in Example 14-1, except that ForCo determines that it should have a representative in the United States for its camera and optical products. Accordingly, ForCo enters a distribution agreement with an unrelated U.S. distributor of such products (3PDistCo). This agreement provides that 3PDistCo has the exclusive right to purchase and resell products bearing the ForCo brand name in the United States.
>
> In this example, ForCo may or may not have U.S. source income from the sale of tangible goods to 3PDistCo, depending on the terms of the transactions. It is possible that 3PDistCo will pay royalties, interest, or other amounts to ForCo in connection with the overall business relationship that may have a U.S. source.

The third situation that may result in U.S.-source income not effectively connected with a U.S. trade or business is present in all situations other than portfolio or business transaction income.

> **Example 14-3**
>
> The situation is the same as in Example 14-1, except that ForCo has determined that it should invest some of its funds in a U.S. real estate development, which is conducted through a U.S. partnership.

Withholding at the Source

The mechanism that Congress has provided to ensure the reporting and payment of U.S. tax on non-effectively connected U.S.-source income is withholding at the source—payment of the tax by the payor of the income. The tax is typically imposed on the gross amount of the income. Withholding matters frequently pose difficult issues to payor-withholding agents, foreign payees, and the Internal Revenue Service.

> **Example 14-4**
>
> The situation is the same as in Example 14-2. It is also agreed that 3PDistCo will license certain intangibles from ForCo and pay a royalty to ForCo in a fixed amount of $10,000 per year.
>
> The payment of the royalty will be subject to a 30 percent withholding tax liability that will be an obligation of 3PDistCo, the payor, subject to treaty provision. DistCo will become a withholding agent. In structuring the license agreement, the question of which party will bear the burden of the withholding tax should be addressed. If ForCo bears the tax, then it will receive a net payment of $7,000 ($10,000 less a 30 percent tax, unless the rate is reduced by a treaty). On the other hand, if it is agreed that ForCo is to receive a net amount of $10,000, then 3PDistCo will have to increase the payments so that the net amount received by ForCo, after withholding tax, is equal to that amount.

The Code imposes withholding obligations on payors of certain types of income to foreign payees under certain circumstances. The basic U.S. tax policy is to collect taxes from the payors of such income so that the payees cannot fail to pay. If the payor fails to withhold and the foreign payee does not pay the tax, the Internal Revenue Service has a domestic party with direct liability to pursue for payment of the tax. In some cases, foreign payees who desire anonymity may prefer to avoid the U.S. withholding net because of concern that the Service will share information with foreign governments pursuant to treaty obligations or otherwise.

If the payor-withholding agent fails to withhold tax, the agent may be directly liable for failure to withhold U.S. tax and subject to interest, civil, and possibly criminal penalties.

Withholding is required in a variety of situations. These situations are listed below.

Non-Effectively Connected Fixed or Determinable Annual or Periodic (FDAP) Income

Tax is imposed on certain types of income earned by foreign persons at a flat rate basis of 30 percent, and must be collected and paid over by the payor. Withholding is required on income from U.S. sources paid to foreign payees where the income is not effectively connected with the conduct of a U.S. trade or business.

Partnership Allocations

A domestic or foreign partnership with taxable income that is effectively connected with the conduct of a U.S. trade or business is required to withhold tax with respect to that portion of effectively connected taxable income allocable to foreign partners.

Real Property

If a foreign person disposes of a U.S. real property interest, the transferor is required to withhold a tax equal to 10 percent of the transferor's amount realized on the disposition. The amount withheld should not exceed the transferor's maximum U.S. tax liability, and the Service will provide a withholding certificate stating the maximum tax liability under certain circumstances.

Anti-Conduit Financing

In 1993, Congress enacted an anti-abuse regime to prevent certain uses of intermediary companies in international financial arrangements. Under these provisions, the IRS is permitted to disregard participation of one or more persons in a conduit-financing arrangement and to withhold tax if the participation is part of a tax avoidance plan (and certain other requirements are satisfied).

Non-Effectively Connected FDAP

The income items covered are defined, in part, as "interest (other than original issue discount), dividends, rent, salaries, wages, premiums, annuities, compensations, remunerations, emoluments, or other fixed or determinable annual or periodical gains, profits, and income...."

Thirty percent withholding is generally required on the gross amount of U.S. income items paid to a nonresident alien individual, foreign corporation or partnership. The Code establishes a five-part analysis to determine whether U.S. withholding is required with respect to a certain payment, as shown below.

1.   Is the payment income from sources within the United States?

2. Does the payment include income of the type generally described as "fixed or determinable annual or periodic?"

3. Is the income in question not effectively connected with the conduct of a trade or business within the United States by the foreign payee?

4. Is the foreign payee a foreign corporation?

5. Is the payor or some other person in the transaction a withholding agent (a person having the control, receipt, custody, disposal, or payment of any of the specified items of income)?

If the answer to each question is yes, withholding is required.

If a withholding agent does not withhold the appropriate amount of tax, the agent becomes directly liable for the amount of tax that should have been withheld, subject to interest and criminal penalties.

Interest

The Code generally requires 30 percent withholding on payments of U.S.-source interest to a foreign payee if the interest is not effectively connected with a U.S. trade or business. This withholding applies to the interest payment regardless of the form in which the interest income is paid. For these purposes, the term "interest" has its customary meaning—amounts paid for the use of money—and includes interest on open account indebtedness, shareholder advances to a corporation, and tax refunds by the U.S. government, a state or political subdivision. Withholding generally applies to the gross amount of the U.S.-source interest paid to a foreign payee, regardless of whether the payment represents a return of capital or payment of income. Interest exempt from U.S. income tax is not subject to withholding.

Original Issue Discount

Original issue discount is generally not subject to the 30 percent withholding requirement, but certain original issue discount accrued on an "original issue discount obligation" is subject to the 30 percent withholding requirement. The net result is that 30 percent withholding is required on payments of debt obligations payable more than 183 days after the date of original issue, absent zero or reduced rate withholding under a treaty.

Original issue discount normally accrues to a taxpayer even if the payments are made. By contrast, the foreign payment withholding rules tax foreign persons on original issue discount only when foreign persons receive payments or sell or exchange the original issue discount obligations.

Portfolio Interest

So-called "portfolio interest" is not subject to the 30 percent withholding. The term "portfolio interest" includes interest (and original issue discount) on two groups of obligations.

The first group is comprised of obligations:

1. Issued in bearer form,

2. Arranged to be issued only to foreign persons,

3. Bearing interest payable only outside the United States and its possessions, and

4. Bearing a prescribed legend.

The second group consists of obligations:

1. Issued in registered form and

2. With respect to which the withholding agent receives a prescribed statement certifying that the beneficial owner is not a U.S. person.

Portfolio interest generally does not include interest received by a 10 percent shareholder of the debtor corporation, by a bank extending credit pursuant to a loan agreement entered into in the ordinary course of the bank's business, or by a controlled foreign corporation from a related person.

Branch-Level Interest Tax

If a foreign corporation is engaged in a U.S. trade or business (or has gross income treated as effectively connected with the conduct of a U.S. trade or business), the branch profits tax treats interest paid by the U.S. trade or business as if it were paid by a domestic corporation. Thirty percent withholding generally applies to interest paid by a U.S. trade or business, if received by a foreign payee and not effectively connected with the conduct of a U.S. trade or business. This interest, however, is not subject to withholding if it qualifies under the portfolio interest or bank deposit interest withholding exemptions. A U.S. income tax treaty may also exempt the interest from withholding in certain circumstances.

Treaty Matters

A U.S. income tax treaty may exempt interest from withholding or reduce the withholding rate. The regulations contain special rules for securing an exemption from tax or a reduced rate of tax by reason of a U.S. tax treaty. To secure the exemption, the recipient must file a Form W-8BEN with the withholding agent when presenting the interest coupon for payment. The Form W 8BEN must be completed and signed by the owner of the interest, the owner's trustee, or the owner's agent. The form must include the information required by the form and its instructions, including a statement that the owner of the income is entitled to an exemption or a reduced rate of tax on the interest under a U.S. tax treaty. The withholding agent must retain the Form W 8BEN for at least three years after the close of the calendar year in which the interest is paid.

Dividends

Dividends from U.S. sources are subject to withholding when paid to a foreign payee, unless the dividend is effectively connected with the conduct of a U.S. trade or business of the foreign payee. An advance from a U.S. corporation to its controlling foreign shareholder is subject to withholding only if treated as a dividend, as opposed to a bona fide loan, for U.S. tax purposes.

Similarly, repayment of a loan to a foreign shareholder that is treated as equity for U.S. tax purposes may be subject to withholding.

The general rules regarding U.S. taxation of corporate distributions apply in determining the amount of a dividend distribution subject to withholding. The amount of the distribution equals the sum of the money received at the fair market value of the other property received minus any liabilities assumed by the shareholder in connection with the distribution or any liabilities to which the property distributed is subject.

Under these rules, a dividend is limited to the earnings and profits of the distributing corporation. However, the 30 percent withholding regulations require withholding on the gross amount of any distribution made by a corporation. This rule is unclear when applied to a corporate distribution that is not out of earnings and profits of the distributing corporation because a distribution in excess of the distributor's earnings and profits is treated as a return of capital. It appears that any portion of a distribution that is not characterized as a dividend for U.S. tax purposes is exempt from withholding.

The Service has taken the position that all corporate distributions are subject to withholding. In Revenue Ruling 72-87, the Service ruled that withholding is required on the portion of a corporate distribution treated as a sale or exchange.

What is the appropriate amount to be withheld when the earnings and profits are not sufficient at the time of the transaction, but could be at the end of the distributor corporation's taxable year in question?

Example 14-5

USCo is a calendar year U.S. taxpayer. USCo has accumulated earnings and profits of $1,000,000, and current earnings and profits of $50,000 as of June 30, 2010. USCo distributes a dividend of $50,000 to its sole shareholder, ForCo, a foreign corporation, on June 30, 2010.

In this example, the issue is whether USCo must withhold on the full amount of the distribution ($50,000) or only on the amount that is a dividend on the date of the distribution ($15,000 on June 30). The Service has proposed regulations that allow the distributing corporation to make a reasonable estimate of the amount of its earnings and profits, subject to review at year-end.

Effectively Connected Dividends

Thirty percent withholding generally does not apply to a foreign payee's dividends that are effectively connected with a U.S. trade or business. Moreover, a foreign corporation that has effectively connected income may be subject to the branch profits tax.

Redemptions, Stock Dividends, and Exchanges

A redemption of stock that is substantially equivalent to a dividend, not disproportionate (in relation to other shareholders), nor a complete termination of a shareholder's interest is treated as a dividend. To the extent that such a distribution is treated as a dividend and has a U.S. source, the distribution is taxable to a foreign payee. The gross amount of the distribution is subject to 30 percent withholding.

A stock dividend is a nontaxable distribution payable in stock or stock rights. It is exempt from withholding. A distribution that is treated as a distribution in part or full payment in exchange for stock is also exempt.

Section 304 Distributions

Section 304 of the Code is intended to treat redemption transactions from certain related corporations as dividends. The potential applicability of Section 304 is demonstrated by Example 14-6.

Example 14-6

USCo is a U.S. subsidiary of ForCo, which also has a foreign subsidiary (MafCo) in Mafonia, a foreign country. USCo purchases the stock of MafCo from ForCo for $50,000.

Under Section 304, the purchase of the MafCo stock is treated as a dividend from USCo to ForCo.

The Service has ruled that the payment of a deemed dividend under Section 304 to a foreign corporation by a domestic corporation is subject to 30 percent withholding to the extent that the divi-dend is from U.S. sources. The Service has also ruled that the payment of a deemed dividend under Section 304 to a foreign corporation by a foreign corporation is subject to 30 percent withholding unless the dividend can be clearly determined to be from foreign sources. The 30 percent withholding tax rate may be reduced under an income tax treaty between the United States and the country in which the selling corporation is organized and is a resident.

Section 306 Distributions

Section 306 of the Code characterizes amounts paid to redeem so-called "Section 306 stock" as a corporate distribution subject to normal rules of taxation of corporate distributions. If the redeeming shareholder is a foreign person and the redemption is paid by a U.S. corporation, the redemption should be subject to 30 percent withholding.

Amounts realized upon a disposition of Section 306 stock, other than by redemption, are taxed as ordinary income. The amount characterized as U.S.-source ordinary income is treated as FDAP for purposes of the 30 percent withholding rules and is therefore exempt from 30 percent withholding.

80/20 Corporations

If at least 80 percent of the corporation's gross income from all sources is foreign-source income derived from the active conduct of a trade or business in a foreign country or in a U.S. possession for the three-year period prior to the payment of a dividend, a specified percentage of any dividend paid by the corporation is exempt from 30 percent withholding. If the 80 percent threshold is met, the portion of the dividend exempt from withholding is the percentage of the corporation's foreign-source income for the three-year period to the corporation's total gross income from all sources for that period. If the 80 percent threshold is not met, all of the U.S.-source dividends paid by the corporation are subject to 30 percent withholding.

Treaty Matters

An applicable tax treaty may reduce the usual 30 percent withholding or eliminate withholding altogether on dividend income. In regard to dividend income, if a treaty applies, a foreign shareholder is not required to file Form W-8BEN with the withholding agent to secure the benefit of a reduced rate or an exemption from tax. In determining whether to withhold less than 30 percent by reason of a treaty provision, a withholding agent is generally able to use the address system depending on the terms of the particular treaty and any regulations issued under the treaty.

The Service has proposed regulations that eliminate dividend withholding based on the shareholder's address of record. These proposed regulations coordinate the withholding on dividend rules with the withholding rules applicable to interest. Specifically, the proposed regulations require the foreign shareholder to file a Form W-8BEN (executed under penalties of perjury) with the withholding agent in order to obtain the benefit of a reduced tax rate or exemption under a tax treaty. These proposed regulations generally provide that a withholding agent may, absent actual knowledge or reason to know otherwise, rely on a claim that a beneficial owner is entitled to a reduced rate of withholding based on an income tax treaty.

Royalties

The regulations, courts, and the IRS have treated U.S.-source royalties as subject to 30 percent withholding. For this purpose, the term "royalties" includes consideration received by a foreign person for know-how and other similar types of intangible or intellectual property.

Gains from the sale or exchange of any interest in patents, copyrights, secret processes and formulas, goodwill, trademarks, trade brands, franchises, and similar property are subject to withholding to the extent that the gains are from payments contingent on the productivity, use, or disposition of the property or interest sold or exchanged and from U.S. sources.

If a foreign person licenses a patent for use in the United States and relicenses the same patent to another foreign person, the Service has taken the position that all the royalties are subject to U.S. taxation and withholding because use of the intangible is in the United States.

Thirty percent withholding generally does not apply to royalty income that is effectively connected with a U.S. trade or business conducted by a foreign payee. Treaties typically reduce the rate of withholding (in some cases to zero) on royalty income.

Rents

Thirty percent withholding generally applies to U.S. source rents paid to a foreign payee. For this purpose, the term "rents" includes amounts paid by a lessee under a net lease arrangement for taxes, repairs, maintenance, and other expenses of the lessor, in addition to payments stipulated as rent. Thirty percent withholding generally does not apply to rental income effectively connected with a U.S. trade or business conducted by a foreign payee. A U.S. income tax treaty may reduce the rate of withholding on rental income or exempt the rental income from withholding altogether.

If there is a withholding obligation with respect to the rent payment in question, the payor has an obligation under the 30 percent withholding rules that cannot be negotiated by the parties. In the absence of a reduction by treaty, the payor is obligated to withhold and pay over 30 percent of the rent payment. In planning for this payment, the parties should negotiate whether the payor or foreign payee will incur the economic cost of the U.S. withholding tax.

Compensation for Services

Nonresident Alien Individuals

Thirty percent withholding is generally required if salaries, wages, and compensation are derived from U.S. sources and paid to a foreign payee. Thirty percent withholding also applies to a nonresident alien individual's compensation for services performed in the United States as an independent contractor, even though the individual may pay U.S. tax on this compensation, less any deductions related to the compensation and with credit for the withheld amount.

Thirty percent withholding is not required from compensation for personal services performed in the United States by a nonresident alien individual as an employee. The general withholding requirements of the U.S. Internal Revenue Code apply in this situation.

Foreign Corporations and Partnerships

Thirty percent withholding generally does not apply to compensation income for services performed by a foreign corporation or partnership. This income is generally effectively connected with a U.S. trade or business and is included on the U.S. income tax return filed for the effectively connected U.S. trade or business.

A U.S. payor may pay compensation income to a foreign corporation or foreign partnership for services in the United States actually performed by a nonresident alien individual hired by the foreign entity. The foreign entity then pays the nonresident alien individual for the services performed. Whether 30 percent withholding applies to these payments depends on whether the foreign entity or the nonresident alien individual should be treated as the real earner of the compensation income paid by the U.S. payor.

Other Types of FDAP Income

Thirty percent withholding applies to fixed or determinable annual or periodic gains, profits, and income (FDAP). The specific items of income listed are not meant to be exclusive. The regulations offer the following definitions.

Fixed

Income is fixed when it is to be paid in amounts definitely predetermined.

Determinable

Income is determinable when there is a basis of calculation by which the amount to be paid may be ascertainable.

Annual or Periodical

Income is paid periodically if it is paid from time to time, whether or not at regular intervals. Under the regulations, FDAP also include a single lump sum. The fact that the payments are not made annually or periodically or that the time period of payments may be altered does not, in and of itself, prevent the payments from qualifying as FDAP.

The regulations offer three specific examples of FDAP income—royalties, monthly commissions on sales, and payments by a tenant for taxes, interest and insurance premiums. There are also other types of income that may be so treated depending on the facts and circumstances of the situation, including premiums, annuities, alimony, and other items.

Gains from Sale of Personal Property

Income derived from the sale of real or personal property generally is not FDAP income and is not subject to 30 percent withholding regardless of whether the character of the gain is ordinary or capital.

Effectively Connected Income Exemption

Thirty percent withholding is not required for income other than compensation for personal services, so long as the income is effectively connected with the conduct of a U.S. trade or business and is included in the gross income of the recipient for the taxable year.

A withholding agent must make the withholding determination as to whether income is effectively connected to a U.S. trade or business at the time of payment. Withholding is not required if (1) the income is effectively connected with a U.S. trade or business of the person entitled to the income, (2) the income is includable in the person's gross income, (3) the foreign payee files a statement with the withholding agent indicating that the income is effectively connected.

The foreign payee must file with the withholding agent a statement, in duplicate, that the income described is, or is expected to be, effectively connected with the conduct of a U.S. trade or business and that the income is includible in gross income for the taxable year. The statement must list the following information: (1) the name and address of the withholding agent and the person entitled to the income, (2) the taxpayer's identifying number, (3) the nature of the item or items of income with respect to which the statement is filed, (4) the trade or business with which such income is or is expected to be effectively connected, and (5) the taxable year in respect of which the statement is made. IRS Form W-8ECI is specifically authorized by the regulations for this purpose, and is the customary means of compliance.

A statement is effective only for the taxable year to which the statement applies, so a new statement must be filed with the withholding agent before payments are made in a later taxable year. The statement must also be filed with the withholding agent before the payment in question. The exemption from 30 percent withholding may not apply if the statement is filed after the income has been paid. If circumstances change during the taxable year so that the income will no longer be effectively connected, the foreign payee must amend the statement. The withholding agent should retain one copy of Form W-8ECI. The other copy should be filed with the Service along with IRS Form 1042S.

In *Casa de La Jolla Park, Inc. v. Commissioner*, the Tax Court held that a withholding agent could not rely on the exemption from 30 percent withholding for effectively connected income because the agent had failed to obtain the requisite withholding certificate prior to making the interest payments in question. The facts involved a U.S. corporation that, through its U.S. bank, made payments of interest to a nonresident alien with respect to a loan from the nonresident alien to the corporation. The U.S. corporation failed to withhold at the rate of 15 percent (the reduced rate under the applicable treaty).

The Service asserted that, as a result of its failure to withhold, the U.S. corporation was liable for the tax. The U.S. corporation argued that it was excepted from the 30 percent withholding rules because the interest in question was effectively connected with a U.S. trade or business conducted by a nonresident alien. Further, the U.S. corporation argued that it had satisfied the requirement for an exemption certificate because in 1983 the corporation had received an exemption certificate from the nonresident alien for the taxable year 1982. The U.S. corporation asserted that it was entitled to rely on the exemption certificate for both 1982 and 1983.

The Tax Court never addressed whether the income was effectively connected with the conduct of a trade or business in the United States. The court stated that the U.S. corporation was not entitled to rely on that defense because it had not complied with the exemption certificate requirements. The court stated that, pursuant to the regulations, the exemption statement is required to be filed before payment of the income to which it applies. In addition, the court pointed out that a new certificate was required for each taxable year. Because the U.S. corporation had filed a form late for 1982 and had not filed a form at all for 1983, the court ruled that it had failed to satisfy the exemption statement requirement for both years. As a result the Tax Court held that the U.S. corporation was liable for the entire amount the corporation had failed to withhold in both 1982 and 1983.

Anti-Conduit Financing Arrangements

A traditional element of international tax planning for multinational businesses is the use of finance companies to facilitate or coordinate financing of the worldwide group. In the inbound context, a foreign-based multinational located in a country not having a treaty with the United States may seek to establish a finance company in a low-tax jurisdiction having an effective treaty network. The offshore finance company may loan funds to and receive interest from a U.S.-related entity, and such interest is deductible for U.S. tax purposes and is subject to little or no U.S. withholding tax under applicable treaty provisions.

In order to combat such arrangements, all recent U.S. tax treaties contain comprehensive "limitation on benefits" articles that generally prevent the use of treaty benefits by corporations not substantially owned by treaty country residents. The Service has warned taxpayers that the use of treaty-protected finance companies that receive interest and flow parts of the interest through to another related company will be challenged by the Service.

In 1993, Congress was concerned about the use of international multiple party financing arrangements and expanded the Service's authority to deal with certain types of transactions. Specifically, the 1993 anti-conduit rules authorize the Service to recharacterize any multi-party financing transaction as a transaction directly between any two or more of such parties where the Secretary determines that such recharacterization is appropriate to prevent avoidance of any tax imposed by this title.

Scope and Purpose

The stated purpose of the anti-conduit regulations is to provide rules that permit the Service to disregard participation of one or more intermediate entities in a financing arrangement if the entities are conduit entities. Once the transaction is recharacterized, the tax and withholding provisions of the Code are applied. However, the recharacterization applies only for purposes of the 30 percent withholding provisions and not for other parts of the U.S. Internal Revenue Code.

The Service has considerable authority to determine whether an entity is a conduit entity or whether multiple entities are acting together as one conduit entity. In certain circumstances, unrelated parties such as banks and other financial intermediaries can be treated as conduit entities.

The anti-conduit regulations provide the following specific definitions and rules for conduit treatment.

Conduit Entity

An intermediate entity is a conduit entity with respect to a financing arrangement if

- Participation of the intermediate entity (or entities) in the financing arrangement reduces the withholding tax on payments made in financing transactions as compared to the tax that would be imposed under the conduit regulations;

- Participation of the intermediate entity in the financing arrangement is pursuant to a tax avoidance plan; and

- Either

  - The intermediate entity is related to the financing entity or the financed entity; or

  - The intermediate entity would not have participated in the financing arrangement on substantially the same terms but for the fact that the financing entity engaged in the financing transaction with the intermediate entity.

Financing Arrangements

A financing arrangement consists of a financing entity that advances funds to an intermediate entity, which in turn advances funds to a financed entity.

If there is more than one intermediate entity there has to be a chain of financing transactions linking each intermediate entity. If the chain of financing arrangements is broken by an equity investment, there is no financing arrangement. However, the Service may be able to collapse two entities into one entity in order to find a financing arrangement.

A financing transaction includes

1.   Debt;

2.   Stock or a similar interest in a partnership or trust (common stock is normally excluded; certain redeemable types of stock are included as financing transactions); or

3.   Any lease or license.

Standard for Conduit Treatment

The regulations set forth the circumstances in which the Service can treat an intermediate entity as a conduit entity, and thereby disregard it as a party to a financing arrangement.

Multiple Intermediate Entities

If there are multiple intermediate entities, the Service can treat two or more entities as conduit entities. When there are two financing transactions involving two related parties, which would form part of a financing arrangement but for the absence of the linking financing transaction (because of an equity wall in between), the Service may treat the related persons as a single intermediate entity. This can be done only if one of the principal purposes is the avoidance of this provision of the regulations. This situation is illustrated in an example in the regulations.

A foreign parent company (FP) is incorporated in Country Y, which has no treaty with the United States. FP makes a loan of $10 million for a 10-year note at 8 percent interest to its subsidiary (ES) in Country X, which has a tax treaty with the United States under which interest is exempt from tax. On the next day, ES contributes $9.9 million to its wholly owned subsidiary (FS2), also incorporated in Country Y, in exchange for common stock, and lends FS2 $100,000. One year later, ES, which is a holding company whose principal asset is FS2, lends the U.S. subsidiary of FP $10 million on an eight-year note at 10 percent interest. Assume that one of the principal purposes of structuring the transaction between ES and FS2 as equity is to avoid recharacterization.

Under these circumstances, the Service may treat ES and FS2 as a single intermediate entity. This has the effect of eliminating the equity wall between ES and FS2 and creates a linking financing transaction between FP and FS2.

Unrelated Intermediate Entities

If the intermediate entity is not related to either the financing or financed entity (for example, a bank or other financial institution), the financing arrangement will not be recharacterized unless the intermediary entity would not have participated in the financing arrangement on substantially the same terms but for the fact that the financing entity made a loan or deposit in the bank or other financial institution or entered into a lease or license with it.

No definition of "substantially the same terms" is provided by the regulations. However, the effect of a financing company guarantee provided to the unrelated intermediate entity raises a presumption that the unrelated entity would not have participated in the financing on substantially the same terms. That presumption can be rebutted by clear and convincing evidence to the contrary. If such evidence is provided, the unrelated entity will not be treated as a conduit entity, even though its participation in the financing is pursuant to a tax avoidance plan.

Tax Avoidance Plan

For conduit treatment to apply in related-party situations, there is an objective test (the actual reduction in 30 percent withholding) and a subjective test (whether there is a tax avoidance plan).

The term "tax avoidance plan" is defined as a plan that has as one of its principal purposes the avoidance of the 30 percent withholding tax. This is a facts and circumstances matter. The circumstances to be considered in determining a principal purpose are as follows:

1. Whether participation of the intermediate entity significantly reduces the 30 percent withholding tax. This is done by comparing the withholding rates between the intermediate entity and the financed entity to the rate of the financing entity. The fact that an intermediate entity is resident in a treaty country is not itself sufficient to establish a tax avoidance plan. Furthermore, in comparing the amount of any tax reduction resulting from the use of the conduit entity, the taxpayer may show evidence that the financing entity is itself an intermediate entity and that another entity should be treated as the financing entity for the purpose of applying the tax reduction test.

2. Whether the intermediate entity would have been able to make the loan out of its own funds.

3. The period between the financing transactions. In one example, a 12-month period between the two loans is evidence of a tax avoidance plan. There is a one-year period in most of the examples.

4. Whether the financing transaction is in the ordinary course of a complementary or integrated business. No tax avoidance plan exists if the intermediate entity is related to the financed entity, whether or not the financing transaction has the purpose of financing an active trade or business of the intermediate entity that is complementary to, or integrated into, a trade or business of the financed entity. However, a loan will not be considered to occur in the ordinary course of an active conduct of a complementary or integrated business unless the loan is in the nature of a trade receivable or the parties are actively engaged in a banking, insurance, or financing business, consisting predominantly of transactions with unrelated customers.

There is a presumption of the absence of a tax avoidance plan when certain significant financing activities are performed by a related intermediate entity. These activities are listed in the regulations:

1.   Rents and royalties earned in an active trade or business as defined under the foreign personal holding company provisions of the Internal Revenue Code.

2.   In cases involving financing activities by cash management intermediaries and similar activities, officers or employees of the intermediate entity must actively and materially participate in arranging the intermediate entity's involvement. These activities must be conducted in the country of incorporation or tax treaty residence country.

The employees must exercise oversight and decision-making and must actively manage the currency and interest rate risks on an ongoing basis, in contrast to taking out a long-term hedge to eliminate all risk.

Conduit Treatment

The regulations confer broad authority on the Service to determine whether an intermediate entity should be disregarded for purposes of the 30 percent withholding rules. The Service has discretion to determine how the standards for conduit treatment are applied, including which financing transactions and which parties compose the financing arrangement. Although some guidance is given in the regulations, the Service's determination will generally be based on facts and circumstances. There is no central review procedure by the Service at the National Office level. The legislative history indicates that courts will review the Service's determination only for abuse of discretion.

Once the Service has determined that an intermediate entity is a conduit entity, there are several consequences. If the Service has recharacterized an intermediate entity as a conduit entity, the entity is disregarded for the purposes of the 30 percent withholding rules, and payments made by the financed entity are treated as made directly to the financing entity. The recharacterization also applies for purposes of taxation of nonresident alien individuals, branch profits tax, withholding tax on payments to nonresident aliens and withholding tax on payments to foreign corporations. The recharacterization does not otherwise affect a taxpayer's U.S. income tax liability under other provisions of the Internal Revenue Code. The recharacterization only applies to payments made by the financed entity that are deductible, such as interest and rents. The recharacterization does not, for example, apply to dividends.

The disregarded conduit entity is in general treated as an agent of the financing company with respect to any payments made by it. The disregarded conduit entity is responsible for withholding tax under the 30 percent withholding rules. If the financed entity is paying interest and principal to an unrelated lender in the arrangement, the regulations provide that the lender is not liable for tax unless the lender knows or has reason to know of the recharacterization. However, the intermediate entity remains liable to act as a potential withholding agent.

Relationship to Other Withholding Rules

The purpose of the anti-conduit financing provisions is to prevent the use of complex international structures to minimize U.S. tax obligations. The anti-conduit financing provisions determine the parties and flow of payments and income subject to 30 percent withholding involved in the financing arrangements in question.

> **Example 14-7**
>
> DC is a U.S. corporation that is in the process of negotiating a loan of $10 million from BK1, a bank located in country N, a country that does not have an income tax treaty with the United States. Before the loan agreement is signed, DC's tax accountants point out that interest on the loan would not be subject to withholding tax if the loan were made by BK2, a subsidiary of BKI that is incorporated in country T, a country that has an income tax treaty with the United States that prohibits the imposition of withholding tax on payments of interest. BK1 makes a loan to BK2 to enable BK2 to make the loan to DC. Without the loan from BK1 to BK2, BK2 would not have been able to make the loan to DC.
>
> In this situation, the loans from BK1 to BK2 and to DC are financing transactions, constitute a financing arrangement and BK2 is a conduit entity under the anti-conduit provisions. DC is a party to the transactions, knows of the arrangement and must withhold tax under the 30 percent withholding rules. If DC fails to perform its obligations as a withholding agent, BK2 is responsible.

Withholding Obligations and Procedures

The 30 percent withholding rules broadly require that all persons (including foreign corporations), having the control, receipt, custody, disposal, or payment of certain items of income of a foreign payee must withhold tax from such income items. Responsible persons may be acting in any capacity, including lessees or mortgagors of real or personal property, fiduciaries, employers, and all officers and employees of the United States.

The withholding agent is generally the last person to have control of income before payment to the foreign payee subject to U.S. income tax liability. Any person who pays or causes to be paid an item of income subject to 30 percent withholding to a foreign payee may be a withholding agent. These broad provisions may require either domestic or foreign persons to withhold.

Obligation to Withhold—Withholding Agent

The 30 percent withholding regulations define the term "withholding agent" as "any person who pays or causes to be paid an item of income to (or to the agent of) a nonresident alien individual, a foreign partnership, a foreign fiduciary of a trust or estate, or a foreign corporation, and who is required to withhold tax from such item of income."

The withholding obligations imposed by 30 percent withholding rules are broad and can cause harsh results if withholding is required but not accomplished. The payor of income must withhold tax from income when the payment of that income is within the payor's control, regardless of whether the income is paid directly or constructively to the foreign payee.

A withholding obligation may also apply to a receiving agent if (1) the agent receives income payable to its principal who is a foreign person and (2) the payor of the income has not withheld. Further, if the payor of the income knows that a U.S. recipient is acting in an agency capacity and that the principal is a foreign person, the payor must withhold on payments to the agent. If the payor does not know that the U.S. recipient is acting in an agency capacity for a foreign principal, the liability of the payor may depend on whether the payor (1) thought that the agent was the true owner of the income or (2) knew that the recipient was acting in an agency capacity and simply failed to discover that the principal was a foreign person.

The 30 percent withholding rules require withholding only with respect to gross income from sources within the United States. If a withholding agent fails to withhold tax because the payee appears to be a U.S. person, the income appears to be foreign-source, the income does not appear to fall within one of the types of income subject to 30 percent withholding or for some other reason, there is no protection for the agent from liability for underwithholding. Moreover, there is no general certification procedure to allow the withholding agent to rely on a statement of the payee or any other party that the income is not subject to withholding.

If the withholding agent determines that withholding is not required and is wrong, for any reason, the agent is liable for the tax that should have been withheld. In this regard there is also no good-faith exception.

Similar concepts are applied with respect to withholding agent responsibilities when the anti-conduit financing provisions apply. A financed entity or other person required to withhold tax under the 30 percent withholding rules with respect to a financing arrangement that is a conduit financing arrangement is required to withhold under the 30 percent withholding rules if all conduit entities that are parties to the conduit financing arrangement should be disregarded. The withholding agent may withhold tax at a reduced rate if the financing entity establishes that it is entitled to the benefit of a treaty that provides a reduced rate of tax on a payment of the type deemed to have been paid to the financing entity.

A person that is required to deduct and withhold tax but fails to do so is liable for the payment of the tax and any applicable penalties and interest. However, in a conduit financing arrangement, a withholding agent is not liable for failing to deduct and withhold, unless the agent knows or has reason to know that the financing arrangement is a conduit financing arrangement. This standard is satisfied if the withholding agent knows or has reason to know of facts sufficient to establish that the financing arrangement is a conduit financing arrangement, including facts sufficient to establish that the participation of the intermediate entity in the financing arrangement is pursuant to a tax avoidance plan. The regulations provide that a withholding agent who knows only of the financing transactions that comprise the financing arrangement is not considered to know or have reason to know that the financing arrangement is a conduit financing arrangement.

Timing of Obligation to Withhold

The obligation to withhold generally arises when a payor pays income subject to withholding to a foreign payee or applies such income for the foreign payee's account.

There has been uncertainty regarding whether actual payment is required in order for a withholding obligation to arise. In *Casa De La Jolla Park, Inc. v. Commissioner*, the Tax Court rejected, in dicta, the theory that actual payment and receipt are necessary to trigger a withholding liability under the 30 percent withholding rules. The court implied that constructive payment may be sufficient.

Payees Subject to Withholding—Foreign Persons

Thirty percent withholding generally applies only to payments to certain foreign persons. U.S. persons are not subject to withholding. In order to prevent withholding, a U.S. person may supply the withholding agent with a written statement (IRS Form W-9) that the recipient is a U.S. person. The withholding agent may rely on this statement as proof that the recipient of the income is not a foreign person. If a withholding agent erroneously withholds tax from a U.S. person's income, the U.S. person must either credit the amount withheld against the tax shown on the income tax return for the year in question or file a timely refund claim.

Amount Subject to Withholding

The 30 percent withholding rules require that tax be withheld at the applicable rate from the gross amount of a payment to a foreign payee. There are few exceptions.

If a payment to a foreign payee consists of part U.S. and part foreign-source income, only the portion of the payment constituting U.S.-source income is subject to 30 percent withholding. If, however, no reasonable basis exists for allocating the payment between U.S. and foreign sources, the Service takes the position that the entire payment is subject to withholding.

Withholding is required only with respect to the "gain" element of certain types of income. The regulations allow the withholding agent to rely on a statement supplied by the foreign payee concerning the amount of the payment that represents gain, unless the agent has reason to believe to the contrary. There is no specific form for the statement, but it must be signed by the foreign payee under penalties of perjury and contain certain information required by the regulations. If the withholding agent does not know the amount of the gain, either because the foreign payee does not supply a statement or the agent has reason to believe that the statement is unreliable, the regulations require the agent to withhold such amount as may be necessary to assure that the tax withheld will not be less than 30 percent of the recognized gain.

While it may be that only a portion of a payment is properly subject to withholding, the practical problem for the payor-withholding agent is to determine the appropriate amount. In light of the problems posed by underwithholding, this can be a sensitive issue. If the amount of the income or gain cannot be determined, the withholding agent generally should withhold 30 percent of the gross amount of the payment to the foreign payee.

Withholding Rates

The 30 percent withholding rules generally require the withholding agent to withhold tax at a flat rate of 30 percent of the gross amount of the income paid to the foreign payee. The 30 percent rate, however, does not apply in certain cases. A U.S. treaty may provide a lower rate of withholding with respect to certain income of residents of a foreign country.

If the withholding rate changes between the time that the foreign person earns the income and the time the income is actually paid, the applicable withholding rate is the rate in effect when the income item is paid.

Effect of Treaties on Withholding

A U.S. income tax treaty may exempt an item of income from U.S. tax or reduce the 30 percent withholding tax rate. The presence of such treaty provisions is not self-executing, meaning that a withholding agent or foreign payee is not automatically entitled to benefits provided in a treaty. In order for a specific foreign payee to be entitled to the benefits of a treaty in regard to U.S. withholding obligations, the foreign payee must meet certain criteria.

Treaty Entitlement of Foreign Payee

A foreign payee's entitlement to the benefits of the treaty in question must first be established. Each of the modern U.S. treaties contains an article that limits its benefits to the class of taxpayers intended by the contracting states. This is typically referred to as the "limitation of benefits" article, which is intended to prevent treaty benefits from being bestowed upon persons not intended to be benefited by the treaty, so-called treaty shoppers. The regulations contain procedures to provide a withholding agent with some assurance that the owner of the certain types of income qualifies under a treaty.

Foreign Payee Performing Personal Services

A foreign payee that is a nonresident individual performing personal services desiring to take advantage of the benefits of a treaty must file a separate IRS Form 8233 for each taxable year. The form must be signed by the recipient of the income and verified by the recipient's declaration that the statements in the form are made under penalties of perjury. The regulations require that the recipient supply various information on Form 8233, including the tax treaty and provision under which the recipient claims the withholding exemption and the recipient's country of residence.

After receiving Form 8233, the regulations require the withholding agent to examine the form before accepting it and to reject the form if the agent knows that any assertions on the form are false or that the eligibility of the individual's compensation for the exemption cannot be readily determined. If the withholding agent feels the form may not be relied upon, tax must be withheld from the recipient's compensation. Also, if the form does not include all the information required by the regulations, the withholding agent may not rely on it and the treaty exemption does not apply.

If, after review of the form, the withholding agent is satisfied that the withholding exemption applies, the agent may accept the statement by making a certification on the form under penalties of perjury. The certification must state that the withholding agent (1) has examined the form; (2) is satisfied that a withholding exemption is warranted; and (3) does not know or have reason to know that the individual's compensation is not entitled to exemption or cannot readily determine whether the compensation is eligible for exemption. The regulations require that the agent mail one copy of the statement to the Service's director of the foreign operations district within five days after accepting the statement and that the agent retain one copy.

The regulations also require the agent to notify the Service's director of the foreign operations district if a withholding agent accepts the form but later discovers that one of the assertions on the form is false or that the eligibility of the recipient's income for the exemption cannot be readily determined. In addition, the regulations provide that the agent cannot continue to rely on the form. The withholding agent must withhold tax or risk personal liability for underwithholding.

If the Service's director of the foreign operations district notifies the withholding agent that eligibility of the recipient's compensation for exemption is in doubt, the regulations state that the withholding exemption does not apply.

Foreign Payee Receiving Effectively Connected Income

Where a foreign payee receives income that is believed to be exempt from withholding because the income is effectively connected with a U.S. trade or business, the foreign payee is required to file Form W-8ECI.

Foreign Payee Receiving Other Types of Income

In order to secure a reduced rate of withholding or an exemption from withholding for other types of income, the foreign payee must file Form W-8BEN with the withholding agent. The withholding agent must receive a separate Form W-8BEN for each type of income. It is not clear whether the payee has to file Form W-8BEN with the withholding agent before the income is paid. The regulations provide that the Form W-8BEN must be filed as soon as practicable.

Form W-8BEN generally applies for a period of three calendar years. However, if the foreign payee ceases to qualify under the treaty, the payee must promptly notify the withholding agent. The withholding agent must retain Form W-8BEN for at least four years after the end of the last calendar year in which the income is paid. The withholding agent is not required to file a copy of the Form W-8BEN with the Service.

If a foreign payee makes a false statement on Form W-8BEN and the withholding agent does not withhold tax in reliance on the false Form W-8BEN, the withholding agent is liable for the underwithheld tax only if the withholding agent knows or has reason to know that the Form W-8BEN is false.

Treaty-Based Return Position

The treaty-based return position reporting requirements do not apply to a withholding agent with respect to the agent's withholding functions.

Procedures for Withholding

Payment of Tax

The regulations require a withholding agent to deposit taxes withheld in a designated financial institution, within a short time after the taxes are withheld, as opposed to on a calendar quarter or other basis. The regulations treat amounts withheld as paid on the last day prescribed for filing IRS Form 1042 with respect to such taxes.

When the income that is subject to withholding is payable in property other than cash (in kind), the regulations provide that the withholding agent must not release the property to the payee until a sufficient amount of the property has been converted to cash in order to satisfy the tax withholding requirement. Alternatively, the payor can provide the withholding agent with sufficient cash to satisfy the withholding obligation.

The amount of income may be calculated in U.S. dollars but be payable to the foreign payee in a foreign currency at the rate of exchange on the date of payment. In this situation, the withholding agent must withhold and pay to the Service a tax equal to the amount of the income calculated in U.S. dollars multiplied by the appropriate tax rate on that date.

Filing of Returns by Withholding Agent

A withholding agent must file an annual return of the tax required to be withheld on IRS Form 1042. Form 1042 states in summary fashion the tax withheld as shown on Form 1042S (reporting items paid to foreign persons) for the calendar year. The withholding agent generally must file the original copy of Form 1042 on or before March 15 of the year following the calendar year in which the tax was required to be withheld. If the regulations require the withholding agent to file Form 1042S with respect to any payments made during the year, the agent generally must file Form 1042S even if no additional tax is required to be withheld.

If the total amount of tax required to be shown on Form 1042 has not been deposited, the withholding agent must pay the balance of tax due for the year to the Service Center in Philadelphia when filing its Form 1042. Along with Form 1042, the withholding agent should file the original copies of all Forms 1042S that were prepared by the withholding agent during the previous calendar year (including any forms reporting income exempt from withholding) with the Service Center in Philadelphia, with a duplicate copy to the payee by March 15. Form 1042S is an information return that shows certain items of income paid during the previous calendar year to foreign persons.

The withholding agent should file the original Form 1042S, accompanied by Form 1042.

U.S. Tax Return Filing by Foreign Payees

A foreign payee must include in its U.S. gross income the gross amount of the income that is subject to withholding, unless an exclusion or exemption applies to that income. The foreign payee may credit the tax withheld against the U.S income tax liability shown on its U.S. income tax return. If the U.S. income tax liability of a foreign payee is fully satisfied by withholding at the source, the foreign payee is not required to file a U.S. return. This exemption does not apply if the foreign payee is engaged in a U.S. trade or business. The filing of a return starts the running of the statute of limitations on assessment by the Service.

To obtain a refund of the overwithheld amount, the foreign payee should file a refund claim within the time generally prescribed for filing such claims.

Refund of Overwithheld Taxes

If a withholding agent withholds too much tax from a foreign payee's income and deposits that tax with the Service, the foreign payee is entitled to a credit or refund. The Service generally does not credit or refund the overwithheld tax to the withholding agent, because the withholding agent is not the taxpayer.

The regulations provide two ways for a withholding agent to correct an overwithholding error. First, the withholding agent may reimburse the foreign payee by applying the overwithheld amount against other withholding taxes required with respect to other payments to the same payee. This application must be made before the due date for filing Form 1042 for the year of the overwithholding (March 15 of the calendar year following the year of overwithholding). The withholding agent makes a corresponding reduction in the taxes deposited with the Service.

Second, the withholding agent may return the overwithheld amount to the foreign payee before the due date for filing Form 1042 for the year of overwithholding (March 15 of the year following the year of overwithholding). In this event, the withholding agent, not the foreign payee, is entitled to a credit or refund from the Service. The withholding agent may then use the overwithheld amount as a credit against later federal tax deposits for the calendar year in which the overwithholding occurred, or for the year following the overwithholding year, if the agent continues to act as a withholding agent during those years. If these procedures are impossible, then the foreign payee must file the claim for refund.

If a withholding agent overpays tax to the Service but does not overwithhold, the withholding agent is the proper party to claim a refund of the overpaid tax and the Service will credit or refund the overpaid tax to the withholding agent.

Penalties for Failure to Withhold

A withholding agent that fails to file the withholding tax return may be assessed a civil penalty of 5 percent per month (but not more than a total of 25 percent) of the tax required to be shown on the return. The penalties are not applicable if the withholding agent shows that the failure to file was due to reasonable cause and not willful neglect. If the failure to file is fraudulent, a monthly penalty of 15 percent (but not more than a total of 75 percent) of the tax shown on the return may be assessed.

If the withholding agent fails to pay the amount of tax shown on the return before the due date of the payment, the withholding agent is liable for a civil penalty, assessed for each month that the payment is late up to a total of 25 percent of such tax. No penalty is imposed if the failure to pay is due to reasonable cause and not willful neglect.

There are also a formidable array of other penalties that may apply to the withholding agent, depending on the facts and circumstances of the matter.

Accuracy-Related Penalty

If a withholding underpayment results from the withholding agent's negligence or disregard of rules or regulations, the withholding agent may be subject to a civil penalty equal to 20 percent of the portion of the underpayment attributable to negligence. There is also a 20 percent substantial-understatement penalty which, however, most likely does not apply to the amount of tax underwithheld by a withholding agent.

Fraud Penalty

If the withholding agent's underpayment of the withholding tax shown on the return is fraudulent, a penalty of 75 percent of the portion of the underpayment attributable to fraud may be applicable. If the Service shows that any portion of an underpayment is attributable to fraud, the entire underpayment is generally tainted. The fraud penalty does not apply to any portion of the underpayment that the taxpayer shows is not attributable to fraud.

Penalty for Failure to Deposit Taxes

A withholding agent may be subject to a civil penalty equal to the applicable percentage of the amount of tax not deposited by the due date of such deposit, based on the number of days the deposit is late. This penalty does not apply if the withholding agent shows that the failure to deposit was due to reasonable cause and not willful neglect.

Liability for Uncollected or Unpaid Tax

If the withholding agent, or an officer or other responsible person of the withholding agent, willfully fails to collect the tax required to be withheld or willfully attempts to evade or defeat the tax, there may be liability for the total amount of the tax evaded, or not collected, or not accounted for and paid over.

Criminal Penalties

If convicted of willfully failing to collect or pay over the tax required to be withheld, a withholding agent may be subject to criminal penalties of up to $10,000 in fines, the costs of prosecution, and not more than five years of imprisonment.

Backup Withholding

The so-called backup withholding provisions require a payor of certain payments to deduct and withhold a 20 percent tax. Congress adopted backup withholding principally to prevent domestic taxpayers from failing to pay taxes on certain types of income, such as dividends and interest. On the other hand, the 30 percent withholding rules apply to payments to foreign persons. Overlap between the backup and 30 percent withholding rules arises where there is uncertainty as to whether the payee is a domestic or foreign person.

> **Example 14-8**
>
> USCo is obligated to make an interest payment to ForCo, a lender with an address in Paris, France.
>
> If ForCo is a foreign person there is no backup withholding obligation. However, if USCo cannot obtain adequate proof of foreign status, there may be a backup withholding issue.

Obtaining proof that a payee is a foreign and not a domestic person is often difficult, because many foreign persons desire anonymity. The Service has adopted rules to accommodate a foreign person's desire for privacy in certain transactions.

Backup withholding may be required in the international context if there is a reportable payment. The principal types of reportable payments include

1.   Interest;

2.   Dividends;

3.   Miscellaneous fixed or determinable gains, profits, and reportable income;

4.   Amounts reportable by brokers; and

5.   Reportable royalties.

Backup withholding in the international context is likely to be triggered because either the foreign payee fails to furnish the payor with its taxpayer identification number or the payee fails to certify under penalties of perjury that the payee is not subject to backup withholding because of prior underreporting.

Certification of Taxpayer Identification Number

A payor can eliminate the risk of backup withholding by requiring that the payee furnish the payee's taxpayer identification number and, if the payee is receiving dividends and interest, certify that backup withholding does not apply because of prior underreporting. A payor can obtain both the payee's number and the payee's certification on IRS Form W-9.

Certification of Foreign Status

Backup withholding often does not apply if the foreign payee certifies that the foreign payee is not a U.S. person. The Service has issued Form W-8BEN for this purpose. A properly filed Form W-8BEN prevents backup withholding with respect to interest and original issue discount in general, as well as on portfolio interest on registered obligations. Backup withholding is not required if the foreign payee supplies a completed Form W-8BEN (treaty qualification) or Form W-8ECI (U.S. trade or business), both of which show foreign status.

Corporate Status of Payee

In general, backup withholding does not apply to any payment made to a corporation. In the international context, the payor needs to establish that the foreign payee is a corporation. Presumably, similar certification procedures as discussed for foreign status may be used for corporate status. If the payee desires to remain anonymous, obtaining appropriate certification could be difficult for the payor, in which event the payor may decide to withhold.

Withholding Agreements

In light of the potential severe liabilities and penalties for failure to comply with withholding, paying over, return filing, and other requirements of the U.S. tax law, a prudent withholding agent may consider entering a specific agreement with a foreign payee with respect to U.S. withholding matters. Similarly, a foreign payee may determine that the economic cost of the U.S. withholding requirements is a matter solely to be incurred by the U.S. payor. If so, the foreign payee may also want to consider entering a specific agreement with the U.S. payor defining respective responsibilities with respect to U.S. withholding matters.

The essential issue to be addressed in the agreement is which party will bear the economic cost of the U.S. withholding requirements.

> **Example 14-9**
>
> ForCo is a Foronia-based multinational engaged in developing, manufacturing, and marketing cameras and other optical products on a worldwide basis. USCo, an unrelated manufacturer of cameras, approaches ForCo seeking a license of new optical technology developed by ForCo that USCo wants to use to produce a new line of copiers. ForCo has not developed this application of its technology and ForCo is interested in seeing whether USCo can successfully do so. Accordingly, ForCo agrees to license its optical technology to USCo in exchange for a stated royalty rate based on net sales generated by the technology.
>
> USCo and ForCo must resolve which party will bear the economic cost of any U.S. withholding obligation and how this agreement will be documented.

Withholding Cost Incurred by Foreign Payee

The U.S. law is not unique in requiring withholding from payments made to foreign persons. The tax laws of many countries provide the payee with a domestic credit for foreign taxes incurred in other countries, including withholding taxes. Accordingly, in many circumstances, the foreign payee expects to incur a withholding obligation on payments from a United States payor and accepts the economic cost of the withholding tax.

> **Example 14-10**
>
> The situation is the same as in Example 14-9. In discussing the terms of a license agreement, USCo is authorized to satisfy any U.S. withholding obligations that may apply with respect to royalties that USCo pays to ForCo.
>
> Here, the parties could include appropriate provisions in the licensing agreement to authorize USCo to withhold and ForCo to provide any certificates or other documentation required by USCo in order to comply with its U.S. withholding obligations.

If there is any possibility that a payor may have a withholding obligation under the 30 percent withholding rules, it may be appropriate to include in the pertinent documentation (1) an acknowledgment that a withholding obligation may exist and (2) an authorization for the payor to withhold, if the payor believes that it has a duty to do so.

Withholding Cost Incurred by Payor

In some circumstances, the foreign payee may not be willing to incur the economic cost of the withholding. Often this occurs when the payee is not able to obtain a credit for the withheld tax.

> **Example 14-11**
>
> The situation is the same as in Example 14-10, except that ForCo states that ForCo will not accept the economic cost of a U.S. withholding tax. USCo is authorized to satisfy any U.S. withholding obligations that may apply with respect

> to royalties paid by USCo to ForCo and USCo is to incur the economic cost of any such tax.
>
> Here it may be appropriate to include in the pertinent documentation (1) an acknowledgment that a withholding obligation may exist and (2) an authorization for the payor to withhold, if the payor believes that it has a duty to do so.

A gross-up provision should be included to place the economic cost of any withholding on the payor. This provision provides that the amount of the distribution will be grossed up so that the amount received by the payee, net of the U.S. withholding tax, will be the initially agreed amount of the payment. Under this provision, the payee gets the agreed amount and the payor satisfies the withholding tax obligation.

Withholding Cost Incurred by Payor beyond Foreign Tax Credit Benefit to Foreign Payee

A foreign payee may recognize that there are withholding requirements in the U.S. tax law but not be willing to incur the economic cost of the withholding unless the payee is able to obtain a foreign tax credit for the taxes withheld. If a foreign tax credit is available, the payee will not incur an incremental cost as a result of the U.S. withholding. However, many countries have severe restrictions on the amount of credit that may be claimed. Any amount of the U.S. withholding tax that is not creditable by the payee will represent an incremental cost to the payee.

> **Example 14-12**
>
> The situation is the same as in Example 14-11, except that ForCo states that it will not accept the economic cost of a U.S. withholding tax except to the extent allowed as a foreign tax credit in its country. USCo is authorized to satisfy any U.S. withholding obligations that may apply with respect to royalties paid by USCo to ForCo and USCo is to incur the economic cost of any such tax except to the extent ForCo is entitled to a foreign tax credit for such withholding tax.
>
> The parties will need to limit the gross-up provision included in the documentation to the amount of foreign tax credit available to the payee.

No Authorization to Withhold and Indemnity Agreements

In some circumstances, the foreign payee may recognize that there are withholding requirements in the U.S. tax law but desire that no filing be made with the Service with respect to the payments. The foreign payee may desire anonymity or have other reasons.

> **Example 14-13**
>
> The situation is the same as in Example 14-11, except that ForCo wants USCo to make no reporting of any kind to the Service with respect to the royalty payments made to ForCo.
>
> This places USCo, the U.S. payor, in a difficult position. If there is a withholding obligation and if USCo fails to satisfy that obligation, the liabilities and penalties are severe.

If a payor underwithholds and is ultimately liable for the tax, the law is unclear regarding whether the payor could successfully sue the foreign payee. The Internal Revenue Code and regulations do not address the matter and there is no case law guidance.

Partnership Allocations

Withholding on distributions to foreign partners is required from a foreign partner's share of the partnership's effectively connected taxable income without regard to actual distribution by the partnership.

Definition of Foreign Partner

A foreign partner is any partner that is not a United States person—a nonresident alien individual, foreign corporation, foreign partnership, foreign trust, or foreign estate. Revenue Procedure 89-31 contains rules under which a partnership can determine that a partner is not a foreign person by obtaining a certificate of nonforeign status from the partner. A partnership is not liable for underwithholding if the partnership relies in good faith on a certificate of nonforeign status provided by the foreign person even if the partner who provided the certificate is later found to be a foreign person. The partnership may not rely on such a certificate if the partnership has actual knowledge that the certificate is false.

Revenue Procedure 89-31 proscribes no particular form of certificate but contains several samples of acceptable certificates for this purpose. A certificate must contain certain information and be signed under penalties of perjury.

A partnership may rely on a partner's certification of nonforeign status until the end of the third year after the partnership's taxable year during which the certificate is obtained unless during that time the partnership receives notice from the partner that the partner has become a foreign person or obtains actual knowledge that the partner is or has become a foreign person. The partnership must retain a certificate of nonforeign status until the end of the fifth taxable year after the last taxable year in which the partnership relies on the certificate.

If a partnership later acquires actual knowledge that a certificate of nonforeign status is false, the partnership cannot continue to rely on the false certificate to avoid underwithholding liability. The knowledge of a general partner that a certificate is false is imputed to the partnership. The knowledge of a limited partner that a certificate is false, however, is not imputed to the partnership based solely on that partner's status as a limited partner.

A U.S. partnership may determine a partner's nonforeign status by means other than a certificate under Revenue Procedure 89-31, but the withholding agent remains liable for the withholding tax if the determination of nonforeign status turns out to be wrong. A partnership is not required to rely on means other than a certificate of nonforeign status and may demand that the partner provide the certificate. If the partner fails to do so, the partnership must withhold tax.

Effectively Connected Taxable Income of Partnership

A U.S. partnership's effectively connected taxable income equals the partnership's taxable income that is effectively connected with the conduct of a U.S. trade or business, with certain adjustments. In order to determine the amount of its withholding obligation, a partnership must ascertain (1) whether it was engaged in a U.S. trade or business during the taxable year, (2) the amount of gross income that was effectively connected (or treated as effectively connected) with a U.S. trade or business, and (3) the allowable deductions that can be allocated to the effectively connected income. A U.S. partnership's taxable income for this purpose is determined under the rules in the partnership tax provisions with certain adjustments.

The amount of a U.S. partnership's effectively connected taxable income allocable to foreign partners for the taxable year equals the partner's distributive share of effectively connected gross income for the year.

Withholding Agent's Payment and Reporting Requirements

A U.S. partnership must withhold tax on U.S. partnership income that is effectively connected taxable income allocable to foreign partners. Revenue Procedure 89-31 provides that the general partners of a partnership are jointly and severally liable as withholding agents for this purpose.

The Service requires a U.S. partnership to make quarterly installment payments of withholding tax based on the amount of the partnership's effectively connected taxable income allocable to foreign partners regardless of whether the partnership makes distributions. Upon making an installment payment of withholding tax, the partnership must notify each foreign partner of that partner's allocable share of tax paid.

The partnership files IRS Form 8813 with its quarterly payments of withholding tax on U.S. effectively connected income. The partnership generally must file this form and pay to the Service a portion of its estimated annual payment for each foreign partner on or before the fifteenth day of the fourth, sixth, ninth, and twelfth months of the partnership's taxable year for U.S. tax purposes. Payments of this withholding tax must be made in U.S. dollars. The partnership must pay any additional amounts of withholding tax due with its annual return on IRS Form 8804 and attach IRS Form 8805.

Penalties are imposed for failure to pay withholding tax installments on U.S. effectively connected income similar to the penalties imposed on corporations for failure to pay estimated tax.

A partnership reports its total liability for withholding tax on U.S. effectively connected income on IRS Form 8804. The partnership generally must file these forms and pay any remaining withholding tax on U.S. effectively connected income on or before the fifteenth day of the fourth month following the close of the partnership's tax year.

Treatment of Foreign Partner's Share

Each foreign partner may credit its share of withholding tax on U.S. effectively connected income against its U.S. income tax liability. The partner may claim the credit for the taxable year in which or with which the partnership's taxable year for which the tax was paid ends. A foreign partner's share of the withholding tax paid by the partnership is treated as distributed on the earlier of the day on which the partnership pays the tax or the last day of the partnership's taxable year for which the tax was paid. The deemed distribution of this credit reduces the partner's basis in the partnership interest as of the date of the deemed distribution.

Penalties for Failure to Withhold

A partnership that fails to withhold the required tax on U.S. effectively connected income is liable for the amount of the tax, interest and any applicable penalties. A person that is required to pay the tax but who fails to do so may also be liable for civil and criminal penalties. Officers or other responsible persons of a corporation such as a general partner or any other withholding agent may be liable for an amount equal to the amount that should have been withheld.

Coordination with Other Withholding Regimes

The 30 percent withholding rules require a domestic partnership to withhold tax on the foreign partners' distributive shares of items of partnership income that are subject to 30 percent withholding. Because each partner's share of the partnership's gross income cannot be determined until the end of the partnership's taxable year, the partnership must withhold tax on all distributions to foreign partners that consist of items of income that are subject to 30 percent withholding. If the partnership withholds on a foreign partner's share of gross income before it is distributed, the partnership need not withhold again when the income is distributed to the partner.

The U.S. effectively connected income withholding rules apply only to a partnership's effectively connected taxable income.

Branch Profits Tax

A foreign corporation with a U.S. trade or business may also be subject to the branch profits tax which would be applicable to a foreign corporation if it were to operate the assets as an unincorporated branch operation.

The branch profits tax also applies to foreign corporations that have effectively connected income through an interest in a partnership that is engaged in a U.S. trade or business. A foreign corporation that is a partner in a partnership is treated as having a U.S. asset in an amount equal to the product of the foreign corporation's adjusted basis in the partnership interest and the ratio of its distributive share of partnership gross income for the taxable year that is effectively connected with the conduct of a trade or business in the United States over its distributive share of all partnership gross income for the taxable year.

HIRE Act

The Hiring Incentives to Restore Employment Act of 2010 (HIRE Act) was signed by President Obama March 18, 2010, and as its name suggests, provides businesses with tax incentives to hire and retain new employees. The Foreign Account Tax Compliance Act (FATCA) was added to the HIRE Act to raise tax revenues to finance the HIRE Act tax incentives. FATCA's purpose is to "detect, deter and discourage offshore tax evasion through use of financial institutions outside the U.S. and to close certain information reporting loopholes that permitted U.S. taxpayers to avoid reporting offshore assets and income.

Key FATCA Provisions

The FATCA legislation:

- imposes a 30 percent withholding tax on all payments to "foreign financial institutions" (FFIs) and certain "non-financial foreign entities" (NFFEs);

- creates a personal liability for any person required to deduct and withhold tax on any withholdable payment who fails to do so as well as new penalties for zero and underwithheld tax on unreported payments to FFAs;

- extends the statute of limitations for failures to report material income amounts in connection with FFAs;

- requires that FFIs file electronic returns to disclose withholding on foreign transfers;

- creates new rules for "dividend equivalent" payments and

- creates additional reporting rules with respect to "foreign financial assets" (FFAs).

Credits and Refunds Under U.S. Internal Revenue Code or Double Tax Treaties

The FATCA provisions do not create new tax liabilities for foreign recipients of U.S. source income. The FATCA rules apply only to withholding.

Foreign recipients of U.S. source income (nonresident aliens and foreign corporations) continue to be taxed in the U.S. under two systems:

1. income and expense effectively connected with the conduct of a U.S. trade or business or other taxable permanent establishment as defined in U.S. tax treaties or

2. non-effectively connected income that is investment or portfolio income or

    a. U.S. source income not effectively connected with a trade or business other than portfolio or business transaction income, and

    b. Non-effectively connected income that does not rise to the level of a U.S. trade or business.

An NFFE can file a U.S. tax return to claim a refund (or credit) for overpayment. As under existing law, the beneficial owner of a U.S. source payment eligible for reduced withholding under a U.S. tax treaty is eligible for a refund or credit of the excess amount withheld. Likewise, if a payment is not subject to U.S. tax, because, for example, the payment represents gross proceeds from the sale of stock or interest exempt from U.S. tax under the portfolio exemption, the beneficial owner of the payment is eligible for a credit or refund of the full amount of tax withheld.

Withholding on Payments to FFIs and NFFEs

The HIRE Act requires withholding agents to withhold 30 percent tax from "withholdable payments" to FFIs and certain NFFEs.

"Withholdable payments" are defined, alternatively, as:

- any payment of interest, dividends, rents, salaries, wages, premiums, annuities, compensation, remuneration or emoluments from U.S. sources

- any other fixed or determinable annual or periodical gain, profit and income from a U.S. source, and

- any gross proceed from the sale of any property that could produce interest or dividend income from a U.S. source.

The 30 percent withholding requirement from property sales gross proceeds applies without regard to gain or loss recognized.

An FFI is any "financial institution" that is a foreign entity. For this purpose, a financial institution is:

- any entity that accepts deposits in the ordinary course of a banking or similar business;

- any entity engaged in holding financial assets for account of others; or

- any entity engaged (or representing itself as engaged) in investing, reinvesting or securities trading, partnership interests, commodities or any interest (including a futures or forward or option contract) in securities, partnership interests or commodities.

In addition to banks, FFIs include insurance companies, hedge and private equity funds.

Penalties For Underpayments Attributable To Undisclosed FFAs

FACTA imposes an accuracy-related penalty of 40 percent on any understatement of tax liability attributable to an undisclosed foreign financial asset, which includes all assets for which a taxpayer does not provide required information. An understatement is attributable to an undisclosed foreign financial asset if the understatement is attributable to any transaction involving the asset.

Modification of Statute Of Limitations for Significant Omissions Of Income Attributable to FFAs

The assessment limitations period on understatements of FFA income is six years. FACTA tolls the limitations period for assessment if a taxpayer fails to provide timely information returns.

No Withholding For Qualified FFIs

Withholding is not required if an FFI agrees to be treated as a qualified FFI (QFFI) and complies with certain reporting requirements.

Specifically a QFFI must:

- annually report certain information with respect to any U.S.-owned account, and

- withhold 30 percent of any pass-through payment made to a "recalcitrant" account holder or a non-QFFI or a QFFI that has elected withholding with respect to the portion of a payment allocable to a recalcitrant holder or a non-QFFI.

A "recalcitrant" account holder is any account holder that (1) fails to comply with reasonable requests for information necessary to determine if the account is a U.S.-owned account; (2) fails to provide the name, address and tax identification number of each specified U.S. person and each substantial U.S. owner of a U.S.-owned foreign entity; or (3) fails to provide a waiver of any foreign law that would prevent the QFFI from reporting any required information.

QFFI ANNUAL REPORTING REQUIREMENT

QFFIs must report account numbers, balances or values, gross receipts and withdrawals as well as names, addresses and tax identification numbers of account holders and substantial U.S. owners of account holders that are specified U.S. persons or U.S.-owned foreign entities.

A specified U.S. person is any U.S. person other than a publicly traded corporation, tax-exempt organization or individual retirement plan or bank, regulated investment company and certain trusts (including real estate investment trusts).

A "U.S.-owned foreign entity" is any foreign-owned entity with one or more "substantial" U.S. owners who own more than 10 percent (vote or value) of the outstanding stock, or, with respect to a partnership, who own more than 10 percent of partnership profits or capital, or, with respect to a trust, any specified U.S. person treated as a trust owner under the U.S. "grantor trust" rules.

The 10 percent ownership minimum does not apply with respect to corporations or partnerships in the business of investing, reinvesting or trading in securities or partnership interests—any U.S. ownership in corporations or partnerships so engaged is considered substantial.

Dividend-Equivalent Payments Received By Foreign Persons Treated As Dividends

The dividend equivalent payment provisions were developed to clarify withholding tax requirements with respect to dividend payments in connection with securities lending transactions. A dividend equivalent payment is:

- any substitute dividend

- a payment under a "special notional principal contract" directly or indirectly contingent on, or determined by reference to, a U.S. source dividend payment

- any other substantially similar payment.

Payments treated as dividend equivalent payments will be the gross amounts used to compute any net amounts transferred to or from the taxpayer.

FFA Disclosure Rules

Individual taxpayers who own an interest in a depository or custodial account at FFIs, and, if not held in a financial institution account, stocks or securities issued by foreign persons, any other financial instrument or investment contract issued by or with a counterparty who is not a U.S. person or any interest in a foreign entity are required to attach a disclosure statement to their income tax returns for any year in which the aggregate value of all such assets exceeds $50,000. This disclosure must include:

- asset identifying information and value;

- account number and address of institution holding the account;

- name and address of the issuer of any stocks or securities and any other information required to identify the stock or security and its issuance terms, and

- information necessary to identify the nature of other instruments or contracts or interests in foreign entities.

FFIS MAY BE REQUIRED TO ELECTRONICALLY FILE RETURNS DISCLOSING WITHHOLDING ON FOREIGN TRANSFERS

Under FACTA, the IRS may require magnetic media filing for any return filed by a "financial institution" even if that financial institution files fewer than 250 returns per year. Forthcoming IRS regulations may grant exemptions from the magnetic media requirement for funds held by one or few U.S. account holders.

QFFI ELECTION TO REPORT AS A U.S. FINANCIAL INSTITUTION

A QFFI may elect the same reporting requirements as a U.S. financial institution. If made, this election requires the QFFI to report each specified U.S. person or U.S. owned foreign entity. As a result, both U.S. and foreign source amounts are subject to information reporting whether paid inside or outside the U.S. The benefit of this election is that a QFFI, by electing the same reporting obligations as a U.S. financial institution, would not need to disclose non-U.S. account holders to the IRS.

QFFI Withholding Election

QFFIs may elect to have a third party U.S. withholding agent to another QFFI withhold. This election is an alternative to acting as a withholding agent for payments to non-QFFIs, other electing QFFIs or recalcitrant account holders.

The electing QFFI must notify third party withholding agents and provide information required to determine the appropriate withholding amount. Also, the electing QFFI must waive any treaty rights with respect to amounts withheld.

This provision permits QFFIs to delegate withholding responsibilities to global custodians and other institutions capable of dealing with withholding issues on a large scale.

Witholdable Payments to NFFEs

The HIRE Act requires withholding agents to withhold 30 percent of witholdable payments to NFFEs (foreign entities that are not financial institutions) except for payments to publicly traded corporations. NFFEs may avoid withholding by providing the withholding agent with either

- the name, address and tax identification number of each U.S. owner of the NFFE or

- a signed certificate that the NFFE does not have a U.S. owner.

Instructions for Form W-8ECI

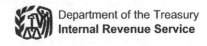

Department of the Treasury
Internal Revenue Service

(Rev. February 2006)

Certificate of Foreign Person's Claim That Income Is Effectively Connected With the Conduct of a Trade or Business in the United States

General Instructions

Section references are to the Internal Revenue Code unless otherwise noted.

Note. For definitions of terms used throughout these instructions, see *Definitions* beginning on page 2.

Purpose of form. Foreign persons are generally subject to U.S. tax at a 30% rate on income they receive from U.S. sources. However, no withholding under section 1441 or 1442 is required on income that is, or is deemed to be, effectively connected with the conduct of a trade or business in the United States and is includible in the beneficial owner's gross income for the tax year.

The no withholding rule does not apply to personal services income and income subject to withholding under section 1445 (dispositions of U.S. real property interests) or section 1446 (foreign partner's share of effectively connected income).

If you receive effectively connected income from sources in the United States, you must provide Form W-8ECI to:
• Establish that you are not a U.S. person,
• Claim that you are the beneficial owner of the income for which Form W-8ECI is being provided, and
• Claim that the income is effectively connected with the conduct of a trade or business in the United States.

If you expect to receive both income that is effectively connected and income that is not effectively connected from a withholding agent, you must provide Form W-8ECI for the effectively connected income and Form W-8BEN (or Form W-8EXP or Form W-8IMY) for income that is not effectively connected.

If you submit this form to a partnership, the income claimed to be effectively connected with the conduct of a U.S. trade or business is subject to withholding under section 1446. If a nominee holds an interest in a partnership on your behalf, you, not the nominee, must submit the form to the partnership or nominee that is the withholding agent.

If you are a foreign partnership, a foreign simple trust, or a foreign grantor trust with effectively connected income, you may submit Form W-8ECI without attaching Forms W-8BEN or other documentation for your foreign partners, beneficiaries, or owners.

A withholding agent or payer of the income may rely on a properly completed Form W-8ECI to treat the payment associated with the Form W-8ECI as a payment to a foreign person who beneficially owns the amounts paid and is either entitled to an exemption from withholding under sections 1441 or 1442 because the income is effectively connected with the conduct of a trade or business in the United States or subject to withholding under section 1446.

Provide Form W-8ECI to the withholding agent or payer before income is paid, credited, or allocated to you. Failure by a beneficial owner to provide a Form W-8ECI when requested may lead to withholding at the 30% rate or the backup withholding rate.

Additional information. For additional information and instructions for the withholding agent, see the Instructions for the Requester of Forms W-8BEN, W-8ECI, W-8EXP, and W-8IMY.

Who must file. You must give Form W-8ECI to the withholding agent or payer if you are a foreign person and you are the beneficial owner of U.S. source income that is (or is deemed to be) effectively connected with the conduct of a trade or business within the United States.

Do not use Form W-8ECI if:
• You are a nonresident alien individual who claims exemption from withholding on compensation for independent or certain dependent personal services performed in the United States. Instead, provide Form 8233, Exemption from Withholding on Compensation for Independent (and Certain Dependent) Personal Services of a Nonresident Alien Individual, or Form W-4, Employee's Withholding Allowance Certificate.
• You are claiming an exemption from withholding under section 1441 or 1442 for a reason other than a claim that the income is effectively connected with the conduct of a trade or business in the United States. For example, if you are a foreign person and the beneficial owner of U.S. source income that is not effectively connected with a U.S. trade or business and are claiming a reduced rate of withholding as a resident of a foreign country with which the United States has an income tax treaty in effect, do not use this form. Instead, provide Form W-8BEN, Certificate of Foreign Status of Beneficial Owner for United States Tax Withholding.
• You are a foreign person receiving proceeds from the disposition of a U.S. real property interest. Instead, see Form 8288-B, Application for Withholding Certificate for Dispositions by Foreign Persons of U.S. Real Property Interests.
• You are filing for a foreign government, international organization, foreign central bank of issue, foreign tax-exempt organization, foreign private foundation, or government of a U.S. possession claiming the applicability of section 115(2), 501(c), 892, 895, or 1443(b). Instead, provide Form W-8EXP, Certificate of Foreign Government or Other Foreign Organization for United States Tax Withholding. However, these entities should use Form W-8BEN if they are claiming treaty benefits or are providing the form only to claim exempt recipient status for backup withholding purposes. They should use Form W-8ECI if they received effectively connected income (for example, income from commercial activities).

Cat. No. 25902V

• You are acting as an intermediary (that is, acting not for your own account or for that of your partners, but for the account of others as an agent, nominee, or custodian). Instead, provide Form W-8IMY, Certificate of Foreign Intermediary, Foreign Flow-Through Entity, or Certain U.S. Branches for United States Tax Withholding.

• You are a withholding foreign partnership or a withholding foreign trust for purposes of sections 1441 and 1442. A withholding foreign partnership is, generally, a foreign partnership that has entered into a withholding agreement with the IRS under which it agrees to assume primary withholding responsibility for each partner's distributive share of income subject to withholding that is paid to the partnership. A withholding foreign trust is, generally, a foreign simple trust or a foreign grantor trust that has entered into a withholding agreement with the IRS under which it agrees to assume primary withholding responsibility for each beneficiary's or owner's distributive share of income subject to withholding that is paid to the trust. Instead, provide Form W-8IMY.

• You are a foreign corporation that is a personal holding company receiving compensation described in section 543(a)(7). Such compensation is not exempt from withholding as effectively connected income, but may be exempt from withholding on another basis.

• You are a foreign partner in a partnership and the income allocated to you from the partnership is effectively connected with the conduct of the partnership's trade or business in the United States. Instead, provide Form W-8BEN. However, if you made or will make an election under section 871(d) or 882(d), provide Form W-8ECI. In addition, if you are otherwise engaged in a trade or business in the United States and you want your allocable share of income from the partnership to be subject to withholding under section 1446, provide Form W-8ECI.

Giving Form W-8ECI to the withholding agent. Do not send Form W-8ECI to the IRS. Instead, give it to the person who is requesting it from you. Generally, this will be the person from whom you receive the payment, who credits your account, or a partnership that allocates income to you. Give Form W-8ECI to the person requesting it before the payment is made, credited, or allocated. If you do not provide this form, the withholding agent may have to withhold at the 30% rate or the backup withholding rate. A separate Form W-8ECI must be given to each withholding agent.

U.S. branch of foreign bank or insurance company. A payment to a U.S. branch of a foreign bank or a foreign insurance company that is subject to U.S. regulation by the Federal Reserve Board or state insurance authorities is presumed to be effectively connected with the conduct of a trade or business in the United States unless the branch provides a withholding agent with a Form W-8BEN or Form W-8IMY for the income.

Change in circumstances. If a change in circumstances makes any information on the Form W-8ECI you have submitted incorrect, you must notify the withholding agent or payer within 30 days of the change in circumstances and you must file a new Form W-8ECI or other appropriate form. For example, if during the tax year any part or all of the income is no longer effectively connected with the conduct of a trade or business in the United States, your Form W-8ECI is no longer valid. You must notify the withholding agent and provide Form W-8BEN, W-8EXP, or W-8IMY.

Expiration of Form W-8ECI. Generally, a Form W-8ECI will remain in effect for a period starting on the date the form is signed and ending on the last day of the third succeeding calendar year, unless a change in circumstances makes any information on the form incorrect. For example, a Form W-8ECI signed on September 30, 2005, remains valid through December 31, 2008. Upon the expiration of the 3-year period, you must provide a new Form W-8ECI.

Definitions

Beneficial owner. For payments other than those for which a reduced rate of withholding is claimed under an income tax treaty, the beneficial owner of income is generally the person who is required under U.S. tax principles to include the income in gross income on a tax return. A person is not a beneficial owner of income, however, to the extent that person is receiving the income as a nominee, agent, or custodian, or to the extent the person is a conduit whose participation in a transaction is disregarded. In the case of amounts paid that do not constitute income, beneficial ownership is determined as if the payment were income.

Foreign partnerships, foreign simple trusts, and foreign grantor trusts are not the beneficial owners of income paid to the partnership or trust. The beneficial owners of income paid to a foreign partnership are generally the partners in the partnership, provided that the partner is not itself a partnership, foreign simple or grantor trust, nominee or other agent. The beneficial owners of income paid to a foreign simple trust (that is, a foreign trust that is described in section 651(a)) are generally the beneficiaries of the trust, if the beneficiary is not a foreign partnership, foreign simple or grantor trust, nominee or other agent. The beneficial owners of a foreign grantor trust (that is, a foreign trust to the extent that all or a portion of the income of the trust is treated as owned by the grantor or another person under sections 671 through 679) are the persons treated as the owners of the trust. The beneficial owners of income paid to a foreign complex trust (that is, a foreign trust that is not a foreign simple trust or foreign grantor trust) is the trust itself.

Generally, these beneficial owner rules apply for purposes of sections 1441, 1442, and 1446, except that section 1446 requires a foreign simple trust to provide a Form W-8 on its own behalf rather than on behalf of the beneficiary of such trust.

The beneficial owner of income paid to a foreign estate is the estate itself.

A payment to a U.S. partnership, U.S. trust, or U.S. estate is treated as a payment to a U.S. payee. A U.S. partnership, trust, or estate should provide the withholding agent with a Form W-9. However, for purposes of section 1446, a U.S. grantor trust shall not provide the withholding agent a Form W-9. Instead, the grantor or other owner must provide Form W-8 or Form W-9 as appropriate.

Disregarded entity. A business entity that has a single owner and is not a corporation under Regulations section 301.7701-2(b) is disregarded as an entity separate from its owner.

A disregarded entity shall not submit this form to a partnership for purposes of section 1446. Instead, the owner of such entity shall provide appropriate documentation. See Regulations section 1.1446-1.

Effectively connected income. Generally, when a foreign person engages in a trade or business in the United States, all income from sources in the United States other than fixed or determinable annual or periodical (FDAP) income (for example, interest, dividends, rents, and certain similar amounts) is considered income effectively connected with a U.S. trade or business. FDAP income may or may not be effectively connected with a U.S. trade or business. Factors to be considered to determine whether FDAP income and similar amounts from U.S. sources are effectively connected with a U.S. trade or business include whether:
• The income is from assets used in, or held for use in, the conduct of that trade or business, or
• The activities of that trade or business were a material factor in the realization of the income.

There are special rules for determining whether income from securities is effectively connected with the active conduct of a U.S. banking, financing, or similar business. See section 864(c)(4)(B)(ii) and Regulations section 1.864-4(c)(5)(ii) for more information.

Effectively connected income, after allowable deductions, is taxed at graduated rates applicable to U.S. citizens and resident aliens, rather than at the 30% rate. You must report this income on your annual U.S. income tax or information return.

A partnership that has effectively connected income allocable to foreign partners is generally required to withhold tax under section 1446. The withholding tax rate on a partner's share of effectively connected income is 35%. In certain circumstances the partnership may withhold tax at the highest applicable rate to a particular type of income (for example long-term capital gain allocated to a noncorporate partner). Any amount withheld under section 1446 on your behalf, and reflected on Form 8805 issued by the partnership to you may be credited on your U.S. income tax return.

Foreign person. A foreign person includes a nonresident alien individual, a foreign corporation, a foreign partnership, a foreign trust, a foreign estate, and any other person that is not a U.S. person.

Nonresident alien individual. Any individual who is not a citizen or resident alien of the United States is a nonresident alien individual. An alien individual meeting either the "green card test" or the "substantial presence test" for the calendar year is a resident alien. Any person not meeting either test is a nonresident alien individual. Additionally, an alien individual who is a resident of a foreign country under the residence article of an income tax treaty, or an alien individual who is a bona fide resident of Puerto Rico, Guam, the Commonwealth of the Northern Mariana Islands, the U.S. Virgin Islands, or American Samoa is a nonresident alien individual.

Even though a nonresident alien individual married to a U.S. citizen or resident alien may choose to be treated as a resident alien for certain purposes (for example, filing a joint income tax return), such individual is still treated as a nonresident alien for withholding tax purposes on all income except wages.

See Pub. 519, U.S. Tax Guide for Aliens, for more information on resident and nonresident alien status.

Withholding agent. Any person, U.S. or foreign, that has control, receipt, or custody of an amount subject to withholding or who can disburse or make payments of an amount subject to withholding is a withholding agent. The withholding agent may be an individual, corporation, partnership, trust, association, or any other entity including (but not limited to) any foreign intermediary, foreign partnership, and U.S. branches of certain foreign banks and insurance companies. Generally, the person who pays (or causes to be paid) an amount subject to withholding to the foreign person (or to its agent) must withhold.

Specific Instructions

Part I

Line 1. Enter your name. If you are filing for a disregarded entity with a single owner who is a foreign person, this form should be completed and signed by the foreign single owner. If the account to which a payment is made or credited is in the name of the disregarded entity, the foreign single owner should inform the withholding agent of this fact. This may be done by including the name and account number of the disregarded entity on line 8 (reference number) of Part I of the form.

If you own the income or account jointly with one or more other persons, the income or account will be treated by the withholding agent as owned by a foreign person if Forms W-8ECI are provided by all of the owners. If the withholding agent receives a Form W-9, Request for Taxpayer Identification Number and Certification, from any of the joint owners, the payment must be treated as made to a U.S. person.

Line 2. If you are filing for a corporation, enter the country of incorporation. If you are filing for another type of entity, enter the country under whose laws the entity is created, organized, or governed. If you are an individual, write "N/A" (for "not applicable").

Line 3. Check the box that applies. By checking a box, you are representing that you qualify for this classification. You must check the one box that represents your classification (for example, corporation, partnership, etc.) under U.S. tax principles. If you are filing for a disregarded entity, you must check the "Disregarded entity" box (not the box that describes the status of your single owner).

Line 4. Your permanent residence address is the address in the country where you claim to be a resident for that country's income tax. Do not show the address of a financial institution, a post office box, or an address used solely for mailing purposes. If you are an individual who does not have a tax residence in any country, your permanent residence is where you normally reside. If you are not an individual and you do not have a tax residence in any country, the permanent residence address is where you maintain your principal office.

Line 5. Enter your business address in the United States. Do not show a post office box.

Line 6. You must provide a U.S. taxpayer identification number (TIN) for this form to be valid. A U.S. TIN is a social security number (SSN), employer identification number (EIN), or IRS individual taxpayer identification number (ITIN). Check the appropriate box for the type of U.S. TIN you are providing.

If you are an individual, you are generally required to enter your SSN. To apply for an SSN, get Form SS-5 from a Social Security Administration (SSA) office. Fill in Form SS-5 and return it to the SSA.

If you do not have an SSN and are not eligible to get one, you must get an ITIN. To apply for an ITIN, file Form W-7 with the IRS. It usually takes 4-6 weeks to get an ITIN.

If you are not an individual (for example, a foreign estate or trust), or you are an individual who is an employer or who is engaged in a U.S. trade or business as a sole proprietor, use Form SS-4, Application for Employer Identification Number, to obtain an EIN. If you are a disregarded entity, enter the U.S. TIN of your foreign single owner.

Line 7. If your country of residence for tax purposes has issued you a tax identifying number, enter it here. For example, if you are a resident of Canada, enter your Social Insurance Number.

Line 8. This line may be used by the filer of Form W-8ECI or by the withholding agent to whom it is provided to include any referencing information that is useful to the withholding agent in carrying out its obligations. A beneficial owner may use line 8 to include the name and number of the account for which he or she is providing the form. A foreign single owner of a disregarded entity may use line 8 to inform the withholding agent that the account to which a payment is made or credited is in the name of the disregarded entity (see instructions for line 1 on page 3).

Line 9. You must specify the items of income that are effectively connected with the conduct of a trade or business in the United States. You will generally have to provide Form W-8BEN, Form W-8EXP, or Form W-8IMY for those items from U.S. sources that are not effectively connected with the conduct of a trade or business in the United States. See Form W-8BEN, W-8EXP, or W-8IMY, and its instructions, for more details.

If you are providing this form to a partnership because you are a partner and have made an election under section 871(d) or section 882(d), attach a copy of the election to the form. If you have not made the election, but intend to do so effective for the current tax year, attach a statement to the form indicating your intent. See Regulations section 1.871-10(d)(3).

Part II

Signature. Form W-8ECI must be signed and dated by the beneficial owner of the income, or, if the beneficial owner is not an individual, by an authorized representative or officer of the beneficial owner. If Form W-8ECI is completed by an agent acting under a duly authorized power of attorney, the form must be accompanied by the power of attorney in proper form or a copy thereof specifically authorizing the agent to represent the principal in making, executing, and presenting the form. Form 2848, Power of Attorney and Declaration of Representative, may be used for this purpose. The agent, as well as the beneficial owner, may incur liability for the penalties provided for an erroneous, false, or fraudulent form.

Paperwork Reduction Act Notice. We ask for the information on this form to carry out the Internal Revenue laws of the United States. If you want to receive exemption from withholding on income effectively connected with the conduct of a trade or business in the United States, you are required to provide the information. We need it to ensure that you are complying with these laws and to allow us to figure and collect the right amount of tax.

You are not required to provide the information requested on a form that is subject to the Paperwork Reduction Act unless the form displays a valid OMB control number. Books or records relating to a form or its instructions must be retained as long as their contents may become material in the administration of any Internal Revenue law. Generally, tax returns and return information are confidential, as required by section 6103.

The time needed to complete and file this form will vary depending on individual circumstances. The estimated average time is: **Recordkeeping,** 3 hr., 35 min.; **Learning about the law or the form,** 3 hr., 22 min.; **Preparing the form,** 3 hr., 35 min.

If you have comments concerning the accuracy of these time estimates or suggestions for making this form simpler, we would be happy to hear from you. You can email us at *taxforms@irs.gov.* Please put "Forms Comment" on the subject line. Or you can write to Internal Revenue Service, Tax Products Coordinating Committee, SE:W:CAR:MP:T:T:SP, 1111 Constitution Ave. NW, IR-6406, Washington, DC 20224. Do not send Form W-8ECI to this office. Instead, give it to your withholding agent.

Form **W-8ECI**

(Rev. February 2006)

Department of the Treasury
Internal Revenue Service

Certificate of Foreign Person's Claim That Income Is Effectively Connected With the Conduct of a Trade or Business in the United States

▶ Section references are to the Internal Revenue Code. ▶ See separate instructions.
▶ Give this form to the withholding agent or payer. Do not send to the IRS.

OMB No. 1545-1621

Note: *Persons submitting this form must file an annual U.S. income tax return to report income claimed to be effectively connected with a U.S. trade or business (see instructions).*

Do not use this form for:

Instead, use Form:

● A beneficial owner solely claiming foreign status or treaty benefits W-8BEN

● A foreign government, international organization, foreign central bank of issue, foreign tax-exempt organization, foreign private foundation, or government of a U.S. possession claiming the applicability of section(s) 115(2), 501(c), 892, 895, or 1443(b) . . . W-8EXP

Note: *These entities should use Form W-8ECI if they received effectively connected income (e.g., income from commercial activities).*

● A foreign partnership or a foreign trust (unless claiming an exemption from U.S. withholding on income effectively connected with the conduct of a trade or business in the United States) . . . . W-8BEN or W-8IMY

● A person acting as an intermediary W-8IMY

Note: *See instructions for additional exceptions.*

Part I   Identification of Beneficial Owner (See instructions.)

1 Name of individual or organization that is the beneficial owner

2 Country of incorporation or organization

3 Type of entity (check the appropriate box): ☐ Individual ☐ Corporation ☐ Disregarded entity
☐ Partnership ☐ Simple trust ☐ Complex trust ☐ Estate
☐ Government ☐ Grantor trust ☐ Central bank of issue ☐ Tax-exempt organization
☐ Private foundation ☐ International organization

4 Permanent residence address (street, apt. or suite no., or rural route). **Do not use a P.O. box.**

City or town, state or province. Include postal code where appropriate.

Country (do not abbreviate)

5 Business address in the United States (street, apt. or suite no., or rural route). **Do not use a P.O. box.**

City or town, state, and ZIP code

6 U.S. taxpayer identification number (required—see instructions)
☐ SSN or ITIN ☐ EIN

7 Foreign tax identifying number, if any (optional)

8 Reference number(s) (see instructions)

9 Specify each item of income that is, or is expected to be, received from the payer that is effectively connected with the conduct of a trade or business in the United States (attach statement if necessary)

Part II   Certification

Sign Here

Under penalties of perjury, I declare that I have examined the information on this form and to the best of my knowledge and belief it is true, correct, and complete. I further certify under penalties of perjury that:

● I am the beneficial owner (or I am authorized to sign for the beneficial owner) of all the income to which this form relates,

● The amounts for which this certification is provided are effectively connected with the conduct of a trade or business in the United States and are includible in my gross income (or the beneficial owner's gross income) for the taxable year, **and**

● The beneficial owner is not a U.S. person.

Furthermore, I authorize this form to be provided to any withholding agent that has control, receipt, or custody of the income of which I am the beneficial owner or any withholding agent that can disburse or make payments of the income of which I am the beneficial owner.

Signature of beneficial owner (or individual authorized to sign for the beneficial owner)   Date (MM-DD-YYYY)   Capacity in which acting

For Paperwork Reduction Act Notice, see separate instructions.

Cat. No. 25045D

Form **W-8ECI** (Rev. 2-2006)

Instructions for Form W-8BEN

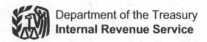

Department of the Treasury
Internal Revenue Service

(Rev. February 2006)

Certificate of Foreign Status of Beneficial Owner for United States Tax Withholding

General Instructions

Section references are to the Internal Revenue Code unless otherwise noted.

For definitions of terms used throughout these instructions, see *Definitions* on pages 3 and 4.

Purpose of form. Foreign persons are subject to U.S. tax at a 30% rate on income they receive from U.S. sources that consists of:

- Interest (including certain original issue discount (OID));
- Dividends;
- Rents;
- Royalties;
- Premiums;
- Annuities;
- Compensation for, or in expectation of, services performed;
- Substitute payments in a securities lending transaction; or
- Other fixed or determinable annual or periodical gains, profits, or income.

This tax is imposed on the gross amount paid and is generally collected by withholding under section 1441 or 1442 on that amount. A payment is considered to have been made whether it is made directly to the beneficial owner or to another person, such as an intermediary, agent, or partnership, for the benefit of the beneficial owner.

In addition, section 1446 requires a partnership conducting a trade or business in the United States to withhold tax on a foreign partner's distributive share of the partnership's effectively connected taxable income. Generally, a foreign person that is a partner in a partnership that submits a Form W-8 for purposes of section 1441 or 1442 will satisfy the documentation requirements under section 1446 as well. However, in some cases the documentation requirements of sections 1441 and 1442 do not match the documentation requirements of section 1446. See Regulations sections 1.1446-1 through 1.1446-6. Further, the owner of a disregarded entity, rather than the disregarded entity itself, shall submit the appropriate Form W-8 for purposes of section 1446.

If you receive certain types of income, you must provide Form W-8BEN to:
- Establish that you are not a U.S. person;
- Claim that you are the beneficial owner of the income for which Form W-8BEN is being provided or a partner in a partnership subject to section 1446; and

- If applicable, claim a reduced rate of, or exemption from, withholding as a resident of a foreign country with which the United States has an income tax treaty.

You may also be required to submit Form W-8BEN to claim an exception from domestic information reporting and backup withholding for certain types of income that are not subject to foreign-person withholding. Such income includes:
- Broker proceeds.
- Short-term (183 days or less) original issue discount (OID).
- Bank deposit interest.
- Foreign source interest, dividends, rents, or royalties.
- Proceeds from a wager placed by a nonresident alien individual in the games of blackjack, baccarat, craps, roulette, or big-6 wheel.

You may also use Form W-8BEN to certify that income from a notional principal contract is not effectively connected with the conduct of a trade or business in the United States.

A withholding agent or payer of the income may rely on a properly completed Form W-8BEN to treat a payment associated with the Form W-8BEN as a payment to a foreign person who beneficially owns the amounts paid. If applicable, the withholding agent may rely on the Form W-8BEN to apply a reduced rate of withholding at source.

Provide Form W-8BEN to the withholding agent or payer before income is paid or credited to you. Failure to provide a Form W-8BEN when requested may lead to withholding at a 30% rate (foreign-person withholding) or the backup withholding rate.

Additional information. For additional information and instructions for the withholding agent, see the Instructions for the Requester of Forms W-8BEN, W-8ECI, W-8EXP, and W-8IMY.

Who must file. You must give Form W-8BEN to the withholding agent or payer if you are a foreign person and you are the beneficial owner of an amount subject to withholding. Submit Form W-8BEN when requested by the withholding agent or payer whether or not you are claiming a reduced rate of, or exemption from, withholding.

Do not use Form W-8BEN if:
- You are a U.S. citizen (even if you reside outside the United States) or other U.S. person (including a resident alien individual). Instead, use Form W-9, Request for Taxpayer Identification Number and Certification.
- You are a disregarded entity with a single owner that is a U.S. person and you are not a hybrid entity claiming treaty benefits. Instead, provide Form W-9.

Cat. No. 25576H

- You are a nonresident alien individual who claims exemption from withholding on compensation for independent or dependent personal services performed in the United States. Instead, provide Form 8233, Exemption from Withholding on Compensation for Independent (and Certain Dependent) Personal Services of a Nonresident Alien Individual, or Form W-4, Employee's Withholding Allowance Certificate.

- You are receiving income that is effectively connected with the conduct of a trade or business in the United States, unless it is allocable to you through a partnership. Instead, provide Form W-8ECI, Certificate of Foreign Person's Claim That Income Is Effectively Connected With the Conduct of a Trade or Business in the United States. If any of the income for which you have provided a Form W-8BEN becomes effectively connected, this is a change in circumstances and Form W-8BEN is no longer valid. You must file Form W-8ECI. See *Change in circumstances* on this page.

- You are filing for a foreign government, international organization, foreign central bank of issue, foreign tax-exempt organization, foreign private foundation, or government of a U.S. possession claiming the applicability of section 115(2), 501(c), 892, 895, or 1443(b). Instead, provide Form W-8EXP, Certificate of Foreign Government or Other Foreign Organization for United States Tax Withholding. However, you should use Form W-8BEN if you are claiming treaty benefits or are providing the form only to claim you are a foreign person exempt from backup withholding. You should use Form W-8ECI if you received effectively connected income (for example, income from commercial activities).

- You are a foreign flow-through entity, other than a hybrid entity, claiming treaty benefits. Instead, provide Form W-8IMY, Certificate of Foreign Intermediary, Foreign Flow-Through Entity, or Certain U.S. Branches for United States Tax Withholding. However, if you are a partner, beneficiary, or owner of a flow-through entity and you are not yourself a flow-through entity, you may be required to furnish a Form W-8BEN to the flow-through entity.

- You are a disregarded entity for purposes of section 1446. Instead, the owner of the entity must submit the form.

- You are a reverse hybrid entity transmitting beneficial owner documentation provided by your interest holders to claim treaty benefits on their behalf. Instead, provide Form W-8IMY.

- You are a withholding foreign partnership or a withholding foreign trust within the meaning of sections 1441 and 1442 and the accompanying regulations. A withholding foreign partnership or a withholding foreign trust is a foreign partnership or trust that has entered into a withholding agreement with the IRS under which it agrees to assume primary withholding responsibility for each partner's, beneficiary's, or owner's distributive share of income subject to withholding that is paid to the partnership or trust. Instead, provide Form W-8IMY.

- You are acting as an intermediary (that is, acting not for your own account, but for the account of others as an agent, nominee, or custodian). Instead, provide Form W-8IMY.

- You are a foreign partnership or foreign grantor trust for purposes of section 1446. Instead, provide Form

W-8IMY and accompanying documentation. See Regulations sections 1.1446-1 through 1.1446-6.

Giving Form W-8BEN to the withholding agent. Do not send Form W-8BEN to the IRS. Instead, give it to the person who is requesting it from you. Generally, this will be the person from whom you receive the payment, who credits your account, or a partnership that allocates income to you. Give Form W-8BEN to the person requesting it before the payment is made to you, credited to your account or allocated. If you do not provide this form, the withholding agent may have to withhold at the 30% rate, backup withholding rate, or the rate applicable under section 1446. If you receive more than one type of income from a single withholding agent for which you claim different benefits, the withholding agent may, at its option, require you to submit a Form W-8BEN for each different type of income. Generally, a separate Form W-8BEN must be given to each withholding agent.

Note. If you own the income or account jointly with one or more other persons, the income or account will be treated by the withholding agent as owned by a foreign person if Forms W-8BEN are provided by all of the owners. If the withholding agent receives a Form W-9 from any of the joint owners, the payment must be treated as made to a U.S. person.

Change in circumstances. If a change in circumstances makes any information on the Form W-8BEN you have submitted incorrect, you must notify the withholding agent or payer within 30 days of the change in circumstances and you must file a new Form W-8BEN or other appropriate form.

If you use Form W-8BEN to certify that you are a foreign person, a change of address to an address in the United States is a change in circumstances. Generally, a change of address within the same foreign country or to another foreign country is not a change in circumstances. However, if you use Form W-8BEN to claim treaty benefits, a move to the United States or outside the country where you have been claiming treaty benefits is a change in circumstances. In that case, you must notify the withholding agent or payer within 30 days of the move.

If you become a U.S. citizen or resident alien after you submit Form W-8BEN, you are no longer subject to the 30% withholding rate or the withholding tax on a foreign partner's share of effectively connected income. You must notify the withholding agent or payer within 30 days of becoming a U.S. citizen or resident alien. You may be required to provide a Form W-9. For more information, see Form W-9 and instructions.

Expiration of Form W-8BEN. Generally, a Form W-8BEN provided without a U.S. taxpayer identification number (TIN) will remain in effect for a period starting on the date the form is signed and ending on the last day of the third succeeding calendar year, unless a change in circumstances makes any information on the form incorrect. For example, a Form W-8BEN signed on September 30, 2005, remains valid through December 31, 2008. A Form W-8BEN furnished with a U.S. TIN will remain in effect until a change in circumstances makes any information on the form incorrect, provided that the withholding agent reports on Form 1042-S at least one payment annually to the beneficial owner who provided the Form W-8BEN. See the instructions for line 6 beginning on page 4 for circumstances under which you must provide a U.S. TIN.

Definitions

Beneficial owner. For payments other than those for which a reduced rate of withholding is claimed under an income tax treaty, the beneficial owner of income is generally the person who is required under U.S. tax principles to include the income in gross income on a tax return. A person is not a beneficial owner of income, however, to the extent that person is receiving the income as a nominee, agent, or custodian, or to the extent the person is a conduit whose participation in a transaction is disregarded. In the case of amounts paid that do not constitute income, beneficial ownership is determined as if the payment were income.

Foreign partnerships, foreign simple trusts, and foreign grantor trusts are not the beneficial owners of income paid to the partnership or trust. The beneficial owners of income paid to a foreign partnership are generally the partners in the partnership, provided that the partner is not itself a partnership, foreign simple or grantor trust, nominee or other agent. The beneficial owners of income paid to a foreign simple trust (that is, a foreign trust that is described in section 651(a)) are generally the beneficiaries of the trust, if the beneficiary is not a foreign partnership, foreign simple or grantor trust, nominee or other agent. The beneficial owners of a foreign grantor trust (that is, a foreign trust to the extent that all or a portion of the income of the trust is treated as owned by the grantor or another person under sections 671 through 679) are the persons treated as the owners of the trust. The beneficial owners of income paid to a foreign complex trust (that is, a foreign trust that is not a foreign simple trust or foreign grantor trust) is the trust itself.

For purposes of section 1446, the same beneficial owner rules apply, except that under section 1446 a foreign simple trust rather than the beneficiary provides the form to the partnership.

The beneficial owner of income paid to a foreign estate is the estate itself.

Note. A payment to a U.S. partnership, U.S. trust, or U.S. estate is treated as a payment to a U.S. payee that is not subject to 30% withholding. A U.S. partnership, trust, or estate should provide the withholding agent with a Form W-9. For purposes of section 1446, a U.S. grantor trust or disregarded entity shall not provide the withholding agent a Form W-9 in its own right. Rather, the grantor or other owner shall provide the withholding agent the appropriate form.

Foreign person. A foreign person includes a nonresident alien individual, a foreign corporation, a foreign partnership, a foreign trust, a foreign estate, and any other person that is not a U.S. person. It also includes a foreign branch or office of a U.S. financial institution or U.S. clearing organization if the foreign branch is a qualified intermediary. Generally, a payment to a U.S. branch of a foreign person is a payment to a foreign person.

Nonresident alien individual. Any individual who is not a citizen or resident alien of the United States is a nonresident alien individual. An alien individual meeting either the "green card test" or the "substantial presence test" for the calendar year is a resident alien. Any person not meeting either test is a nonresident alien individual. Additionally, an alien individual who is a resident of a foreign country under the residence article of an income tax treaty, or an alien individual who is a bona fide resident of Puerto Rico, Guam, the Commonwealth of the Northern Mariana Islands, the U.S. Virgin Islands, or American Samoa is a nonresident alien individual. See Pub. 519, U.S. Tax Guide for Aliens, for more information on resident and nonresident alien status.

 Even though a nonresident alien individual married to a U.S. citizen or resident alien may choose to be treated as a resident alien for certain purposes (for example, filing a joint income tax return), such individual is still treated as a nonresident alien for withholding tax purposes on all income except wages.

Flow-through entity. A flow-through entity is a foreign partnership (other than a withholding foreign partnership), a foreign simple or foreign grantor trust (other than a withholding foreign trust), or, for payments for which a reduced rate of withholding is claimed under an income tax treaty, any entity to the extent the entity is considered to be fiscally transparent (see below) with respect to the payment by an interest holder's jurisdiction.

For purposes of section 1446, a foreign partnership or foreign grantor trust must submit Form W-8IMY to establish the partnership or grantor trust as a look through entity. The Form W-8IMY may be accompanied by this form or another version of Form W-8 or Form W-9 to establish the foreign or domestic status of a partner or grantor or other owner. See Regulations section 1.1446-1.

Hybrid entity. A hybrid entity is any person (other than an individual) that is treated as fiscally transparent (see below) in the United States but is not treated as fiscally transparent by a country with which the United States has an income tax treaty. Hybrid entity status is relevant for claiming treaty benefits. See the instructions for line 9c on page 5.

Reverse hybrid entity. A reverse hybrid entity is any person (other than an individual) that is not fiscally transparent under U.S. tax law principles but that is fiscally transparent under the laws of a jurisdiction with which the United States has an income tax treaty. See the instructions for line 9c on page 5.

Fiscally transparent entity. An entity is treated as fiscally transparent with respect to an item of income for which treaty benefits are claimed to the extent that the interest holders in the entity must, on a current basis, take into account separately their shares of an item of income paid to the entity, whether or not distributed, and must determine the character of the items of income as if they were realized directly from the sources from which realized by the entity. For example, partnerships, common trust funds, and simple trusts or grantor trusts are generally considered to be fiscally transparent with respect to items of income received by them.

Disregarded entity. A business entity that has a single owner and is not a corporation under Regulations section 301.7701-2(b) is disregarded as an entity separate from its owner.

A disregarded entity shall not submit this form to a partnership for purposes of section 1446. Instead, the owner of such entity shall provide appropriate documentation. See Regulations section 1.1446-1.

Amounts subject to withholding. Generally, an amount subject to withholding is an amount from sources within the United States that is fixed or determinable annual or periodical (FDAP) income. FDAP income is all income included in gross income, including interest (as well as OID), dividends, rents, royalties, and compensation. FDAP income does not include most gains from the sale of property (including market discount and option premiums).

For purposes of section 1446, the amount subject to withholding is the foreign partner's share of the partnership's effectively connected taxable income.

Withholding agent. Any person, U.S. or foreign, that has control, receipt, or custody of an amount subject to withholding or who can disburse or make payments of an amount subject to withholding is a withholding agent. The withholding agent may be an individual, corporation, partnership, trust, association, or any other entity, including (but not limited to) any foreign intermediary, foreign partnership, and U.S. branches of certain foreign banks and insurance companies. Generally, the person who pays (or causes to be paid) the amount subject to withholding to the foreign person (or to its agent) must withhold.

For purposes of section 1446, the withholding agent is the partnership conducting the trade or business in the United States. For a publicly traded partnership, the withholding agent may be the partnership, a nominee holding an interest on behalf of a foreign person, or both. See Regulations sections 1.1446-1 through 1.1446-6.

Specific Instructions

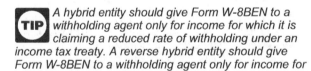 *A hybrid entity should give Form W-8BEN to a withholding agent only for income for which it is claiming a reduced rate of withholding under an income tax treaty. A reverse hybrid entity should give Form W-8BEN to a withholding agent only for income for which no treaty benefit is being claimed.*

Part I

Line 1. Enter your name. If you are a disregarded entity with a single owner who is a foreign person and you are not claiming treaty benefits as a hybrid entity, this form should be completed and signed by your foreign single owner. If the account to which a payment is made or credited is in the name of the disregarded entity, the foreign single owner should inform the withholding agent of this fact. This may be done by including the name and account number of the disregarded entity on line 8 (reference number) of the form. However, if you are a disregarded entity that is claiming treaty benefits as a hybrid entity, this form should be completed and signed by you.

Line 2. If you are a corporation, enter the country of incorporation. If you are another type of entity, enter the country under whose laws you are created, organized, or governed. If you are an individual, enter N/A (for "not applicable").

Line 3. Check the one box that applies. By checking a box, you are representing that you qualify for this classification. You must check the box that represents your classification (for example, corporation, partnership, trust, estate, etc.) under U.S. tax principles. Do not check the box that describes your status under the law of the treaty country. If you are a partnership or disregarded entity receiving a payment for which treaty benefits are being claimed, you must check the "Partnership" or "Disregarded entity" box. If you are a sole proprietor, check the "Individual" box, not the "Disregarded entity" box.

 Only entities that are tax-exempt under section 501 should check the "Tax-exempt organization" box. Such organizations should use Form W-8BEN only if they are claiming a reduced rate of withholding under an income tax treaty or some code exception other than section 501. Use Form W-8EXP if you are claiming an exemption from withholding under section 501.

Line 4. Your permanent residence address is the address in the country where you claim to be a resident for purposes of that country's income tax. If you are giving Form W-8BEN to claim a reduced rate of withholding under an income tax treaty, you must determine your residency in the manner required by the treaty. Do not show the address of a financial institution, a post office box, or an address used solely for mailing purposes. If you are an individual who does not have a tax residence in any country, your permanent residence is where you normally reside. If you are not an individual and you do not have a tax residence in any country, the permanent residence address is where you maintain your principal office.

Line 5. Enter your mailing address only if it is different from the address you show on line 4.

Line 6. If you are an individual, you are generally required to enter your social security number (SSN). To apply for an SSN, get Form SS-5 from a Social Security Administration (SSA) office or, if in the United States, you may call the SSA at 1-800-772-1213. Fill in Form SS-5 and return it to the SSA.

If you do not have an SSN and are not eligible to get one, you must get an individual taxpayer identification number (ITIN). To apply for an ITIN, file Form W-7 with the IRS. It usually takes 4-6 weeks to get an ITIN.

An ITIN is for tax use only. It does not entitle you to social security benefits or change your employment or immigration status under U.S. law.

If you are not an individual or you are an individual who is an employer or you are engaged in a U.S. trade or business as a sole proprietor, you must enter an employer identification number (EIN). If you do not have an EIN, you should apply for one on Form SS-4, Application for Employer Identification Number. If you are a disregarded entity claiming treaty benefits as a hybrid entity, enter your EIN.

A partner in a partnership conducting a trade or business in the United States will likely be allocated effectively connected taxable income. The partner is required to file a U.S. federal income tax return and must have a U.S. taxpayer identification number (TIN).

You must provide a U.S. TIN if you are:
• Claiming an exemption from withholding under section 871(f) for certain annuities received under qualified plans,
• A foreign grantor trust with 5 or fewer grantors,
• Claiming benefits under an income tax treaty, or
• Submitting the form to a partnership that conducts a trade or business in the United States.

However, a U.S. TIN is not required to be shown in order to claim treaty benefits on the following items of income:
• Dividends and interest from stocks and debt obligations that are actively traded;
• Dividends from any redeemable security issued by an investment company registered under the Investment Company Act of 1940 (mutual fund);
• Dividends, interest, or royalties from units of beneficial interest in a unit investment trust that are (or were upon issuance) publicly offered and are registered with the SEC under the Securities Act of 1933; and
• Income related to loans of any of the above securities.

 You may want to obtain and provide a U.S. TIN on Form W-8BEN even though it is not required. A Form W-8BEN containing a U.S. TIN remains valid for as long as your status and the information relevant to the certifications you make on the form remain unchanged provided at least one payment is reported to you annually on Form 1042-S.

Line 7. If your country of residence for tax purposes has issued you a tax identifying number, enter it here. For example, if you are a resident of Canada, enter your Social Insurance Number.

Line 8. This line may be used by the filer of Form W-8BEN or by the withholding agent to whom it is provided to include any referencing information that is useful to the withholding agent in carrying out its obligations. For example, withholding agents who are required to associate the Form W-8BEN with a particular Form W-8IMY may want to use line 8 for a referencing number or code that will make the association clear. A beneficial owner may use line 8 to include the number of the account for which he or she is providing the form. A foreign single owner of a disregarded entity may use line 8 to inform the withholding agent that the account to which a payment is made or credited is in the name of the disregarded entity (see instructions for line 1 on page 4).

Part II

Line 9a. Enter the country where you claim to be a resident for income tax treaty purposes. For treaty purposes, a person is a resident of a treaty country if the person is a resident of that country under the terms of the treaty.

Line 9b. If you are claiming benefits under an income tax treaty, you must have a U.S. TIN unless one of the exceptions listed in the line 6 instructions above applies.

Line 9c. An entity (but not an individual) that is claiming a reduced rate of withholding under an income tax treaty must represent that it:
• Derives the item of income for which the treaty benefit is claimed, and

• Meets the limitation on benefits provisions contained in the treaty, if any.

An item of income may be derived by either the entity receiving the item of income or by the interest holders in the entity or, in certain circumstances, both. An item of income paid to an entity is considered to be derived by the entity only if the entity is not fiscally transparent under the laws of the entity's jurisdiction with respect to the item of income. An item of income paid to an entity shall be considered to be derived by the interest holder in the entity only if:
• The interest holder is not fiscally transparent in its jurisdiction with respect to the item of income, and
• The entity is considered to be fiscally transparent under the laws of the interest holder's jurisdiction with respect to the item of income. An item of income paid directly to a type of entity specifically identified in a treaty as a resident of a treaty jurisdiction is treated as derived by a resident of that treaty jurisdiction.

If an entity is claiming treaty benefits on its own behalf, it should complete Form W-8BEN. If an interest holder in an entity that is considered fiscally transparent in the interest holder's jurisdiction is claiming a treaty benefit, the interest holder should complete Form W-8BEN on its own behalf and the fiscally transparent entity should associate the interest holder's Form W-8BEN with a Form W-8IMY completed by the entity.

 An income tax treaty may not apply to reduce the amount of any tax on an item of income received by an entity that is treated as a domestic corporation for U.S. tax purposes. Therefore, neither the domestic corporation nor its shareholders are entitled to the benefits of a reduction of U.S. income tax on an item of income received from U.S. sources by the corporation.

To determine whether an entity meets the limitation on benefits provisions of a treaty, you must consult the specific provisions or articles under the treaties. Income tax treaties are available on the IRS website at *www.irs.gov.*

 If you are an entity that derives the income as a resident of a treaty country, you may check this box if the applicable income tax treaty does not contain a "limitation on benefits" provision.

Line 9d. If you are a foreign corporation claiming treaty benefits under an income tax treaty that entered into force before January 1, 1987 (and has not been renegotiated) on (a) U.S. source dividends paid to you by another foreign corporation or (b) U.S. source interest paid to you by a U.S. trade or business of another foreign corporation, you must generally be a "qualified resident" of a treaty country. See section 884 for the definition of interest paid by a U.S. trade or business of a foreign corporation ("branch interest") and other applicable rules.

In general, a foreign corporation is a qualified resident of a country if any of the following apply.
• It meets a 50% ownership and base erosion test.
• It is primarily and regularly traded on an established securities market in its country of residence or the United States.
• It carries on an active trade or business in its country of residence.
• It gets a ruling from the IRS that it is a qualified resident.

See Regulations section 1.884-5 for the requirements that must be met to satisfy each of these tests.

 If you are claiming treaty benefits under an income tax treaty entered into force after December 31, 1986, do not check box 9d. Instead, check box 9c.

Line 9e. Check this box if you are related to the withholding agent within the meaning of section 267(b) or 707(b) and the aggregate amount subject to withholding received during the calendar year will exceed $500,000. Additionally, you must file Form 8833, Treaty-Based Return Position Disclosure Under Section 6114 or 7701(b).

Line 10

Line 10 must be used only if you are claiming treaty benefits that require that you meet conditions not covered by the representations you make in lines 9a through 9e. However, this line should always be completed by foreign students and researchers claiming treaty benefits. See *Scholarship and fellowship grants* below for more information.

The following are additional examples of persons who should complete this line.
• Exempt organizations claiming treaty benefits under the exempt organization articles of the treaties with Canada, Mexico, Germany, and the Netherlands.
• Foreign corporations that are claiming a preferential rate applicable to dividends based on ownership of a specific percentage of stock.
• Persons claiming treaty benefits on royalties if the treaty contains different withholding rates for different types of royalties.

This line is generally not applicable to claiming treaty benefits under an interest or dividends (other than dividends subject to a preferential rate based on ownership) article of a treaty.

Nonresident alien who becomes a resident alien. Generally, only a nonresident alien individual may use the terms of a tax treaty to reduce or eliminate U.S. tax on certain types of income. However, most tax treaties contain a provision known as a "saving clause." Exceptions specified in the saving clause may permit an exemption from tax to continue for certain types of income even after the recipient has otherwise become a U.S. resident alien for tax purposes. The individual must use Form W-9 to claim the tax treaty benefit. See the instructions for Form W-9 for more information. Also see *Nonresident alien student or researcher who becomes a resident alien* later for an example.

Scholarship and fellowship grants. A nonresident alien student (including a trainee or business apprentice) or researcher who receives noncompensatory scholarship or fellowship income may use Form W-8BEN to claim benefits under a tax treaty that apply to reduce or eliminate U.S. tax on such income. No Form W-8BEN is required unless a treaty benefit is being claimed. A nonresident alien student or researcher who receives compensatory scholarship or fellowship income must use Form 8233 to claim any benefits of a tax treaty that apply to that income. The student or researcher must use Form W-4 for any part of such income for which he or she is not claiming a tax treaty withholding exemption. Do not use Form W-8BEN for compensatory scholarship or fellowship income. See *Compensation for Dependent Personal Services* in the Instructions for Form 8233.

TIP *If you are a nonresident alien individual who received noncompensatory scholarship or fellowship income and personal services income (including compensatory scholarship or fellowship income) from the same withholding agent, you may use Form 8233 to claim a tax treaty withholding exemption for part or all of both types of income.*

Completing lines 4 and 9a. Most tax treaties that contain an article exempting scholarship or fellowship grant income from taxation require that the recipient be a resident of the other treaty country at the time of, or immediately prior to, entry into the United States. Thus, a student or researcher may claim the exemption even if he or she no longer has a permanent address in the other treaty country after entry into the United States. If this is the case, you may provide a U.S. address on line 4 and still be eligible for the exemption if all other conditions required by the tax treaty are met. You must also identify on line 9a the tax treaty country of which you were a resident at the time of, or immediately prior to, your entry into the United States.

Completing line 10. You must complete line 10 if you are a student or researcher claiming an exemption from taxation on your scholarship or fellowship grant income under a tax treaty.

Nonresident alien student or researcher who becomes a resident alien. You must use Form W-9 to claim an exception to a saving clause. See *Nonresident alien who becomes a resident alien* on this page for a general explanation of saving clauses and exceptions to them.

Example. Article 20 of the U.S.-China income tax treaty allows an exemption from tax for scholarship income received by a Chinese student temporarily present in the United States. Under U.S. law, this student will become a resident alien for tax purposes if his or her stay in the United States exceeds 5 calendar years. However, paragraph 2 of the first protocol to the U.S.-China treaty (dated April 30, 1984) allows the provisions of Article 20 to continue to apply even after the Chinese student becomes a resident alien of the United States. A Chinese student who qualifies for this exception (under paragraph 2 of the first protocol) and is relying on this exception to claim an exemption from tax on his or her scholarship or fellowship income would complete Form W-9.

Part III

If you check this box, you must provide the withholding agent with the required statement for income from a notional principal contract that is to be treated as income not effectively connected with the conduct of a trade or business in the United States. You should update this statement as often as necessary. A new Form W-8BEN is not required for each update provided the form otherwise remains valid.

Part IV

Form W-8BEN must be signed and dated by the beneficial owner of the income, or, if the beneficial owner is not an individual, by an authorized representative or officer of the beneficial owner. If Form W-8BEN is completed by an agent acting under a duly authorized power of attorney, the form must be accompanied by the power of attorney in proper form or a copy thereof specifically authorizing the agent to represent the principal in making, executing, and presenting the form. Form 2848, Power of Attorney and Declaration of Representative, may be used for this purpose. The agent, as well as the beneficial owner, may incur liability for the penalties provided for an erroneous, false, or fraudulent form.

Broker transactions or barter exchanges. Income from transactions with a broker or a barter exchange is subject to reporting rules and backup withholding unless Form W-8BEN or a substitute form is filed to notify the broker or barter exchange that you are an exempt foreign person.

You are an exempt foreign person for a calendar year in which:

• You are a nonresident alien individual or a foreign corporation, partnership, estate, or trust;

• You are an individual who has not been, and does not plan to be, present in the United States for a total of 183 days or more during the calendar year; and

• You are neither engaged, nor plan to be engaged during the year, in a U.S. trade or business that has effectively connected gains from transactions with a broker or barter exchange.

Paperwork Reduction Act Notice. We ask for the information on this form to carry out the Internal Revenue laws of the United States. You are required to provide the information. We need it to ensure that you are complying with these laws and to allow us to figure and collect the right amount of tax.

You are not required to provide the information requested on a form that is subject to the Paperwork Reduction Act unless the form displays a valid OMB control number. Books or records relating to a form or its instructions must be retained as long as their contents may become material in the administration of any Internal Revenue law. Generally, tax returns and return information are confidential, as required by section 6103.

The time needed to complete and file this form will vary depending on individual circumstances. The estimated average time is: **Recordkeeping,** 5 hr., 58 min.; **Learning about the law or the form,** 3 hr., 46 min.; **Preparing and sending the form to IRS,** 4 hr., 2 min.

If you have comments concerning the accuracy of these time estimates or suggestions for making this form simpler, we would be happy to hear from you. You can email us at *taxforms@irs.gov*. Please put "Forms Comment" on the subject line. Or you can write to Internal Revenue Service, Tax Products Coordinating Committee, SE:W:CAR:MP:T:T:SP, 1111 Constitution Ave. NW, IR-6406, Washington, DC 20224. Do not send Form W-8BEN to this office. Instead, give it to your withholding agent.

Sample Form 14-2

Form **W-8BEN**

(Rev. February 2006)

Department of the Treasury
Internal Revenue Service

**Certificate of Foreign Status of Beneficial Owner
for United States Tax Withholding**

▶ Section references are to the Internal Revenue Code.   ▶ See separate instructions.
▶ Give this form to the withholding agent or payer. Do not send to the IRS.

OMB No. 1545-1621

Do not use this form for:	Instead, use Form:
● A U.S. citizen or other U.S. person, including a resident alien individual	. W-9
● A person claiming that income is effectively connected with the conduct of a trade or business in the United States	.W-8ECI
● A foreign partnership, a foreign simple trust, or a foreign grantor trust (see instructions for exceptions)	W-8ECI or W-8IMY
● A foreign government, international organization, foreign central bank of issue, foreign tax-exempt organization, foreign private foundation, or government of a U.S. possession that received effectively connected income or that is claiming the applicability of section(s) 115(2), 501(c), 892, 895, or 1443(b) (see instructions)	W-8ECI or W-8EXP

Note: *These entities should use Form W-8BEN if they are claiming treaty benefits or are providing the form only to claim they are a foreign person exempt from backup withholding.*

● A person acting as an intermediary	. W-8IMY

Note: *See instructions for additional exceptions.*

Part I   Identification of Beneficial Owner (See instructions.)

1 Name of individual or organization that is the beneficial owner

2 Country of incorporation or organization

3 Type of beneficial owner: ☐ Individual   ☐ Corporation   ☐ Disregarded entity   ☐ Partnership   ☐ Simple trust
☐ Grantor trust   ☐ Complex trust   ☐ Estate   ☐ Government   ☐ International organization
☐ Central bank of issue   ☐ Tax-exempt organization   ☐ Private foundation

4 Permanent residence address (street, apt. or suite no., or rural route). **Do not use a P.O. box or in-care-of address.**

City or town, state or province. Include postal code where appropriate.

Country (do not abbreviate)

5 Mailing address (if different from above)

City or town, state or province. Include postal code where appropriate.

Country (do not abbreviate)

6 U.S. taxpayer identification number, if required (see instructions)
☐ SSN or ITIN   ☐ EIN

7 Foreign tax identifying number, if any (optional)

8 Reference number(s) (see instructions)

Part II   Claim of Tax Treaty Benefits (if applicable)

9 **I certify that (check all that apply):**

a ☐ The beneficial owner is a resident of _____ within the meaning of the income tax treaty between the United States and that country.

b ☐ If required, the U.S. taxpayer identification number is stated on line 6 (see instructions).

c ☐ The beneficial owner is not an individual, derives the item (or items) of income for which the treaty benefits are claimed, and, if applicable, meets the requirements of the treaty provision dealing with limitation on benefits (see instructions).

d ☐ The beneficial owner is not an individual, is claiming treaty benefits for dividends received from a foreign corporation or interest from a U.S. trade or business of a foreign corporation, and meets qualified resident status (see instructions).

e ☐ The beneficial owner is related to the person obligated to pay the income within the meaning of section 267(b) or 707(b), and will file Form 8833 if the amount subject to withholding received during a calendar year exceeds, in the aggregate, $500,000.

10 **Special rates and conditions** (if applicable—see instructions): The beneficial owner is claiming the provisions of Article _____ of the treaty identified on line 9a above to claim a _____ % rate of withholding on (specify type of income): _____ .

Explain the reasons the beneficial owner meets the terms of the treaty article: _____

_____

Part III   Notional Principal Contracts

11 ☐ I have provided or will provide a statement that identifies those notional principal contracts from which the income is **not** effectively connected with the conduct of a trade or business in the United States. I agree to update this statement as required.

Part IV   Certification

Under penalties of perjury, I declare that I have examined the information on this form and to the best of my knowledge and belief it is true, correct, and complete. I further certify under penalties of perjury that:

1 I am the beneficial owner (or am authorized to sign for the beneficial owner) of all the income to which this form relates,

2 The beneficial owner is not a U.S. person,

3 The income to which this form relates is (a) not effectively connected with the conduct of a trade or business in the United States, (b) effectively connected but is not subject to tax under an income tax treaty, or (c) the partner's share of a partnership's effectively connected income, **and**

4 For broker transactions or barter exchanges, the beneficial owner is an exempt foreign person as defined in the instructions.

Furthermore, I authorize this form to be provided to any withholding agent that has control, receipt, or custody of the income of which I am the beneficial owner or any withholding agent that can disburse or make payments of the income of which I am the beneficial owner.

Sign Here ▶

_____   _____   _____
Signature of beneficial owner (or individual authorized to sign for beneficial owner)   Date (MM-DD-YYYY)   Capacity in which acting

For Paperwork Reduction Act Notice, see separate instructions.   Cat. No. 25047Z   Form **W-8BEN** (Rev. 2-2006)

✳ *Printed on Recycled Paper*

14-47